THE TWO DUCHESSES

ALSO AVAILABLE FROM FONTHILL MEDIA

Dearest Bess—Elizabeth Duchess of Devonshire
Dorothy M. Stuart
ISBN 978-1-78155-005-2
£16.99 $25.95

Georgiana, Duchess of Devonshire
The Face without a Frown
Iris Leveson Gower
ISBN 978-1-78155-557-6
£16.99 $25.95

THE TWO DUCHESSES

Georgiana, Duchess of Devonshire, Elizabeth, Duchess of Devonshire

Family correspondence of and relating to Georgiana, Duchess
of Devonshire, Elizabeth, Duchess of Devonshire, Earl of Bristol
(Bishop of Derry), the Countess of Bristol, Lord and Lady Byron,
the Earl of Aberdeen, Sir Augustus Foster, Bart., and others,
1777–1859

VERE FOSTER

FONTHILL

Fonthill Media Limited
Fonthill Media LLC
www.fonthillmedia.com
office@fonthillmedia.com

First published in the United Kingdom
and the United States of America 2018

British Library Cataloguing in Publication Data:
A catalogue record for this book is available from the British Library

ISBN 978-1-78155-015-1

Typeset in 10.5pt on 13pt Sabon
Printed and bound in England

Publisher's Introduction
to the 2018 Edition

It should be stated at the outset that Vere Foster (1819–1900), philanthropist and educationist, was the son (the third son) of Sir Augustus John Foster, first baronet (1780–1848), and more to the point, grandson of Elizabeth Cavendish, Duchess of Devonshire (1758–1824). Foster, through the obvious family connections, had access to much material. This material is now housed in the United States of America, mainly at the Library of Congress, but also at the Huntington Library, California. Obviously Vere Foster had all of these papers at his fingertips in Ireland, long before they crossed the Atlantic.

He entitled the book *The Two Duchesses*, and although this is understandable, his family papers were largely of one duchess—his grandmother, Bess. He did not go out of his way to cultivate his Devonshire House or Chatsworth relations for additional material, and indeed he already had plenty to write about. As a consequence, this book is largely a Foster book, but notwithstanding this, it is a mine of information. Before describing Vere Foster's work in more detail, it may be helpful to explain the American angle.

Augustus Foster first arrived in Washington in 1804 as an assistant to the British minister, Anthony Merry. His stay was of four years and on his return to Europe in 1808, he was appointed *chargé d'affaires* at Stockholm. He was in Sweden for only two years and was expelled by order of Napoleon who had entered into an accord with the Swedes. In 1811, he was appointed once more to the United States, but this time as minister, and returned to Washington with rigid instructions that gave him little room for manoeuvre. This is not the place to explain the causes leading to the War of 1812, but needless to say, Foster was not able to placate the warhawks and the United States declared war on Great Britain on 18 June 1812. As a consequence, Foster returned to England.

Foster may not have been the ideal candidate to have dealt with the Americans, but it would have been an impossible task for anyone, and he harboured a quiet grudge at the inferences cast upon him that he had failed. What he had done during his total of six years in America was to have made voluminous notes. In later life, spurred on by the success of books such as Fanny Trollope's *Domestic Manners of the Americans* (1832), he spent a great deal of time and effort turning these notes into a book. A few extracts were published in the *Quarterly Review* in 1841, but apart from that, the manuscript remained in the cupboard at Glyde Court, the Foster home in County Louth.

The American interest in the Foster papers was due to the fact that historians were aware of the manuscript's existence because of the extracts published in 1841. In the early years of the twentieth century, Dr John Franklin Jameson came to head the historical section of the Carnegie Institution of Washington, and interested himself in the early diplomatic relations of Great Britain and the United States. He found the *Quarterly Review*'s extracts of the work 'so capable an observer and so interesting a narrative' that he made a prolongued but unavailing search for the manuscript. In 1929, however, just about the time Dr Jameson transferred from the Carnegie Institution to the Manuscripts Division of the Library of Congress, an assortment of Foster's Papers—letters, notebooks, and diaries—were offered for auction in London, and were secured for the Library. The manuscript of the *Notes on America* was not among them, but four years later, it was found in the cupboard at Glyde Court of which the lock had been broken, and the Library promptly purchased it from Augustus Foster's grandson, Vere Foster's nephew.

What Dr Jameson did not know was that the efficient and somewhat secretive collector, Henry E. Huntington, had acquired an alternative manuscript of the *Notes*, along with other Foster material as early as 1926. Eventually, the scholar Richard Beale Davis carefully compared the Huntington Library manuscript against the Library of Congress manuscripts, and the work was finally published by the Huntington Library in 1954 under the title *Jeffersonian America, Notes on the United States of America Collected in the Years 1805–6–7 and 11–12 by Sir Augustus John Foster, Bart*. A new edition of this book will shortly be published by Fonthill.

Late in 1954, shortly after the publication of *Jeffersonian America*, the article 'Augustus Foster and his Book' was published by the scholar Donald H. Mugridge. The following quote is of interest:

In 1898, Foster's surviving son Vere Foster, published a substantial volume of family correspondence, entitled *The Two Duchesses*, which contains many letters exchanged by Foster and his mother, in whole or in part. So far as I can discover Vere Foster, although he omitted much, altered nothing, and his texts, so far as they go, are quite accurate—no small achievement in view of the fact that neither Lady Elizabeth nor her son wrote a good hand, and at time they could scrawl abomimably.

Vere Foster is very cautious in his notes and does little to assist the reader with the family's interesting background. He hardly touches on the notorious *ménage à trois* and the reader—if not already aware of the facts—is left to read between the lines. The exact relationship between Georgiana and Bess will never fully be known, but it seems likely that in addition to their heterosexual life, they enjoyed some form of special friendship that was probably lesbian in nature. As for the duke, he does not seem to have ever been particularly close to Georgiana, but in Bess he found a chemistry that mixed much better with his own. The end result to all of this was a remarkable bond between the three, which was broken only by death; first of Georgiana in 1806. Three years after Georgiana died, Bess married Cavendish to succeed her 'best friend' as Duchess of Devonshire. She herself was widowed just two years later and eventually left England behind and went to Rome, where she lived happily as a patron of the arts. On the anniversary of Georgiana's death, Bess herself passed away and was returned to England to be interred in the Cavendish vault beside her husband and the woman who had been her most faithful friend.

As for Bess, her early 'bond' with the duke resulted in two illegitimate children: Caroline Rosalie Adelaide (1785–1830), who later, as Caroline St Jules, married George Lamb; and Admiral Sir Augustus William James Clifford, 1st Baronet, CB (1788–1877). To avoid gossip, Bess bore both children in quiet retirement in France, away from prying eyes.

As for Georgiana, her loveless marriage led her momentarily astray, and following a liaison with the much younger Charles Grey, 2nd Earl Grey (1764–1845), she followed Bess's example, or more to the point, was purposely exiled by the duke, and bore her illegitimate daughter, Eliza Courtney (1792–1859), at Aix-en-Provence in France.

Vere Foster is very careful how he handles his material, to a point that we might find prudish in the twenty-first century, but which was normal during the staid later nineteenth century. As a result, some interesting asides that might have added to our knowledge of the family are sadly lacking. Even so, the work is a very welcome additional to the library of anyone fascinated by the remarkable 'Two Duchesses' and their extended families.

Most of the preface written by Vere Foster to the first edition of this work has been made redundant by a combination of time and by the fact that this edition contains different, but better versions of illustrations than he could find; furthermore, they are in colour rather than poor-quality black and white. However, Foster's truncated preface does contain a few relevant paragraphs:

I have given to this book the title of *The Two Duchesses*, because its contents are mainly composed of poetry and correspondence written by, or to, one or other of the two last Duchesses of Devonshire, one of whom, Georgiana, was daughter of John, Earl Spencer, and the other, Elizabeth, was daughter of Frederick Augustus Hervey, fourth Earl of Bristol, and Bishop of Derry.

These two ladies were inseparable companions, and lived under the same roof for nearly a quarter of a century. They travelled together in Switzerland and Italy; Georgiana, usually referred to as the beautiful Duchess, writing an account of their travels in verse addressed to her children, and pieces of poetry addressed to her friend, while Elizabeth illustrated Georgiana's poetical narrative by numerous landscape paintings of her own composition. Georgiana died in 1806, and Elizabeth became the second wife of the fifth Duke of Devonshire in 1809, and died in 1824.

The letters quoted in the correspondence are mainly written by the following persons:

Frederick Augustus Hervey, Earl of Bristol, Bishop of Derry, to his daughter, Lady Elizabeth Foster.

The Countess of Bristol to her daughter, Lady Elizabeth Foster.

Lady Elizabeth Foster, afterwards Duchess of Devonshire, to her son, Augustus Foster.

Augustus Foster, afterwards the Right. Hon. Sir Augustus J. Foster, Bart., to his mother.

The Earl of Aberdeen to Augustus Foster.

Lord Byron to Elizabeth, Duchess of Devonshire.

Lady Byron to Vere Foster, third son of Sir Augustus Foster, and compiler of this correspondence.

The Hon. Mrs. George Lamb to Augustus Foster.

Frederick Thos. Foster to his younger brother, Augustus Foster.

There are also single letters written by Gibbon; Sheridan; Fox; the Prince Regent; General Moreau; Alexander, Emperor of Russia, to Madame Moreau; Canova; Thorwaldsen; Baron d'Armfelt; and Count Cape d'Istrias, President of the Greek Republic.

I give in an Appendix some particulars culled from reliable sources about the Earl of Bristol, Bishop of Derry, Sir Augustus Foster, and Lord Aberdeen, who, next to Lady Elizabeth Foster, afterwards Duchess of Devonshire, are the principal parties in the correspondence here published.

The biography of Lord Byron is so well known that I would think it an impertinence to offer any information on the subject beyond the three letters addressed by himself to my grandmother; and I do not feel at liberty to publish anything about Lady Byron, except as regards the episode connected with my father's attachment to her prior to the advances of Lord Byron, and the few interesting letters addressed by her to myself.

The attachment here referred to, which met with the full approval of Sir Ralph and Lady Milbanke, as stated in the Duchess Elizabeth's letters to my father, came to my knowledge as a surprise, and will probably be new to all my readers.

In conclusion, I should mention that none of these letters have ever been published before, except a very few which appeared a few months ago in an Irish provincial newspaper, the *Belfast Northern Whig*, and that the present occasion of their publication arises from the fact that I have recently had access to a mass of family correspondence of which I was previously unaware, dated mostly about the end of the last and commencement of the present century. As the Duchesses moved, Georgiana for more than twenty, and Elizabeth for upwards of forty years, in the highest circles of society in London, Paris, and Rome, and were intimate with many eminent persons, and a great number of these letters relate to memorable contemporary events and subjects of public interest, I have copied some entire and made extracts from others, and, with the kind permission of my grandnephew, Sir Vere Foster, and encouraged by the very favourable reception of the letters already referred to, I have at the special request of many friends put them in print, adding notes of my own as to dates, and in explanation, where apparently required, of the text.

Owing to illegible writing, to fading of ink, to the torn and fragmentary state of much of the correspondence, and to the absence of dates in hundreds of cases, it has been found very difficult to preserve continuity, and I must claim the indulgence of my readers for such mistakes as they may discover.

Belfast, December, 1897,
Vere Foster

It is worth adding that the very final letters—those from Lady Byron to Vere Foster—were an unusual addition to the work, but obviously meant a great deal to Foster. Lady Byron was a great philanthropist and took a keen interest in the potential for the abolition of slavery on the USA. As for Foster himself, (1819–1900), philanthropist and educationalist, some have called him one of the greatest Irishmen ever. He was born at Copenhagen on 25 April 1819, while his father was serving as British Minister to Denmark. He was educated at Eton and Oxford and after graduation, entered the Foreign Office where his promising career as a diplomat was put aside once he returned to Ireland, in 1847. He contributed towards building school houses in rural Ireland—he devised cheap but very effective school books, and tried to better the lot of the poorly paid Irish school teachers. He was among the original promoters of the Belfast School of Art where, in addition to his annual donations, he guaranteed the headmaster's salary for a number of years. Several young students were put through college at his expense. The Royal Victoria Hospital in Belfast was another institution that benefited from his generosity. For over forty years, Vere Foster gave freely of his own money until his death in 1900. During his life, he assisted around 25,000 people to start a new life in the Americas and it is believed he spent approximately £100,000—a huge amount in the late nineteenth century—on other charitable endeavours while he himself lived on the equivalent of £100 a year. He died, 21 December 1900, in a cheap lodging house in Belfast.

As for Glyde Court, the Foster family home mentioned several times above, it is now a sadly derelict skeleton of a house at risk of collapse and in need of immediate attention before it descends to dust.

There are two final points to make. First, Foster's notes are very brief, and there are some points he did not contribute notes upon at all. In order to make this work more accessible to the reader, I have taken the liberty of adding extra endnotes, and these are denoted as 'Editor Note'. I have also completely re-illustrated the work.

Alan Sutton FSA
April 2018

THE TWO DUCHESSES

The Hon. Mrs. Hervey[1]
To Mrs. John Thomas Foster.[2]

Brussels, *June 6, 1777*

Voici déjà vendredi et je ne fais que prendre men écritoire pour la premiere fois depuis que ma chère fille m'a quitté. Mais pourquoi en *français* dit *Monsieur le sage?*[3] C'est vrai mais il a coulé de ma plume toute-fois comme je n'ai point besoin de vous dire *des choses.* I may in plain English tell you a plain truth, that I love you with all my heart, that I think of you continually, and that your whole conduct since your marriage has given me the most perfect satisfaction. Don't misinterpret this expression: it does not mean the most distant censure on your behaviour *before it*; but the *16th of December*[4] is your *grand epocha*, and may you date from it, dear Bess, every possible happiness. I shall be impatient to hear you did not suffer materially by the heat, fatigue, and distress of the first day. The rain and change of air we flatter ourselves made the second more pleasant, and this very night, perhaps, or tomorrow, you will breathe the pure air of your own dear country. I have been so mauled by the suffocating heat here that I have not been able to stir off the couch these two days; but I hope to get out this morning, and Monday the 9th is fixed on for our going to Antwerp. I find your sister[5] writes by this post, so I shall not touch upon the la rue des étoiles, and I could almost forbear to say anything myself (out of economy, that a packet of foreign letters may not add to your continental expenses), but that I have a mind to meet you in London and show you that my heart and mind are with you, but I expect you to rely upon this and not to expect frequent repetitions. You will have a thousand new objects, and I the important one of preparing and removing ourselves.

Whilst Mary is here, too, I know she will mention us. When we separate I will try to make you amends. Your father continues to *complain* and *do nothing*, but I think a journey will soon set him all right. Assure Mr. Foster of my sincere affection. He loves you too well for me not to feel a true regard for him, and I flatter myself that a well-founded esteem and perfect harmony will subsist amongst us all as long as we live. Adieu. Je vous sers sur mon cœur, and I repeat to you to take care of yourself, and above all to be *at home* in time. Remember what I said of a *false calculation*, and avoid its consequences. Present my compliments to Doctor Foster,[6] and *obey* as well as love. Your most affectionate mother.

Louisa[7] sends a thousand loves.

> *The Hon. Mrs. Hervey*
> *To Mrs. J. Th. Foster.*

> Liège, *June* 22, 1777

I am afraid my dear Bess will think I have made a long interval between my first and second letter. I feel it so myself, but as I knew Lady Erne wrote as punctually as if she had nothing else to do, I contented myself with doing everything else without writing, and indeed I found the business and the civilities belonging to our departure quite enough for me; however, I thank God, here I am tolerably well, and the journey thus far delightful, having your sister still with me, but we are drawing towards the moment of separation, which must be endured. Miss Creightons were received into the Convent yesterday in form, with all the black things hovering about them, but we are all vastly pleased with their present situation; they are well lodged as to conveniency, cleanliness and air, have a room and two little beds to themselves, a garden, a view to the country, and the cheerfulness of a great many pensioners, who seem perfectly well attended to.

The house is five stories high, and they carried us into every part of it, and nothing in Holland was ever cleaner.

Monday, the 23rd. Your sister and I were up this morning by six o'clock in order to go and make a visit to a Mrs. Bond, a cousin, at about 115 miles distance, but as I sent an express yesterday to give her notice of it, fearing to appear abruptly before an infirm woman of *eighty*, she just now has sent to decline it on account of her health, which mortifies me extremely, as I had a high opinion of her sense, manners, and excellence of mind.

Lord Erne was so good as to *propose* himself that Mary might go with me. I hope we shall keep together to-day notwithstanding our disappointment, but to-morrow, I fear, must be the day of *execution*, and poor *Dodd*[8] scarce dreads it more, for now I am bereaved of my children, and even *little Benjamin* cannot make up the loss—à propos, think of Louisa's being ready to stay in the Convent, and being quite at her ease amongst the nuns, and singing both English and French to them. The Lady Abbess is a cousin of Mr. Dennel's, and very like him, less fine, but a more soft, benign angelic countenance.

And now, my dear love, let me thank you for your letter from Bethune, and assure you of the pleasure I receive from every mark and expression of your affection to me. We all do you the justice to believe that you or Mr. F. wrote on your arrival at Dover and London, but your letters did not arrive from either place, and the delightful news of your being safe and well in London came accidentally from L. M. Fitz. Since that your father has received one, and you will easily imagine how we have all rejoiced in your welfare, amusement, and *good luck* in finding so many of your relations together. I must, before I forget it, tell you that your maid's letters to *Joseph* have been constant, so I suppose she has more care in putting them into the post-office than your other servants. As your stay in London was so precarious I will direct this to Bury, as my brother[9] can frank it to you if you should have left. I cannot yet give you that to Pyrmont,[10] but when I can find it out you shall have it. Pray always mention your health and how you go on, describe your meeting with Doctor F., tell me where you have been and are to go, and in general everything which belongs to you down to your watch. I had intended the foldings[11] for Mr. F., but since I have run into them unawares, I beg you will thank him in my name for his *little scribble*, which was very welcome to me, but his constant and kind attention to you I shall never forget—assure him of it and of my sincere affection. Adieu. The Padre's[12] blessing and the love of this party attend ye both. Ever your affectionate mother.

The Ministers did not quit us to the last, and a petit soupé, with a *Harp* and *arrêter sous cet ombrage* was our parting.

The Hon. Mrs. Hervey
To Mrs. J. Th. Foster.

Pyrmont, *July* 15, 1777

My dear Elizabeth, though I have been as good as my word in *not* writing to you, my thoughts have accompanied you through your several journeys, meetings, &c., and I also guarded as well as I could against any anxiety which you might have on my account by desiring my sister[13] to inform you of my welfare, which, I thank God, has been uninterrupted by any material accident. I found your letter here on my arrival on the 5th, which gave me great pleasure. Your expedition to London seems to have fully answered in point of *amusement*, and to have exceeded our expectation in your reception in the family, which is doubly satisfactory. I see, too, with content, that you have not forgot my friends, and I flatter myself that you have made them yours. I entirely approve of your going first to Sh.[14] with Dr. F., and wish that he remained in England to carry you over with him, for though you seem to *intend* being in time, I know *the young ff's*[15] are dreadfully irresolute, and I should depend more upon the old one.

I daresay you have had a little notice before this, but if not (for it is very weak in some people), do not be tempted to retard your journey. A propos, I hope you will remember that you have many *necessary things to provide*, but don't do it without a person of prudence to advise you, for finery and expense in these matters is very ridiculous for a private station. I am glad to find your health is at all better, but your account of yourself is not altogether satisfactory. I hope you are attentive to take your pills, and to prevent your being overheated; that you do not exercise *too much*, or sit up very late; as to the rest you must arm yourself with fortitude against a time which I hope will be of as little suffering as possible, and *that* abundantly made amends for by the *fruit of it*. As to unwieldiness, nobody ever heard or talked of such a thing in the *first instance*, not even *dear poppy*; you cannot be pincé, to be sure, any longer, but I advise you, when you are a mother, to be one in good earnest.

Your second letter from Sheffield is arrived, for which I thank you, and your father commissions me to assure you that his silence does not proceed from want of affection, which is as *cordial as ever to you*, but from a rambling life first, and then from the inability which these waters give to all reasonable employment. I am now transgressing positive orders, but I hope to come off for a *red nose*, whereas others pay the heavier tax of a headache. He has drunk these waters nine days, and I think with great benefit, which would be still greater if the weather was not worse than ever you saw it even in Derry; constant rain, and dirt, and puddle, and yet in spite of all he is well and cheerful, and the gouty pains fly before them. The lounging life agrees with him also, and he finds great amusement from the company's being quite new to him. Our Princess of Brunswick[16] is here, and vastly good to us. We dine with her quite en famille. Two of the Queen's brothers, too (one with his Princess), the Prince Augustus of Saxe Gotha, and many people of rank with whom one lives upon the easiest terms; the Prince of Waldeck[17] (who is Prince of the territory), vastly obliging, too, and all speak a little French. We have regulated our hours to theirs, and breakfast little, dine at half an hour after 12, sup between 8 and 9, and go to bed by ten. I have not yet said a word of myself, but I think you will not be contented without it, and I can with truth say that I feel better and stronger than I did before I came. I now and then pass

an agreeable hour with somebody that I discover to my taste, and I have
no material complaint. The village is very pretty. There are lovely walks
by the well, and the country is very picturesque, but the roads by which
we came were so dangerous that we do not care to return the same way. I
believe it will be difficult to find any that are good, but many schemes are
in agitation. The hereditary Princess wants us to go by Brunswick. She may
possibly be the reigning Princess by that time, as the Duke[18] is dangerously
ill, but what we shall determine on is quite uncertain.

I thank you, my dear love, most tenderly for your dear little present
by La. M., and am very sorry I did not stay long enough to receive it. I
am in hopes of a letter soon from Bury with an account of your having
spent your time very happily at Sheffield[19] amongst *friends* toute faite,
and some of them at least to your taste. What a wilderness the world is
without them, and how I miss you and your sister every day and every
hour. We have no news yet from Canada.[18] Louisa sends her kindest love
to you. I have been unlucky about a governess, for that *Aigle* would not
come at last. *Scott* was a little piqued, but behaved vastly well in the end,
and has come with us, making the best of all difficulties, and serving as
intepreter through Westphalia. Adieu, my dear child, my best affection to
Mr. F.,[20] and your father's blessing to you both. He says he will write to
you, but don't be uneasy if he does not. I hope f.[21] continues well, happy,
and satisfied. I believe Mr. Gifford has at last a living; he wrote your father
a letter of 3 *lines only* to notify the vacancy without asking for it. Dearest
Bess, I am your most affectionate mother. I know nothing yet of Mary, but
that she has got a lodging to her mind.

> *The Hon. Mrs. Hervey*
> *To Mrs. J. Th. Foster.*
>
> Pyrmont, *July* 30, 1777

My dear child, I received your letter of the 13th from Sheffield Place
yesterday, and am extremely concerned to find that you have had so much
apprehension on my account. I had warned you against expecting frequent
letters, and the constant change of place on your side as well as ours has
been a great hindrance to our correspondence. What can have interrupted
your sister's active mind and *pen* I can't guess, but it ought not to have
increased your alarm, because as we were not together it could not arise
from the cause you suspected. I fear, my dear Bess, that you have inherited
your mother's anxious temper about those you love, but conjure you, by
the well-known suffering of it, to struggle hard against it while you have
youth and spirits to do so, and to incline as much as you are able to the

best side of every object. You have, I hope, long before this received the letter I directed to Bury, either there or elsewhere. I meant it to secure the satisfaction to you, by which I fear I delayed it, but as you will find by it how perfectly free we have been from all *accidents fâcheux* I hope you will be more backward for the future to suspect them. The posts seem to be very ill regulated, too, and your letter from Dover of the 9th of June came only two days sooner than that of the 13th of July, but when once we are in Italy and you in Ireland we shall have a more regular intercourse.

We are to leave this place about the 8th or 10th, and go to Frankfort, and perhaps to Mayence, and so embark on the Rhine, and carry Ma^lle to Cologne, to put her en pays de Conoissance on her way to Brussels. This will give us an opportunity of pulling down that river for so far, by seeing the finest part of its banks. We shall take our carriages and come back by land, and so proceed to Frankfort again, Darmstadt, Manheim, Spier, Stutgard, Ulm, Augsbourg, Munich, Inspruck, Trent, Verona. This route through Germany will be new to us, and we hope besides to be in time to drink the waters of Val d'Agno[23] for three weeks. They are something like those which have agreed most wonderfully with your father and done some good to me also. His gout is drove away, and he is the life of the company: he has had but one drawback, by a slight fever brought on by cold, but which he has thoroughly recovered.

We are now reduced to a very small company here. Our Princess and her train set out for Brunswick to-day, which is a great blow, for there was real satisfaction and comfort in her company—a thing not very common with Princes or Princesses. There have been no English except ourselves and Col. Faucit, who is the negotiator for the foreign troops now in our pay. *Hot-hot's* brother is come for a few days, and is grown a quiet, good boy. Lord Bessborough[24] is here, too, who can never grow better or worse or *other* than *he* is. It is incredible what nonsense he talks. People listen and laugh; cela lui suffit, he puts it all down to his credit, and stands like a mountebank with a circle round him, which he entertains with marvellous things much in the same style.

I am glad to find you have passed your time so pleasantly, my dear love, and that your health is mended, of which I hope you have a proper care, and that you do not only *intend* but *determine* to be in Ireland by the very beginning of September. Remember, you have to settle yourself and to provide many things. I have not been able to learn whether Nurse Wilkinson stays for you in Dublin, but I hope so, to prevent the hazard of her going back and returning. I hope there will be no objection to her manner of nursing, as you seem to wish it, and I am certain she is too honest a woman not to tell you if by any weakness in the child a breast should be necessary, which is sometimes the case. N. Byrne, you know, is engaged for yourself, and I advise you to use the hartshorn and oil with hare-skins, as I did, to backen your milk, and remember your promise of guarding your breast from cold on your recovery and first going out, which will be in cold weather. I don't much approve of riding, except you had begun it sooner, but that is now over. I am glad the *infanta* is so *lively*, but I shall chide you if you become a mother so tristement. I had reckoned upon your feeling the full value of it, and I still think that when your fears are over you will think you are well paid for your *pains*. I have *ever* thought so, and I hope my dear child's children will not degenerate. At all events, if you find it too early a care I am ready to take it off your hands. When I return next year send the dear little creature to me with its nurse, and I will make it as hardy and active as a Magilligan kid. As to *names*, *il faut plus de menagement*: one of ours first, if you please, but don't put in too *much of the same ingredient*. D. F.'s present was very handsome, and what is better, very kind. I think you judge perfectly well about the trimming, which is proper, handsome, and lasting.

Your father bids me assure you of his truest, warmest affection: he received your long letter, but the waters have prevented his writing: he says when we are settled that we must take it by turns, and that you shall hear from us every fortnight. Adieu, my dear child. Louisa sends you a thousand loves, and longs for her *nephew*. My sincere affection to Mr. F.; pray mention his health. I will direct my next to Dunleer, and will write as we go on, but remember to allow for the failure of letters, which is very frequent. Adieu once more. I am very well, and most truly your affectionate mother.

> *The Hon. the Bishop of Derry*
> *To Mrs. J. Th. Foster.*
>
> Pyrmont, *July* 30, 1777

Your mother and I, my dearest Elizabeth, have at last agreed to atone for our long silence by writing to you alternately every week, and as she is a little occupied at present and I not at all (unless drinking waters comme un enragé may be so called), I have spontaneously taken upon myself to become the periodical tatler for this time, and to tell you that we are all well and the better for this Helicon of health. Your mother, very fortunately, found upon her arrival Dr. Closius—don't imagine this singular name either an abridgment or a translation of Close:st., whatever affinity there may be between his profession and his title. Such a trouvaille immediately quieted the lady's nerves, and prepared her admirably for the waters, which were deemed specific for her.

The next question was with regard to company, and in that, too, we were fortunate, for there was no canaille, little bourgeoisie, and some persons, not only of great distinction, but of excellent dispositions; and the great parity that is maintained here among all persons gives this little place a spirit of elegant but easy republicanism that is very pleasing, and I am sure contributes much to the salutariness of the waters, and of course to the recovery of the patients. At the head of this motley society of princes, peers, and citizens stands the amiable, the generous, the spirited, the learned prince of the country, the prince of Waldeck, about a stone's throw from the well. He has a soi-disant castle, but a very comfortable casino, built on a eminence which commands a most beautiful country of wood, water, meadow, and hill to a great extent, but to a much greater variety than ever I saw. Here he entertains during a month or three weeks every person successively who either can or cannot entertain him, females alone excepted, for as he is not married he claims an exemption—I am sorry to call it so—from that trouble. This is our commander-in-chief, but our principal citizen in this miscellaneous republick is our Princess Augusta, hereditary princess of Brunswick, with whom we have lived more than with any other person whatever, and from whom we part with a proportionate regret. Her husband came for a few days, but he is of a different character from his wife, more proud, less liant, rusé, some say false, very debauched, but with a kind of decency, and gave no tokens of it here. Grâces aux tempéramens délabrés et epuisés qui s'y trouvent. Among the crowd are expatriated prime ministers, exhausted ministers of the gospel, Lutherans, Calvinists, Hernhuters, Jews, Greeks, &c., who altogether form a good savoury oglio of society, especially as one can pick out of the dish such pieces as are too luscious or too hard for one's stomach, or even such as do not suit one's palate.

As to the Place, it is magical. There are two large and long avenues, flanked on each side with lesser, which are deemed the shilling gallery of Pyrmont, a part for servants. At the end of each of these avenues, which cut each other at right angles, is a decent octagon building which incloses the most salubrious of the most generally efficacious waters perhaps in all Europe. At the back of these avenues a triple range of buildings as singular in their appearance and yet at least as necessary in their use as the octagon itself, and which are calculated to receive these salubrious waters after they have filtrated through all the different vessels which have received them. The avenues are flanked on each side with shops, not very brilliant indeed, but by means of bath apartments said to be very convenient, and in the middle is a long salon where are public breakfasts, dinners, dancings, cards, concerts, and almost all the uses to which the ark of Noe could be put. Such is our situation here, where we shall remain ten days more. From hence into dear Italy once more, to drink the waters of Valdagno and winter at Pisa. Adieu. Be sure not to take the long voyage if you remain late in England; your stomach cannot bear it, and you will fall into the equinoxes. My blessings to your husband.

> *The Hon. the Bishop of Derry*
> *To Mrs. J. Th. Foster.*
>
> Pyrmont, *August* 7, 1777

I am just run home from the walks, my dear Elizabeth, to tell you that our journey for Italy is decided, and that we have the additional satisfaction of carrying with us the Prince of Saxe Gotha, one of those few men who unite familiarity with dignity and science, knowledge, &c., with politeness. We have taken violently to each other; he is to meet us at Frankfort, and from thence he says nous irons au Paradis sur les ailes de l'amitié. On Monday we begin this violent operation. You may trace us on the map to Cassel, Frankfort, Mayence, from thence we embark on the Rhine, descend it as far as Cologne by water, and return by land to Mayence, thence to Manheim, *Immortal Stutgard*, aussi sur que je m'appelle *Charles*, and so on to Ulm, Augsburg, Munich, Inspruck, Trent, and dear Verona. Don't I write like a child upon this subject, yet no wonder, when the very prospect of seeing such a country revives and *rajeunit*; your mother, too, is greatly reconciled to it, and only dreads the penetrating too deep into it, but it is absolutely necessary that she should winter where there is no winter. She will, besides, have the advantage of drinking the waters of Valdagno both in going and returning, and nothing can be more decided than that we shall return to these superexcellent waters; none can be composed with more suitable materials for relaxed constitutions, or for slow circulation of juices. Iron, nitre in small quantities, and a large portion of vitriol or fixed air constitute this salubrious spring; 'tis beyond belief efficacious. May you, my dear child, never want to try them, or if you should, may you never miss to do so. Your mother is marvellously well, walks for above four hours in the day, a is cheerful, sings, and enjoys the place in spite of its present solitariness. Adieu, my dear child; my head is so dizzy I can write no more; my love to your husband. Send for the mare home, as she risques being hurt by the others, being the weakest.

The Hon. Mrs. Hervey
    To Mrs. J. Th. Foster.

Manheim, *August 25, 1777*

My dear Bess, though I wrote to you only a few days ago from Frankfort, yet, as I flatter myself that you are at this moment on the march to Dublin Je me fais un vrai plaisir ma chère d'aller au devant de vous et de nous féliciter de votre arrivée. As it cannot be in person we must be contented with its being by proxy, and I hope you will not let your spirits sink on account of this unavoidable separation. All essential points are settled already, you know, by me for your safety and comfort, and though a mother is not easily replaced, yet I hope you will have such an accession of friends as will make her care and presence unnecessary.

We got here last night from Mentz, where I staid two or three days to wait for your father, who took the opportunity of going down the river as far as Coblentz, as the scenery there has been so much admired. He had the finest weather imaginable for it, and returned satisfied, but not enchanted; in fact, I think the banks, wherever I have seen them, too low to be very fine. I had intended myself this amusement, but he did not think the boats commodious enough for me, nor the road back by land sufficiently good, so I was obliged to give it up.

Take care of your health, my dear Bess, in time; one becomes a sad burthen to oneself from the want of it. The heat, dust, and fatigue of the journey has unravelled great part of the web wove at Pyrmont, and I have been drooping like a new planted cabbage for some days past. However, thanks to some rain, a few grains of I powder, and change of air, I am refreshed, and begin to hold up my head; the weather is fine, the heat moderate, the air seems good, and the town appears a perfect bijou. I am going out to examine it, and will tell you more at my return. Adieu.

Manheim is a vrai bijou; its situation, though flat, is beautiful, almost an island by means of the Rhine and Neckar, over which there are yet but convenient bridges, but when the devastations of the French in the Palatinate are better recovered, and that they are converted into ornaments, it will compleat the scene. The ramparts are pleasant walks which command these rivers, beyond which is a small plain bounded with very picturesque mountains. The town is, great part of it, new built, the streets are perfectly regular and broad, some planted in two rows for a walk in the middle, and a place or two very well laid out; the houses are tirés au cordon, and though the fronts are not uniform, this regularity of the line, together with a neat plaister they are covered with, some German ornaments and jalousies, give a general elegance in the appearance which is very pleasing. The Elector's[25] Palace is an immense building, but there is no good architecture or ornament. A grandeur and magnificence from the extent, and a fine prospect of the river and country from the back front; these are its merits. In the precincts of the Palace are also an Opera House, Tennis Court, Riding House, Library, and various collections of antiquities and natural curiosities in different cabinets.

We are waiting for our Prince, whom we expect every minute. In the meantime we have a very good apartment, with a large room which looks on the Place d'Armes, the prettiest spot in the town. Besides the cheerfulness of its being the parade, you may imagine that your father amuses himself very well here in the midst of these collections, and in sight at least of the mountains to which we are going. The Court are out of town, and we have not been in any society. He has seen and liked the French Minister (who is an Irishman), and last night an Excellence, something *hausen*, who is the Elector's Minister, sat with us for two hours. He is monstrously partial to the English, laments their present situation, and seems to be a sensible, well-minded man. The conversation turned chiefly on politics, on which, as you may imagine, I took little share; but when he got up to go away, the ceremonial was singular enough, with a permettez moi, Madame, de vous baiser la main (he repeated the baiser quick, and I believe as frequent as 20), *saying* jusqu'a cent fois. It was quite new to me, and I was almost ready to laugh, but I can conceive the scene to be sometimes more embarrassing. C'étoit un bon Papa avec un *presque Grandmama*, but I am not clear that *little slimness*[26] would have been easy with such a liberty towards his wife, even from *Nestor*.

We have still very hot weather, but I am much reconciled by rest. What I regret most is that I cannot hear from my children till I get to Verona. I hope to hear there *what time* you were to be at home, and then to believe you arrived. Adieu, my dear child; my best affection to f. Let me know exactly how you are circumstanced, and tell him I don't doubt but he will give me early and frequent news of you when you are confined. Remember you must not use your eyes. Tell N. W. I love her, and trust in her care, and give her Louisa's love, which she will like better. She is perfectly well, and minds neither heat nor fatigue. My compliments to Doctor F. Ever, my dear child, your most affectionate mother. Your father and Louisa send their best affection to you and Betsy.

The Bishop of Derry and Mrs. Hervey
To Mrs. J. Th. Foster.

Augsberg, *Sept.* 5, 1777

Here we are, my dear child, in great spirits, and in the company, I will not say of the most agreeable Prince, because that is almost a contradiction in terms, but of one of the most agreeable men I almost ever met—I mean the Prince Augustus of Saxe-Gotha, first cousin to His Majesty George the Third, K. of Little Britain. He has better talents, more knowledge, and less pretensions than most people—in short, he is a most excellent companion and all the appearance of a most affectionate friend. Your poor dear Mother is as much pleased with him as I am, and as he is perfectly polite and constantly cheerful, he is an equally good companion for both.

Would you believe que déjà nous avons été a Stutgard, seen its mad Sovereign,[27] and been accueilli by him in the civilest manner? He was in the country when we reached his capital. It was necessary to ask his leave in order to see an Academy of his institution, which bears an uncommon character in the rest of Europe. An old Rum professor, to whom I was recommended by a little Rum physician, dispatched an express to solicit his Princely permission, aussi sur qu'il s'appelle Charles. He brought it himself, and sent word that he would have the pleasure of showing it. We met him there with his Comtesse under his arm, and after saluting us with all proper dignity he began exhibiting his lions. A more elegant and orderly Raree-show I never saw. Imagine, my dear, 300 lads from seven years old up to seven-and-twenty, all ranged in different classes, but in the same uniform, same manner of dressing the hair, same hats, stockings, buckles, &c. &c., marching with as regular a step as a regiment of guards, and presenting themselves each before his respective plate, standing stock still till the signal is given for grace, and then each joining most reverentially in the benediction. When that is finished they remain as motionless till the word is given for sitting down, which alone is done with some eagerness. They then eat as methodically as they march, and during the meal the Prince and we marched from class to class, and he distinguished, as his caprice, his interest, or perhaps their merits led him, the different lads of talents. Their dread of him was shocking, though he seemed to do everything to familiarize them with him. After dinner they returned in the same distribution with which they came, and the Prince explained to us the nature of the Society. Lads of every nation, every religion, every age, and even every rank, are here admitted—from the sons of common soldiers up to Barons and Counts. Each follows his genius. We saw rooms for painting, sculpture, drawing, music, Latin, Greek, Hebrew, &c. &c. This is the true secret of education, and it succeeds accordingly. Different geniuses have ripened at different ages, and some premature ones have been blighted when least expected. Those who, after every trial, have shown no talent at all become good dunces; this event never fails. The Prince feeds, clothes, and lodges every one. None is allowed to receive money even from his parents, nor on any pretence to transgress the bounds of the College without an Inspector. Each lies in a separate bed, and fifty of them sleep so cleanlily in one room that the air is as pure within as without. I did not think so perfect a system of education existed anywhere.

To-morrow we go to Munich, then to Inspruck, then to Verona. Your Mother bears all beyond expectation, and Lou[28] in the highest spirits. I have my own horses, so need not say how well I am. Adieu. My love and blessing to your excellent husband; may he always love you as well as he does now, that is, as well as you deserve. I leave the rest of the paper for your mother; but send us all the Irish news you can, and believe me most affectionately.

Added by the Bishop's wife.

I will not let this paper be folded without adding a few lines to my dearest Bess, to confirm your Father's good account of me, and to say that I bear the fatigue of travelling very well, now the heat is over; and though my fat is in great measure melted away, I manage to carry my skeleton through with those who are in better case. Your Father's new friend is indeed a valuable acquisition, infinitely so to him and very agreeable to me. We shall now, I hope, be at Verona in a few days, and, I hope, find there good account of my dear children. I am persuaded that you are at this moment in Dublin, and may all possible happiness attend you there. Darling Lou is well, and sends her best love to You. Pray assure little f.[29] of mine; and great F.[30] of my perfect esteem and good wishes. I flatter myself that your present to him next month will make him very happy. Mention f.'s head, and be assured that I am interested for you both in every article to ye greatest degree, being ever

Your most affectionate Mother.

> *The Hon. Mrs. Hervey*
> *To Mrs. J. Th. Foster.*
> Valdagno, *September* 28, 1777

I think of you so much, my dear Bess, that I must absolutely write pour me décharger le cœur, especially as I have not had a line from you since you left Bury, which I reckon was on the 2nd, and of course 26 days ago. It is a proof, at least I hope, that you did not return to London, and that you are growing every day nearer to your own home though farther from me. That is now my first wish, yet the fear of any accident which may have befallen you on the road in so long a journey is very disquieting; but you have passed all the dangerous epochas for premature births; you have good roads, a good season, a kind, indulgent husband, and, I hope, an attentive servant, all strong guarantees for your good behaviour. I will therefore positively suppose you in Dawson Street,[31] and this is, I think, the fourth letter which I send to you there, and happy shall I be if my dear child receives it with her usual spirits, and with as much health as her situation will allow of. The accounts of you from Bury were very flattering, and Je tâche de m'en bien farcir la tête en attendant your own which I am sure you will not neglect to send me. You cannot be at a loss for a direction, as Danoot remains receiver-general, so that any letters directed to Verona would be sent after us.

I suppose you had des vives entretiens with Mr. Foster upon the beauties of Yorkshire comparatively with those of Brabant, but I flatter myself that he received a total defeat and gave hostages for his good behaviour: in short, I think you went triumphantly through all that riding; when you came to Westmoreland and Cumberland he took a little sly, malicious revenge, and if my poor dear love was not very sick in the passage she repaid him with interest on the other side of the water. I imagine you slept one night at least at Dunleer,[32] where I hope you have many comforts in store, and that you got coolly and quickly to town afterwards. But why do I talk of coolly? Perhaps you poor creatures are already in rain and storm while we are basking in sunshine.

It is a week to-day since we came hither, and we have had the finest weather imaginable, with only some rainy nights that have made the air still more agreeable. Your father continues to ride every morning to the spring, which is four miles from this village, and s'en trouve bien. For my part I readily adopt the Italian manner, and take the waters in bed. I begin about seven, remain in quiet and darkness till near half an hour after nine, and then open my window (behind the curtain), take my chocolate and lie till eleven, and sometimes twelve. This has rested and restored me extremely, and the waters agree perfectly with my constitution in every respect. I cannot positively recollect whether I wrote to you since I left Verona and told you the horrors of our bare walls, black meat, hard bread, &c., but we are all so much in humour with the waters that we scorn to be out of humour with anything else. We have dressed up the ugliness of the house as well as we could, a good appetite makes our peace with the bad food, and health, even in perspective, makes amends for many defects. There are two gentlemen and their wives here, but one family is too good, being always at church, and the other rather too bad: however, we have some communication with this last, though without any hopes of conversion. The lady is handsome, the gentleman very dull indeed, but we let him alone, and she is really agreeable, and having no object of love makes a very good, cheerful companion, with a proper retenue, at least when I am present.

Bittio[32] arrived two days ago, noir comme un maure, and grinning in a most ghastly manner, both at the fright he had been in about some robbers, and the joy to find himself so near home. He has brought a great many fine drawings, and made good remarks on them. We hope to see Mr. and Mrs. Strange here, and think of going back with them to Venice in about a fortnight. We are not quite resolved whether to remain the winter at Padua or to go to Pisa, but Rome and Naples are exploded, and this keeping nearer to you, my love, almost makes me feel as if I should see you sooner. Louisa sends her love to you; she is going on very well now her hours are regulated in the old way. She reads French and gets by heart with the governess, then writes and reads English with me. She has now begged to resume her drawing with Bittio, and she walks every day after dinner attended by a little dog I have given her, which makes her delight. She is perfectly well, and keeps her plumpness still. I have a bed, even here, in my room for her, and Mademoiselle in the next, so that I am a spy upon them, and she no fatigue to me, but much pleasure, and her mind opens daily. Adieu, dear Bess. My love to f. Your father's blessing on you and him, and our compliments to the Doctor. La Belle is almost suffocated for want of somebody to scold, but behaves well, and so do I. Remember me most kindly to Mr. Rich and Miss Bellew....

The Hon. Mrs. Hervey
  To Mrs. J. Th. Foster.

Valdagno, *October 5*, 1777

S'occuper c'est savoir jouir,
L'oisiveté pèse et tourmente;
L'âme est un feu qu'il faut nourrir
Et qui s'éteint s'il ne s'augmente.

You will wonder, my dear, to see my letter begun with poetry, but these four lines of Voltaire were just now repeated to me. I do not recollect to have ever seen them, and if they are as new to you, I think you will not receive less pleasure from them than I have done.

The 6th.—I had got thus far in an idle kind of scribble when I was blessed with my dear child's letter from Dunleer. The winds favoured me extremely and brought me the news of your safe arrival in 24 days. I need not, I cannot, say how delighted I am with it, nor how thankful I am for your preservation from all the accidents which threatened you. You was a good dear thing for giving me this satisfaction so immediately and by your own hand, as no other could have conveyed the same degree of content to me. You seem to have performed the journey in a very short time, but I flatter myself that you wrote truly safe and well, and that you have not suffered from it. The scheme of *ending* your journal at home was an excellent one, but as I received your letter with too great eagerness to see the postmark on the direction, I was much disappointed on finding the date from Bury, and the happiness at the end was such a surprise to me that I was in transports at it. Don't make any apologies to me for the length of your letters, but be assured they are by so much the more welcome, and that there is no circumstance belonging to you so trivial as not to interest me.

Though I have mentioned L. B.'s conduct towards Mr. F. and you in former letters, yet I must repeat my satisfaction as well as surprise at it. I think the £100 was well allotted, but would it not buy 3, instead of 2, pins. I have a notion 30 guineas for each would do very well, and that would be something more, and the number better suited to your use for them. I am glad *Slimness* is a favourite and should wish to hear his remarks and opinion, but not by letter.

My dear Bess, you outdo my best hopes in matronly care. Comment une petite provision; 'twas an excellent wench, and when I love her not chaos is come again. It had often occurred to me to recommend it (so truly have you guessed my thoughts), but the fear of alarming you withheld me, and I believe I never even hinted it. I thank God that this provision was useless, but I figure to myself that my dear child may be at the time she receives this safely and comfortably in her own bed, with the little—removed to other quarters, and in high content, the Doctor in possession of a little grandson, nurse W. in high fun, little Byrne in a notable fidget, and dear Mrs. R., or my friend Miss B., in social chat in the great chair by you. If all this has not already taken place, I flatter myself it is a comfort in store for you. I expect from my dutiful son great discretion, and that he talks no more to you than the women allow of (who are here, for once, the best judges), besides which, I must add that if Poupée is dismissed one moment before her time my heavy hatred shall fall on him; it is a thing of the utmost importance or I would not name it, but who else can do it? You have only to keep my letter en cas de besoin, and I have too good an opinion of the youth to doubt his compliance after such a warning.

We have compleated a fortnight here with satisfaction, that is, with success; the waters continue their good effect, the weather has favoured us, and one week more, before the rains set in, is all we ask. We are then to go to Venice for a short time, and I believe afterwards to Pisa (in Tuscany), but direct always to Danoot for fear of a change of plan.

I have wrote to beg Mrs. Preston's protection for you in Dublin, which I think will please her and make her partial to you, and that you will like her and she you notwithstanding the disparity of age. The poor La. M'D. have played a desperate game. Be sure to let me know your acquaintance and connections; take care of cold on your recovery; cover your *petto*; wear a *châle* all winter, and let me find you blooming next summer. Adieu. My love to f. Your father and Lou's to both; compliments to Dr. F., M. Rich, M. B. Parnello, et tutti quanti, and my blessing on my children and grandchildren. Louisa says she is monstrously happy at your safe arrival, and longs to be an aunt. She sends her love to Nurse. I hope she is stout and well, and little Byrne also.

> *The Bishop of Derry*
> *To Mrs. J. Th. Foster.*
>
> Rome, *January* 28, 1778

I have been writing till my head is almost giddy, and yet I cannot let the post go out without saying one word to my dear Elizabeth. Your mother and Lou are at the opera, from which I exclude myself per decorum. I have the more leisure for other amusements, among the foremost of which, my dear child, is conversing with you. I must, however, begin with commissions. I have bespoke a full-length statue of my late brother,[34] which I mean to have executed by the print we have of him, and beg that you and your husband would visit the work as often as you can. Vanoost, if he is able, is to execute it. The next, my dear, is rather more difficult. I wish you to buy me the handsomest poplin you can find, and of the richest colour, as much as will make the most fashionable gown. This I would have sent to your sister at Paris, which Lady Buckingham can easily contrive for you by one of the many messengers that go to London, or even by the common post to the Secretary of State's office, from whence it can with equal ease be directed to your sister at Lady Stormont's,[35] and your sister will have directions from me to forward it to me at the Cardinal de Bernis' at Rome, where I am on such a footing that he has done this more than once for me.

'Tis incredible how pleasantly I pass my time here, both within the town and without, and how agreeably the first nobility receive strangers. Your mother begins now to mix a little more, and I hope will gain both health and spirits by it, but she dares not attack palaces or antiquities, both on account of the fatigue and the damp. I am impenetrable to both, and have, besides, painters working in my room all the day. 'Tis really a life of Paradise. The sett of English, too, are pleasant enough, and have their balls, their assemblies, and their conversationes, and instead of riots, gallantries, and drunkenness, are wrapt up in antiquities, busts, and pictures. One day or other, perhaps, we may visit it together, but as yet I think the hazard in every respect too great.

"For youth to itself rebels tho' none else near."

I am impatient to hear that something is to be done for the R. Catholics. Pray inform yourself well about it, and then me. The young senator's[36] opinion would weigh much with many people, and he could easily discover their bent; there seems to be no possibility of escaping a French war. They are working with all their might at Toulon, and only getting ready to attack us the better. My intelligence is pretty good, and they are so confident of success they can scarcely veil their faces enough to conceal it. In this case you would see us sooner than we promised, and the Cardinal de Bernis must give us his last favor, a passport. Some of the French are already hurrying home, and a lady of the very first distinction took leave of me to-day, hoping there would be no war, but expecting there would. She is sister of the French ambassador at London. Ireland in this case is undoubtedly their first object, and what a desperate condition is ours if the R. Catholics are not first won over. I tremble to think of it. Why don't you write to us more constantly, and be sure that every trifle that belongs to you or your husband interests us. Adieu. It is an hour later than I thought, but a short letter is better than none, and so I send you this.

The Hon. Mrs. Hervey and the Bishop of Derry
  To Mrs. J. Th. Foster.
                                            Rome, *March* 3, 1778

I waited for the end of the Carnival, dear Bess, in hopes of having something to tell you which was extraordinary and amusing that might dissipate your *natural gravity* for a moment, and lighten the effect of *Irish fogs*; but, alas, my dullness and indolence, and the most perverse and persevering wet weather imaginable has in great measure disappointed my project. The *Saturnalia* is almost over, and nothing memorable has happened that I know of. The public entertainments have been bad operas, masked balls at the theatre at so low a price that you might be in company with your cook, or even your footman, and for the last eight days a horse race in the principal street, which was likewise crowded with coaches and masks. The Roman people are remarkable for an immoderate love of pleasure, yet, though *this* amusement was limited to a few hours only each day, the part they took in it was so moderate that it seemed to consist only in gazing at each other, and throwing sugar plumbs. This *retenue*, however, is, I believe, the effect of guards, constables, and spies, and la Corda[37] (which you may remember described by Bittio) set up in the midst ready to punish any offender sur le champ. The race itself is indeed as little worth seeing, as can be imagined, and as little seen. For imagine to yourself five or six horses let loose to run down a street quite full of people, without riders, and without a place set off for them. The people, who are divided among many objects, make no place for them till the moment they come up, and then, falling back just enough for them to pass, close again the moment after; so that as there is only one heat, it is really only a momentary amusement. What is a greater is the variety of figures that are *piled* up on each side. The windows and balconies tapissés, and full of people. Some fine carriages, and a few open ones; but I have seen nothing so pretty as the procession at Brussels, and there is very little *humour* amongst this great variety of people. The most entertaining of them was one who, in the character of a *petit maître abbé*, went about bowing to all the ladies, and looking at them with his lorgnette. One of our horses happened to fall, and this prétendu abbé ran, amongst others, to our assistance, and after he was got up, he very pompously gave him his *benediction* to prevent future accidents (knowing, as was supposed, your father for a bishop), on which there was general acclamation.

Colonel Dillon (brother to the one who married Miss Phipps) is just come here, and has given us the satisfaction of seeing somebody who has seen your dear sister, which is always more satisfactory even than a letter. I had one at the same time, and she seems going on very pleasantly.

Voltaire[38] is really at Paris, as the newspapers mentioned, but which I could not believe. He lodges upon some quay or open part of the town where there is a crowd every day to stare at him; but what is more satisfactory, he has had a deputation from the Académie des Belles Lettres with some of the first people at their head. The first geniuses in the suite, and above forty in number to compliment him on his arrival and acknowledge those talents by which he has done so much mischief. Imagine his excess of happiness! This man, who has certainly more vanity than almost any other person, has been also proportionably more flattered. His sun sets bright indeed, yet I think that in the midst of his glory his heart smites him. He is going to bring a play upon the stage even now, but I have not heard whether it is likely to be a proof of his strength or of his weakness. I cannot help feeling something on this occasion for poor Rousseau, [39] who, I think, will be ready to dye with envy. He is certainly a more amiable man, and I believe more mad than wicked. In proof of this I must tell you that he has lately made his address to God Almighty, which is not to be published till after his death. He tried several times to deposit it under a particular altar in a church at Paris, but was defeated, and at last determined to find out a *faithful, generous, pitying Englishman*, with whom he might entrust it with this injunction. He has done so. I saw the particular friend of the person to whom it is confided, who told me that R. had read it to his friend with the tears pouring down his cheeks, and that it is a recital of all his hardships and misfortunes, and a most sublime and affecting composition.

God bless you, my child; perhaps we may meet sooner than was intended, for we are in daily expectation of a declaration of war, which must drive us home. My love to f., and a kiss to dear Fred the third. Your father and Lou join in all kind thoughts towards you. Compliments to Doctor F. No account yet of Mrs. Oliver. I write to you almost every week. I hope you receive my letters. I am, dear Bess, your most affectionate mother.

E. HERVEY.

Louisa sends her love to Nurse, to which I add my blessing.

The following supplement is added by the Bishop.

Your mother has left me just room enough to give you a commission, dear Bess. Ships are continually going from Dublin to Leghorn. Send me by the first as much poplin as will make two suits of clothes, one of a grey, and the other of a puce colour. Direct them "à monseigneur le Cardinal de Bernis à Rome". Put them into oilskin, and inclose them "au Consul François à Livourne". I wish I knew what would best please you and your husband from hence. Tell me frankly, but after the second week in April direct to us at *Paris* at Sir John Lambert's. If you like to go and stay at Derry this summer, the house and garden there belong to you and yours.

> *The Hon. Mrs. Hervey*
> *To Mrs. J. Th. Foster.*
> Rome, *March* 15, 1778

From the time of your receiving this letter, dearest Bess, your direction must no longer be to Rome but to Paris, Sir John Lambert. Our route is not absolutely fixed, but the troubles *naissant* in Germany will prevent our returning the way we came, and I hope we may go the other in time to see your sister before she leaves it. They seem quite uncertain about their summer party, indeed we must all be so whilst war hangs over our heads. I have just now your letter *ended* on the third of last month, and am sorry to find that you have had any apprehensions about me, but I cannot account for an *interval of six weeks*, as I think I have seldom been so long as a *fortnight* without writing to you. I have had no confinement all the winter, and though it has rained almost as constantly as in Ireland, there is generally some part of every day not only *practicable* but *pleasant*, and with a mild, soft air and sun unknown to us poor islanders in our own country. The spring is now remarkably forward, and the scene brightens every day. I hope to see some of the environs, and in the meantime our Lent promises to be more cheerful than the Carnival, from the great number of strangers which are now every day returning from Naples. Vesuvius has been so quiet that your father has not been tempted to go there. I hope it will not take a *tantarum* at the time we should go northwards for fear we should make a short turn towards it.

Mr. Dillon, brother to our nephew and colonel of a regiment in the service of France, is here with some other officers who had all received orders for their immediate departure to join their corps, but it is relaxed a little yet, so that they seem in expectation every post of fresh orders. Many jokes pass between him and your father about the invasion of Ireland. The Colonel promises to be careful of the Palace, your father to be *indulgent to the prisoners.*

What you tell me of f. and yourself opens a prospect to me much more delightful than the fairest in Italy. I see very plainly that his conduct towards you has been affectionate and confidential. I know how well you deserve it, and I long to embrace you both; the *rose-lipped cherubim*, too, whom I am prepared to see with an éclat of beauty and its first lovely little endeavours to walk. I regret only that it will be old enough to fly from me, but I trust I shall soon win him over. I hope you will all come to us as soon as we get home and that may perhaps be by the middle of summer, but certainly cannot be later than the end of it. Remember me affectionately to Mrs. Richardson. I am very glad she is in town. I have not heard from her, but notwithstanding your caution, if she tells me you are thin I shall be alarmed. I hope you will take the medicine I have recommended to you pour me soulager. I am sorry for your disappointment in Miss M., but dear Lady Ross makes amends, and I had rather your intimacy were with those older than yourself. La. B.'s civility to you n'est pas peu de chose, for I hear she is haughty. You don't mention the Fitz, so I conclude they don't go on to their credit, but I wonder you say nothing of the youngest brother, married to Miss Butler, Dean Bayley's granddaughter. I hope you have visited her. Your good nature to poor Miss Blackall pleases me, and I believe she is sincerely attached to you and to me, besides that she is unhappy, which is always a claim on a generous gentle mind, and therefore operates, I am sure, upon yours. Your éclat on the birthday, and the *popular acclamation* was charming. I flatter myself that little f. quietly enjoyed both. Adieu, my love. My hours are now much crowded, and I have not leisure for long letters. Your father and Louisa send their love to you both. You know how much you possess the heart of your affectionate mother.

Louisa's love and my blessings to Nurse.

The Hon. Mrs. Hervey
To Mrs. J. Th. Foster.

Rome, *March* 25, 1778

I return you my most affectionate thanks, dear Bess, for all the kind things which you say to me on my birthday. The gift of life to one who feels its true value and tries to attain *its end* is inestimable, whatever may be the rubs which, in the course of it, are allotted to us. But good children are its choicest blessings, and Providence has been bountiful to me in this article, not only giving to me the present enjoyment of them, but the most reasonable hope of their being treasures to society, and furnished with all that can procure their own most everlasting happiness. I can hardly say how much I felt for you on the *alarm* which your dear little boy gave you. They are a *tax* (amongst some others) which nature has laid upon us poor mothers, but then the tenderness of our attachment makes us great amends, from the first innocent smiles of our infants down to their grateful and well-directed affections. I hope these pangs, however, have not been repeated. It is sometimes only the first that are so violent, and as he begins early to cut his teeth I flatter myself they will come the easier. He is, I conclude, before this *decorated* with a coral. The nurse knows that I conformed to this usage, which I think both *ornamental* and *diverting*. I have more reliance on a crust of bread for efficacy. I figure to myself poor f. in a deplorable state, betwixt his anxiety on your account and the dawning of his *fatherly tenderness*, and am sure it cost him many a sigh and stride about the house.

Sir Robert Smyth (the Welshman) is here and his wife, who is a pretty sensible young woman. I talked a good deal to him about f., whom he spoke of with kindness. He said he was sure he would make a good husband, and I don't remember that *we could find any fault* except a little too much reserve and gravity for a young man, but he swore to me that he had seen him at times lively, even to mixing *humour* very agreeably with his conversation. So have at him, dear Bess, and make him laugh without mercy in spite of Lord Chesterfield.[40] I am very glad to hear so good an account of his health, and that he is in *better hands than his own*.

I hope you do not forget that I consulted Dr. Smyth for you in that only illness you ever had, and which overturned your constitution and was the foundation of all that is amiss about you to this day. I mention this because it will make him a better judge than anyone else, having the experience added to family attachment, and perhaps you will take his opinion about the medicine I sent you, for if I find you *thin* and coughing I shall chide you as usual or perhaps more—especially as I find *you take fright and don't dance*. Your letter is a very pleasant account of yourself, my dear, and I follow you about to all your parties…. Had I the face of Mrs. Ferguson at full grin I would sit for my picture, to indulge your affectionate desire of it. The fact is that my face, such as it is, has been very bad, and the medicine of no effect. I had intended it for my brother, and the first sitting is over, but it promises so ill that I believe it will be only fit for my *partial children*, who seem to wish to preserve even the idea of what I am. I hope yours will be well done. Your father's is admirable, and Louisa's, though unfinished, may, I think, be relied on for a pretty picture and strong likeness.

Your sister[41] has fallen not only into the first set of company, but has made some of the *best* acquaintance, and the most creditable imaginable. She is bien repandue dans le monde et parfaitement bien reçue, yet I don't think her at all happy, and I fear, though she does not say it, that Lord Erne keeps his usual restlessness and discontent, and though he requires society more than anybody, is constantly running away from it, and yet is without a fund in himself to supply its place.

We have now determined on making Paris our way home, but whether we shall be in time to catch them there the war will determine. If it breaks out now we must hurry home and go there en droiture, but if not we go to Venice. I write to Mrs. Strange by this post to say that we intend being there by the 18th of May. The 27th April is our day fixed for leaving Rome, and we shall make short stops on our way. I hope you will have calculated for a full month's journey for your letter, and not have directed it here too late. At all events when *this* reaches you let it warn you to direct only to Paris, Sir John Lambert's. All the rest is too uncertain. God bless you, my dear child. I must say a word or two to *Slimness*.[42] Louisa sends you her *unfaded love*, her constant kind wishes to her nurse, and a kiss to her nephew.

I thank you sincerely, my dear Sir, for your satisfactory account of my daughter, and am not a little pleased that you begin already to huff your son. I flatter myself that I shall examine the truth of these articles before it is very long. We are soon to leave the treasures of Rome for the *treasures* of *Ireland*, which are now far greater to me. I confess, however, that this is a charming residence, but as to weather, the winter has been much more rainy than that we passed at Brussels. I thank you for your Politicks, though the most interesting of them is the completion of the circular road, of which I hope you and Bess profit, and perhaps the *dab*.[43] As to f.'s silence in Parliament, it is prudent to begin with it: il se recule pour mieux sauter. Voltaire has been dying at Paris, and has *confessed* and asked pardon of God and the Church. He is now recovering, and I should think would be puzzled to know whether to act Saint or Devil.

The Hon. Mrs. Hervey
   To Mrs. J. Th. Foster.

Rome, *April* 6, 1778

My dear child, your father went out yesterday on a little tour, the first that
he has made (in the four months which we have been here), and has left me
your letter to answer, that is, acknowledge, lest an unusual silence should
alarm you. But acceptable as the commission is to me, I fear I must needs
be brief, for our departure draws very near, and I have left a *mass* of things
to do in his absence, which I thought would have happened sooner, and
which you know is the time I allot for all the *fiddle faddle* of preparation
so *inexplicable* to our *sovereigns*. I have besides to pay my respects to some
of the *principal rarities* here, for I have been obliged to decline the *detail
of them*. I shall only eat what I *can digest* and I hope be the better for, but
the weather has become quite hot, and though I have now the absolute
command of my time, it harasses me a little, but I shall make everything
bend to it and accept of no engagements: all daylight may be put to profit,
and in the evenings our friend the Prince of G.[44] and the Russian general
came and sat with me till eleven, which is my hour of repose.

I have been more vexed than you can imagine at losing the advantage
I had promised myself of the excellent music-master I mentioned to you:
great defects and great perfections are almost always contrasted in the
same person; he is quite a character, but it is not *Bittio's*. In short, an
enthusiasm about a treatise he is writing on music, an attachment to his
country, and a philosophic contempt of riches robs us of this treasure and
perhaps a little love, qui s'en mêle.

I have this moment a letter from your sister, who gives me the triste
nouvelle of Lord Stormont's[45] departure from Paris, Monsr. de Noailles'[46]
arrival there from England, &c., &c., in short, everything but a *formal*
declaration of war, but as that must now follow, I think we have nothing
further to do or to hope for, and I imagine your father, who has had this
account, will return in a few days, and that we shall soon after take the
shortest route to our *unhappy* country.

Adieu! Venice, but would I were already at Paris to counsel poor dear
Mary. One good, at least I trust, is to be drawn from this great evil; I mean
our being all once more together. The English post is come in, but there is
no confirmation of the above news, though I know it to be true. I suppose
it was a day or two before the event. Adieu, dearest child: be in no pain for
us. There is no doubt of a passport and a safe conveyance home, and the
season is now fit for travelling. I look upon America as lost for ever, but I
flatter myself that Lord Chatham[47] will be our minister, and that we shall
punish the *treachery of France* effectually. Ireland is to be invaded, it is

said, but I hope we shall give them other employment. The French officers are all gone off this morning. I embrace the father, mother, and son with true affection. Louisa sends her love to all, and to her nurse par dessus. She is well and happy. I told you before to direct to Paris only—Chevalier Lambert.

The Bishop of Derry
    To Mrs. J. Th. Foster.

Rome, *May* 29, 1778

My dear child, in the uncertainty whether this will find you in Ireland or not, I shall not write as copiously as I would have done last week had I had leisure. When your mother wrote to you, my dear, the fate of war appeared to be fixed, and in that case we were equally fixed to remain at Rome; but since all the appearances now incline for peace, our project changes with that of higher powers, and if the political weather continues fair we shall leave this delicious abode at latest in the autumn. Your mother has imagined that the waters would be almost necessary to you, and if you suspect it, my dear girl, don't delay so pleasant a remedy for a single week, but take up fifty pounds from my banker, Mr. Gleadow, who upon seeing these few lines will be contented with your receipt, and it will at least pay your postage through England.

I must confess to you that if a war should take place between France and us, I am in no little pain about Ireland, as I know to a certainty their great stroke will be at us, as the weakest, the most divided, and the least defended. The Irish regiments in their service are already quartered on the coast and ready to be embarked, and the officers belonging to those regiments who had made an excursion to Rome of a few weeks were returned, recalled in a hurry, and had joined their corps. From these I collected enough, not only to assure myself of their destination, but even of more particulars than they would have chosen *before dinner* to communicate. Their object at Rome at this time was easily guessed. Considering what a number of Irish friars of every denomination abounds here, and how attached our cruel and political laws render them to the Stuart family, nothing could exceed the attention shown by the French Ministers here to these gentlemen. They were lodged in one of their houses, and received daily at their tables, and distinguished constantly from all other strangers, and their elation at the thought of a war was beyond all description. At the close of their visit they scarce made any secret of their destination, and would frequently rally me on my purchases of statues and busts, which they said must one day belong to them. If so perilous a state does not waken our Government to mitigate the penal laws against the Papists, and to win by gentleness whom they cannot subdue by severity, if the most uniform acquiescence under the most impolitic and undeserved oppression that ever disgraced any legislature does not soften our, as yet, inflexible Government, I must confess I shall suspect some treachery, and that there is a latent scheme for driving them out of the island.

You write to us very irregularly, my dear child; I hope your health is not the cause of it. Yet at this distance the omission of a post is of some consequence, and forms a disappointment not easily repaired. Have you received your little mare? Does she suit you, or are you become too timid? Did you ever receive my letter in which I offered you my house either at Derry or the Down Hill,[48] if you wish to change the air? It long preceded our thoughts of staying here, and it is now an age since we have heard. Think that it requires almost two months to return an answer and you will not be so dilatory in sending one. I long to know where you pass your summer, in case you remain in Ireland, what your occupations and what your intentions are.

We are fixed in a delightful habitation twelve miles from Rome which we see every day, but have not yet visited since we left it. The environs of this part are the most delightful that can be imagined. Wood, water, hills, plains, rivers, and the sea, while beautiful buildings decorate all the villages, which are chiefly on eminences, and from our house to Albano the road leads through a bird-cage walk of about a mile, shaded by the largest, the oldest, and the most venerable oaks, as well as chestnuts, that I ever saw. Under the branches of these patrician trees one frequently discovers the principal buildings of Rome, and especially the numerous ruins of ancient ones that fill the immense plain between this hill and the city. In short, a more romantic spot cannot be seen. But I am tired of writing my tenth letter and must break off, not without assuring your husband of my sincerest affection, or without renewing every protestation of the truest love to you and yours. Your mother and Lou are both well, and both at supper in the next room.

The Hon. Mrs. Hervey
To Mrs. J. Th. Foster.

Castel Gandolfo,[49] *June* 28, 1778

As I had flattered myself, dear Bess, so it has turned out, and the last courier from Paris brought me two of your letters, for which I thank you, my love, and for all your punctuality and affection. You say your health is better. Mrs. Richardson writes me word that you seem well, but that your looks are not in favor of that opinion. I hope, however, that the fatigue of the winter and amusements may be the *chief* cause of the alteration; and I think I may rely on you and Mr. Foster for not retarding any measure that may be thought necessary to restore you. Don't you deceive him in your complaints, dearest child, and I think he will not deceive me in his attention to them.

Great events have happened here since the date of your letters: Lord Chatham's loss in the political world, Voltaire's in the literary, and the great long-wished-for toleration passed so nobly in England and so well begun in Ireland; you may imagine how much your father's mind is occupied with such articles. He was very much affected by the death of our great minister and deliverer; but, luckily, the warm part he had taken in bringing about this bill, and the unexpected and rapid success of it, has turned his thoughts into a new channel, and restored his spirits: he now talks of nothing but Ireland, and I only pray God that we may wait till the heats are fairly over before we undertake our journey. The Roman Catholics here and everywhere are in high spirits, and we have already some instances of the good Irish *preparing* to spend their *fortune* and their *lives* in their own country, so that I do not doubt but there will be a very great revolution in favor of it almost immediately.

I conclude that your sister will have told you how infamously Voltaire closed a life which has been a perpetual scandal to mankind; he certainly had very great and agreeable talents, but a corrupt mind, and a mean, unfeeling heart. *F's transport of rage against him* was a *feast* to me, and conveyed such agreeable ideas of his sentiments as I trust he will verify in all his words and deeds. Your account of your *matron manners* does not alarm me, for I lost my wild, youthful spirits as soon as you did; and I know that you may have more satisfaction, and less danger from a more even and quiet temperature, which I hope, however, will not degenerate into *grave*, which does not belong to you. Mrs. Berkeley writes me word that Ranizzini[50] goes over to Dublin, on which I congratulate you, as also on all the pleasant parties which I flatter myself you have had out of town. I can easily conceive you to be a favourite with dear La. Arabella and all who think well; and, what is more, I am convinced that you will always be such, for your character has taken its *plie* and Dieu soit loué for its being a right one. I beg you will reconcile your mind to my passing the summer here, where the air agrees uncommonly well with me, instead of going to Val Dagno, which, being a small town in a small valley, would have suffocated me. I am thinner than ever, and wizened like a winter apple, but I thank God my health is pretty good, my spirits even, and my face better; and if the frequent variation in the father's feelings and schemes did not affect my nerves, I believe I should even grow fat—he begins now to find this air too gross for him, and is going to make a little tour, which at *this season* in *this country* is difficult, but he cannot do without it. Louisa is very well, very amiable, very docile, but without application to anything. She sends her sincere love to you; to f., the darling nephew, and his nurse. Adieu! I embrace you both, my dear children, and am your affectionate mother.

F.'s scrap at the end of your letter was cheering, and I thank him for it. Compliments to the Doctor.

The Hon. Mrs. Hervey
To Mrs. J. Th. Foster.

Rome, *July* 15, 1778

Though I think I wrote to you last Wednesday, dearest Bess, yet, as I find myself at my usual employment here, I must try to snatch half an hour to thank you for a long letter of the 14th of May, which I think came after mine was set out. The time will soon come when I shall begin to talk of the arrangement of our journey, and the time fixed for it: in succession our adventures on the road, and finally, I hope, a rendezvous given in St. Patrick's blessed island.

The heat is increased since I wrote, but is still bearable, and much depends on temperance, patience, and good management. The most disagreeable circumstance is the disappointment. We have the finest sky and sun imaginable, which we dare not enjoy; fruits which are delicious and pernicious; and refreshing evenings which prudence forbids to taste of: my weak frame will not allow me to get up at 4 o'clock in the morning, which is the time of enjoyment, and your father's regularity and strictness with regard to good hours at night takes off the amusement which the freshness of the evening invites to after supper (I mean in the house). This leaves a short space in each afternoon only for going out, &c., but the drives are lovely and invaluable even thus. I have dined at a neighbouring villa; but though it is delightful when once there, it is difficult to get to it without suffering. Thus you see new illusions start up in every path of life; virtue is the only good, and a good conscience the only real, invariable, permanent satisfaction and enjoyment.

Your lamentation and panegyrick on Lord Chatham are very just, dear Bess, yet I confess that, strongly as I feel the publick loss, I think the ruin of his family by a shameful profusion or inattention bears hard on his private virtues as a man.[51] To make a perfect character they must go together, and where they do not, I cannot but suspect brilliant qualities to be without a solid foundation. A man who loves his country preferably to his children appears to me a monster; but I speak more as a woman than as a patriot, notwithstanding I can conceive the virtue of a Brutus (hard as it was); but there must be delinquency and the austere justice of a magistrate; but why a retired statesman should forget he is a father je l'ignore. Rest, however, be to his soul, for it was a great one, and the greatest have perhaps the most striking defects.

I admire your Irish patriotism very much, and hope trade is in a way to have every reasonable advantage, but that sudden qualm has checked the ardor for the Papists, and in the midst of the indulgence to their interests, has made Mr. Gardiner forget their religion. How much more noble is the unlimited toleration of them in England! What says *hum-hum* (Mr. Fortescue)? I know f. is for him, de cœur et d'âme. Pray assure him of my best love and thanks for his readiness to take you to England, which I flatter myself is not so necessary as I had imagined. You have an excellent place for the goats when near you, if that should be proper, as it once agreed with you, and are in time for the second season; but I hope your house, and the country air may suffice. Pray when you write to Mrs. Richardson assure her of my affectionate friendship and gratitude for her kind letter, which I entreat her to forgive my not answering. The heat takes away all strength, and I hope by the end of October to thank her in person. A kiss to your boy, my blessing to his nurse, compliments to Doctor Foster. Finalement je vous serre ma très chère fille sur mon cœur. Your father came home yesterday well. Louisa is perfectly so.

The Bishop of Derry
To Mrs. J. Th. Foster.

Rome, *August 5*, 1778

Though I was rejoiced to see your handwriting, my dearest Bess, yet when I found the contents of your letter I was sorry you had employed it so long after any degree of fever: so long an abode in Dublin and at such a time of the year could scarcely produce anything less. This country, too, has had its fevers, and we have all suffered more or less: mine, as usual, lasted two days—one good struggle and my constitution, like a giant, subdued its adversary. Your mother's, according to her system, lasted longer, but I thank God and her physician (this is more modest than Cardinal Wolsey,[52] who always wrote "I and my king") she is better recovered than ever I saw her, and contemplates her journey and her return to you with great satisfaction. Louisa is still very weak, though in good spirits; she and her mother write billets doux to each other every hour, and I believe this intercourse does them more service than febrifuge drafts or decoction of bark.

At the end of our Campaign, or when the hottest of our Fire was over, Mr. O'Reilly, a gentleman who has passed the summer in the same house, entered upon action with a most violent fever, and began to batter his enemy in the system of the, but, like the Frenchman who attempted to cut his throat and stopped in the middle of the operation, so poor O'Reilly, who is as fat as Dr. Palliser, twice as young, and with a truly Hibernian constitution, when he found himself deluging in sweat and floating in his own grease, whether he regretted losing so much O'Reilly matter, or whether his heart failed him, he changed his system abruptly, called in another engineer, who began immediately to *batter in breech*, and expended by this means so much of the patient's ammunition that he was near falling a victim to his own imprudence and the ignorance of his engineer; another has since been called in, who has wisely turned the siege into a blockade and means to starve the enemy into surrender.

But, to return to business, you will have learned before this both from your sister and from me that we all hope to winter in Ireland, and, if Shanahan will allow us, at the Downhill, but the poverty of the country is so extreme, rents have so entirely failed that the poor tenants are not able to pay even with daily labor, the bankers in Dublin are failing by dozens, famine stares the country in the face, providence itself seems to fight against us, and the crops threaten to be worse than ever. The pitiful concessions made to us by England will not compensate for an hundredth part of the losses which their multiplied blunders have brought upon us. In the meantime I advise your husband to live very frugally, since if the American war continues, it is almost impossible that Irish tenants in the north should pay above two-thirds of their rent. As to the invasion of Ireland, if no relief had been given to the R. Catholics, I believe I know much more of the feasibility of that scheme than either the Viceroy or his Secretary, the place where it was to be executed, the people with whom it was concerted, others, again, the least suspected, by whom it would have been abetted, and the arrangement intended to take place in case of success. If the Government are blockheads enough to imagine that the raw, undisciplined troops transmitted to them from Great Britain, stationed in a part of the country where the French never meant to approach and surrounded by internal ennemies, would have been able to secure you from a descent in the most remote parts among crowds of friends who daily expect them and look up to them as deliverers from the most cruel and unjust bondage that ever oppressed human creatures, it would only convince me there was as much treachery as folly in their counsel. But the countenance of the French ministers in this place upon the first intelligence of the R. Catholic bill was the clearest proof how salutary that measure was, and that the medicine would go, if the fainthearted physician permitted it, to the root of the evil—but remember, dear child,

"Truths would you teach and save a sinking land,
All fear, none aid you, and few understand".

The prejudices of some, the interests of others, the fears of still more, and the indolence, indifference, and supineness of all are barriers which even Lord Chatham found insurmountable. What think you of a button-making king that in the midst of a general conflagration drives about the country drinking tea and coffee with Lords and Ladies at their villas and country houses? Does he imagine the K. of Prussia resists the H[ouse] of Austria by such amusements, or that William Pitt supported his G.father against the whole force of Bourbon[53] by tripping about in such revels?—fie upon't! Whip me such Roitelets[54] into good behaviour, and send 'em to school to learn their lesson. Adieu. My love to your husband, who will say amen to this *Imprecation*.

> *The Hon. Mrs. Hervey*
> *To Mrs. J. Th. Foster.*
> Castel Gandolfo, *August* 15, 1778

I find two of your letters in my writing-table, dear Bess. I do not exactly know how long they have been in my possession, but they would not have been totally unanswered if I had not known that your father had wrote to you, and that I was engaged in a *little experiment upon fevers* in this hot climate and season. In short, I have paid my *usual tax*, and experienced the usual goodness of providence in my recovery, which is going on very well after a very short confinement. The circumstances which attended this event made it a little distressful at the time. Your father had one of his short fevers during the worst part of mine, and Louisa was confined to her bed likewise with an intermitting fever, which is in a very fair way of being subdued; her looks improve every day, the fever is quite gone, and she gains appetite and strength as I could wish. There is only a gallery between my room and hers, and our doors were open night and day, which makes me able to attend in some degree to her; and in some of my good intervals I wrote her joking billets, which kept up her spirits, which the absence of father and mother had rendered very necessary. We had a physician in the house, who attended us very carefully; but I had no confidence in him, though he was from *Ireland's own self*. At the same time a healthy young man in the apartment over ours took a violent fever and died in a week: it has proved since that it was the only circumstance which could have saved his wife from ruin, as he was spending all he had. So after comforting her for a week she has left us, and all melancholy incidents are giving way to the pleasure of returning health, and the satisfactory preparation for our return home, which we mean to do as soon as the heat will let us.

Your father has taken a little alarm about my exposing myself to the blasts of the North of Ireland after being in a state of perspiration for so many months, and has proposed to leave us in England for the worst of the winter months, which I believe may be necessary. I shall quit him with reluctance, and regret much to delay our meeting, dear Bess; but I hope you, Mr. Foster, and the little boy, perhaps also the Doctor, will go to him, and make up for my absence, which I shall make as short as I can. I fancy he will be at Derry first, to *creep* into the Downhill as he can, and I hope that may be an amusement to you. Mrs. Richardson, too, will be in the country, and I trust often with you. I wish Lady Moira would trust you with one of the Lady Rawdons.

I hope our affairs are in a much better position than when you wrote last. I flatter myself that peace is at this moment made with America, and by the French fleet going back into port it is plain the war is not desired with England; and I hope that if Spain can adjust the difference betwixt us that *we* shall not be so absurd as to run into it, but that we shall have the pleasure to find general peace at our return, and poor Ireland emerging from its difficulties.

God bless you, my sweet child. My tender affection is with you and yours. I imagine your father will be at home the end of October. Lady Bristol,[55] who still calls herself D. of K., is just come to Rome, and they say is busy packing up all her effects.

> *The Hon. Mrs. Hervey*
> *To Mrs. J. Th. Foster.*
> Castel Gandolfo, *September* 14, 1778

My dearest Bess, I flatter myself that you will have imputed my long silence to the accidents attending our removal from hence, and our journey towards home, and by this means may have avoided any particular anxiety for us; but here we are still, my love, and just emerging from a scene not a little perplexing; in short, there has been an *influenza* in the air of this country from the heats of the last two months from which scarce any one could secure themselves. Your father and I, Louisa, Finney, Barwick, the

Bn.'s valet de chambre, the child's governess, all have paid the tax; it has been a fever more or less to all; but no one has been so gently treated by it as myself, so that I became the nurse and apothecary to all. I thank God my labors and prayers have been blest with success; all are returning towards health, and for my own part, I am both ready and willing to set out towards you, but I much fear that your father will be inclined to pass the winter in a milder climate than that of Derry, on account of his dreaded gout, for indeed he is much reduced, and it would take him at a disadvantage; but I do not relinquish the hopes of his getting strong enough to *wish himself* to set out, and to have courage to do it. Poor honest Samuel has escaped this scourge, and some of our Italian servants, but most of then, have suffered, and even the assistants to the sick have themselves fallen ill of the disorder; it has not been mortal in this part of the country, yet pretty severe: for the particulars of our woful state I reserve them for our meeting, that I may make you cry and *laugh* at pleasure, for *which I pledge myself*.

I long to hear something of your state and situation, and how little f. settles to a family life in the country. I am glad he is so well entertained in town. I conceive him to be interested in Parliamentary debates, and I was pleased to find him *in the chair*. The notable provision for the country, my dear child, delights me; and I think I see you in the midst of family occupations, with the little *fairy* tripping after you and *bleating* (as ye all used to do) that dear word *Mama*. I have as yet no account of Lord Erne and your sister having left Paris. I am much distressed at her state of health and at his irresolute conduct about Spa; but most of all at the apprehension of being defeated in my scheme of taking her with me to Bath, where I hoped to have recovered her, but man proposes and God disposes. I dread her going to Ireland with her present complaints; the pleasure of seeing you will be a *counter-poison*, but I am afraid it will be the only one.

We have now very pleasant weather, and, notwithstanding my own illness, and that I have suffered on account of other people's, this place certainly has agreed with me, and, some circumstances changed, I should have been very happy in it. It is impossible to say even now whether we shall have war or peace. Poor Keppel[56] has been severely treated for not doing impossibilities. I am *furious* when I hear a brave man condemned hastily for want of success, or an honest man for want of good fortune. I think a character once established should be proof against everything but matters of fact.

Adieu, dearest child. Why are we to be hundreds of miles asunder? My best affection is with you and yours. Dutchess of Kingston still at Rome.

The Bishop of Derry
    To Mrs. J. Th. Foster.

Rome, *September* 19, 1778

My dear child,—I have but a moment to tell you that we are all making great strides towards health, and that at this instant the critical rains are falling, which usually purge this atmosphere of all its impurity; but, alas! a journey to England is impossible till next April. In the meantime, comfort your poor sister[57] all you can, who is exhausted, worn out, and can no more. He tires her to atoms by his silly difficulties, and his endless irresolution. Great God, how ill she is matched! Tell your husband, the antipode of t'other, that I should be much obliged to him for a list of the speakers in our house on the Popish bill, and the sum of the arguments against us; that I wish also to know if the bill to tolerate their religion is to take place, without which I do not know how the multitude are benefited; that I beg him to ply his cousin[58] close on this subject. He is a man of very superior talents, of great weight. If such a bill should pass, I *pledge myself* to bring sixty thousand pounds sterling within eighteen months into the kingdom for the purpose of building cathedrals, churches, and chapels. The Pope will give us five thousand, and one single convent in Bohemia, of Irish friars, subscribes one thousand pounds, the seminaries of *Valladolid* and *Salamanca* as much. There is a Governor MacEgan, is just returned from his government in Peru, an old bachelor with £70,000, who will give us £5000. The Empress of Germany, if this war does not continue, has promised her confessor, Father Kelly, an Irish Recolet, a considerable sum for the benefit of her soul in Purgatory—other lesser subscriptions are numberless, but such a sum would be deeply felt in our exhausted country. Adieu! my dear. You see how much I have this matter at heart. Your husband must never let the prime serjeant rest till he becomes our advocate. I have myself destined one thousand pounds for our chapels in the diocese of Derry, having seen the excellent effects of a reciprocal toleration through all the great towns of Germany, and the bad effects of intolerance through all the great towns of Italy.

The Bishop of Derry
    To Mrs. J. Th. Foster.

Rome, *November* 18, 1778

Your letter of September 6th, my dear Eliza, did not reach me till the last post, as it was directed to Paris, and of course my silence must have kept you in disagreeable suspense; not that it would have been so rigidly observed, but that every little exertion of the brain, during many weeks after this cruel fever, was sure to renew the attack, and even at present writing is occasionally more prejudicial to me than I can well express: however, I cannot forbear giving you some account of the family, unsatisfactory as it may be. Louisa and your mother are already returned to Rome; but having been rendered sensible to the extreme at every impression of air, she has already had two small relapses which, from the recollection of what she has suffered, have disheartened rather than weakened her. Your mother's attendance you may be certain is as uninterrupted as her anxiety, and as she sleeps, or rather lies, in the next room, both are very uniform. What this will produce at the end of the winter, God alone knows; but I fear they will be ill prepared to undertake an early journey, which was my purpose. In the meantime they are better lodged than they were, in a higher atmosphere, in separate rooms, and with the convenience of a third that commands the finest prospect in all Rome. To facilitate their *airings*, and to make them really *such*, I have bought four horses for them, which carries them into the country and out of the suburbs, their former *patrolle*. At dinner we have usually two or three friends, and in the evenings, if Louisa keeps well, we shall have small concerts. With these ingredients, I think it no difficulty to make a good dish of happiness, "animus si nos non deficit aequus": your husband will English this Latin for you, but for fear he should not, it runs thus, "if your appetite be as good as your meat"—for if it be not, 'tis in vain to abuse the cook, and would be more to the purpose to call in the physician, who, if he knows his trade, will brace the body in order to pacify the mind. Fortunately, the physicians in this country are entirely for this system infinitely more honest than ours, for they make no scruple to confess that great towns are the churchyards of the human species.

I must confess myself a little uneasy at your scheme of lying in at Dublin, and would much rather be at the expense of your coadjutor than have you risk yourself in so prejudicial an atmosphere, both to the child and its mother. Air, my dear Elizabeth, is nothing more than a fluid whose purity and impurity depend almost entirely upon the greater or less degree of its elasticity: in great cities and marshes there can be little elastick air, for reasons too obvious to mention to you. Dublin is both a great city and a great marsh; judge, therefore, what a stagnant air it must always contain. Fear it, my dear Ophelia; fear it. A propos to Dublin, send me word what were the colors of the two poplins you forwarded for Paris, but which never reached it. The lady to whom they were destined doubts our taste a little, but has given strong proofs of her own in two most beautiful gowns she was so good as to procure at Paris for your mother, who now deems herself too old to wear them; and if Louisa continues as she has begun, your mother, too, will grow younger and fitter for her gowns.

The air grows delightfully mild, but so changeable that we have daily three seasons within twenty-four hours; and though I am what is called recovered, I dare not stay abroad in the evening. Lord and Lady Lucan, with a most delightful family, are here, and enjoy Rome as much as we enjoy them. To-morrow they dine with us though there are six in family, but 'twill be a family dinner, and probably a cheerful one. The other English here are not worth naming to you, but Lady Berkeley is expected, and we shall have a scene of it. What if the Dutchess Countess[59] should return? How impatient will you be for our letter, and what copious materials we should possess; but fate has no such happiness in store.

Have you seen Lord Erne? Is he on tip-toes? Isn't *Mary* a sweet creature to be at last multiplying herself, and providing comforts for *her* old age and mine? I am in raptures with the thought of seeing you all at the Downhill, and have some thoughts of building barracks for children. Go on, my dear Eliza, and never fear hurting your constitution by honest child-bearing, since for one mother that grows thin with this work, there are five hundred old maids that grow more thin for want of it. My love to your husband, and a thousand thanks to him for the warm part he took in favour of R. Catholicks. Your mother and sister are both asleep, and probably dreaming of you. Send me word frankly what the Primate *says of Downhill*.

> *The Bishop of Derry*
> *To Mrs. J. Th. Foster.*
>
> Rome, *December* 8, 1778

Though I wrote to you so lately, my dear Eliza, yet, as we are making a jaunt to Naples, I just apprize you of our motions. Your mother would have wrote, but having just finished a letter to Lady Erne she is not in a disposition to scribble, and I am grown such a secretary that letters are my pastime. Our weather is growing delicious; our company of English multiplies very much, and some pleasant people among them, especially Mr. Thomas Pitt, nephew to my hero: he resembles him so much both in person and understanding he is quite a treat to me, and having been intimate with him in his last years, becomes twentyfold more interesting. I am purchasing treasures for the Down Hill, which I flatter myself will be a *Tusculanum*, especially that my dear *Tullia* will render its desert Eden. Bid your husband write me constant billets of you whilst you lie in, and be sure you grow a prudent, sober matron, and play no gambols. Adieu, this is a short letter to travel so far, but it is better than none. Louisa and your mother are at the table, and send their love to you and f. You cannot doubt mine.

The Hon. Mrs. Hervey
To Mrs. J. Th. Foster.

Rome, *December* 12, 1778

My dear Elizabeth,—The last post brought me *two letters* from you. I had already destined you one by the courier to-night, but imagine, if I could want anything to stimulate me, how much my dear child's affectionate anxiety for me must have confirmed my intention, and quickened the pleasure arising from this happy invention of communicating one's thoughts and affections. I received your letters, my love, at the harpsichord, in spite of which I read them till the tears poured down my cheeks, and I was forced to cry out, "Oh! love, how painful thou art!" But I hope the pains you have felt from it on our account have been gradually softened down by our repeated good news of the sick, until your mind is settled into a thankful calm for our deliverance. It is true we all suffered much, and myself in the extreme, but God's providence was so manifested in my favor, that in the midst of my calamity I found comfort.

Since we came here this dear child has had two or three very slight relapses, which have determined us to go to Naples for a month for change of air, lest she should otherwise be subject to them all the winter (direct, however, always to Rome). Do not imagine, dear Bess, that she has any consumptive complaints from this, or, indeed, any that I conceal from you. I give you *my honor* that she has *none* but this disposition to a return of fever, but she is grown strong, has got flesh to cover her bones, and eats and sleeps well, rides on horseback, walks a little, is in good spirits, dies to see you, and desires a thousand loves which she had intended to assure you of with her own hand. Her little horse and little dog are her delights, and she is very happy at the thoughts of going to Naples.

As to myself, I continue very well; my red face, indeed, is returned, which I had exchanged for a better hue at Castello, but my health is good. The account of yours, my love, would distress me extremely did I not impute your complaint to your situation, and hope they would go off of course. Your sister has taught me that comfortable lesson, for after thinking her in a very bad state I hear she is growing quite well, and likely to produce a fine child, which I hope you may do too. You both, I find, have an inclination to nurse, but she has taken advice and is confirmed in it. *You* are uncertain. The *principle* in you both gives me the *truest pleasure*, but you must follow her steps, and not do it without proper authority on your own account; it sometimes weakens and sometimes strengthens the constitution. I cannot judge at this distance which is likely, but beg you will be cautious; do the best for your child, and leave the rest to Providence. Perhaps nurse would stay and superintend *Henrietta*, though she might not be equal to the *Laborious part*, as we shall not be at home till the summer: in short, this will depend upon *herself*, because, though she remains in our pay we make no claim upon her; should be glad she could be of any service to you, and would have her equally depend on us for her home. As to reward, my dear, it would be difficult for *me* to name it. Some present, I should think right and best, in money; but you are to consider yourself as Mr. Foster's wife, and not as my daughter. I have set down your commissions in a memorandum sheet for *Paris*—*here* there is nothing. I will add some silk stockings to them, though they are so hard to get over that I believe I must put them on. This will get to you, I suppose, about the time of your confinement, in which I hope you will be *very prudent*. I am heartily glad that you are to be in Dominick Street, which I look upon as in good air; but if you should not recover well, I hope you will meet us next spring in England: your sister stays for us there, and I think it very possible that Jack[60] may be returned home by that time. He writes in great spirits, was on a cruise, and delighted with his station, and determined that *Captain Hervey* of the present time should not be contented with less fame than his uncle[61] had had before him.

Adieu, dear Bess, I have neither time nor place for anything but family matters. Your father wrote to you last post, but as perhaps he might not mention his health, I must tell you that he is well, and everlastingly employed in buying ornaments for the Down Hill, though we *both* think the *greatest* there will be our children—God send us to them. My love to f. I hope he is very good to the poor dear little orphan.[62] and will be able to give her in good health to the arms of her affectionate mother.

> *The Bishop of Derry*
> *To Mrs. J. Th. Foster.*
>
> *November 6, 1779*

Here we are, my dear Eliza, within a few miles of Preston, in Lancashire, and at every stage more impatient to see you and your husband. Perhaps you will be able to meet us at Belfast and settle our winter's campaign, that we may not pass more time asunder than is necessary. I have wrote to your sister for the same purpose, and hope you will be able to settle something. In the meantime I dread some violent convulsion in this country. Very credible reports are circulated that Jamaica is taken. The manufactures of Lancashire and Westmoreland depend chiefly on the cotton which that island produces, and the price of it is already raised 25 per cent: judge how the manufacturers are alarmed. Sugar, tea, and coffee have risen in proportion, and the alarm is universal. I must own that I expect little less than a general insurrection, for there seems to be a determined resolution in some branches of the ministry to reduce us to some fatal extremities, with what view I can better tell than write. No one in London doubts of an union, nor do I believe there will be much difficulty about the terms. The peerage to be incorporated into the British house is to be hereditary, and the remaining Irish peers are to be admissible, as at present, into the lower house. The proportion of each will be a little more difficult to ascertain, but all agree that we Bishops shall remain in our diocese. God grant this may be true. Another scheme has been proposed of leaving the Parliament in Ireland for the internal administration of the kingdom, and assessing it once for all in proportion with England, but I cannot imagine the Irish will endure this: it would reduce them to the insignificance of a mere corporation of aldermen and common council, and would multiply the number of non-residents beyond endurance, for who would condescend to become a member of such a legislature. Write to me, my dear, at Portpatrick, and let me know at large how matters go on. Send me no foreign politicks, for on your side the water you know none. Lord Mountstuart is gone to negotiate a peace with France. Think what a system to close ignominiously a popular war at the expense of maintaining the most unpopular and most unnatural one possible, and what terms can be expected from the insolence of France, and what will they dare to offer to poor America. Cunning, which they call policy, guides all their steps, yet some there are among them of true parts and real probity, but, alass! how few. What is your husband doing? I never hear from either of you, yet I wrote on my landing at Dover, and once again from London.

[The rest of this letter is torn off—V. F.]

> *The Bishop of Derry*
> *To Mrs. J. Th. Foster.*
>
> *November 29, 1779*

I am just arrived here, my dear Elizabeth, and was fully determined to set out to-morrow to meet you and your dear sister either at Dundalk or Barmeath, but the extreme badness of the weather, joined to some alarming symptoms of the gout, which you know operate strongly on me, have determined our immediate course to Derry. It is a little hard to be so near you and not to have the least chance of seeing you, but I shall trust to the chapitre des accidents and endeavour to make it out in some manner. I send you a parcel by a carrier which contains two pair of bracelets, one for your sister and the other for you. I would not let them be sett, that you may do that in Dublin according to your own taste, and when you have done so, without sparing my purse, if you will let me know the amount I will discharge my debt and complete my present. There are also two rings: the Apollo I desire dear Mary will offer in my name to Lord Erne. The *Plato* I hope our philosopher *John Thomas* will accept, and I must rely on your interest for making it acceptable. All your encomiums on Dublin will hardly prevail on me to go there, but I don't know what effort I may make for the sake of passing a week or ten days with Mary in the S.W. room which she has so comfortably offered me, and which is worth a whole apartment in a palace from the cordiality of the offer. I hear from good authority that Buckingham leaves you, and that Lord Hillsborough[63] is bold enough to visit us. This prognosticates real free trade, for it is the object of his ambition.

You press me strongly, my dear child, to return to Dublin, and not deny any longer my assistance to this sinking country. I have given pretty strong proof to the ministry in England and to many of the leading people here that I have been invariably pursuing its interests and investigating the causes of its decline for these last three years. Can any country flourish where two-thirds of its inhabitants are still crouching under the lash of the most severe illiberal penalties that one set of citizens ever laid upon the other? All the errors in our Popish laws have proceeded from one fatal and, as yet, insurmountable piece of ignorance. The Protestants here have universally concluded that every R. Catholic is a Papist, that is, that every man who was fool enough to believe in transubstantiation was wicked enough to hold no faith with heretics and to deny allegiance to his Sovereign the moment that Sovereign was excommunicated by the Pope. In order to discriminate one of these Catholics from the other, I got an Act of Parliament passed in 1774 by which every Catholic that had been educated in the French and Flemish seminaries (where the dangerous doctrines of Popery are exploded) had an opportunity of abjuring them and exculpating himself. Immediately about one-fourth of the R. clergy availed themselves of the occasion, and took the oath which purged them from this imputation, but a very great number from whom I expected the same conduct, because I knew they had received the same education, declined it: nor did I guess the cause till we were at Brussels. There I learned that the hopes of preferment in their miserable hierarchy deterred them from abjuring the prerogatives of their sovereign master the Pope. On this I resolved to visit the fountain head of such a defection and to trace it to its source. I did it so effectually, bribed so many clerks and under-clerks in the different offices that I obtained the whole course of correspondence between Rome and her clergy in Ireland on this topick. I did more. I detected the whole plan of invasion for last year, which could not have been attempted without the assistance of Irish friars conversant in the English, Irish, and French languages, and I have good reason to believe that the whole proceedings in England in favor of the Catholics were grounded on the information I transmitted to Lord North[64] and Lord Hillsborough. Had the French ministry imagined that the Irish Parliament would have done things by halves and omitted the religious indulgence to the people whilst it granted the pecuniary one to the gentry, the invasion would still have taken place last year in Ireland, after Mr. Keppel had so scandalously left the French masters of the ocean. Don't imagine, therefore, my dear girl, that I have been inattentive to the welfare of this kingdom. Your mother can tell you how many wearisome days and studious evenings it has cost me whilst the ignorant and unobserving thought me busied in virtu and occupied by the elegant arts. The *committee* at Rome which governs the religious affairs of Ireland is composed of seven cardinals, who are governed in their consultations as the Commissioners of the Customs are in Dublin, by a *secretary*. They, too, have their Sackville Hamilton. Every member of this committee is as venal as a Board of Aldermen, but in order to bribe them you must buy a picture of one, give a poplin to the niece or the mistress of another, a suit of clothes to the secretary of a third, and so on; so that with a good purse and a liberal hand one may know every tittle of what these Christian Pharisees have sworn not to reveal. It was by means such as these that I discovered the sentiments, the views, the interests and connexion of almost every Popish bishop in Ireland, and that at this instant I know why some have taken the oath of allegiance and why others have declined it. By these means I discovered that the King of France,[65] through his ambassador, the Cardinal de Bernis, got the nomination of three Irish bishops in the course of one year, as the most effectual means of securing the assistance of the Popish clergy and the Popish populace in case of an invasion; and of all this I transmitted immediate information to such as could best avail themselves of it. Whenever that great topick comes to be discussed, I will endeavour to give such council as I am able, but, alass! mankind are little guided by reason, and unless interest or danger excite their attention they are generally deaf. Adieu, my dear girl. I must say a word to your sister, and as I conclude she may still be at Dunleer I shall direct it there.

The Earl of Bristol, Bishop of Derry,
To Lady Elizabeth Foster.
                    Downhill, near Coleraine,   *April* 21, 1780

By some untoward accident, my dear Eliza, your letter of the 14th did not reach me till last night, by which means I was deprived of my option of attending the dissenters' bill; but, indeed, my spirits are so depressed by the loss of dearest Lady Mulgrave[66] that I am totally unfit for anything but the heartless solitude in which "I live and move and have my being". Your mother is every day more urgent with me to go over in order to join with Jack in liberating the estate[67] from the shackles in which it is held, but matters in this country are not sufficiently decided to allow me to quit it. The fever is now coming to a crisis, and whether it will end in a delirium or in the health of the patient and restoration of his constitution, neither you nor I are prophets enough to foretell; but this I can venture to say, that to all appearance the struggle will be great.

Is it possible that the Ch. Governor[68] or any of his friends can think me capable of distressing an administration both in England and Ireland to which I wish so well, and for the sake of which I have separated from some of the oldest and most intimate connexions I have in the world? Believe me, I think their cause too good either to desert it or embarrass them. When I judged them to be better informed than myself, as in all foreign politicks I should without either scruple or reserve deliver my political conscience into their hands; but with regard to their interests in Ireland, and the intrinsick unalienable rights of Ireland itself (which are the rights of mankind), in which I deem myself much better informed than them, having not only taken more pains on the subject, but being likewise an ocular observer on the spot, if either through inattention or presumption they will not take the advice I have given them but persist in the same infatuated system of despotism towards Ireland which has almost lost America—what is then the part of an honest man or a true friend? What would a faithful physician do upon a similar occasion with a struggling patient? Would he, in compliance with the prejudices of the family, concur in administering a medicine which he knows to be improper and suspects to be fatal, and which, if it did not destroy the patient, would at least throw him into strong convulsions, or would he honestly resist the dictates of that family, prohibit the medicine, and encourage the patient to decline it? Would your friends have me act the part in the North which the poor Duke of Leinster[69] has been persuaded to take in the South? The Duke of Leinster may perhaps be sincere in his professions of the dependency of Ireland, but I, who do not deem that dependency legal, nor even that it is either politick in England to assert or useful to exert it, could not either as an honest man or as a real friend to administration, remain silent in such a conflict, much less espouse the opinion I from my head and heart condemn. But suppose for a moment I should—what would be the unavoidable consequence? I should first find myself bereaved of any little influence I have acquired in this part of the country by professing my real sentiments, and afterwards, when the flame breaks forth—as break forth it will, unless some gold dust shall smother it—what would administration naturally say to me? Why remain in the North to give no information of the storm brewing? or why coincide with sentiments which you knew to be prejudicial? Why not at least preserve your own influence in the country to prevent violence and guard against extremities? I think we are at the eve of a civil war, which bids fair for being one of the most sanguinary and most general that this country has known. Parasites and sycophants may talk another language at the Castle, for all governments love to be soothed into an *opinion* of their *safety*, and for real safety heedlessly mistake their own dangerous security (but a real friend will apprize the minister betimes of his danger, and a warm one will do it in warm terms). Their danger at this moment does not arise only from their offensive measures and from the alarm given to the friends of the Irish Constitution, but from a more latent and a more cancerous evil, from an inherent dislike to the religious establishment from the scandalous—

[The rest of this letter is missing.—V. F.]

> *The Countess of Bristol*
> *To the Earl of Bristol, Bishop of Derry.*
> *August* 13, 1780

We drank your health yesterday, but I am much concerned to find, upon pressing Elizabeth on that subject, that it is not altogether so good as, in your ardour for the mountains, you represent it to me; and though Mary says that you have no other complaint than a sore finger, yet she seems to think your spirits low, and I much fear that you have taken too much fatigue for your strength.

We are in hourly expectation of f., who has been more absurd and inconsistent than it is possible to express; and, after fearing to trust anything to writing, has wrote four or five letters by every post of everything; in short, he is a ship totally without ballast, blown about by every gust of passion, a very tiring companion, and an insufficient and unsatisfactory friend.

There has been some thought of dissolving the Parliament, but I flatter myself that it is over for the present. My brother[70] was disappointed of his companion into Devonshire, so turned about from Lewes races, went back to London, from whence he writes me word that he stays choked with dust, he does not know why, but I suppose he will soon be down. Colonel H. is on the road at last, and will perhaps be here to-day or to-morrow, which I am glad of, for I think f., a—, and it may keep him in better order. How could I be so mistaken in him? Yet are not wiser people than myself mistaken every day? Adieu. Lady Hervey still up. Poor Elizabeth better notwithstanding, and eats a little.

The Countess of Bristol
    To Lady Elizabeth Foster.

Ickworth Park, May 17, 1781

My dear child,—I was very sure that my brother would not decline his friendly assistance in your present distressful situation; and I am sorry to find that any delay should have occurred in a thing so necessary for your peace and my satisfaction. As to the message which you have delivered to me from Mr. Foster, I should be surprized at it from anybody else; for he cannot but recollect that I have mentioned the very sums for which he engaged to me; and I am sure that when he is cool enough to have his judgment operate, he cannot term a conduct severe which is only the steady performance of a very painful duty. He will recollect, perhaps, that I once consented to your reconciliation, and tried by uniting you under my own eyes to promote your happiness: his return to me has been a conduct which I confess was the last I should have expected from him; but it has opened my eyes.... With regard to the children, as they are *boys*, I advise you to make no opposition to his desire of having them. I hope poor little Frederick goes on well.

I am, my dear child, your most affectionate mother.

The Countess of Bristol
    To Lady Elizabeth Foster.

St. James' Square, *June* 1782

Lady Mary is much better. I am just come from her, and have had an opportunity of talking to her about the scheme I mentioned to you last night, and she, with her usual kindness and good humour, has assured me of a welcome, if you can take up with such a retirement; and that Mrs. Gordon makes no objection, for they are to lodge and board together: that is, to have no trouble, and each pay the cook 14*s.* a week for themselves, and 7*s.* a week for servants; rooms as at Bath, each person to breakfast alone, and at no time to be a clog on each other. You will not, I am afraid, look favorably on such a party, and I am aware that it will be a dull one, yet your affection for Lady Mary, and the real use and comfort you may be of to her, will, I know, brighten the prospect to you. You would not disturb their Methy proceedings, nor would they intrude them upon you. Thus stands the compact, provided Mrs. Gordon, who is the foundation of the party, is agreeable. The advantages to you would be in a kind relation, an appearance of protection, retirement, a good air, and lovely scenery;

and if you adopt my scheme of Bath for next winter, you would save two expensive journeys. I have this moment received the letters you sent by the Duke of Devonshire,[71] and have caught your father before he could get quite into bed to hold a conversation upon them, the result of which is that I expect you both to leave Bath on Saturday, and to be here on Sunday (as I suppose).

The Duchess of Devonshire's[72] behaviour on this occasion is heavenly, and your distress will have been, I hope, at this very hour that I am writing, relieved by your father's £100. I am so hurried and agitated that I don't know what I say, but we look upon your journey and your summer as most happily allotted. I shall certainly stay in town a little while to see you, though part of the family are gone to Ickworth; and I flatter myself that your sister will be better here than alone: pray tell her this; I am not able to write it. I send two letters which came to-day from your brother. S. H. intended to have wrote to you had she not seem *them*, and desires me to say so, with her best love. Adieu! my dear children. Is it possible that I am so near having you both with me again, and may I look forward to a degree of comfort and happiness for you for this summer? My blessing on this dear woman! I hope you will recollect that you and your sister and *lal lal* will be ill-lodged but affectionately welcomed.

> *The Countess of Bristol*
> *To Lady Elizabeth Foster.*
> Ickworth Park, *January* 5, 1783

My dearest Bess,—I would not write to you till I got hither, as I had a mind to tell you something at least with certainty, and that I thought my letter would certainly travel faster than you. I received your dear little note from Dover, but have not yet the comfort of knowing you got safe to Calais, though it is ten whole days since you left me; however, the weather has been so good that though I am impatient I am not uneasy. I saw your Duchess several times before I left Town. She behaved like an angel in everything, supported her loss with fortitude and felt it with the utmost tenderness, was warm and interested about you to the smallest trifle, and infinitely kind to me on your account. I rely on her for the first possible tidings of you, but I am quite vexed that she should have found a way of writing to you which I did not, and reproach myself for your being solitarily at Dover with a comfort less than I could have given you.

Whilst I was at Devonshire House one morning there came a letter for you directed there. I saw it was from Mr. F. and told her I would open it to save the postage. I did so. There was a repetition of the remittance sent, settlement, your receipt to be given, &c., and at the end what I will now transcribe: "I would ask you, if it should not appear to you as a question of idle and impertinent curiosity, whether since I saw you you have ever received any pecuniary assistance from either of your parents: if it appears to you in the light I have stated you have only to be silent; if otherwise, you will give me an answer. J. T. F." This is so extraordinary that I should advise you to answer him by asking leave to answer his question, by a question, how he thought you had been maintained for the eight months he had left you without a shilling. I pity you for the meeting at Dover, and long to know the result.

The ex is postponed, and will probably never take place. There have been two notes to you from Lord Shuldam, which, as they were about La. H.'s business, I opened and gave to her, and wrote to him that you was gone. I believe the parcel is safe, only they did not know to whom it belonged. I am rejoiced that Mr. Hunter answers so well. I have wrote your father word how I had engaged for him. I have no letter yet. Poor Mrs. Greene is highly satisfied at having been of use to you and with your letter. She has had a great escape. The step of her carriage broke with her, and her leg is slightly hurt and in a very good way, but if the horses had stirred it was over with her. She bears it vastly well, and is all kindness. My sister is very well, sends her love to you, and says as a proof of her forgiveness she has recommended you to the good offices of a friend of hers at Nice, a Mr. Morice, who was long her tenant, at last bought her house, and has always behaved in a very gentlemanlike manner. I expect Fred to-morrow, have asked the poor Plumpa for a week. Augustus Phipps is now playing at backgammon with Louisa, and desires his love and good wishes to you. I shall have the pleasure, I hope, of seeing all these young people happy. You see I write very close to make as much as I can of a letter. I saw Captain Finch just before I left town, who had left your brother in good health and spirits at Madeira. La. H. and your sister are at Bath; saw the poor little Dillons in their way, and were delighted with them. I shall be happy to hear that Louchee improves upon you, for a disagreeable object so repeatedly present is horrid, but I know you will turn to the best side of her. Lady Emily Ker is going to be married. Lady Ma, the Duchess of Devonshire, and I are in agony of expectation for a return of favor, but La. Ma, who knows her best, says we must let it work alone. God bless you, my dearest. Thank you for your promise. Louisa asks for the foldings.

The Countess of Bristol
 To Lady Elizabeth Foster.

Ickworth Park, *Feb.* 7, 1783

I thank you, my dearest Elizabeth, for your two letters from Lyons, for which I had been long impatient, as the winter was so far advanced. Your stay there for some time seems absolutely necessary after so much fatigue, at which I am the more disappointed as I had flattered myself the roads were good, and that, being totally your own mistress, to stop when you would, that you would have escaped it: however, bless Ma^lle. Bertin's five wits who has preserved you from cold à la Chinoise, and as to the pole, springs, &c., though they are teasing accidents, and, what is worse, expensive ones, I dare say you bore them very coolly, but I confess that your expedition on the water alarms me, nor shall I be easy till I hear of you on dry ground again.

I am sorry Mr. Hunter does not turn out the economist I expected, and if he continues his princely ideas, which are just opposite to what I expected from him, it may become necessary for you to send him back and to take a servant more suitable to your situation; but I am still more vexed about Mrs. Ashburner, who, I see, can never be more than tolerated by you, and yet I do think it necessary that you should have a person of character and conduct about you, and not a pert, gallant, corrupt femme de chambre, who may overturn your best plans of prudence.

I am sorry I did not write to Lyons, but you will have found my letters, I hope, at Nice. I cannot think of troubling the Duchess of Devonshire with them except on any particular occasion, so direct them *en droiture.* I am surprised at your recollection of that town, though it is very striking. I trust that you have found no difficulties on the road, and this peace will now have put all sides in good humor. I hope, too, that it will have relieved your mind of part of its burthen.

I am sorry that my situation has sat so heavy on it, for I can give you no comfort on that subject except by assuring you that my mind is quite above and out of the reach of the oppression I receive and the insults which accompany it, and that I have pride enough to bear being told that my advice is presumption, and that I am a being so made up of vanity and ostentation as not to be capable of cooperating in so laudable a plan without feeling the least humbled by it; and even my resentment is softened down into compassion for the frailties of human nature, and for the wreck which warring passions bring upon it: my own happiness has long been an empty sound, and I now am only intent on drawing all the good possible out of this evil in favor of Louisa ... and to acquire in solid advantages to her mind and character what she loses in accomplishments, which are more easily taken up at any time and of infinitely less consequence.

In the meanwhile we pass our time cheerfully, each considering the other: she is become a dear, amiable companion: we read and work together in the evenings, and they do not appear long; and now the general[73] is come, I make him take his turn; we chuse pleasant books, and we are all in good humour with one another. She is at present very busy in clothing a girl that she is to put to school, and is to be the beginning of one kept by your music master, who is come to settle at Horringer. Dearest Lou loves you with the sincerest affection, and begs I will say so. The house in town is let for three years to Lord Paget for £600 a year. I have sent servants up to-day to prepare for his coming in. God knows what is your father's plan. Your brother, I fear, will be much mortified; but perhaps it may help to settle his affairs, and all may yet turn out well for those I am most anxious about. I suppose he will come home now to settle. I must write a line or two to your dear Duchess. Adieu, my dear Bess....

The Countess of Bristol
To Lady Elizabeth Foster.

Ickworth Park, *Feb.* 7, 1783

My dearest Bess,—I have to thank you for your great attention in writing to me so frequently on your journey. I received your letter from Calais (though late), two from Paris, two from Lyons, one from Aix, (none from *Avignon*, as you mentioned), but one welcome one indeed from Nice. Welcome, my love, indeed, not only from your having passed all dangers and fatigues, from your being pleased with the place, well accommodated, well received, &c. &c., but infinitely dear to me from the change brought about in your sentiments. Do not lament any longer my *situation* or late disappointment, but be assured that there is none whatever which could have given me half the satisfaction which I feel on this occasion; and appease the reproaches of your own mind on the uneasiness you have given me (which I confess has been great) by reflecting that you have it still in your power to make me amends for it. For thou art the sheep that was lost and is found again, and I will rejoice over thee. This calm of mind, my dear child, will wonderfully assist the climate and the sweet retirement you describe; and bring you back happy yourself and capable of making your friends so.

Your heavenly friend is every day more and more the object of my admiration and love. *What a note!* from a person apparently absorbed by every worldly pursuit and gratification. It is so sweet that the *sense akes at it*. I saw her often before I left town, and always with fresh pleasure; and on my coming hither she had the goodness to take up *my protégé*; Mr.

Parkison, in order to serve him by means of the Duke of Portland,[74] but her humanity to him, condescension, and real attention to his affairs have been beyond any possible description, as I learn from himself, and I am in hopes he will succeed at last.

As you had received but one of my letters when you wrote, I hope you have had since in their order those of the 23rd of January and 7th of February. I did not write to you on the road, as I always fear the loss of my letter.

I suppose I have repeatedly told you my situation, &c., but I believe it is since my last that Lord Paget has actually hired the house in St. James' Square for three years, and is now in possession of it. I have had many reproaches for the vanity and levity of my character that made me unwilling to adopt so fine a scheme, but not one word of excuse or concern at the supposed necessity for it. I own I have never *condescended to answer these accusations*. I leave my whole life to do so. In the meantime I have accounts from time to time of his great spirits and happiness in everything that is going on in Ireland, and he seems quite unconcerned at having placed me here without a plan, view, object, or improvement of any sort to occupy a mind so much harassed; but I thank God I have objects that are out of his reach, and from which my mind receives such daily comfort that I hope you will not be uneasy for me. I have converted this disappointment, I trust, entirely to the advantage of Louisa. I have called forth all the best feelings of her excellent heart, and to turn her from a *selfish* and *pining* discontent, I endeavoured to *make myself her object* whilst she is mine. It has answered my wish—her case is to lighten *my solitude*, et vous pensez bien ma chère qu'elle n'y perd rien. I have convinced her that she is at an age not only to bear but to profit by it, and that it is only severe in the *decline of life* when *prospects* are no more. She has adopted the idea, redoubled her attention to me, endeavoured to improve herself, is in good spirits, reads, writes, plays, works, rides, and joins very intelligently in all I read to her. I had the precaution before I left town to make her dancing master promise to come down for a month in the summer if I did not return; and I hope poor Salvatore will come likewise; but of all this I say not a word to Ireland. It might be thought too expensive, and as I am determined to lay out *nothing on myself*, I think I have a *right to it*.

Fred[75] has been here to keep her birthday; he must be removed from Mr. F., who has not *behaved well*, and I am trying with your F. to get him to school, and am uneasy whilst he balances between that and a private tutor. I have reconciled Fred's mind more to a school than ever I had been able to do before; he is a dear boy, and I hope I shall save him. Mr. F.'s letter is very ex: *I think as you do*, and approve so highly of your answer that I could not help telling the purport of it to Fred and Lou: a disposition of that sort in him is favorable to yr cha, though you do not avail yourself of it: he certainly means me, mais n'importe. I have lately had a letter from your brother; vastly well; likes the warm sun as well as you do; is in spirits, and will be more so when he knows that a peace brings him home. I should think that S. E. and S. H. would wait for him at B.; and I should imagine that if things are not properly settled for him that they will go abroad, and probably you will *all meet*. Pray remind Lady Rivers of me, and assure her that I have not forgot a *beautiful, amiable* woman, whom I knew first in *this house*. Remember me, too, to Miss Danby, Mr. Morice, and the B.'s. My Aunt Greene is quite recovered, and sends her love to you. My sister well. General H. here for this month past. I make him hear me read the first part of the evening, and read to me the latter part. I am quite troubled about Louchee, and angry with Mr. P., but you must dispose of her, and if she would draw *a veil over her ugliness*, it would do very well. I fear Mr. H., too, has not economized sufficiently, and that your journey has cost you more than we allotted for it; however, I hope all these matters may be arranged. Louisa desires me to add her tenderest love. You have that of your most affectionate mother.

I send this to the dear Duchess. Thank you for your orange flowers; they gave me agreeable ideas of your *villa*.

The Countess of Bristol
   To Lady Elizabeth Foster.
                              Ickworth Park, *March*. 13, 1783

I was just going to write to you, dearest Bess, when your two letters of the 16th and 22nd arrived by the means of your invaluable friend. It would be impossible for me to describe the tender emotions they have raised in me, but of this be assured that I have no sufferings but what are infinitely over-balanced by the sentiments you express, provided that you pursue them steadily. You take my admonitions so well that I have nothing to add upon that subject, and I am extremely pleased with the arrangements of your retirement and the limited acquaintance you receive at your house; something decisive in your conduct was necessary to make an impression and to put you upon a new footing, and I expect the best consequences from it; yet I should be glad to know how you pass your evenings, and whether they do not hang heavy on you who have been used to constant society. I perceive that your spirits are very low, and I am disappointed at your not feeling more relieved by so great a change of climate in three weeks. You say your stomach is a little better, but you do not mention your breast, side, or cough, and you complain of fever. How do you like Mr. Farquhar's friend, and what has he directed besides orange juice? What is your diet? Do you keep good hours? and don't you write too much? I am glad you ride, but how do you manage it, and what does it cost you, and your house and servants, &c.? Pray send me a little plan of all your doings, that I may attend you in them.

Your father in his last letter to me says he intends to add £50 a year to your income, and perhaps £100 if you conduct yourself prudently. I beg you will be very cautious, in speaking of him to others, how you throw any blame on him on my account. I leave him to Heaven and to those thorns that in his bosom lodge to prick and sting him. I give you my honor that my situation here is a less painful one than you imagine it. I own I had promised myself great comfort in being in town, but I have bent my mind to my circumstances. I have laid out my disappointment to Louisa's advantage, and though I should be very happy indeed (believe it, my dear Bess) with you amidst your orange trees, yet there are several things of consequence transacting here in which I think I may be able to serve your brother and poor Fred materially, and I find great satisfaction in the idea of it—il y a une fâcheuse pilleule que je n'ose pas nommer, une insensibilité dans certains moments critiques et une philosophie si baroque qu'il y a de quoi se désesperer, mais il n'y a point de remède, et on s'établit en maître sans se faire prier; il faut donc tirer parti comme on peut et vivre au jour la journée. I shall long for you to obtain the, request you made to Mr. F. My poor child, I have always said that you was made for domestic happiness and domestic duties.

What you tell me of the Duchess goes to my heart, and will, I hope, be a real comfort to yours. You have done well, most certainly, to leave your interest in her hands; for where could it be so well? But I am pleased at your growing indifference to those matters, and do not doubt but that your affairs will be made easy in some way or other. The Duchess and I do not correspond, but we write sometimes occasionally. She is vastly obliging to me, and treats me like your mother, and I love her as your friend, and, besides that, am charmed with her disposition and character. She has promised me a print of herself, and I gave her my sweet miniature of Susanna, which she liked. I hear she advances happily, which I hope you know long before this.

The Polignacs are certainly a great acquisition for you, and I think your stay at Paris and renewal with them on your return will depend upon circumstances, of which now I dare say you will judge properly. I am glad to find Lady Rivers so comfortable to you, notwithstanding her deafness. One of her daughters, I believe, is preferable to the other. How do you like Mrs. Stuart? and have you no acquaintance with Lady Eliott? Pray write the dangerous Italian's name a little plainer for I can't make it out; but avoid him by all means—their whole composition is intrigue. Poor Miss Danby! I am sorry she has exchanged one bad complaint for another. You don't mention Lady Craven, so I hope she is gone some other way. You must have no intercourse at all there. She is quite undone, and has not an atom of character left.

I hope Miss W. will answer to all your care and their hopes, and then it will be a pleasant circumstance between you; but I am sorry she requires strictness: that is against the bent of her indulgent governess, but perhaps even that may have a good effect, and give to a soft heart a firmer texture.

I have heard nothing about H., but I hope that all is en train to open the eyes on both sides. You have now no further solicitude about his destination, and seem to have fixed your conduct upon very proper principles.

Poor Fred told me he had made you his confidant. I cannot get any decisive direction about him, and he is not well placed where he is. Mr. F. has behaved ill, and has been led into it, I believe, by distressed circumstances. Mark that, and fear it, my dear Ophelia, as much as anything.

I mention no politics, because you have them fresher from Devonshire House, but never was poor nation in so distressed and contemptible a situation.

My Aunt Greene is very well, and your warm friend always. My sister, too, was softened to tears at the perspective I showed her from your present plan; continue it, my love, and return to the arms and grow for ever to the hearts of your family. My brother is still in town acting like an honest man in the midst of all this faction. I have not the least hope of going up; now the house is gone I could not. Mr. D.' A.—comes Ambassador, Your sister and I agree that we feel ashamed that he should find us without an hotel. She has got little benefit from Bath, poor thing! Always something to fret upon wears out the machine. Louisa is well, and loves you tenderly; goes on well, and keeps up her spirits. Your uncle W. still here, having, I believe, fixed it as a part of his grand plan not to be in the hay market till such a day of such a month of the year 1783, Is Mr. Wollaston at Nice? and how is he? My compliments to La. Rivers, Mr. Morice, Miss D., and the Birbecks. I am glad my letters come easy, and will write oftener, being, my dear child, your most affectionate mother.

The Countess of Bristol
To Lady Elizabeth Foster.

Ickworth Park, *April.* 12, 1783

I have two of your letters, my dear Elizabeth, and one, so late as the 19th of March, I should have hoped might have brought me the comfortable news of your amendment, but I search for it in vain, as I do also for the real cause of your complaint. Is it that we have been so unlucky as to choose a wrong climate? You seem to think so, and if it is confirmed to you, for God's sake change it; or is it still the effects of your long journey, and the scene you went through; or a wound that is still festering, though you think it healed; or the absence from your friends; or the severe judgment you are passing on yourself?

For your bodily complaints, my dearest Bess, you must be governed by others, and if you must remove, I suppose La R. has decided you in favor of Lyons. It is a long journey, but if Nice is thought improper for next winter you may as well be there as anywhere else, except you could find a cool place nearer to where you are to pass the next winter. I should hope you would not be determined by the motive you mention of hearing sooner of your friend, dear as she is, and natural as it is for you to make it an object, but I beg your health may be the first, and the more as you are doing everything which can make it valuable to yourself and your friends. Lyons, too, is a little Paris, and I don't know how you could live there en retraite.

As to Italy, though at this time one cannot think of it without horror, yet I am very sensible that after un tal sfuogo it may be next year safer than ever: but it is a terrible journey; you are alone, and I do not see how in your unfortunate circumstances you can either profit of the advantages, or bear the expence of it, and though you say that Miss W. would go with you, and lessen the expence of it, yet I confess I think it is one thing to carry her with you for health to a place of retirement, and another to act as a mother to her all over the world; neither do I think it would put you in a proper light in Italy, but I am too far off to wish you to rely absolutely upon me. I would have you do what is best, but circumstances and good opinions must decide you—only remember L. A. P., and how often people advise and persuade what in their serious judgment they disapprove. I could not help making many reflections on that approbation which you forced from him for having refused what he had solicited. I hope you made some too, but I am sure you did, for all you say gives me hope and comfort.

I am sorry that my banishment should sit so heavy upon you, my dear Bess; the manner of it was, to be sure, cruel, but I hope I shall turn it all to good account; and as to the mere solitude, you know nobody minds it less than I do. I assure you upon my honor, that my health and spirits are good, and that if I have now more time for reflection, I have also subjects of more content for it. You, my dearest child, make a great part of this, for I cannot but flatter myself that you are getting into port again, though the current may be a little against you, and oblige you to work for some time at the oar; but I do earnestly beg of you not to be discouraged, and to endeavour to steer safely between two dangerous points of too much confidence and too much fear and distrust of yourself. The one would make you imprudent and careless, and the other too anxious and unhappy. You have, I trust, a solid principle on which to form your conduct: you have now some experience on which to rectify your sentiments, and I think you have good sense and steadiness enough to lay down the coquette without adopting the prude, and to give an example of a reform which may set your character in its true light and give it all the dignity of virtue, without the severity which would be necessary to a heart viciously inclined, but which is totally improper for yours.

I have just received a few lines from your dear Duchess, whom I rejoice to find goes on well, but I am afraid she has been sadly hurried by the D. of P.[76] being in the house at this time. At last all is settled, however, I hope lastingly so, but that seems to be doubted. I don't yet know who goes to Ireland. I hope not the D. of D.,[77] for I think they could get nothing but vexation by it.

Salvatore has been here for a week and behaved vastly well, and I have settled everything to his mind for his summer attendance on Louisa: he is to come next month, and has engaged a lodging at Bury, from whence he is to come every morning. He has wrote his whole story relative to the imprisonment: it is well drawn up, and shews that he has been cruelly and unjustly treated. Louisa is very happy at this arrangement, and has been very eager with some new music which he brought down. She goes on in every respect as I could wish, health, spirits, sentiments, application, &c., loves proper reading, shews taste in it, and never finds her time upon her hands, &c.

I am sorry to say that I have not the same satisfaction with poor Fred, though he has no fault in it; but your father has determined on sending for him to Ireland, and having a private tutor. I have said everything that was possible to dissuade him from it, even to pointing out his improper treatment of him, for this was my duty, coûte que coûte; he has taken it very well, ne s'est point offensé, calls it good sense but reasoned on false principles; and, in short, desires me finally to leave him to him, so there is an end of it, and I can do nothing but wish and pray that he may do well.

I know the Sir Rob. S. you mention a little, and think him very sensible, but odd tempered. La. M. Fitz talks of going to Ireland next month. Mr. Fitz is out of confinement. I suppose you hear often from Bath. Lord Rodney[78] is now there, and they are both inamorato morto di lui; he says your B.[79] may be at home next month. Pray remember me to my old admirer, &c. Pray say something pretty to Madame Birbeck: I thought she had been dead, but tell her I am very glad to hear she is so much better than when I had the pleasure of knowing her at Marseilles, &c. Poor soul, I believe she was unhappy there, and that he was a Birbo,[80] so pray soothe her a little. Adieu. I send this by the dear Duchess. What heavenly good nature and attention she shewed to you in that £20! Do you know whether she ever sees Mrs. Cosway? I think I could one day prove to her that she is unworthy of her notice, and I wish you would mention it. God bless you! ...

> *The Countess of Bristol*
> *To Lady Elizabeth Foster.*
>
> Ickworth Park, *April.* 16, 1783

The inclosed letter from your brother, my dear Bess, arrived last night, and I hasten to send it to your charming friend to forward to you. I have one by the same pacquet, and as mine is wrote in very low spirits, I must caution you against any infection from yours, and desire you to recollect how the news of the peace (which he had not then heard) will have rejoiced him, together with some other circumstances which are in his favor more than he expected.

I thank you, my dear, for your frequent letters, and for your pretty account of the dedication of the fountain, which was a rural compliment very well turned, and what, I think, may, without any self-reproach, give you half-an-hour's pleasure; but if the attentions you mention are really in so respectful a style—I mean generally so, and not from a designing individual like Eh (who sacrificed the very character he pretended to revere)—I think you have the greatest reason to be pleased and the strongest inducement to go on in your new system.

I am sorry you think of leaving Nice so soon, but, as I said before, it is impossible to give advice at this distance. I have only to hope that you do not sacrifice great points to lesser ones. I have just heard from Barmeath[81] your dear little boys are vastly well. Dr. Foster has been given over, but is better again. I long to hear whether that letter of Mr. F. to you is to produce anything.

Adieu! my love. I cannot write to-day, having a thousand embarras, servants inoculating, others ill, contrivances, orders, &c. I expect my brother from London, too, to-day, and we will talk of you. I do not ride, for, if I had a mind to do it, your father has taken my horse without saying a word to me. Salvatore is not yet here. I expect him next month; he is to be at Bury, and come up every morning. Louisa desires her love. I will take care to make all your excuses about writing. I wish you was not so punctual in that article with H., for by that means you make absence no advantage, and you are still the dupe of his expressions. The Duchess of

Devonshire assures me that she is vastly well, and, as she has been all the time so prudent and manageable, I think there is nothing to fear.

I long for your Italian letters, the verses, and Mr. Robertson's answer, as also for further particulars of your travelling scheme, which I do not comprehend. You will not forget that Switzerland and Geneva are dear places for strangers. Adieu! Ever affectionately yours.

> *The Countess of Bristol*
> *To Lady Elizabeth Foster.*

Ickworth Park, *Dec.* 26, 1783

I received your letter from Rome of the 27th November, my dear Bess, a little before that of the 10th from Florence; I don't know by what accident, but the dear Duchess who sent it to me said she supposed the French Ambassador had had it some time in his hands; and, as she did not mention having received one of an earlier date, I wrote to her to say what I knew of you, and I knew she would be glad to hear. She is comforting her poor mother[82] at St. Albans, and I am happy to find is so well recovered herself as to be able to go on with her nursing, and to succeed extremely in it.

This overturn of the ministry will, I am afraid, vex her, but in the present moment of confusion it is hard to say what may be the consequence of it, or whether they may not come in again stronger than before. On an expectation of the Parliament being dissolved, your brother came down to me to try again at Bury; but as that is not to be, he is spared some trouble, and myself much disquiet, from the difficulty of acting in all matters so as to content your father. We are going to set out together for Valentine, and by being so near London I shall hear more frequently how the arrangements and negotiations go on, and whether Mr. Pitt can form an administration to go on with him: Lord Mul[83] is one of his adherents.

I am very sorry, my dear Bess, if anything I have wrote to you has given you the smallest idea of my being refroidi towards you. No, my poor suffering child, my tenderness is always the same; nay, more, my reliance on your good intentions, and on the desire you have to throw a drop of comfort into my bitter cup, which, I repeat to you, is always in your power; but when I see you borne away by the defects in your character, or blinded by your own approbation acting so as I think will provoke the censure of the world, I must tell you of it. I hope it is not with aigreur, but I own it is with strong feelings, because I see you in a situation in which you have everything against you. I am grieved to say that your father's very extraordinary conduct has given rise to many ill-natured reflections on the whole family.

I have lost poor Mrs. Ashburner's letter and direction, but if you wish me so much to write to her, and will send it to me, I will certainly do it. I do not understand Lady Cow's[84] situation by your account of her. Pray explain it, and how you found poor, dear Emily, and if she mentioned having heard from me. I am glad you saw things so agreeably there, but I was impatient to have you out of that climate, which I know is a bad place for you late in the year. You will soon have the Emperor, I find, in Italy, so you will have an opportunity of seeing many crowned heads and extraordinary characters.

I am not surprised at the avidity with which you have gone to the great objects of curiosity and admiration at Rome; and to tell you the truth, am glad Mr. Byres was absent, because I think Mr. Jenkins will be a pleasanter cicerone, as he knows as much, and will communicate his instruction less en routine. You will find him in all things, I hope, an intelligent, useful, and friendly man; and, indeed, he has already given a proof of it in the circumstance you mention. Pray remember me very particularly to him. I shall never forget his attention to me in my distresses at Castello. I will not write to him till I return.

I find your father has not paid him the last year's pensions he is so good as to distribute for him. I wish it may be only forgetfulness, but for some time past everything has been neglected on this side of St. George's Channel. He took some of them begun by me out of my hands (I believe) for fear I should have the merit of it.

I don't know how I expressed myself about Salvatore, for he is in London, and of course cannot be employed by you, but may be served by your good report. I am glad you find people at Rome that speak favorably of him. I was afraid that that scandalous imprisonment had hurt him there. I wonder Cardinal Bernis should speak of me whom he never saw; and not of your father, whom I supposed he had admired and saw often....

    The Countess of Bristol
      To Lady Elizabeth Foster.
                    Ickworth Park, *January* 26, 1784

My dear Elizabeth,—I have two of your letters from Rome, one of which I received at your brother's, and one since my return home. I thank you for the account of what you see. The principal things I remember; but I had not the advantages you have, nor any guide given me, much less so good a one as Mr. Jenkins. Indeed, he does not act in that capacity, and it is a particular attention to you. I am glad you made my message more acceptable to him by making it public. I would give him every testimony of my regard, for I was in misery, and he helped me. As to Cardinal Bernis, I don't wonder at your surprise that I should not even know one with whom your father was so much acquainted, but I soon found that we could not go together. I wished much to have seen him, am sure I should have liked him, and have my disappointment unexpectedly made up to me by his kindness to you.

The footing you have put yourself upon, my dear Bess, gives me great pleasure, and Mr. I. confirms it to me, but do not rely upon the praises of one who has acted so different a part. They are false: pursue your own plan, and give her no opportunity of intimacy to overturn it. I dare not name names, but I dare say you will understand me; if not, your cicerone can explain the living as well as the dead; but since all is quiet at Naples, and since you must go there, I rejoice much at your Danish friend, who is probably of a different character from any other woman you see; but I almost envy you the opportunity of knowing the Emperor[85] and King of Sweden,[86] two characters which have excited my curiosity extremely, and which you seem to have sifted so well. All is safe, too, at Venice. Well, I am rejoiced at it; and if you have tolerable weather, you have escaped from the most severe winter I ever saw, and must be a gainer, I hope a great one, in many points; but you still complain of your chest. Êtes vous sage, ma chère fille? Do you avoid cold? do you keep to regimen? do you follow Pipot? Above all, don't let even S. tempt you to sing.

I sent you word of Sir R. Smyth's death; his son was with him to the last, but he made no alteration in his favor: he has left him nothing; but what falls to him, and what he had before, gives him an income of about £1400 a year. Mrs. Brand has behaved very handsomely to him, and he very unkindly to her.

I have to inform you of the death of one which will affect you more— poor Dr. Foster—which account came very kindly to me from Miss Bellew in order to transmit to you. I know you will be very uneasy about the poor boys, but I think Mr. Foster will be inclined to leave them there, and that if you request it of the Marshalls that they will keep them; as to what you ask me about your father and Mr. Foster, I suppose they have quarrelled, for I wrote to him when he was in Dublin to beg he would get your settlement registered, and his answer was that he would have nothing more to do with Mr. F. I will let you know whatever I hear from Dunleer. In the meantime do not let your imagination be too busy, for our real evils are enough and more than we can well cope with.

I must not finish this letter without saying something of Valentine: it is really a pretty place and very comfortable house, but there are some inconveniences belonging to it, and I wish your brother, if possible, to get rid of it. Lady Hervey[87] is not very well, and they talk of going to Spa early in the season; and your sister, who is not at all so, has promised me to go whether they go or no. Your brother is grown fat and looks vastly well, and the two little cousins are au mieux.

I will say nothing of Irish politics, and English ones are in such a state of confusion at this moment that nothing can be said of them.

I will remember you to your Aunts when I see them, and to my brother, who is in the country; but we are all shut up by the snow. Your uncle William is with me, and has just done a very friendly thing by your brother. He and Louisa send their love to you. Remember me to Mr. Jenkins. Have you never been at Batoni's? [88] I am well and calm though I live in a storm, and evermore your affectionate mother.

Richard Brinsley Sheridan[89]
To Georgiana, Duchess of Devonshire..
Crewe, *October* 29, 1786

My dear Duchess,—I have waited with the greatest impatience for the hour of liberty to remind you and Lady Elizabeth of one who never thinks of either of you without a mixture of pleasure and pain. I hope it is not necessary for me to entreat you both not to forget me. I am more interested in your happiness than half those who, with fine speeches and cold hearts, impose on your natural openness and sincerity; and, though it is impossible for those who know you at all not to love you, yet I will be confident in saying they cannot feel towards you as I do and must, after all that passed at C.

I passed two days at Capethon, with its inhabitants, and Sir George and Lady Warren. I wandered about all day alone, and by recalling the past made the present less disagreeable. It is not often I indulge myself in these solitary rambles; though it is most pleasing to me in general, it unfits me for the part I am too often obliged to act; but I could not find words to answer all the fine speeches and pressing invitations of Lady Warren. My eyes were so dazzled by the glitter of her diamonds and trinkets, and the sound of her voice almost convinced me I was at a crowded assembly in town. I fled from the idea and from her, and, if wishes had wings, you would have seen me again at C.

We came here Friday morning; there are many people in the house, but, as I am quite sure they are quite as uninteresting to you as to myself, I will not mention them. I must except Mr. Hare,[90] who must be pleasant anywhere; his business is put off, I find, for he does not talk of going away. Charles Greville likewise is here, but I do not find he has been talking, consequently he has no suspicion of what you imagined, otherwise you may be assured Mrs. C. would have been acquainted with them. She has asked me a thousand questions of various kinds, to all which I have answered as I would to the town Cryer if I was questioned by him. I believe she feels that my heart is shut against her, and behaves accordingly; but I dare not complain, nor would it be of any service to me if I did; she is of an unhappy disposition, and there are moments when, in spight of her behaviour, I feel inclined to pity her: for my own part all situations are pretty much the same to me when there are cribbage or whist parties; there at least I escape observation; a grave look may denote a bad hand, and an, accidental sigh may be that of regret for getting out a wrong card; here I find it doubly necessary to be so occupied, for the attention of Friendship does not suffer a word or look to escape, and by officious enquiries of my health or spirits point out an occasion for reproach to him whom I wish always to see happy by appearing perfectly so myself.

When shall I hear from you? I am very anxious to know how you are, and how things are going on. I see by the papers the Duke is gone. I hope you have influence enough over him to persuade him to resign. I am sure he ought. Pray when you write assure him of my regard and *Friendship, indeed no more.* Tell him the only thing in the world that would give me the greatest satisfaction is to think him perfectly happy, and in that wish I know I shall be joined by you. God bless you, my dear Duchess; pray believe that my heart is anxiously interested in all that concerns you, and that my warmest prayers are offered up for your happiness, let it depend on what it will. Pray believe this, and that I am, with the greatest affection and sincerity, ever yours,

SHERIDAN.

My best love to Lady Elizabeth; tell her Mrs. C.'s greatest insight to me is the having expressed myself as I feel about her.

> *The Countess of Bristol*
> *To Lady Elizabeth Foster.*
>
> Bruton Street, *Jan.* 22, 1792

My dear Elizabeth,—I found a letter from Mrs. Bellew when I arrived here two days ago which I eagerly opened, as it was to answer my inquiries after your poor boys. The account is so pleasing a one that I will give you her own words, her letter is of the 8th of this month: "I had the pleasure of seeing the dear little Fosters here yesterday. They spent the day with us, and are perfectly well now, and both very fine boys. Frederick is very sentimental, sedate, and sensible; he had for a time severe chillblains, but is now well of them; the youngest seems arch, lively, and sensible, and I think has much of Lord Bristol in him, and they are very good-natured boys, and always seem happy to see us; indeed, the father seems very fond of both, and takes great care of them." I was in a hurry to write this, my dear Bess, though it could not reach you the sooner, and trusted to having time to finish my letter to-day, but the great racket and perplexity of arranging things and people, Louisa's being ill of a cold and cough, and a number of little plagues leave me but little time for it; however, I will just add that I think everything is settled for the mutual advantage of all parties. I was going to have explained to you, but Louisa tells me she has done so, and I will therefore only say that I have got a very good bed-chamber myself, and that hers is next to it, at which I know you will rejoice for me. We have not stirred from the house on account of her cold and my business, and, on account of both, have made our arrival so little known that we have seen but few people. I have just sent to Devonshire House. How vexatious that your poor little muso[91] is not there, and where is it? for that I cannot figure to myself. I do wish it out of France—for though I think war further off than ever, I do not like to have you exposed to the accidents belonging to the present anxiety of it, but I must have patience per force....

Edward Gibbon[92]
To Lady Elizabeth Foster.

I know not whether you are already informed of the sudden death of poor Lady Sheffield[93] after four days' illness, but I am sure that your feeling, affectionate mind will not be surprized to hear that I set out for England next week, and that a journey undertaken at the call of friendship. All the dragons of the way have already vanished. I go by Basle, Frankfort, Cologne, Brussels, and Ostend, and I flatter myself that the success of our allied arms will contribute every week to open my passage; it is even possible, though scarcely probable, that I may embark from the English town of Calais. Your answer to my last letter is doubtless on the road and will follow me, but you must write immediately to Sheffield Place, and I promise you a speedy and sincere account of our afflicted friend. I wish to hear of your motions and projects. I now sigh for your return to England, and shall be most bitterly disappointed if I have not the pleasure of seeing you in that happy island—yourself and the most amiable of Dutchesses before the end of the autumn. I cannot look with confidence beyond that period. My friend and your Chevalier will guard me as far as Cologne or Frankfort; his tender attachment to his mother, who is still very melancholy, will recall him from thence to Lausanne, but in the course of next winter he has thoughts of visiting England. The circumstances of the times, which impoverish every one, have persuaded him to listen to my advice of conducting on his travels some English pupill of fashion and fortune. Such a pupill will be fortunate in finding a real gentleman, and I trust that the Dutchess and yourself will exert your omnipotence in providing some connection equally honourable and advantageous for my friend and your sincere Votary. Adieu. Excuse brevity, and address a Classic prayer in my behalf before some statue of Mercury, the god of travellers.

Lausanne, May the 4th, 1793.

The Earl of Bristol, Bishop of Derry
To Lady Elizabeth Foster.

Naples, *March* 6, 1796

Dearest Elizabeth,—I did not expect a second letter of yours from Goodwood[94] without a plan and elevation of that *model* of a house you admire so much and prefer to mine. A few guineas, my child, would have procured it, and you know I am not niggard of them, especially where architecture is concerned. I am certain, on your speaking to the Duke of Richmond, he will order it immediately; you may fold it up in a large letter, and I receive it time enough to adopt any improvements it contains.

You beg me on your knees that Ickworth house may be built of white stone brick. You know, my dear, what Ranger says to his cousin, and upon my knees I beg you too. What, child, build my house of a *brick* that looks like sick, pale, *jaundiced* red brick that would be red brick if it could, and to which I am certain our posterity will give a little rouge as essential to its health and beauty? White brick always looks as if the bricklayers had not burnt it sufficiently, had been niggardly of the fuel; it looks all dough and no crust. I am ever looking out for its crust, so, my dear, I shall follow dear impeccable Palladio's rule, and as nothing ought to be without a covering in our raw damp climate, I shall cover house, pillars, and pilasters with Palladio's *stucco*, which has now lasted 270 years. It has succeeded perfectly well with me at *Downhill* on that temple of the winds, and as well at my Casino of Derry—that temple of *Cloacina*. It has resisted the frosts and the rains of Vicenza c'est tout dire, and deceives the most acute eye till within a foot.

We have Lord Macartney[95] here these eight days. They had him at Court twice, and have squeezed this *China orange* so close they left him nothing but the pulp. What restless perturbed spirits he has, that in the course of his short life he has visited Petersburgh and Grenada, Madras and Pekin, and is now reduced to a mock embassy to a mock king. A propos I passed two hours and a half with this *King of Candides*; he is no *Carnival* King, however, that is certain, but un vrai Roi de Carême. I never conversed with a more pleasing, cheerfuller, easier, better-informed man in any country. Adversity has not soured but sweetened him, and turned all his vinegar to oil.

I am truly delighted you are so much so with the picture I sent Louisa. 'Tis a real bijoux, and just fit for her breakfast-room, but you say nothing of the *Berlin dejeun*é which I reckon a great cadeau, and when it stands on a tripod of *Siberian malachite* will be impayable.

What say you to my idea of a gallery of German painters contrasted with a gallery of Italian painters, from Albert Durer[96] to Angelica Kauffman,[97] and from Cimabue[98] to Pompeio Battoni,[99] each divided by pilasters into their respective school—*Venetian* for colouring, *Bologna* for composition, Florence for designs, Rome for sentiment, and Naples for nothing at all? But the *Homer* of Painting is in my mind in *Germany, Rembrandt,*[100] and the author of the Descent from the Cross[101] at Antwerp. Raphael[102] and all Italian painters are the Minor Poets of Painting, the Garths,[103] the Gays,[104] the Priors,[105] but there is not a *Shakespeare*[106] among them. Michael Angelo[107] is mad, not sublime; ludicrous, not dignified. He is the *Dante*[108] of painters as Dante is the Michael Angelo of poets. The picture of the last judgment is so tragi-comical 'tis difficult to say what passion it excites most; and St. Barthlemé, all flayed, who holds up his skin as his ticket of admittance into Heaven, is worthy only of *Bartholomew* fair. Adieu. This is the fortieth day I am in bed unremittingly, reduced to a shadow, yet devouring like a *shark*. My pulse is a pulse of *threads* scarce to be felt. The King and Queen supply me with game, and I make game of everybody. The House—The House—The House.

The Earl of Bristol, Bishop of Derry
To Lady Elizabeth Foster.

Pyrmont, *August* 1, 1796

Dearest Elizabeth,—Though I would not for the world itself disappoint your poor brother's[109] hopes if his noble and generous heart be really engaged, nor even diminish of one obole the allowance I should be able to make him, which is exactly the same I gave your poor dear eldest brother, yet I must confess it would half break my heart to see his fixed on any other than the beautiful, elegant, important, and interesting object I have proposed to him.

At least, dearest Eliza, if you have any interest with him, induce him, beg him, my dear, not to decide before he is able to chuse. She would bring into our family £5000 a year, besides a Principality in Germany, an English Dukedom for Frederick or me, which the King of Prussia[110] is determined to obtain in case the marriage takes place, a perpetual relationship with both the Princess of Wales[111] and her children, as also with the Duchess of York[112] and her progeny, the Embassy to Berlin, with such an influence and preponderance in favor of dear England as no other could withstand. Add to all this, the King is so bent upon it, from his great partiality to me, that I doubt not his doubling the dot in case F. desired it, which indeed I should not. We are, besides, all determined to go and meet him the moment we hear of his debarking, which he may notify by estafette. In short, nothing would be more brilliant, or flattering, or more cordial than his reception in case he can think with us; and indeed, dearest Elizabeth, the examples he has before his eyes in and within his own family ought fully to determine him against a love match; 'tis so ominous a lottery, so pregnant with blanks, so improbable a success. In short, dearest Elizabeth, write to me soon; above all, *See him.* All I desire of him is not to resolve against us; not to throw away a Pearl richer than all his tribe; let him but see before he decides, let him weigh all we offer to his ambition, his ease, his comfort, his taste, and his pocket.

> *The Earl of Bristol, Bishop of Derry*
> *To Lady Elizabeth Foster.*
>
> Pyrmont, *August* 4, 1796

Dearest Elizabeth,—I have wrote warmly and fully to your dear brother on my project of marrying him to one of the prettiest, sweetest, most delicate, and innocent, as well as accomplished little women I ever saw, endowed with £100,000 down, besides the reversion of a landed property in Germany, with the promise of a Dukedom to him or me, as the King of Prussia can obtain it from our King. On the contrary, though, God forbid I should negative his inclinations, poor fellow, at his time of life, and in his state of health, [I wish] to dissuade him all I can (and I entreat your assistance, sweet Elizabeth) from his present pursuit. *She* has little or no fortune. Your brother by the last act of settlement can make no provision for either her or her children, and if he should die within five or six years—which the perturbed state of his mind might easily produce—what must be the consequence to his widow and her orphans? Once married and the first heat of passion allayed, what must be the state of an anxious debilitated mind?

Dearest Elizabeth,—Farquhar[113] himself could not ensure his poor life for a year more after black and melancholy ideas should begin to possess his mind. Relief would neither be in his power nor in mine, and medicine would be the more ineffectual as the malady would be in the mind.

If you care, my dear child, to accompany your brother to Pyrmont, and from thence to pass the winter at Naples, I will gladly pay your expenses, and be glad of your company for the winter. The King of Prussia has been good enough to write by Express to the Directory at Paris requesting a passport for Lord Hervey and his suite to land at Ostend and pass through the Low Countries to Pyrmont.... [Torn.] At any rate, my dear Elizabeth, try to dissuade him from a passion and a pursuit so pregnant with evil consequences to the quiet of his mind and the health of his body, whilst on the other hand I offer a real Cornucopia.

The Earl of Bristol, Bishop of Derry
To Lady Elizabeth Foster.

Pyrmont, *August* 16, 1796

You nasty little Imp of Silence! What are you doing that one can hear no more about you than if one did not care for you, and yet who do I care for more?

I wrote your brother that he might bring your ugly face with him, and we would all go to Naples, where I have, without exception, the handsomest and best situated house there; fourteen rooms on each floor all hung with Rafaels, Titians,[114] and what not. Then how happy the queen to see you, and the delicious evenings we should pass with her. Your brother is to receive by estafette a passport from the Directory to land at Ostend and come to me through Brabant. That would be the road for you, eight hours' sail and no more. Then, what a journey together, and a month's residence at Sans Souci, which the king has just lent me with his cooks, his manors, library, gallery, &c. Oh! if I can accomplish my heart and soul's desire to join your dear brother's hand with La Comtesse de la Marche[115]—£5000 a year down, £5000 more in reversion, an English Dukedom, probably the embassy to Berlin—por Dio che piacere. The King gave me his honor to pass next summer at Ickworth if there be a peace.

The Earl of Bristol, Bishop of Derry
To Lady Elizabeth Foster.

Pyrmont, *August* 27, 1796

Dearest Elizabeth,—Are you alive or dead, or are you on a journey? Or perchance she sleepeth? If so, at least dream a little, or walk in your sleep, or talk in your sleep, for I have no patience with your long, very long, silence. I proposed to your dear brother to bring you with him first to Pyrmont, then to Naples, where you know what pleasures, intellectual and sensual, await you, and neither your journey nor your abode shall cost you one farthing; and I think the climate, to say nothing of other circumstances, would do ye both service. What I have most at heart in this moment is your brother's marriage with The Comtesse de la Marche, the King of Prussia's daughter, of which I have wrote to you so fully; but I would not on any account have you teaze him about it how ardently soever I may wish it, especially as he seems inclined to another project. But see the difference:

On my side.	On, his side.
£5000 a year down.	No fortune.
£5000 a year in reversion.	Wife and children beggars
An English Dukedom, which the	for want of settlement.
King pledges to obtain.	No connexion.
Royal connexion—Princess of Wales,	A love match, like all others for
and Duchess of York.	four generations before him.

Sweet Elizabeth, when occasion serves, help me to accomplish my project. I cannot, if I would, afford him more than £2000 a year whilst my house is building and furnishing. What is that in London?

But on my plan.	On, his plan.
£2000 from me.	£2000.
£5000 Dowry	Wife and children, and no settlement.
£3000 Embassy to Berlin or Munich	
———	
£10,000	

The Earl of Bristol, Bishop of Derry
To Lady Elizabeth Foster.

Pyrmont, *September* 11, 1796.

Dearest Elizabeth,—Your are a dear, amiable little girl not to have called on me for your sugar plums in this year of distress and confusion, for by the last balance of my accounts with Messrs. Gosling[116] there remained but one hundred pounds in their hands, and several of my own drafts from Italy have been protested, which is both expensive and disgraceful, so that you see, my dear child, I had little left to be generous with, having scarce withal to fill the duties of justice.

Lord Hervey.

And now, my dear child, for poor, dear Frederick's affair; and it amazes myself when I recollect the object the nearest to my heart for these last twelve or fourteen years. I thought I could be content to vegetate for the remainder of my *green old age* among painters and sculptors, masons and bricklayers, and was not aware of the very deep interest this warm, sensible heart of mine was likely to take in any project whatever; but I own to you the idea of fixing a son of your brother's superior and preeminent qualities, both moral and intellectual, in a station worthy of him and *of us all* has kindled anew the almost extinguished sparks, the very embers of my expiring and effete ambition. To see him in possession of a station where his interest can be as independent as his spirit, and take a bond of Fate; to see him fixed where he can essentially and proudly serve the greatest country that ever reared citizens, and the ablest minister[117] that ever served a country, was a prospect to which my dim eyes did not yet reach: then to see that project tumbled down to a Château d'Espagne in the regions of love and fancy; to see him a bankrupt in the most problematical and disadvantageously fascinating Lottery with 500 blanks to one prize, would put even my philosophy, triumphant as it yet is, to the proof. Aid me, therefore, my dearest child, to eradicate, if possible, his own project from his mind, and then to establish mine. The first object is to get him abroad, where, if you can, I dare say you will, accompany him; then to secure his health of body and tranquillity of mind: a winter passed in England at this period of his malady, both of mind and body, cannot but be fatal; whereas a warm air bath at Naples, in that most balmy of all atmospheres, amidst music, friends, and dissipation, will be as soothing to his mind as the climate to his body; and as I, on account of my own horses, never travel above 25 or 30 miles a day, and have always saddle-horses at hand, he can not fear fatigue. As to his love project, thus stands our account:

	On, his plan.
1. A lady without fortune, without connexions.	1. A lady with £10,000 a year instead of £5000 and five more in reversion.
2. No possible settlement on my part nor on Lord Hervey's	2. An English Dukedom.
3. All my Irish leasehold estates entailed long ago on H. Bruce[118] and his children;	3. The highest and most desirable of all connexions.

on Theo. Bruce and his children; on
your two sons; on Caroline; and finally
on Frederick, with a clause in favor of
myself.

4. Peace of Mind for me and
himself.
This is your brief, and I
expect you to plead with
eloquence the cause of us all.

4. Therefore poverty, famine, and omnipotent
love for her and her children.

He says his honor is engaged; so it is—not to entail poverty and famine
on her and her younger children. Your late brother has left me a debt of
£15,000 to pay—£10,000 to his daughter and £5000 to his creditors:
judge of my means, and believe me, as ever, yours.

> *The Earl of Bristol, Bishop of Derry*
> *To Lady Elizabeth Foster.*
> Pyrmont, *September* 11, 1796.

If I have anything to ask of you, my dearest Elizabeth, it is that in case your
brother gets a *cough* in the course of the winter, you beg of Lord Spencer[119]
a frigate, and send him off directly to me at Naples, ever yours, B.
P.S.—Nothing can equal the Deroute of the damned Blackguard, pilfering,
plundering, pillaging Republicans. Neither Minden[120] nor Rosbach[121] can
compare with it: all their artillery, all their baggage, all their waggons
loaded with contributions, all taken: we have here two *officers* and the
son of our apothecary just arrived from Frankfort, who not only confirm
all this, who were ocular witnesses to these ourang outangs running like
themselves without shoes, stockings, or breeches, and the exasperated
peasants knocking them down, like real monkeys, their prototypes,
with bludgeons, pitchforks, staves, all that came to hand, "furor arma
ministrat" 12,000 dead on the road or the field, 900 waggons loaded with
wounded, that is 9000 wounded, and the Austrians in Frankfort before
the rear guard left it.

> *The Earl of Bristol, Bishop of Derry*
> *To Lady Elizabeth Foster.*
> Frankfort, *Sept.* 26, 1796.

Dearest Elizabeth,—Here is the most consolatory Gazette I have read of a
long time, and I inclose it as a receipt to cure you of a migraine. Nothing
can be more brilliant than the successes of our two heroes, the Archduke

Charles,[122] and the Prince Frederick of Orange, except their own exertion to obtain them. They are idolized by their armies, and amply supported by their courage. The last accounts I have seen of Moreau's[123] defeat near Munich carry the number of dead up to 15,000 the wounded 9000, and the prisoners 7000. If the Austrians can carry the fort of Kehl, Strasburg, entirely commanded by it, must fall, and then France will begin to feel the iron hand of Austria.

I leave this at 4 o'clock to-day, and shall reach Pyrmont in three days, which I left only to get a sight of the armies. From Pyrmont straight to *Sans Souci*, where I pass a month with my dear Countess and her beautiful, elegant, decent, mild, gentle Daughter. Would to God she were also mine. I have so set my very heart and soul on this union that no event whatever could give me equal satisfaction, and when poor dear Frederick perceives the absolute impracticability of his own project, [I have no doubt] but he will, according to the tenor of his last letter, readily adopt mine. Ce qui me mettra à la joie de mon cœur, for a young woman more calculated by nature, as well as education, to make a virtuous man happy, I never yet saw, and I am certain you would doat on her.

The Earl of Bristol, Bishop of Derry
To Lady Elizabeth Foster.

Cassel, *Sept.* 30, 1796.

Dearest Elizabeth,—I am now returning to Pyrmont from my military expedition, for you know, child, we have Church militant as well as Church visible—Low Church and High Church. The affaire at *Alten Kirchen*[124] near Dillembourg, which is near Marpurg, was bien sanglante. The Ourang Outangs or Tyger monkeys lost the few shirts and breeches they had. That modern hero, Prince Frederick of Orange (observe, my dear, all the great men of this century are Fredericks[125]); this hero, who united the phlegm of Hannibal with the activity of Scipio, cut them to pieces like a sailor's biscuit. They have recrossed the Rhine, and evacuated Dusseldorf. On the Upper Rhine the bravery of the Austrian soldiers had taken Fort Kehl, which commands Strasburg; and the stupidity, indiscipline, and rapacity of the officers lost it. They were plundering the stores when they ought to have been raising the Drawbridge—quelles bêtes—Landau is known to have only 600 men or boys in it. The Archduke marched with 13,000 men to take it, and here ends my Budget and letter, and so adieu, dearest Eliza.

To-morrow for *Sans Souci* and my dearest Countess, de qui je soucie beaucoup in spite of my *Goliah* = Rival, whom little *David* no longer fears.

From Georgiana, Duchess of Devonshire,
   To Frederick Foster.

Devonshire House, 18th *Nov.*, 1796

I have hitherto refrained from claiming the privilege of an old acquaintance, and writing to you, not only from the dreadful complaint I have had on one eye, which has occasioned my being forbid writing, but also, Dear Frederick, from thinking that your time must be very much taken up. I can, however, refrain no longer, and I write now to assure you of the warm interest I take in everything that concerns you, and my impatience to see you. Your appartements, and your brother's, are quite ready at Devonshire House. I hear you are to set out 20th. I do most earnestly *entreat* you to let your journey suffer no further delay. Your Dear Mother's heart is so full of anxiety and expectation that any disappointment or delay in the expected moment would be fatal to her health. You will find many friends impatient to see you, and none more so than your new Uncle, Lord Hawkesbury.

I do not know if you remember me, but I assure you that I never have forgot you since Bath. You must excuse this bad writing, as I am still half blind, but, truly and affectionately, yours,

   G. DEVONSHIRE.

To Lady Elizabeth Foster, from Georgiana, Duchess of
   Devonshire, when she was apprehensive of
      losing her eyesight—1796.

The Life of the Roebuck was mine,
      As I bounded o'er Valley and Lawn;
I watched the gay Twilight decline,
      And worshipped the day-breaking Dawn.

I regret not the freedom of will,
      Or sigh, as uncertain I tread;
I am freer and happier still,
      When by thee I am carefully led.

Ere my Sight I was doomed to resign,
      My heart I surrendered to thee;
Not a Thought or an Action was mine,
      But I saw as thou badst me to see.

Thy watchful affection I wait,
     And hang with Delight on Thy voice;
And Dependance is softened by fate,
     Since Dependance on Thee is my Choice.

Lines by Georgiana, Duchess of Devonshire,
on Lady Elizabeth Foster.

Untutored in the Pencil's Art,
My Tints I gather from my Heart,
Where Truth and Love together trace
The various Beauties of thy face;
Thy Form acknowledged fair and fine,
Thy Smile, the antidote to Pain,
Thy Voice that never spoke in vain;
As diamonds on the Crystals trace
In Lines no Efforts can efface:
To please for ever is thy Lot
Once seen, once loved, and ne'er forgot.

On Lady Elizabeth Foster, by Georgiana,
Duchess of Devonshire.

Portrait d'Elizabeth.

A la beauté enchanteresse,
     Elle unit l'attrait de l'esprit;
Par un regard elle interesse,
     Par un sourire elle seduit.
A la finesse du langage,
     Du gout parfait le rare don;
Elle réunit 1'avantage
     De la bonte et de la raison.
Mortels, craintifs fuyez ses charmes,
     Fuyez son pouvoir enchanteur;
La cruelle impose les peines,
     An lieu de dormer le bonheur.
                    G. DEVONSHIRE

To my Children,
     By Georgiana, Duchess of Devonshire.

THE PASSAGE OF THE MOUNTAIN OF *SAINT GOTHARD*.

Ye plains where three-fold harvests press the ground,
     Ye climes where genial gales incessant swell,
Where art and nature shed profusely round
     Their rival wonders—Italy farewell!

Still may thy year in fullest splendor shine!
     Its icy darts in vain may winter throw!
To thee, a parent, sister, I consign,
     And wing'd with health, I woo thy gales to blow.

Yet, pleas'd Helvetia's rugged brows I see,
     And thro' their craggy steeps delighted roam,
Pleas'd with a people, honest, brave and free,
     Whilst every step conducts me nearer home.

I wander where Tesino madly flows,
     From cliff to cliff in foaming eddies tost;
On the rude mountain's barren breast he rose,
     In Po's broad wave now hurries to be lost.

His shores, neat huts and verdant pastures fill,
     And hills where woods of pine the storm defy;
While, scorning vegetation, higher still,
     Rise the bare rocks coeval with the sky.

Upon his banks a favor'd spot I found,
     Where shade and beauty tempted to repose;
Within a grove, by mountains circled round,
     By rocks o'erhung, my rustic seat I chose.

Advancing thence, by gentle pace and slow,
     Unconscious of the way my footsteps prest;
Sudden, supported by the hills below,
     St. Gothard's summits rose above the rest.

Midst tow'ring cliffs and tracts of endless cold
     Th' industrious path pervades the rugged stone,

And seems—Helvetia let thy toils be told—
    A granite girdle o'er the mountain thrown.

No haunt of man the weary traveller greets,
    No vegetation smiles upon the moor,
Save where the flow'ret breathes uncultur'd sweets,
    Save where the patient monk receives the poor.

Yet let not those rude paths be coldly trac'd,
    Let not these wilds with listless steps be trod,
Here fragrance scorns not to perfume the waste,
    Here charity uplifts the mind to God.

His humble board the holy man prepares,
    And simple food and wholesome lore bestows,
Extols the treasures that his mountain bears,
    And paints the perils of impending snows.

For whilst bleak Winter numbs with chilling hand—
    Where frequent crosses mark the travellers' fate—
In slow procession moves the merchant band,
    And silent bends where tottering ruins wait.

Yet 'midst those ridges, 'midst that drifted snow,
    Can nature deign her wonders to display;
Here Adularia shines with vivid glow,
    And gems of chrystal sparkle to the day.

Here, too, the hoary mountain's brow to grace,
    Five silver lakes, in tranquil state are seen;
While from their waters many a stream we trace,
    That, scap'd from bondage, rolls the rocks
between.

Hence flows the Reuss to seek her wedded love,
    And with the Rhine, Germanic climes explore;
Her stream I mark'd, and saw her wildly move
    Down the bleak mountain, thro' her craggy shore.

My weary footsteps hop'd for rest in vain,
    For steep on steep in rude confusion rose;

At length I paus'd above a fertile plain
     That promised shelter and foretold repose.

Fair runs the streamlet o'er the pasture green,
     Its margin gay, with flocks and cattle spread;
Embowering trees the peaceful village screen,
     And guard from snow each dwelling's jutting shed.

Sweet vale! whose bosom wastes and cliff surround,
     Let me awhile thy friendly shelter share!
Emblem of life! where some bright hours are found
     Amidst the darkest, dreariest years of care.

Delv'd thro' the rock, the secret passage bends,
     And beauteous horror strikes the dazzled sight;
Beneath the pendent bridge the stream descends
     Calm—till it tumbles o'er the frowning height.

We view the fearful pass—we wend along
     The path that marks the terrors of our way—
Midst beetling rocks, and hanging woods among
     The torrent pours and breathes its glittering spray.

Weary at length, serener scenes we hail—
     More cultur'd groves o'ershade the grassy meads,
The neat, tho' wooden hamlets deck the vale,
     And Altorf's spires recall heroic deeds.

But tho' no more amidst those scenes I roam,
     My fancy long each image shall retain—
The flock returning to its welcome home—
     And the wild carol of the cowherd's strain.

Lucernia's lake its glassy surface shews,
     Whilst nature's varied beauties deck its side;
Here rocks and woods its narrow waves enclose,
     And there its spreading bosom opens wide.

And hail the chapel! hail the platform wild!
     Where Tell directed the avenging dart
With well strung arm, that first preserv'd his child,
     Then wing'd the arrow to the tyrant's heart.

Across the lake and deep embow'd in wood
      Behold another hallow'd chapel stand,
Where three Swiss heroes lawless force withstood,
      And stamp'd the freedom of their native land.

Their liberty requir'd no rites uncouth,
      No blood demanded and no slaves enchain'd;
Her rule was gentle and her voice was truth,
      By social order form'd, by laws restrain'd.

We quit the lake—and cultivation's toil,
      With nature's charms combined, adorns the way,
And well earn'd wealth improves the ready soil,
      And simple manners still maintain their sway.

Farewell, Helvetia! from whose lofty breast
      Proud Alps arise, and copious rivers flow;
Where, source of streams, eternal glaciers rest,
      And peaceful science gilds the plain below.

Oft on thy rocks the wondering eye shall gaze,
      Thy vallies oft the raptur'd bosom seek—
There nature's hand her boldest work displays,
      Here bliss domestic beams on every cheek.

Hope of my life! dear Children of my heart!
      That anxious heart to each fond feeling true,
To you still pants each pleasure to impart,
      And more—oh transport!—reach its Home and You.

The Earl of Bristol, Bishop of Derry
    To Lady Elizabeth Foster.
               Dresden, *December* 6, 1796.

Did I not tell you, my dearest Elizabeth, that they would bungle the affair with the King of Prussia, and so it has happened? Mr. Elliott[126] here assured me he had seen all Mr. Hammond's papers, and to himself it was clear as daylight that the King and his ministers had acceded to all the preliminaries, whilst Mr. Hammond, who has a much greater *hesitation* in his brain than in his speech, was persuaded the preliminaries have not been acceded.

The King himself, Bishopswerder,[127] and Moellendorf[128] were all of Mr. Elliot's opinion, and the King himself told me in presence of my friend that he never was so surprised as when he heard that Mr. Hammond was decamped. I repeat it to you, let them send Frederick to Frederick William. I will give him *la grâce prevenante* with my Countess, and I will pledge myself he, with his talents, his manners, and his activity, will render it *la grâce efficace*. 'Tis a shame, dearest Elizabeth, that Frederick, with such endowments as his, both natural and acquired, should sacrifice so all to indolence, prepossession, and mere Egoism, whilst by entering into a career equally suited to his birth, to his talents, and to his education, he can render himself so extensively useful to the noblest country that ever did or ever can exist, respectable to his friends, and highly, permanently, and solidly serviceable to himself. Add to all that it is inconsistent with that noble character of independence which I suppose him to possess, to throw himself on the shoulders of a father already sinking under the weight, whilst by a manly and vigorous exertion of talents, for which he is responsible, he might prove an honor to his country, a comfort to his family, and a solace to himself.

Lord Elgin[129] is tired to death of Berlin, and would be so of any other station where he could not exercise his fox-hunting spirit, but Ratisbon was the station I wished your brother to accept, at this hour the very best diplomatick school in Europe, where the interests of all the empire are daily discussed, where he might learn his lesson in the best company. Mr. Elliot, who began with those rudiments, assured me yesterday it was to that school he owed all the diplomatick knowledge he possessed, and regretted infinitely with me that Frederick had Declined what he should have Conjugated. He empowered me at the same time to say that if Frederick could procure him any desirable exchange, he would resign Dresden to him. At all events, be sure your brother is not aware of the false step he is taking by declining the diplomatick line; according to all experience he cannot miss with his Birth, his Talents, his Connexions, and his assiduity becoming Secretary of State in ten or twelve years. Either he is, or he is not, calculated for public speaking; if he is, ministry will be as glad as him to give him a Semestre for the Parliament month (?) to avail themselves of him; if he is not, he cannot be better employed than at the *Desk*, where he has already given proofs of his prowess and powers in handling Mr. Thomas Paine[130]—and so adieu, sweet Elizabeth. I have done my duty; let Frederick now do his. Pour moi j'irai mon train, and if I cannot be the Caesar nor the Cicero,[131] I will be a less splendid but a more usefull Cityzen, the Lucullus[132] of my time, the Midwife of Talents, Industry, and hidden virtues. Sweet Elizabeth, adieu.

A luminous idea has just struck my mind which I only propose to you, and of which you may dispose as you please; if your eldest son[133] was sent abroad whilst I remain so he might live with me, and Mr. Lovel for one or two hundred a year might be his mentor—no one better for it, either for the morals or intellect of your son. I do but propose; do you dispose.

The Earl of Bristol, Bishop of Derry
To Lady Elizabeth Foster.

Dresden, *December* 28, 1796.

I do not expect peace to be signed by that blundering attorney, Lord Malmesbury[134] too cunning to deceive and too crafty to be trusted, but in case I should be disappointed and the French tygers submit to our terms, I think it is worth Frederick's while in time to speak for the embassy to the Hague, which is so near England, he is almost at home, and may ever be so in 24 hours; but here are my politicks, and if ever you canvass with the Duke and Duchess or other *Plenipo*, pray start the question and let me know the result. My idea is to annihilate *Holland* as a blackguard, mean, low, shabby, rival power, and sink her, as she was formerly, into the 17 provinces of Brabant, &c., &c., then give them altogether to Bavaria, and the Palatinate to the old Elector, an ignorant enthusiast, and a Papist whose nonsense, as Bishop Burnet[135] says, suits their nonsense. Brabant will at length have a Resident Sovereign. The Palatinate east of the Rhine I would give to a young branch of our Royal family as being Protestant; but west of the Rhine, and including all the iniquitous, profligate, debauched bishopricks and their infamous chapters, I would cede to the Republick on condition, and for this condition I would spend the last drop of blood and money, that they cede all the Provinces south of the Loire to Louis 18. Here is France as a maritime and commercial nation sunk for ever; the two governments eternally at war together, and doing the business for England; but if France is to remain entire—oh! judge of her future energy by her past, and dread the fatal moment when that restless people, having recruited her strength, pour all upon England: at all events, dear Elizabeth, I hope your *torpid* friends, for such I must call them, will not forget to secularize the two very lucrative but tyrannical bishopricks of Paderborn and Hildesheim in favour of two younger sons of our Royal family. The Bishops expect it, the people pray for it, and all Westphalia applaud it. Perhaps that *Log*, Lord Grenville,[136] does not know that they exist nor has ever heard of the secularization of the opulent bishoprick of Magdeburg in favour of the house of Brandenburg[137] after the 30 years [war], for, by all accounts from my diplomatick friends, a more ignorant blockhead does not exist; but, dearest Elizabeth, in case these torpid gentlemen assume the courage to secularize Hildesheim and Paderborn, let them not over look the small, low-lived, ignorant convent of English Benedictines at Lambsheim (?) worth, £3000 a year in the heart of that bishoprick, and now possessed by a whole sty of groveling, grunting, Epicurean hogs drawn out of the counties of Lancashire, Westmoreland, and West Riding of York. If your friends have the courage to look at such an enterprize you may give them a memorandum for their consideration. In the bishoprick of Paderborn there is another convent of Dominicans which I have also visited, and may be worth £2500 a year, and is in the centre of the bishoprick. The act of secularization depends entirely on the Emperor, who can refuse England nothing. The Chancellor of Hanover assured me that, to his knowledge, that corrupt, abandoned scoundrel, Lord Bute,[138] had absolutely the offer of a secularization in 1762, but refused it. 'Tis supposed he pocketed £20,000 for this infamous refusal, and the younger sons in consequence remain a burthen on England. Oh! if your brother were now Minister at Berlin what a blow he might strike! since I know for certain and past a doubt that my landlord of Sans Souci wishes nothing so much as to join in crushing the tigres-singes. What a blunder the sending of Hammond, whom nobody could understand, and who did not understand neither himself or others, and as to the present [Rest of this letter missing.]

The Countess of Bristol
    To Lady Elizabeth Foster.

On both my children's arrival in England, to Lady E. Foster.

Wimbledon, Monday, 1796.

How can I express to you, my dear Elizabeth, the feeling I have for you at this moment and the share I take in your happiness. In every respect your letter gives me great satisfaction. You happy will be a novelty indeed, but you have been patient under your sufferings as a wife, you have done your utmost to perform your duty as a mother, and I doubt not but that Providence has in store a reward for you, *more especially* as you think yourself undeserving of it, for an humble confidence in God is acceptable to Him.

God reads the language of a silent tear
And sighs are incense from a heart sincere.

I had just written you a note to beg you would moderate your agitation, and I still hope you will try to do it, but to-morrow is so near, it will be difficult. We had been a little distressed lest you should see that an Irish packet had been lost, and not observe that it was going *from* England; however, I thought it best not to mention it, and here they are safe. I thank you, my dear Elizabeth, for sending the earliest notice, and congratulate you most warmly on it. Pray assure them of my best affection, and believe that I shall be most sincerely glad to receive you and them together on Thursday if that suits, but if the House of Commons and Louisa's health should be likely to disturb your Wednesday's party, let me know it, and bring them here, if you like it better, on that day. Adieu, most affect.

I send you, my dearest Elizabeth, as to one of the few persons capable of relishing a great idea worthy of either Cromwell[139] or Chatham, but perhaps unintelligible to your dull, formal, pedantick, uncomprehending, and incomprehensible Minister of Foreign affairs, to which department he is as inadequate as to the Home, witness the insults offered to the British Lion by the Cubs of Genoa, or the Foxes of Tuscany. I send you, I say, a copy of my letter to Frederick William, which has been infinitely better understood and far more relished by him than by that impenetrable and unpenetrating blockhead Lord Grenville.

Chère amie, je te confie par une main très sûre un projet qui m'est d'autant plus cher que je me flatte qu'il s'agit des véritables intérêts d'un des plus vertueux Souverains de' Europe entière, et sans contredit des intérêts de celui à qui par goût, comme par reconnaissance je suis le plus attaché.

C'est beaucoup dire pour un Anglais et, pour un Anglais aussi fier que moi.

Il s'agit donc chère amie de mettre la France hors de combat: cette Nation inquiète et inquiétante sera tranquille pour au moins un siècle.

Il s'agit de la partager en deux—France Républicaine et France Monarchique, l'une au nord de la Loire, l'autre au midi.

La Nature s'y prête et la Politique s'y prête, car au sud de La Loire il n'y a pas Fortresse quelconque si vous en exceptez La Rochelle—et Antibes et Toulon, toutes les deux dégarnies de leur artillerie pour subvenir au siége de Mantoue.

Ajoutez que la proportion des Aristocrats a toujours été et subsiste toujours d'un supériorité énorme à la proportion Démocratique.

La France dans ce moment est terrassée; elle est aux abois et à peine peut-elle se soutenir.

Pour effectuer ce projet de partition il y'a deux partis a prendre.

Ou de s'allier avec le nouvel Empereur de Russie et de concert avec lui, et avec lui seul sur un Principe purement Monarchique, conduire le Roi Louis 18, avec la petite, mais brave et loyale armée de Conde travers la Suisse et le Piémont sans façon quelconque et le proclamer Roy de la France méridionale tout en entrant dans la Provence.

Ou bien de s'allier avec l'Angleterre qui fera la moitié des frais, et aideroit avec sa flotte pour seconder le même système.

Mais je crains un Cabinet aussi lâche, aussi équivoque, aussi indécis que celui de Londres, et je préfererois toujours un Cabinet dont 1'alliance seroit sympatétique et où les intérêts de la Monarchie serait commun aux deux Monarques.

Alors je prétens que d'après les connaissances que 25 ans de voyages m'ont donné, les frais de la guerre doivent être annuellement aux dépens de la France Méridionale.

Dans les années 1766 et 1767 j'assistais a la tenue des Etats de Languedoc.

Cette Province accorda au Roi chaque année la somme de £300,000 livres Sterlines.

Les Provinces de Guienne et de Gascogne avec la ville de Bordeaux payerent en impôts la valeur de £600,000 livres sterlines.

Les Etats de Dauphiné et de Provence avec la ville de Marseilles accordaient au Roi la somme de £500,000 livres sterlines—disons donc.

Languedock, ...	£500,000
Guienne, &c., ...	£600,000
Dauphiné, &c., ...	£500,000
	£1,600,000

Doublons cette somme par le droit de guerre nous aurons la somme complette £3,200,000 sterlines. Je me flatte qu'avec les contributions ordinaires cela suffirait pour entretenir les deux armées.

Il s'agit à present du Bien qui resulterait a votre ami de ce projet et du Mal qui doit resulter de sa negligence.

Par la division de la France en Republicaine et en Monarchique elle devient Puissance tres secondaire, par consequent hors de combat—encore plus si le caractere inquiet de la Nation faisait remuer la Republique. Voilà le Monarque tout de suite à son dos pour revendiquer ses anciens droits, et lui arracher quelque province—en tout cas son aide comme Puissance secondaire serait tres mince, tres equivoque et pen à craindre.

Mais—laisser échapper ce moment et que la République reste—une et indivisible—quel en est le triste et fatal resultat?

La France République devient mille fois plus énergique, plus terrible, plus dangereuse et plus séduisante durant la paix que durant la guerre.

Les commis voyageurs, les négotians, les émissaires, les apôtres de la liberté répandront à droit et à gauche ces principes de la liberté qui étouffent toute liberté et tres-sûrement bouleverseront les Monarchies actuelles et les Gouvernmens Monarchiques.

Et dites moi quel sera l'antidote à ce poison.

Les Pays-Bas seront-ils cédés à la République ou non? S'ils sont cédés quel colosse de Puissance et où est donc Wesel? Juliers? Cleves?

En cas qu'ils ne sont pas cédés trois ans après la paix voilà le duplicat du traité de ce Fanfaron Kaunitz.

Cédez-moi les Pays-Bas dira la République qui vous chicanent tant, vous insultent tant, et foncièrement vous rendent si peu, et je verse tous mes forces pour vous donner un équivalent dans la Silésie, la Pologne, &c.

Mais on me répliquera—La Russie ne le permette pas—La Russie l'a déjà permis une fois; donc la Russie le peut encore permettre. Il ne lui faut qu'un Ministre corrompu—dans une Nation la plus corrompue de toute l'Europe—ou bien accorder à la Russie pour sa neutralité Dantzig, &c., et qui me répondra de son amitié fidèle?

Vaut il la peine de risquer les évènements de la guerre de sept ans? Ne vaut-il pas mieux secouer ses plumes, aiguiser son bec, et deployer ses griffes, et fondre une fois pour tout sur cet ennemi abattu—terrassé mais toujours inquiet perfide et rusé, et lui ôter tout pouvoir de se relever— Divide et impera.

Dearest Elizabeth,—my friend writes me it has made the deepest impression, and raised the most vigorous resolutions, but alas I know him. One hour in the Lap of his *Danseuse,* and he lies there the shadow of a king—yet at such a moment if your brother, with all his energy and all his insinuation, was on the spot to keep this momentary energy alive to secure to his interests she who now opposes hers, to back all my friend's exertions,—to warm this lump of inert matter and breathe into it a permanent fire with 233,000 men at his back—at this critical decisive moment what might not this Colossus effect, and what honor to himself, and what permanent, extensive, substantial benefit to his country might not Frederick achieve: but I am talking to the Deaf. Dearest Elizabeth, make your friends speak out, if possible, to the purport of this memorial— read well yourself, read with Frederick—state the objections—at Dresden at Berlin the idea has more than pleased: perhaps the magnitude of the object deters. It would not have deterred Lord Chatham, but alas he did bestride this narrow world like a stage Colossus, and these petty men do but Peep between his legs.

*The Countess of Bristol
     To Frederick Foster.*

Wimbledon, Oct. 19, 1797.

My dear Frederick,—I imagine this will find you at Oxford; and though I am not a *very good* correspondent when you are in the *midst* of your friends, I hasten to you in your Solitude that you may see that you and your Interests are ever present to my mind. I beg, therefore, that you will tell me how you like your new situation, as soon as you can form any judgement of it, and whether you have any acquaintance there. I wish I could have given you an introduction to anybody likely to prove a Companion and friend to you, for that is what you want, and, indeed what is necessary to everybody for their comfort and happiness. You will remember *one Person* whom I cautioned you not to receive upon a footing of Intimacy, or *easily to believe* what He may tell you either of himself or other People. At the same time I hope you will keep upon *civil terms* with him, for I dare say he will be full of profession; but you must learn early to keep certain Characters at a distance, whilst I hope you will take Polonius's advice and *grapple* those friends thou *hast* to *thy Soul* with *hooks of Steel*. Tell me how you like your rooms, and your reception. I shall really feel very anxious till you have got over the first fortnight, and then I hope you will begin to distinguish some of your Companions, and to enjoy some Society.

I rejoice with you, my dear Frederick, on our late glorious Victory over the Dutch[140] Fleet, which has been very compleat, and conducted with as much skill and gallantry as possible. The English have, now defeated the three Fleets of the Allies separately, and, I believe, indisposed them very much to engage further with us: this is supposed to be the most material defeat of the three, and it will, I hope, be the preservation of your Country.

I conclude you passed your time very pleasantly a Chatsworth, and that you was struck with the Place, as it was probably the finest you had ever seen. I don't know whether you love Country Sports, but I suppose you had them in perfection. Lady Hervey, Lady Erne, and their Daughters are still at Tunbridge. Your Uncle is, I believe, at Weymouth, but he has gone by the Coast, and stopped at different places for bathing. I am afraid he will return to Town with great regret for the meeting of Parliament. Lord and Lady Hawkesbury[141] mean to be there about the 28, and are to leave Dunleer on Monday. Adieu! dear Frederick: as I have been very ill, writing fatigues me, so I will only add that I am ever your affectionate G. Mother.

I am so glad that your mother appears to be well, and Augustus quite happy with his Colours. I hear he has at last the approbation of his guardians.

*The Earl of Bristol, Bishop of Derry
To Lady Elizabeth Foster.*

1797.

Sans Souci and Sans Souci for ever, my dearest Elizabeth! At last, on the 30th of October—Sunday, noon—here I am truely worthy of this Philosophic Mansion, without care, and almost without thought, so consummately am I Germanized.

Nothing, no, nothing, not even the plains of Thetford or of Brandon can equal the aridness of this situation, nor even the Terrace of Weybridge surpass the beauty and luxuriancy of the prospect. Hesperian gardens surround the house: grapes worthy our best hothouses, pine apples as plenty as crabs in Devonshire or apples in Herefordshire; we can eat 1200 in a year, and every week at Pyrmont we received a dozen or more. Then for game, the Basse-cour at Chatsworth does not supply more fowl, ducks, geese, and capon than we have—partridges, grouse, woodcock, &c; but, alas! to-morrow we enter the eve of November, and I have those accumulated Purgatories of the Alps to pass before I can enter that earthly paradise, Naples. So to-morrow we decamp, bag and baggage, and no bad baggage is mine: geese, turkies, ducks, shoulders and legs of mutton alternately, preceded by two graduate cooks, masters of arts, who arrive just one hour before us—quanto basta, to find our dinner as ready as our appetites. Lo, here is our diary: At seven help Hyperion to his horse, and then mount our own; trot away 15 or 18 miles sans y penser; find excellent coffee, and better cream, and two eggs ready for a rapacious stomach, with all its "suc gastric" afloat, ready to consume whatever it receives.... After two hours' rest, but not of our tongues, for we babble like parrots or starlings, though our converse be not quite sterling; on horseback anew, and even so we dispatch 15 or 18 miles more through this ocean of sand, with now and then a village to make the remaining solitude more sensible; at close of day we close our labors, and then here is our recompense:

Soupe.
Bouilli of duck or goose.
Mutton shoulder or leg.

and a large bowl of punch, in which we bury all fatigue, and at length all thought, and then, as the clock strikes eight, enter the warming pan, et tout est dit, and all night sleep in Elysium without one single ghost in our dreams. And so, sweet Elizabeth, not to put you to sleep, I close my narrative: to-morrow for Berlin, next day for Werlitz, next Dessau, Leipzig, and Dresden, &c., &c. Yours affectionately, du fond de mon profond cœur. B.

> *The Earl of Bristol, Bishop of Derry*
> *To Lady Elizabeth Foster.*
>
> *March* 20, 1798.

Dearest Elizabeth,—Now or never perhaps may you most essentially serve me. All my effects at Rome are under sequestration to the amount of £20,000 at the very least, Could Mr. Pitt be induced to send a Minister to congratulate the Roman people on their emancipation, and appoint me to the Embassy, he would do himself and me a most essential service: me, because I should save all that immense, valuable, and beautiful property of large mosaick pavement, sumptuous chimney pieces for my new house, and pictures, statues, busts, and marbles without end, first-rate Titians and Raphaels, dear Guidos,[142] and three old Carraccis[143]—gran Dio! che tesoro; and himself, because such an embassy would wrench the Republick off the hands of their tyrant's dispoiler and merciless taskmaster, restore us the ports of Ancona and Civita Vecchia for our manufactures and codfish, and lay the foundation of a treaty of commerce, the most beneficial perhaps of any in Europe.

Now, if either your friend, Lord Spencer, or, above all, your greater friend, the Duke of Devonshire, or the Duchess, would effectually join in this lottery, you see, dearest Elizabeth, I should literally get the £20,000 prize.

Dear girl, do what you can for me. As to the Duke of Richmond, I do not suppose he has now any interest, else he could refuse you nothing.

I am on thorns till I hear from you. A ransom was offered by General Berthier,[144] but that is now suspended.

> *Lady Elizabeth Foster*
> *To Augustus Foster.*[145]
>
> *December* 4, 1798.

You are eighteen this day, my own dear Augustus—many many happy years may you see, and may those encreasing years ripen every virtue in your breast and bring them to their full maturity. Let not this anniversary of your birth, my dearest boy, pass without forming new resolutions for the year to come. Examine your own character; see what you think you find there to alter or amend. You are young enough to counteract any wrong tendency, yet old enough to be soon in danger from the influence of habits and custom; indulge in a fault to-day it will be harder to resist it to-morrow; the fault which you acknowledged to me, that of too easily giving way, would insensibly make you act not only according to the errors of your own judgment but those of others; be on your guard against this, dearest Augustus, yet the contrary extreme, an unyielding disposition, is still less amiable. Be firm, therefore, only when the pure dictates of your heart tell you that you are wrong, and if ever wrong, fear not to acknowledge it; above all, fear it not to me; some means of reparation a friend may generally point out, but where can you find a friend so true and so affectionate as your mother. All the great fundamental qualities of your character I trust are right. I have never known you fail in them; strict inviolable truth, a religious observance of one's promise, a sacred observance of another's secret, and prudence for one's own; as your situation and connections in life enlarge duties increase also, and amongst the foremost I hope you will ever feel the purest [torn out] women, and never risk their happiness to gratify your vanity or even passions. I was pleased to hear W. Lamb[146] say with earnestness that if he felt a growing passion for his friend's wife he would fly to the further end of the earth to resist the danger. Dear, dear Augustus, I fear I have bored you, but my heart is anxiously watchful over you, and this day encreased the feeling. May Heaven ever guide, bless, and direct you.

LINES ON THE BATTLE OF ABOUKIR
By GEORGIANA, DUCHESS OF DEVONSHIRE (1799)

"Hush! forbear to tell the Story
    Full of Horror, Full of Fear.
Talk not to a wretch of Glory,
    Or of Hated Aboukir.

Whilst I shrink from every morrow,
    Whilst kind death alone I claim,
Conquest cannot cure my sorrow,
    Nor Despair be soothed by Fame.

I am wretched, past retrieving;
    He is lost and I'm undone;

All my life will pass in grieving
        For the battle we have won.

Cease those cruel exultations,
        Cease this mockery and boast;
What's to me the fate of nations,
        When to me my Love is lost."

Whilst poor Laura's frenzied ditty
        Mingled with the sounds of glee,
Many a heart, subdued to Pity,
        Altered said, I pity thee.

Gallant was thy Lover's story,
        Bravely did he Life resign.
Cheer thee, maid, he died for glory,
        But his latest sigh was thine.

Lady Elizabeth Foster
        To Augustus Foster.
                Devonshire House, *February* 2, 1799.

… Mr. Pitt's admirable speech, though firm, is not so strong an appeal to
the good sense of the Irish, and so far from any violence that no violent
measures need be apprehended; and it makes me regret the more that a
question of such importance to the welfare of a whole country should have
been, by the efforts of party, refused a fair hearing. I think your reasoning
upon it very just. I do not find that Lord Hawkesbury acknowledges Lord
Castlereagh[147] to be in any scrape, so I hope the fears I heard expressed
were exaggerated; the violence in the House was very great....

Augustus Foster
        To Lady Elizabeth Foster.
                Weimar, *March* 19, 1799.

… I introduced myself to Kotzebue[148] at our ball, for he was invited with
his wife there. I talked a good deal to him since about his plays; he says
he likes always the last written of them the best. He has entered into an
engagement with Harris of Covent Garden. Harrison had been desired by
Sheridan to treat with him, but Kotzebue told me that he had heard that

Sheridan was not remarkably strict in paying his debts, and he thought it better receiving half sure from Harris than double from Sheridan. I promised to send him Pizarro in a day or two, for he has not seen it yet. It is droll that Rolla has had very bad success in Germany.

... Kotzebue, when he heard that Miss E. Gore was going to get the portrait of him copied in order to give me for you, proposed sitting himself again for another portrait, as he was discontented with the first.

> *Lady Elizabeth Foster*
> *To Augustus Foster.*
>
> Colchester, *August* 7, 1799.

We left Ickworth yesterday a little after twelve and arrived about six; we travelled rather with heavy hearts, for there had been unpleasant letters from my father, and my dear mother was low and unwell. I cannot tell you at present what they were, but most certainly he is a cruel man.... General Hervey and Lady Erne are there, and I hope the Hawkesburys are going next week. My mother has need of all the comfort which her children can give her, and it is the most sacred duty we can fulfill.... Dear Lord Howe[149] is dead. There is a brave man lost to his country: it is at a momentous time too. The combined fleets are out 40 strong and sailing from Cadiz northwest; supposed, therefore, for Ireland. What our Channel fleet is I don't know, but Lord Keith, it is said, was not far behind; the extraordinary thing is how they can have missed them. The secret expedition is near its embarkation. A camp of 18,000 men is now on Barham downs.

Thursday, 8th.

Lord Hawkesbury, whom we met going to town the day we came here, is now returned. He brings us very particular news. It was supposed that the French meant to get into Brest harbour with the Spanish fleet, to be prepared for an attack on Ireland, but we shall soon have a fleet of full thirty sail of the line in the channel. Lord Keith[150] is trying to get up to him. Lord Chatham—is going with this expedition, some are already embarked, and the others are to go as soon as possible, but Lord H. swears that nobody knows where it is going except the directors of it; you will soon know of its disembarkation.... Sheridan's Pizarro I think you must like; 17,000 copies have been sold. Sheridan is now adapting the Virgin of the Sun for the stage. It seems again doubtful whether the Duke of York goes with this secret expedition. Lady Anne Fitzroy is to be married this day to Cullen Smith, so they are both of them consoled for their faithless former loves....

Augustus Foster
       To Lady Elizabeth Foster.

Weimar, *Nov.* 22, 1799

... I don't know if I may risk telling you as news that Buonaparte[151] has overthrown the whole of the French Constitution. His life was attempted in the Council of 500 at St. Cloud, where he and the Antients have assembled them, by the deputy Aréna,[152] who threw himself upon Buonaparte with a dagger in his hand, and, if it was not for a grenadier officer, who received the blows in his coat, would have killed him. He, Sieyès, and Roger Ducos[153] form the new triumvirate—but it is foolish telling you all this, for you must have it already in your papers. B. is an extraordinary man indeed; he will fill up many pages in history. What if he should act the part of Cromwell or Julius Caesar?[154] but I'm afraid he wants the talents. Mounier don't know what to think of it. He supposes that there may be perhaps a Constitution like that of America....

Lady Elizabeth Foster
       To Augustus Foster.

Dec. 6, 1799.

... I envy you having got acquainted with Kotzebue. I should have liked to have told him that if fame came into his calculation that he had better have received half from Sheridan than any sum from Covent Garden. Pray tell me what he says to Sheridan's Pizarro. I suppose you have frequently met at Weimar. I do wonder that Rolla should not have succeeded in Germany. Don't fail to bring his picture....

Augustus Foster
       To Lady Elizabeth Foster.

Weimar, *Dec.* 14, 1799

I wonder you have not in any of your letters mentioned anything about Bonaparte's return, and the changes in France. I should have thought you would all have been enthusiastic about him in England, Lady Anne Hatton particularly, who was so dazzled with him. Notwithstanding what you say about the Expedition, [155] and the courage of the troops, I can't help thinking that from what we hear on this side, the Expedition was but badly conducted, and that they might have made a better and more creditable retreat. You ask me Mounier's opinion about the late

Revolution. He liked it at first, because it was at least a change, and that Sieyès and Bonaparte seemed more moderate and cleverer men than the others; but, since the violent transportation of so many Jacobins, without form or process, into Guiana, he thinks there's as little liberty as ever.... I sent Pizarro the other day to Kotzebue, for he had not yet read it. It was an odd idea of Sheridan's, but I am told that he got Pizarro translated into German, and sent it as a present to Kotzebue.

There are three new tragedies coming out here this winter: Mary Queen of Scots by Kotzebue, Gustavus Vasa by Schiller,[156] and a translation of Mahomet by Goethe.[157] ...

> *Lady Elizabeth Foster*
> > *To Augustus Foster.*
>
> > > > *Dec. 27, 1799.*

I Suppose, dearest Augustus, that you are now at Minden. I do not wonder that you went, for the review of such an army must be a fine sight. The eagerness for news increases in proportion to the importance of the crisis, and, particularly, everybody here is anxious for news of the fleets. Lord St. Vincent[158] has with him probably at this moment 50 sail of the line. How mean and pitiful of the French the sending the unfortunate Pope[159] to an hospital in France at 80, not to allow him to end his days in a convent in his own country; but the French do not know the greatness of treating humanely a fallen foe. Mr. Henry Foster and his adopted daughter went with me to the opera. Pizarro the 21st night has been as full nearly as the first. Pray send me any anecdotes you can pick up about Kotzebue. There is no other subject scarcely of conversation, by which you will understand that there are various opinions on the subject. The violent Ministerialists are angry that Sheridan should have such applause; the violent oppositionists are as angry at the loyalty of the Play; and the rigid and censorious are suspicious of such pure morality and mild religion from the pen of a person esteemed profligate. To bring up the rear, authors are jealous of his success, and cry out it is Kotzebue and not Sheridan's merit: so Sheridan says—I am but a translator: but then, such a translation! As soon as it comes out I will send it to you. William Lamb foolishly distrusts it—foolishly, because it is attributed to pique at the failure of the Epilogue; the poetry of this was pretty, but it wanted strength. I dined yesterday at Richmond House with the Melbournes[160] and there it had a grand discussion.

... A very odd story has just come out. Lady Holland[161] yesterday restored to Sir G. Webster a child whom she had always told him was dead: it is a little girl, whom she lay in of in Italy, and when she was coming home, conscious that she was to be parted from Sir Godfrey, and being doatingly fond of this child, she contrived to have it pass for dead, and had it brought to England under a feigned name, and has constantly seen it; but at last, convinced she was acting in a most unjustifiable manner both to Sir Godfrey and the child, she owned the whole thing, and the child, now six years old, is restored to its father, who received it with transport; but did you ever hear of so odd a thing? ...

21st.

You will be surprized to hear that I, who never go to balls or assemblies, went to the masquerade. Lady Bessborough[162] said she would not unless I did, and Lady Anne would not go with her. We let everybody go, and then disguised ourselves very well indeed, and went half an hour after them. I was not found out the whole night. When Lady B. was discovered, they took me for Lady Anne, and it was good fun to hear Lord Morpeth[163] say low to Lady Bessborough, "She can't disguise herself; her way of fanning herself betrays her". I assure you I did not know I was so good a mimick, and Cullen Smith said, "There is Lady Anne taking off Lady Elizabeth". We attacked the Duchess, [164] and she did not know us for a long time. The masquerade was a good one, but the house was not quite lighted enough....

>   *Augustus Foster*
>   *To Lady Elizabeth Foster.*
>   [Fragment of a letter.]

... He[165] was dressed in a blue coat faced with white, two gold epaulets, white waistcoat, &c., and English riding boots, no ornament in his hat; he is a very dirty [illegible] and his hair looks as if it never was combed. When the officers had withdrawn, Buonaparte retired to put on his Consular dress, scarlet with rich gold embroidery, and soon after we were all of us, with the different Ambassadors, ushered into the Salle des Ambassadeurs, where we found Buonaparte and his two inferior Consuls:[166] I was presented one of the first after Lord Cowper, but it was done in such a hurried manner by Mr. Jackson, who generally answered the questions made by Buonaparte himself, that we had none of us, except Mr. Blayden, an author, the honor of a conversation. To him he spoke a good deal about Sir Joseph Banks,[167] who, he said, was much esteemed in this country. I ought to give you a description of his person, but I don't know anybody he resembles unless it is to my uncle a little, I think. He is under the middle size, has light gray eyes, brown hair and light-coloured eyebrows, sallow complexion and nearly a straight nose. I think he would be good-looking if he had complexion. He has, in my opinion, the air of a gentleman, and certainly the manners of one. When he came near the American minister, who is deaf and don't speak French, he asked him how he did in French. The American, straining every sinew in his ear in vain, turned for explanation to his interpreter, who shouted out amazing loud, "The First Consul, Sir, asks you how you are". The gravity of the man's manner in delivering this made everybody laugh. The Prince of Orange was there, and seemed considerably chagrined. The Consul spoke more with him than anybody else. None of the English dined with him but such as had been already presented the last time. Yesterday the Bishops were restored, or at least the treaty with the Pope to that effect published.

> *Countess of Erne*
> *To Frederick Foster.*
>
> Ickworth Park, *Oct.* 20th, 1800.

I send you a line, my dear Frederick, to acquaint you with the grievous loss we have all sustained in the death of the best beloved Mother. It happened suddenly early yesterday morning from a spasm in her stomack. What my grief and suffering is, no words can say, as no mother could be a greater loss to a daughter than she is to me. I am sure you will share in it, my dear lad, and lament her who was every way so deserving of affection and veneration from every part of her family.—Yours sincerely and affectionately,

MARY C. ERNE.

> *Lady Elizabeth Foster*
> *To Frederick Th. Foster.*
>
> Devonshire House, Saturday, 1801.

I wrote to you yesterday, dearest Frederick, in the greatest hurry and vexation. Your uncle had been with me a great while, and though I admire, as I always have done, his motives, yet I regret to the greatest degree his decision. However, it is done now, and I shall close my lips and comfort myself with the conviction that in any and every situation he will do himself credit. The danger has been owing to Pitt's high sense of honor. He had pledged himself, I hear, to the Catholic emancipation. He could not carry his point in the Cabinet; the King had been firm, and Pitt sent in his resignation. His first idea and wish was to go out alone in order to preserve to the country the measures and system he thought essential to it, but a large proportion of the Cabinet Ministers resigned with him, and several of his friends; he has, however, urged many to remain, and this occasions much conversation, and has created a kind of third party, as Lord Hawkesbury, Addington,[168] &c., say they are Pitt's real friends, and the others are Canning's party. This is hard on those who, as Canning[169] says, sacrifice their interest to their principles. Canning says Addington ought to fall at the King's knees and ask pardon for his annoyance. It is, indeed, most extraordinary. You have no idea of the state of party, and all the variety of conjectures formed. I think Pitt has acted nobly, but almost too much so. He is advising and helping his successor, and opens the budget himself, so that he only goes out Thursday. Lord St. Vincent is first Lord of the Admiralty, Lord Hawkesbury, Secretary of State for the Foreign Department....

> *Lady Elizabeth Foster*
> *To Augustus Foster.*
>
> *Feb.* 19, 1801.

My dear Child, ... I think it a shame that Addington has accepted the situation that William Pitt held, because his merits are confined to those which were necessary and sufficient as a Speaker, and yet which are very inadequate to being Prime Minister; a mild, well-tempered, candid, upright man forms a good Speaker, but where are the talents, the abilities, the wonderful resources with the genius of Mr. Pitt to be found? Who is there can say that they look up with confidence to Mr. Addington, or indeed to any one of the new administration, except Lord St. Vincent and the law department; besides was not Addington Pitt's creature? and though Pitt, with a romantick disinterestedness, has urged all these people to stay in, does not one's heart prefer those who have gone out? Mr. Elliott, Lord Heathfield's son, alas, is desired by his father to stay in. I don't think that all who have remained in have done so from interested motives, but yet I think that had not their hearts leaned that way they would have felt at once that if Pitt resigned because he could not carry this measure which he thought so essential, that they who would certainly have supported him in it should have gone out too, and then perhaps the King would have yielded. The bishops and archbishops got hold of him, and persuaded him that Catholic emancipation would endanger the Protestant religion. Pitt felt himself pledged to Ireland, and nobly went out upon it. It is supposed that, sanguine as he is, he did not fully take the king's opinions till it was too late. Some people think the new administration will try for peace; they expect some good news from the Mediterranean and of the French squadron. I have given you a full dose now....

> *Frederick Foster*
> *To Augustus Foster.*
> St. Petersburgh, *January* 10, 1802.

My dear Augustus, ... The weather has been at times extremely cold, 20 and 23 degrees, and several people have been frozen, and it is not an uncommon thing to have one's cheek or ear or tip of the nose frozen; the remedy is to rub it instantly with snow, for, if neglected, it may mortify... The other day I went to see the Palace of St. Michael, which the Emperor Paul[170] built. It is an immense pile, something like the Queen's House in London, but twice as large. The inside is very fine, several of the rooms inlaid with Porphyry, Marble, Lapis Lazuli, and Malakite. It was in this Palace that he was murdered, and by the greatest chance in the World, for his favorite had received a letter with an account of the whole Conspiracy, and the names of all the Conspirators, which he neglected to open; and even when they did come, Paul had concealed himself behind a screen, and the Conspirators were going away in despair when one of them perceived his legs; nay, further, though discovered, yet so accustomed had they been to fear him that he had completely awed them, and was going away, when a Georgian chief flung a club at his head and knocked him down, upon which the others ran in and completed their work. An Hanoverian, of the name Benixin,[171] was the man who conducted the whole, and most probably if he had not been in the room Paul would have escaped. The present Emperor was immediately proclaimed.

> *John Leslie Foster, afterwards Baron F.*
> *To his sister Harriet, afterwards Countess de Salis.*
> Paris, *April* 6, 1802.

My dear Harriet, ... I hope the last long letter I wrote to you found you perfectly recovered, and there is at least one letter from you on its road to me. I send you an account of pomps and vanities, and what you will think my great good fortune. I was yesterday presented to Buonaparte, but, before I give an account of your Protegé, you shall endure a chronological history of the means that brought me there. The 15th of every month the first Consul receives in the Court of the Tuilleries the Consular guard, that is a selection of 5000 or 6000 men from all the armies of France accoutred at an expense and with a magnificence that I suppose was never before lavished on an equal number of soldiers. After that he holds a Levée of the French Generals, the Foreign Ambassadors, and such strangers as they present to him. The Etiquette of a Court and Court dress are strictly observed, and every one agrees that the splendour of the Court of the Tuilleries is much greater than ever was the old Court of France. Having an introduction to our Minister, I was, of course, among the Anglais to be presented. At a previous ceremony we were all introduced to Talleyrand-Perigord, Minister for Foreign Affairs, the day before. I shall not delay you with an account of the Renegade Bishop of Autun. He is not worth it; it is enough to say of him that he was pompous, awkward, and uncivil. The scarlet and silver in which he was dressed only made him appear to greater disadvantage. His person is as crooked as his principles, and his face, unhappily for his beauty, a faithful Picture of his Heart. The next Day, Monday the 5th, Augustus and I went to the Tuilleries at eleven o'clock, and were, luckily for us, by mistake admitted into the Salle des Generaux instead of the Salle des Ambassadeurs, which gave us an additional two hours' contemplation of Buonaparte. At twelve we passed through the Room to the Parade. It lasted but an Hour. Buonaparte, mounted on a noble white Horse, and surrounded by his Aides de Camp and Generals, formed the first Part of it. At one o'clock he returned to the Salle des Generaux. He spoke to almost every one in it, and with a Grace for an account of which you must wait a little longer. I followed him everywhere in the Crowd, and hardly lost an expression of his countenance. At two he retired to change his dress previous to receiving the strangers, who were supposed to be all the time in the Salle des Ambassadeurs. I went down to them to fall into the Ranks, found about 20 Anglais, among them Lord Blayney, Lord Cowper, Lord Arch. Hamilton, Mr. Cust, a Cambridge friend, Luttrell, &c. The Ambassadors were all there. Among them were three celebrated characters; D'Armfeldt the Swede, Markoff the Russian, and Lucchesini the Prussian. The Prince of Orange was also there. The most brilliant of the company was Demidoff, a Russian nobleman. He had on his breast a single Diamond valued at £30,000. In half an hour we were shown upstairs, found a large Circle, and were taken by the first Consul in the order that we stood. The Ambassador of each Nation presented his own countrymen; the first Consul said something to almost every one, and not much to any one. Now for his Person, what is he like? I will first tell you what he is unlike. In the first place he is unlike every other Person in the World, and in the second place he is perfectly unlike every Painting, Print, and Bust that has been taken of him. I cannot say why so many artists have so entirely failed, but if we may judge from the past, Posterity will have no idea of the countenance of Buonaparte; if Painting has failed, no words can succeed. However, I am bound to tell you what I think of him. He is about 5 feet 7 inches high, delicately and gracefully made; his hair a dark brown crop, thin and lank; his complexion smooth, pale, and sallow; his eyes grey, but very animated; his Eye Brows light brown, thin and projecting. All his Features, particularly his Mouth and Nose, fine, sharp defined and expressive beyond description; expressive of what? Not of anything percé as the Prints expressed him, still less of anything méchant; nor has he anything of that Eye whose bend doth awe the World. The true expression of his countenance is a pleasing melancholy, which, whenever he speaks, relaxes into the most agreeable and gracious smile you can conceive. To this you must add the appearance of deep and intense thought, but above all the predominating expression a look of calm and tranquil Resolution and Intrepidity which nothing human could discompose. His address is the finest I have ever seen, and said by those who have travelled to exceed not only every Prince and Potentate now being, but even all those whose memory has come down to us. He has more unaffected dignity than I could conceive in man. His address is the gentlest and most prepossessing you can conceive, which is seconded by the greatest fund of levée conversation that I suppose any Person ever possessed. He speaks deliberately, but very fluently, with particular emphasis, and in a rather low tone of voice. While he speaks his features are still more expressive than his words....

> *Augustus Foster*
> *To Lady Elizabeth Foster.*
>
> Paris, *April* 13, 1802.

I thank you a thousand times for your kind letter, and many, many thanks for letting her[172] send a few lines enclosed in it. If you knew how happy it made me when I saw her handwriting; but, however, as you think there may be an impropriety in their being frequent, I yield, only I hope it would not appear wrong my writing a little message now and then just to say that I am *alive*. I long very much to hear about her mother's answer, which will decide in a great measure whether I am to be happy or not.... Lord Cowper I dined with to-day. He is not very well, and talks of not going to Italy till next year. He has quite had his *dose* of Paris, and now says that he shall probably go back to London in May. How very little one's happiness depends on the quantity of gold or silver dross one has in one's pocket:

he, with all his riches, rank, and titles, seems to ennuy in every place he happens to be in. At London he wished to go to Paris and Italy, and at Paris he wants to go back again to London. I am sure any situation is better than that of a discontented rich man, because with all the idea that he ought to be happy he never is so.... I have not seen Bonaparte since the presentation, but there is to be a grand ceremony next Sunday that I shall move Heaven and Earth to get at—the celebration of the Peace, and of the re-establishment of Religion, together, in the Cathedral of Notre Dame. The Consuls are to attend, the Legates, Cardinals, &c., and the Archbishop of Aix is to preach the sermon.... The people here seem to think of nothing but how they may amuse themselves most. I wonder if any Englishman ever yet preferred France or any other country for living in to England? As for me, I only feel the superiority of England everywhere I go, and if I had a large fortune I think I should never stir out of it. Madame de Stael[173] said t'other day that there were only two countries free in the World, l'Angleterre et l'Amerique. Menou is expected daily at this Hotel with his Egyptian spouse.... I dined at Madame de Stael's yesterday. I was the only Englishman. We had a bad dinner at a little, narrow table, many of the men in boots. I don't admire Madame de Stael much; she may have a vast deal of esprit, but shews a vast deal too much of it, I think; or, in other words, is a great *bavard*, and in my humble opinion is a very disgusting woman.... I have taken great pains to find out whether the people here, in passing the Place de la Concorde, where Louis was guillotined, took off their hats, and I can assure you that I never saw any one do so, and have, on inquiry, never heard that any one did. It is surprizing why people will circulate such lies in London. It would, at any rate, be a very equivocal proof of their loyalty, as the Jacobin would equally have reason to doff his hat to the place which gave him liberty.... Remember me to all my friends at Devonshire House, and tell Corise that I have read her little note over at least 20 times.

> *Augustus Foster*
> > *To Lady Elizabeth Foster.*
> *April,? 1802?*
> > > > *[A Fragment.]*

Paris must be much changed since you have been here, for several buildings have been pulled down, particularly about the Tuileries, and in many parts new streets and fine hotels have been erected. Shocking marks of devastation among the chateaux and churches all along the road from Calais. At St. Denis the Cathedral has been pillaged and every statue or ornamental monument demolished; the sepulchres torn open, and the bodies of the Kings of France taken and burnt with lime and buried in the churchyard. I saw the ruins of Chantilly, where I stopped one night. That magnificent building, which cost near 4 millions with the gardens, sold to a carpenter and ironmonger for 130,000 livres! They employed 2000 men to destroy it in order that they might sell the materials before they were deprived of them by a new revolution. The gardens were ruined by the inhabitants of a village opposite the chateau, and who lived by the Prince's bounty. It is astonishing how the French bear their misfortunes; some of them live in miserable little holes, perhaps near their former magnificent hotels, and yet they are as lively and gay as ever, and even laugh at their ...

Monday, *April 5*, 1802.

I have delayed sending this in order that I might acquaint you of my presentation, which took place to-day. Yesterday there were about sixteen English in all presented to Talleyrand[174] Perigord: he is a shocking ugly fellow, with both his feet turned inwards. This morning I repaired in full dress at half past 11 to the Tuileries with J. Leslie Foster.[175] The troops were fast assembling; we, contrary to custom for foreigners, but much to our own advantage, and indeed from ignorance, went up the grand staircase into the Salle des Officiers Generaux instead of going below into a little room, where we should have seen nothing. There were assembled all the great generals and whole Etat major. Moreau was not there, but I saw Massena,[176] and many others of note whose names I could not find out. Their uniforms surpassed my ideas far—all in blue, richly embroidered with gold. I did not see the parade very well, but, however, the passing of the regiments before the 1st Consul I saw pretty well from the windows. Previous to his mounting he passed through the Salle, where we were, with a quick step, and a little after we saw him on his beautiful dun horse riding among the ranks attended by eight or ten officers and one Mameluc richly dressed; it rained hard, unfortunately, but, however, it was a magnificent sight. As for me, it appeared to me like a dream to find myself in the midst of the conquerors of Italy and Germany, with Buonaparte at their head. The famous regiment which stood the brunt at the battle of Marengo was among them. There were about 4000 men, Cavalry and Infantry, all very simply but very well dressed. This lasted for an hour, when Buonaparte returned to receive petitions and talk to the generals, and I am sure no King or Emperor ever went through a levée better: he seemed to speak to every one, and not a repetition of the same fulsome stuff to each, but something which appeared adapted to each person, and evidently sent them away pleased with him and themselves. He is like the picture that was in Piccadilly, but that gives him a severer countenance than he has, for I think his face, which don't give me the idea of heroic courage so much as of cool intrepidity and collectiveness, is very expressive of good nature. He has a very unaffected dignity in my opinion, and appears perfectly at his ease, and never at a loss for anything to say. He had several petitions given him, which he read all on the spot. I shall write to you to-morrow about my presentation. At the time of his receiving the petitions he put me in mind of Julius Caesar the day he was assassinated. I am quite enthusiastic about him.

> *Augustus Foster*
> > *To Lady Elizabeth Foster.*
> > > > > Paris, *April* 18, 1802.

Vive l'effronterie; sans elle je n'aurais rien vu de la fête. On m'a repoussé de porte en porte me disant que men billet d'entrée ne valoit rien à chaque endroit au quel je me presentois, et enfin j'ai mis l'important et je leur criois, Messieurs je ne puis pas passer si vous ne me faites pas de place, je suis de l'Ambassade Angloise, laissez moi passer s'il vous plait. Alors me voyant aussi dans un riche uniforme les soldats se sent empressés de me faire de la place. John Leslie que j'avois ammené avec moi me suivois en me tenant, et nous sommes arrivés heureusement à l'endroit où se placaient les Ambassadeurs dans le fond de Notre Dame vis à vis de la Chaire. Now, in plain English, I can only write a few lines to tell you that it was a very magnificent and unique sight; but to me it appeared that the idea of Religion was not in the least connected with it. There was a great crowd in the body and galleries of the Church—on both sides of the altar were the Canopies; one on the right, crimson and gold for the legate Caprera; on the left gold and crimson canopy supported by five pillars, and underneath three chairs, the middle for the First Consul, the other two for the secondary Consuls. It is now midnight and a half. P. goes at three. Therefore I shall send you a longer account to-morrow. The Archbishop of Aix, now of Tours, preached an excellent sermon, in the opinion of several not enough thankful to the Government, but attributing all to the powerful effect of Religion and the natural consequence of things. Bonaparte and the other two walked under a crimson canopy supported by four priests—the Archbishop of Paris, Dubelloy, holding the Cross before him—all yielded hommage.

Augustus Foster
  To Lady Elizabeth Foster.

Paris, *April* 19, 1802.

… Yesterday, as I wrote you word, was the great ceremony of celebrating the peace and the establishment of Religion. Mounier, Camille Jourdan,[177] and most of that set consider it as a deathblow to the hopes of Louis 18,[178] who is now called le Pretendant, as he went till now hand in hand with religion, and as religion was the principal link which connected his interests with those of the Honnetes Gens of France, because Atheism was encouraged and Piety laughed at. Now that the Government proclaims Liberty of Conscience, that the bishops have taken the oath of preserving the Constitution and religion, and that they see that they may pray without the aid of Louis, it will weaken his interest very much in the country. The ceremony was very magnificent and well ordered, but it struck me as resembling anything rather than a religious ceremony, and the strange medley of military, armed cap a pied, and of priests in petticoats was very ridiculous. Buonaparte ordered beforehand that no Minister or Ambassador should go to Notre Dame without four horses to his carriage—he himself had eight—and besides, six saddle horses, led each by a Mameluc before the carriage, there were only the other two Consuls with him. The people, who would cry Vive to a Dog if a Dog were an amusement to them, shouted Vive Buonaparte! Vive la Republique! When he got to the door of Notre Dame four priests met him, supporting a sort of Canopy under which he went, and behind him Cambaceres and Le Brun, and thus he marched, preceded by Dubelloy, Archbishop of Paris, who held the Cross, through the aisle to the throne, drums beating, arms presented, and organs playing; it was altogether very fine. The Bishops all took the oaths before him, and bowed to him and the Cross; he himself took the oath and kissed the book to preserve the religion. The Archbishop of Aix read the sermon extempore; it was very good, but the noise so great scarce half of it could be heard. Many reckoned it too little complimentary to Buonaparte; he seemed to consider it as a matter of right and necessity the return of religion into the country. I spoke to him after it was over. Poor old man, he thought nobody heard him. I pleased him by telling him that I heard tolerably well. I saw Massena and M'Donald.[179] The last resembles Lord Morpeth, I think; he is fair faced and gentlemanlike-looking. Massena is blackfaced and seems a scoundrel. Buonaparte I still admire. His face was perfectly grave during the whole ceremony. After it was over he pleased everybody by his condescension in speaking to them. What was rather mockery, I think—I did not see it myself—but Camille Jourdan told me that he crossed himself several times as well as Cambaceres. That was *trop fort* for one once a professed Turc. Madame Buonaparte dresses very lightly; seems to have been pretty; she, with Madame Joseph,[180] I think her daughter, and Madame Murat,[181] her sister-in-law, and Louis Buonaparte[182] with several ladies, was placed in a gallery a little above the altar on the left; she only came with two horses to her carriage. The Duchess of Cumberland[183] is here; the princes of Orange and Weimar.... Don't let Corise forget me, and tell her that she is never absent from my thoughts in the middle of all this bustle....

> *Augustus Foster*
> > *To Lady Elizabeth Foster.*

... What say you to the Catholic Question? In my opinion no one solid argument has been brought forward against the Emancipation. Grattan[184] was a flower of eloquence, but I fear sadly they will lose Ireland by the refusal, if so 'che sfortunato Re'. Nelson has been displaying his great name in the Western World. He has appeared and gone again like a comet without doing mischief, but I sadly fear they will get to Ireland before him.... The Americans are sending across the continent to find the source of the great river Missouri, the elder branch of the Mississippi, and their people have written from t600 miles up its banks.

> *Augustus Foster*
> > *To Lady Elizabeth Foster.*
> > > Boyukdere, *June* 10, 1803.

... I should not forget to tell you that I saw the slave market about three days ago: an officer of the Reis Effendi[185] took us in there. There were great numbers of blacks enforced to sale in the halls and whites within the rooms; there was no one very handsome, they all, I thought, looked excessively rnelancholy. I got our Dragoman to question a white lady, not ugly, that was sitting cross-legged in one of the rooms. She told us that she was a Circassian. He said that we came with a commission to see and buy slaves, and she begged that we might take her; however, it is not permitted to a Christian to buy, he may commission his Janizary to purchase for him; it would be rather a bore, however, to depend upon his taste, and beauties are bought up before they land for the pashas and Grand Signors; it is very seldom that any very handsome are to be found in the market. Our Turk had promised that we should see one more lovely than a Sultana, or in other terms, as he expressed himself, one so fair that, as she drank water, one might see it gurgle down her pearly throat; the price of such a one may be about £1000; the common run of pretty ones is from £300 to £600, and a black may be had for £50. As we were returning we saw a man who, discontented with his slave, was refusing her upon the plea that she was sickly, desiring the merchant to feel her pulse and examine her hand; the other vociferated that he ought to stick to his bargain. The girl, by her motions, was explaining what she was fit for—sewing, working, washing, &c. She was a very pretty slender Circassian. I could have beat the man for his bad taste in giving her back; it is quite like a sale of horses, or any other cattle. The Blacks are innumerable, according to the different nations, more in features distinguished from one another than I thought such complexions would admit of. The market place has four sides, and a sort of booth or collection of coffee-houses in the middle. We examined and even entered into the halls and rooms on three sides, but on the fourth some Turks rather roughly objected to our going into the rooms as the Firman did not mention that; however, we saw all that was worth seeing. This and the printing office at Scutari are among the most curious things that I have seen. The Turks have learned from us to make Geographical Charts; the first they ever did.

Charles James Fox[186]
To Georgiana, Duchess of Devonshire.
1803. St. Anne's Hill, *August* 12.

My dear Duchess,—I have no intention to abuse you for a neglect which was in itself so unimportant, but am very sorry you have such an excuse to make as Lady Georgiana's illness. I should have had no curiosity, much less anxiety, upon the matter if it had not been that I wished to know whether the language, which I knew Sheridan would hold to him, had any effect and what. I think I can see by the newspaper accounts of the debate that Sheridan disliked Francis[187] pressing him on the subject of the Prince very much, and that if there was any difficulty he got very well out of it.

I am very sorry the Duke has so bad a fit of the gout. I do not believe the French will come: if they do, by what I see they will find us as unprepared as ever owing to the last foolish manoeuvres of the Doctor.[188]

Yours ever,
C. J. Fox.

P.S.—I hear an admirable quotation of yours upon S. and his prepared Uniform. Motley your only wear should be his motto.

The Earl of Aberdeen[189]
  To Augustus Foster.

Edinburgh, *August* 14, 1804.

Dear Augustus,—You will participate in my grief when I tell you that I arrived last night at Edinburgh, which is of all places the most horrible. There is a most plentiful crop of grass in the streets, which the painter of the panorama has omitted, much to the injury of the *Rurality* of the scene.

I am going to-morrow into Aberdeenshire. Do not imagine I shall really die, for I shall contrive to vegetate and give you accordingly some signes de Vie.

Pray remember me to Lady Elizabeth and to the Duchess when you see them next, and tell them that if any wayward friend is obstinately bent upon visiting our northern wilds to send him to me, and I will do my best to entertain him, that is to say, give him good shooting. Bid them think what a state the Belle Nature of that country must be in, when murder is the only amusement.

Were I not in possession of a calendar, but was to judge from my sore lips and red nose, I should be tempted to set out instantly for London, thinking Christmas past; reflection, however, informs me that five or six gloomy months must pass. Although I cannot in strict justice say

> Ye gods, annihilate both time and Space
> And make two *lovers* happy,

yet I am persuaded that no Lover ever preferred the request with more fervency. Having now poured forth my sorrows, I beg you will write to me, and about your own plans, when you go to *your* Exile and how. My direction is Haddo House, Aberdeenshire. I shall also expect to hear from you as soon as you have touched Philadelphia ground.

Believe me, ever most truly yours,
Aberdeen.

P.S.—If I am not lost and benighted in my own deserts, I will write shortly after my arrival, in hopes of its finding you still in England. Adieu.

The Earl of Aberdeen
    To Augustus Foster.

Cromarre,[190] *August* 20, 1804.

Dear Augustus,—I wrote you from Edinburgh a letter Which might be called the Lamentations of Jeremiah, so dismal were the contents; however, I am now rejoiced at the intelligence that you are not to Columbize, for I this evening received your letter after a mountain massacre.[191] I do not find this country so horrible as I imagined, or as you seem to think, and there is a sensible pleasure at standing to look around one and being able to see nothing but one's own.

What can you be about at Gell's?[192] I hope and trust you will come down here: throw yourself into the Mail and you will arrive at Aberdeen in three days and a half. Nothing would give me half so much pleasure as to see you. My Constantinopolitan plan is in statu quo, that is to say, nothing certain, at all events it probably is stopped until next Spring. London must be wretched at present, which makes me hope you will not be so averse to quit it, therefore (Si quis adhuc precibus locus) come. Congratulate Lady Elizabeth from me at your escape from eating entrails, like the Esquimaux, or bedaubing your face with Tallow, like the Iroquois. I should think there could not be much difficulty in despatching you *eis tēn polin*,[193] and that you will soon be restored to the beauties of the Bosphorus.

I am now midst "Mountains vast and Bogs Serbonian", but am going into the low country in a few days. In the meantime, pray write, and tell me all the news. Farewell, and believe me, with the greatest sincerity,

Aberdeen.

The Earl of Aberdeen
    To Augustus Foster.

Kinrara,[194] *Sept.* 22, 1804.

Dear Augustus,—I have for the last month been speculating as to your fate, which, when you wrote last, appeared to be as uncertain as one could well desire. I send you this epistle in order to be informed both of it and a variety of events. I am here at the Duchess of Gordon's cottage in the Highlands for two or three days: she means to reappear in London next winter if she can procure a house large enough for the magnificent fêtes which she proposes to give. From this I go to Blair (the Duke of Athol's) in order to massacre a few red deer, but shall quickly proceed to my own retreat of Vall Ombrosa, near Dunira, than which nothing can be more beautiful. With regard to any external motions, I am very uncertain if I shall again walk the olive groves of Academia,[195] or freeze midst hyperborean snows, or inhale the smoke of London—perhaps the last. Is Gell gone to Zante, as the time which he proposed for departing is arrived? Tell me what is doing in Babylon,[196]—though I suppose you will say nothing, but that is not sufficient. Your ancient flame is at last gone, and I can only hope that you have none of the veteris vestigia flammae remaining. Are the French come? for it would appear as if you expected them every day.

But perhaps you are already gone, and this missive may find you after an interview with his most Catholic Majesty at the Buen Retiros or L'Escurial. God knows, however, if you may not have crossed the Atlantic and heard the muddy notions of the Americans about Liberty, how unlike our Athens; but wherever you may be, believe me to be, with great friendship,

Aberdeen.

Should you perchance be still in London, I beg to be remembered to Lady Elizabeth and the Duchess.

The Earl of Aberdeen
   To Augustus Foster.

Haddo,[197] *Nov.* 20, 1804.

Dear Augustus,—I long very much to know how you are satisfied with the Terra Australis, and how you like your situation; if you are content I shall *feel* real pleasure. Tell me something about your Society: in what does the haut ton Americain consist? You see that I am still buried in these Northern Wilds, but am now meditating a flight to London, where I shall stay five or six months, at the end of which I should hope to be able to undertake the Grecian expedition. Gell is gone with Mercer and Baker.

I have always been of opinion that Russia will do nothing, and, though I hope not, yet fear that idea will be confirmed. I understand that the King has not been quite so well of late, but at all events the reconciliation between him and the Prince has done much good. I cannot speak with certainty as to the appointment of Lord Moira and Tierney[198] in Ireland: if Lord Moira wishes it he will get it certainly; but I do not apprehend that he is anxious about it.

I belong this winter to the Duchess's boxes at the Play, where, however, I shall but too often miss you; it is really lamentable the great distance at which you are, which so entirely precludes all my exertions to see you....

If there is anything you wish done with dispatch, accuracy, and good-will, pray write to me, and you may depend upon my doing everything to show you with what sincerity of friendship I am, and shall be, ever yours,

Aberdeen.

Lady Elizabeth Foster
   To Augustus Foster.

December 5, 1804.

We have been in town now but a few days, and we removed from Chiswick sooner than we expected, in consequence of the melancholy event that happened there. Poor John Brown, the Duke's faithful servant, fell from his horse in an apoplectic fit, and died the fourth day. It was very shocking, and he is sincerely regretted by all the servants. I have been nervous and hurried for some time past owing to an arrangement that is about to be made for the payment of the Duchess's debts. There never was anything so angelic as the Duke of Devonshire's conduct, and the many conversations I had with him on the subject, though it made me so nervous at the time, have made me happier now, and, if possible, increased my admiration and attachment to him. I feel secure now that she will avoid things of this kind for the future, and though the sum is great, yet it will end well I am convinced. I know so well your feelings about them that I have a pleasure in telling you what has passed.

As for politicks, though every day an account of Bonaparte's coronation and Russia's decision is expected, nothing hardly is seen or talked of but this young Roscius.[199] I saw him his first night as Achmet or Selim in Barbarossa; I saw him last night as Norval in Douglas. He is but thirteen, and yet I never saw anything to compare to him; his is the inspiration of genius, with the correctness of taste belonging generally to experience and study alone, feeling far beyond his years, and a knowledge of the stage equal to any performer, and far more graceful: in short, he has changed the life of London; people dine at four, and go to the Play, and think of nothing but the play. How I wish you were here! Frederick is just returned from Ickworth, but I have not seen him. I have sent to ask him to the Play. The Hawkesburys stay in town for this boy's acting all next week. Sheridan took him to Carleton House, and the Prince told me that his manner was perfect; it was simple, graceful, and unaffected. As to the applause, the Pit, which is filled with men, not content with applauding, over and over again cry out Bravo! Bravo! I don't suppose such applause could ever be exceeded....

> *Lady Elizabeth Foster*
>   *To Augustus Foster.*
>   Devonshire House, *Dec.* 18, 1804.

... I suppose before the day that the Mails are closed for America that the Spanish War will be officially declared.... Parliament meets the 15th, and the Session is expected to be stormy; some rumours, however, are still afloat of peace, general peace, and that France will make the overtures. Pitt will have to contend with a strong opposition probably, though probably also he will have enticed over some of those who never could resist the attraction of power, place, or Court favor. I should not be surprised if an Earl nearly connected with Devonshire House should
be one. He is under the influence of the love of those three things just named, and also that of a fair lady, whose yearly visits at his Country House have often directed his Politicks, and a little Scotch blood in her veins makes her sensible to the good things of this world. I beg dear Lord Aberdeen's pardon for this reflection: he has only the good, and none of the bad, of Scotch inheritances.

                                        December 19.

... All politicks have given way to admiration and interest and curiosity about young Roscius. The most unbelieving, like General Fitzpatrick,[200] have, on seeing him, confessed that he is admirable as an actor, and cease talking of him as a boy. General Fitzpatrick wrote to Charles Fox that he had been astonished and delighted. Mr. Fox came to town to see him, but the dear boy was ill and confined to his bed. Every precaution was taken to prevent any tumult from disappointment, and Wroughton read the physician's letter, in which he said the boy could not act without great risk, and Mr. Jordan acted in both play and farce. How I wish you could see him! It is the inspiration of genius with perfect nature and a grace of action unequalled, never forced in any character.

> *Lady Elizabeth Foster*
>   *To Augustus Foster.*
>   *December* 25, 1804.

I must begin by hoping that this may have been a happy Christmas to you, and many may you see. There have been so many rumours of changes here that I waited a little to know what was truth before I wrote again. Two days ago the Prince of Wales sat some time with me in my room, and told me that Addington and Pitt shook hands, and had dined at Lord Hawkesbury's. This seemed so strange that I thought it one of those rumours with which people about him amuse his idle hours, but yesterday it was declared, and the papers at least attribute the reconciliation to the King. That men who have opposed each other violently should become friends is not a matter of surprise or novelty, but to forgive cold, unpitying scorn and contempt has been hitherto unheard of, and the *Morning Chronicle* will not let it be forgot that Pitt applied the most contemptuous terms to Addington and his administration. If the Doctor comes into office he will have a majority of the Cabinet, and I should not be surprised if he in a few months turned out Pitt. The report is also that Lord Hawkesbury returns to the foreign department. All I feel to care for in this is whether it is a favorable change to you. Kind as Lord Harrowby was, I should hope relationship might do still more—at least it is a fair claim for promotion. Poor Lord Harrowby fell down stairs as I told you, but he was sufficiently recovered to be removed yesterday. The Princess Charlotte[201] of Wales is at Carleton House, and played, poor little thing, on the Pianoforte to the Prince to-day. She is pretty, I hear, and clever. The King wanted to have her given up to him. The Prince does not consent to that, but appoints as nearly as he can all the persons whom the King would have named about the little Princess.

I believe that Miss Trimmer will be sub-preceptress. The Duke of Portland has been in a very bad state of health and retires, What the King's real state is I don't know, but he went to the Play in an admiral's uniform, which he never did before. Sometimes he wears the uniform of the Oxford Blues, and the other day received Sir Charles Poole on some naval business in an old naval uniform of Lord Howe's time, These are facts which tell, yet what is to be done whilst he can talk collectedly on business? Young Roscius is still ill; that is the worst news, and very ill....

26th.

The Morpeths, Lady Bessborough, Lord Cowper, and Mr. Ward supped here. Mr. Ward toldHenry Dillon he was afraid the fame of his pamphlet would outlive the stability of his principles, and Lord St. Vincent wrote to a friend three days ago, "Addington in opposition is a very different man from what he was in power; he will be firm and steady," è *ben trovato*. Canning and Lord Granville[202] will be miserable at this; it lowers so Pitt's fine, lofty mind.

Corisande is still unmarried. Ossulston[203] is gone to Cambridge for a
week or ten days. I daresay he won't marry till March, because he then
expects a little money, but it is sad dawdling.

Augustus Foster
        To Lady Elizabeth Foster.

                                        Washington, *Dec.* 30, 1804.

... I have at last reached this soi-disant city, as you perceive, and am settled
with *Toujours Gai;*[204] but such a place; you can have no imagination of it,
it is so unlike every other sort or description of a heap of human abodes
calling itself a city. I made a visit yesterday to the only pleasant family
in the place, who live five miles off—a Mrs. Barry, an Irish woman, who
has got a pretty daughter (that I mean to carry with me as cara sposa
all' Inghilterra); the badness of the weather and the roads, and the
wretchedness of the carriages, will be the most powerful obstacles to this
intention of mine. I wrote to you from Norfolk last. At Baltimore I got into
a round of assemblies for five or six days that I stayed there, and among
the rest beheld Madame Jerome[205] Buonaparte, who has not a good figure,
but a very delicate shin, and, I think, very pretty little features. Jerome[206]
was confined. They have both been sadly tantalized about getting away.
They were shipwrecked once, and are afraid to go out in a frigate that
lies in the Chesapeake. The French Minister did not return his visit, so I
suppose that he is in high disgrace with the Emperor. This is a sad distance
to be at from all the civilized world, and whenever I think of Europe, I
always think I see an immense swell of sea between me and it. This place
looks like—what, in fact, it is—an infant colony. Every man has built his
house of wood or brick just where his fancy chose, so that there are hardly
six buildings together in the whole of this immense space. I was presented
to the President,[207] who behaved to me very civilly in general. Merry says
he has not spoken to others he introduced to him. He is dressed and looks
extremely like a very plain farmer, and wears his slippers down at his heels:
only think what must have been poor Toujours Gai's embarras when at
his first audience he went all bespeckled with the spangles of our gaudish
Court dress: the door opened suddenly too. He thrust out his hand to
me as he does to everybody, and desired me to sit down. Luckily for me I
have been in Turkey, and am quite at home in this primeval simplicity of
manners. However, they ought to establish some rule for foreign ministers
if they will copy at all the customs of civilized Courts. As to this variegated
nation—composed of British of all descriptions, of French, Dutch, Swiss,
Africans, &c., I can form not the least idea as yet: all I know is that I

have been disappointed in some things, particularly in their want of land eternally, and their thieving, which is carried to such an extent that there is no keeping even standing corn at a distance from your house here. Poor Mr. Merry is in perpetual alarm lest his disorder should return, and Mrs. Merry has had a very violent fever with which she still is confined to her bed. He really is a very good man, though [not?] the most methodical in the world. We live pretty well, but I have only got one room, and unluckily I sent my books and most of my things from Norfolk up the Potomac, so that they are not yet arrived....

*Lady Elizabeth Foster
To Augustus Foster.*

1804.

... The cultivation of the muses would most agreeably occupy your leisure moments, and lead you to a study of all that can form and refine your taste; it would encourage also the enthusiasm which I think so necessary to your happiness in every situation ... a really true enthusiastic mind will never want an object for its enthusiasm: you may be an enthusiast in friendship, an enthusiast in lore, in the forming of one's own character to the practice of every virtue and the fulfilling of every duty; and enthusiasm is, in fact, what, well directed, leads to the attainment of every virtue, and enables the possessor of it to walk out of the common track of common characters who rest satisfied with doing what is required of them, but never are equal to that most generous, most rare of all qualities l'oubli de soi même (unselfishness): it also leads to a great indulgence for others, and a great severity to one's self. In short, enthusiasm appears to me (perhaps you will say I am pleading my own cause) the vivifying heat that must bring forth the seed of all that is good in our natures, and lead to the imitation of all we see good in others. The enthusiasm which inspired you with some of those very beautiful lines on the deserted plains of Thebes would, if cherished, equally fill your mind at home with admiration of the Duke of Devonshire's admirable taste and understanding, and constant friendship of Mr. Hare, and the various excellencies of Mr. Fox's patriotism and transcendent abilities, Mr. Pitt's wonderful talents, &c., &c., and would also make you determine to distinguish yourself.... I shall perhaps write again and again on this subject, for pray remember, when you say that my enthusiasm has had a fair and wellshaped channel, that I was younger than you when I was without a guide; a wife and no husband; a mother and no children; travelling for my health, which was impaired by sorrow, and by myself alone to steer through every peril that surrounds a young woman so situated:—books, the arts, and a wish to be loved and approved; an enthusiastic friendship for these my friends; a proud determination to be my own letter of recommendation; these, with perhaps manners that pleased, realized my projects, and gained me friends wherever I have been—but adieu, I must go. Read Candide as an amusement, but Voltaire will only amuse but never improve except in tragedies—a firm and manly trust in the providence of God will give you happier hours than ever Candide's philosophy can. Heaven bless and direct you.

ON THE DEATH OF JAMES HARE.
BY GEORGIANA, DUCHESS OF DEVONSHIRE, AND LADY
ELIZABETH FOSTER.

Mark! 'twas the Knell of Death! What spirit fled
And burst those shackles man is doomed to bear?
Can it be true, and midst the senseless Dead
Must sorrowing Thousands count the Loss of Hare?

Shall not his Genius Life's short Date prolong—
Pure as the aether of its kindred Sky?
Shall Wit enchant no longer from his Tongue
Or beam in vivid Flashes from his Eye?

Oh, no, that mind for every Purpose fit
Has met, alas, the universal Doom.
Unrivalled Fancy, Judgment, Sense, and Wit
Were his, and only left him at the Tomb.

Rest, Spirit, rest, for gentle was thy Course;
Thy Rays, like temper'd Suns, no Venom knew;
For still Benevolence alloy'd the Force
Of the keen Darts thy matchless Satire threw.

Yet not alone thy Genius I deplore;
Nor o'er thy various Talents drop the Tear;
But weep to think I shall behold no more
A lov'd Companion and a Friend sincere.

[James Hare, 1749–1804, was a friend of the Two Duchesses, of Charles James Fox, and of many others of his eminent contemporaries.]

ON THE PEERAGE.
EPIGRAM BY GEORGIANA, DUCHESS OF DEVONSHIRE.

When a Peerage they give to some son of the earth,
Yet he still is the same as before;
'Tis an honour if gained as the premium of worth,
But exposes a blockhead the more.

Lady Elizabeth Foster
To Augustus Foster.

February 4, 1805.

... The ferment continues about Young Roscius, and to-morrow he acts Octavian again. It is the only character I have seen him in in which the beauties of his acting could not surmount the disadvantages of his extreme youth. He spoke, and the tones of his voice went to the heart as a man reduced to madness from unhappy love; but he looked a boy, and they had made Mrs. St. Leger, who acts in Valentine and Orson, do the part of Floranthe with him—she is six feet high.

5th.

I ought to talk of politicks to you, but all conversation begins and ends with Roscius. There never was anything like the beauty of his acting last night, yet it is a wretched play. Mr. Fitzpatrick went to the boy's room to be acquainted with him. His manners are those of a young man of the first fashion and good breeding. He is an astonishing creature, and you would admire him, I am sure. Think of his feeling, too. When he first rehearsed Hamlet, he had so worked himself up that when, in the closet scene, he says, "On him! on him! look how pale he glares!" he fainted in the arms of his friend. Mr. Hough, the prompter, caressed and soothed him, and said he should rehearse no more that night; and next day he said, "What, my dear boy, moved and affected you so last night?" "Why," he said, "I thought I did see my father's ghost." Caroline Wortley tells me that his acting Hamlet is the finest piece of acting she ever saw or can conceive.

Well, now, as to other things. Pitt is said to have written two letters to the King urging the making Prettyman Archbishop of Canterbury, which he refused doing, and Sutton is appointed. Lord Melville is said to have recommended Admiral Cochrane to go out to the West India Fleet, and this is not done. The rumour for some days was that Pitt must go out, but I do not think it. You will see a contradiction of the

statement in Cobbett's[208] paper about Canning. I have avoided asking
about it out of delicacy to the Hawkesburys, but I believe there were
friends of Canning's that would not let it rest so. I believe Wallace has
been indiscreet, else I know not how Cobbett could have had possession
of the transaction, or, at least, of what was said of it. Next Friday Mr.
Grey's[209] motion on the Spanish papers comes on. They are rejoicing it
is not Thursday, as Roscius acts Romeo! Opposition will divide strong,
I should think.... All here is as you left it. Corisande still unmarried, and
Ossulston without money to marry: how long he thinks he can go on so I
know not: it makes her, poor little thing, feel very uncomfortable. Dunc.
seems a little smitten with your friend Mrs. Payne; but her manner is quite
proper. B. North looks in despair; I believe she has cut him quite; and Lord
and Lady Villiers look happiness itself. Lady Boringdon very handsome
and happy, and he seems proud and fond of her. H. Dillon has hid
himself.

> *Augustus Foster*
> *To Lady Elizabeth Foster.*
> Washington, *February* 8, 1805.

... Though I have not as yet seen much of this country, I have seen enough to
be convinced that it will not do to stay a great while in it. This, undoubtedly,
is a miserable place, but the elect of all the States are assembled in it; and
really such a gang to have the affairs of an Empire wanting little of the size
of Russia entrusted to them makes one shudder. Imagination is dead in
this country; wit is neither to be found nor is it understood among them;
all the arts seem to shrink from it, and you hear of nothing but calculation
and speculation in money or in Politics. When I am introduced to a person
here, I am quite at a loss what to converse with him upon. Their depth of
reading generally goes no further than Tom Paine's muddy pamphlets, or
more generally their own still more muddy political newspapers. If they
go as far as books of travels and magazines it is a very great deal. I have
frequently attended their Congress. There are about five persons who look
like gentlemen; all the rest come in the filthiest dresses, and are well indeed
if they look like farmers, but most seem apothecaries and attorneys. There
is only one man who can speak well; he is the leader of the Republicans,
or, as the Federalists call them, Democrats—Randolph.[210] He is, I believe,
going to England and to France with a little nephew who is deaf and dumb,
but extremely intelligent, to take him to Lizard. I shall give him a letter for
you, for, though the strangest-looking Demagogue you ever set eyes on, he
is very gentlemanlike, and, for this country, a prodigy. He has a little of the

affectation of a self-taught and late-taught politician, but he is certainly clever, and, as a descendant of the Indian Queen Pocahontas,[211] you will be interested about him.... I do not think that this ever will become a great city. The Demon of speculation has already fixed himself here; and, instead of giving premiums for building, the land is very dear. There is no commerce whatever, and all the increase arises from the demand for houses for the members of Congress, and those whom they bring here; but I heard so bad an account of this wretched settlement, that the only thing I was disappointed in was the hope of finding great forests of fine trees, instead of which the land is mere waste in the city, and all the trees have been cut for fire. In short, if I don't fall in love very soon the dullness that stares you in the face in this letter will irrevocably get hold of me. I do nothing but read the Tempest and Midsummer Night's Dream and Virgil to try and keep alive the embers of imagination; but really there is in this demi-city demi-wilderness so lovely a damsel of parti-coloured extraction—Irish and Portuguese—that I won't quite be sure of not melting a little; if so, I shall be destined to be always falling in love with Roman Catholics. She is the most determined devotee in existence, almost starves herself on fast days, but certainly is beautiful; however son ancora intatto per sicuro.

> *Augustus Foster*
> *To Lady Elizabeth Foster.*
> Washington, *February* 15, 1805.

I saw Jerome Bonaparte last night. You seem to be interested about him in England. Those letters are undoubtedly authentic, though he tries to persuade Madame and his friends that they are forgeries. He has made several attempts to go away, and now says he will go with her in three months. He is in size rather smaller than Napoleon, and very like Lord Bristol in figure.[212] He is only like Bonaparte in the lip. The French Minister and his affect to call his wife Miss Patterson in speaking to others of her. They are both, I think, very much to be pitied; and though he has been extravagant here, yet he has in general conducted himself in company modestly and unassuming; but that and his youth cannot save him from the ill-nature of these most ill-natured renegades from all countries under the sun, the American inhabitants of towns. His daughter is wife of an Irish refugee, who came over here in a very low situation, indeed, as some say, hostler; but at present against his character there is not the least imputation: however, truth is hard to be got at here....

Lady Elizabeth Foster
  To Augustus Foster.

March 3, 1805.

... Miss Drummond is in love, they say, with Young Roscius, so that all her lovers must despair. He is truly, as Mr. Pitt says, a prodigy, and I do grieve that you are not here to see and admire him. It has made a change in London life, and the theatre is now the great topic of conversation and the favorite amusement. Even Grassini complains that he has spoiled the Opera,[213] and is the great attraction to all people. I assure you that the great politicians consult what day he acts that they may not give their dinners on those days. We saw him the other day at Lady Abercorn's. Lady Hamilton did her attitudes, and the Boy was asked to recite. He refused a great while. At last his father asked him. He said, "I must do whatever my father desires me," and came, not over-pleased, to the room where people were waiting to see him, and then he recited a speech of Hassan's.

The Earl of Aberdeen
  To Augustus Foster.

March 4, 1805.

My dear Augustus,—It is but two days since I emerged from obscurity and resumed my place amongst the constellations which adorn Babylon. That you wallow in space is most true, but that you embrace the Heavenly Goddess of Liberty I beg leave to doubt; it must be a painted representation, no more like her than a Volunteer is to a Soldier. Your Republic is certainly in her childhood, but she has nothing of infancy but its frowardness, and instead of the strength and vigour of youth she has nothing but its insolence and ignorance. The resemblance of Washington to Rome is a good burlesque. As for my Plans they are far from being decided, whether I go to Happy climes or remain here, whether I roam in Liberty amongst the Beauties of the Day or content myself with the possession of one object. The thermometer of my affections is not very far from the freezing point, and, what is worse, I fear the mercury is still sinking. I saw your former flame at Devonshire House looking very well, but no Ossulston.... It is a great consolation that your women are pretty. As for their expecting you to be enamoured at the first glance it is no objection, provided they comply equally soon; Whittington desires to be remembered. The tooth of a Mammoth would highly gratify him. If you meet with the seeds of plants which are very rare in this country send me a few for a beautiful Dame who has nothing but vulgar roses and lilies in her cheeks. Write me, and believe me your most sincere and faithful friend,

ABERDEEN.

Lady Elizabeth Foster
　　　To Augustus Foster.
DEVONSHIRE HOUSE, *March* 25, 1805.

... Dear Lord Aberdeen really seems quite anxious (about the illness of Georgiana, Duchess of Devonshire). He had been one of the few infidels about the young Roscius, but he is, I hear, won over, and acknowledges his merit. Mr. Crawford saw him for the first time, and in Hamlet, the other night. He said that he expected to be disappointed, having, heard so much and remembering Garrick so perfectly, but that he was astonished and delighted, and that in many parts he thought him not even inferior to Garrick.[214] There never certainly was so extraordinary a being, and the more one thinks of it the more extraordinary it appears. Sir Walter and Dr. Blane have just been here.[215] The Duchess is really better, but yet they think there must be more pain, but not so bad as before—at least I am willing to think not. They had a budget of news. Lord Chatham has the government of Plymouth vacant by the death of Lord Lennox; that the Russians will certainly co-operate with us and send 100,000 men into the field, and that Sir S. Craig is to command the expedition: he is first to take Minorca, and then proceed to Malta to combine where to meet the Russians and their future operations. Of all the Convoy, it is now known that the French took three ships, and allowing to the bravery of the Arrow sloop and Acheron brig....

March 28.

The publick go on being delighted with young Roscius, Parliament discussing the Militia, the papers are dwelling on the tenth report, and Buonaparte is adding more crowns to his Imperial Diadem. It is a fortnight, I believe, since I have stirred from home, so I can only give you outlines of news. A poem has just appeared of Walter Scott's,[216] which is said to be good, but till I hear a little more of it I shall not send it as it is very long.

Lady Elizabeth Foster
　　To Augustus Foster.

April 5, 1805.

The fifth representation of Hamlet has filled the house more than I have yet seen it. I never saw him act so well as to-night, and Lord Aberdeen was quite delighted with him, of course, you know that I mean Roscius.... I am afraid Lord Aberdeen is vexed about Lord Melville, I send you the paper with his letter. The tenth report is as yet too large,[217] but when the extract or abridgement comes out I will send it you. Lord Suffolk chose to move in the House to-night for the authentic letter, the one which has been published in the papers being, he said, a forgery, as it criminated Lord M. more than he was before it. Some think it clears him at least from having speculated for himself.

News is come of the French attack on Dominica. The Toulon fleet was said to have passed the straits of Gibraltar in order to join the Rochefort squadron in the West Indies, but some reports say that it is gone back. The present moment is not a bright one for Ministers. They are in need of some coup d'état to help them on. One of the rumours of the day is that Lord Wellesley has declared himself Sovereign of India;[218] then he and Holkar may fight it out.[219] Your friend Lord A.[220] braves the Duchess of Gordon,[221] and flirts with Harriet more than ever.[222] I admire his spirit, but I am sorry the papers have got hold of it, and amiable and delightful as he is, he would not be a good match for her. Lord Tankerville has not relented, and I have no guess how that will end.[223] ... Speaking of Jerome "yet he has in general conducted himself in company modestly and unassuming", it should be either *modestly and unassumingly*, or in company he is *modest and unassuming*. These are only little inaccuracies and inelegances which you require to avoid, by having the habit of writing correctly at all times, and this would prevent your having even any trouble in avoiding them, and as you seem to have acquired a love and habit of study and application, do, my dearest child, put this time to profit in every way, and the very dullness you naturally complain of will then turn to your advantage—set doggedly to, as Johnson called it, not only to translate Cicero, but to transcribe Lord Chesterfield. Transcribing forms the style as translating does the judgment and taste. If you acquire a habit of correct and elegant writing now it is done for life; your style is natural and agreeable; the construction of your phrases is all that requires attending to; whatever is simplest is best, but then the grammatical part should be pure and correct to the utmost. You must forgive these criticisms, the consequence of *materno affetto* which is watching over you most anxiously. Let me know where you are likely to go in the spring that I may follow you on the map. You will hear of the reverses in India, and the shocking fate of Colonel Monson's detachment. Lord Cornwallis is going to give peace,[224] as I hope, to that desolated country; would the olive branch could be extended over Europe.

> *The Earl of Aberdeen*
> > *To Augustus Foster.*
> > > WATIER'S CLUB, *April* 6, 1805.

My dear Augustus,—I heard of you lately from Lady Elizabeth, and am sorry that you continue to dislike the Metropolitan residence of Washington, although in one respect it should give me pleasure, as it will lessen the impediments to your return. There is nothing of great consequence. I am not sanguine about Russia, but combined expeditions are talked of, and we have already despatched some thousand men. The most atrocious virulence which ever disgraced a party has been exerted against Lord Melville, but he will ultimately triumph—Magna est Veritas et praevalebit. The Duchess, you will have heard, has been very ill, but is now much recovered. Your old flame is still in statu quo,[225] although Lord Tankerville, I understand, now consents. I think Grantham is very far gone with Miss Pole, who is certainly the prettiest girl in London. Au reste there have been produced but few beauties this spring. Lady Charlotte Gower will be pretty; there are two Lady Fitzgeralds greatly celebrated, but without much reason....

> > > > ABERDEEN.

> *Lady Elizabeth Foster*
> > *To Augustus Foster.*
> > > DEVONSHIRE HOUSE, *April* 10, 1805.

... I finished the last letter on Monday the 8th. That eventful day![226] we received in the course of the evening several notes from the House of Commons saying that the opinion of the House seemed to go very much with them (opposition) and that Pitt had spoke without one solitary cheer, a thing, I suppose, unknown to him before. Lord, Henry Petty spoke admirably, and Lord John wrote us word that he thought that they would divide 170, a strong division for opposition. Mr. Pitt was keeping his friends together saying that the next question he should have to carry was so and so; whatever it was I forget it now. The question was called for before five; a great and awful silence ensued. The Speaker rose and said that the motion for a secret committee had appeared to him to be a fair and equitable measure, but that the charge which had been brought before him was so strong he must, according to his conscience, give his vote for the question. The ayes have it. They had divided equally, and he gave the casting vote. He was pale as ashes, and you might have heard a pin drop; it is an event that occupies every creature. The House sat again to-day. I saw my sister in the morning; she was extremely low. I told her what I really feel, that I was nervous and agitated, and that I believed whoever knew Lord Melville felt concern and regard, and I for my own part feel a disbelief that he would have profited by the peculation, however wrong it was to pass it over in another so lightly. She said certainly it was very wrong, but that she hoped nothing more would be done, as the national justice might now be satisfied. I saw her and Mr. Grey to-day, but I don't know what they mean to do. Only think of Lord Melville being obliged to have a great dinner on the next day. How I do feel for them. Lady Hawkesbury said they got through it pretty well.

Night.

Mr. Whitbread's motion, you will see, he consented to withdraw, and only moved that the resolutions should be carried up to the King to-morrow. This Pitt agreed to. The debate was animated. Mr. Grey, Duncannon, and Lord Ossulston supped with us afterwards. Mr. Grey said that Canning's had been the most intemperate attack upon him and very unexpected, as lately there had been much intercourse between them of a very friendly kind, and certainly what he advanced had nothing to do with the present case. The temper of the House was milder. Wilberforce said that as the national justice was satisfied he wished the question not to be pressed further. Fox's was very brilliant and very severe. How sorry I am for Lord Aberdeen; he will feel this, I am sure, deeply. Lord Melville was so kind to him, and he has so much heart. The impression is beyond the giving you an idea of.

CHISWICK, *April.*

Lord Aberdeen called on me to-day. On taking my hand, I felt his as cold as marble; he threw himself on a chair and said what miserable sad things have passed since I saw you. It made me so nervous I could hardly speak, but I told him that I could not express to him how much I felt for Lord Melville; that those who, like me, had seen him in his private life must feel a regard and affection for him that nothing could alter; and I owned also that I felt a disbelief that he ever enriched himself, though I own I thought opposition right in doing what they had done. Oh! good God, yes, he said; he was condemned on his own confession of breach of an Act of Parliament and allowing Trotter to speculate with the publick money;[226] it was right, it was necessary he should go out and that there should be this censure. I should not have mentioned this, but I cannot, cannot bear that a suspicion should rest on anybody's mind that he could enrich himself. Those who knew him will not believe he did. I said I hoped it might be proved, but thought Pitt's speech had been a weak one. He said he was frightened for the first time in his life; dismay and horror were in his looks, he never raised his eyes from the ground, and next day when he called on Lord Melville he was some time without uttering. I asked him how Lord Melville bore it; he said well; that he reproached them for their melancholy countenances, and said it looked as if they thought him guilty; indiscreet he had been, but he had not been more. I do assure you, dear Augustus, I was nervous and agitated to a great degree. I felt for him as his and as your friend, and I am sorry for Lord Melville; it is the deathblow to his greatness. He falls, as Wolsey did, never to rise again, and like him with too much of former power and with some great and good qualities. The impression on the public mind is beyond all belief; it occupies everybody and all day long; it is a fearful example of the vicissitude of human prosperity. He was a man who had a real pleasure in obliging and in doing a kind thing. I hear that he will be regretted in the navy, where every thing went on well and with kindness to the officers and men. Adieu, my dearest Augustus. As this is a chance letter, I will say no more now. I asked Lord Aberdeen to find out for me if they would like to receive me as they are going to Wimbledon, and I would drive there from here, though it would be a nervous visit. Adieu, adieu. I never remember a question in which I thought opposition right would give me so much pain.

> *Lady Elizabeth Foster*
> *To Augustus Foster.*
>
> CHISWICK, *April* 22, 1805.

Lord Aberdeen dined here yesterday, and was introduced to the Duke, who I heard liked him very much. I had a wretched sick headache from crying at the play of Zara, in which Roscius in the last Act outdid himself, and I was so undone by it I could not leave my room, but Caro told me it all went off very well: he was shy, to be sure, and during dinner did not, I am told, talk much, but that is no fault, young as he is, and after dinner he was at his ease, and Caro, Harriet, Georgiana, and he had a great deal of conversation, and you know how good his conversation is. Mr. Bennet dined here, and the Duchess wanted Lord A. to sleep here, but he was going on to Wimbledon: his feeling, yet candour, about all that business of Lord Melville, is most amiable. He told me that it was going on rather better, and that Trotter now was willing to make an affidavit that Lord Melville had no share.

25th.

The Duke has been to the Installation. It was a very magnificent sight, and it all went off very well. Nothing extraordinary in the King's behaviour except wearing the most wonderful wig ever seen, and which attracted every body's notice as soon as he appeared.... Next day the Prince and Duke of Clarence dined at Chiswick.[228] Pitt is to anticipate the motions which opposition meant to bring forward, and moves for continuing the naval commission and instituting inquiries into the war department. Sir Charles Middleton is to be First Lord of the Admiralty, but he is supposed to be a creature of Lord Melville.

27th.

Lord Aberdeen, Ossulston, Lord H. Petty, W. Lamb, and Lord Brook supped here after the Opera. The news of the day, and this Lord R. Spencer had told me before dinner, is that Addington and Lord Buckinghamshire have resigned. I asked Lord Henry P., and he said he believed it was certain, and on the grounds that Pitt required a support of Lord Melville which Addington could not conscientiously give. Lord Aberdeen told me that some condition for favouring Lord St. Vincent had not been complied with, and that he imagined that they certainly would go out, for their conversation, he says, does not agree with the votes they give, nor were those votes of all their friends. It excites some curiosity, as you may believe.

28th.

All this morning the resignation appeared certain, but Pitt was known to have gone to Richmond (where Addington lives), and conferences of various kinds were held. Four of the Cabinet Ministers were sent for from the Academy dinner yesterday to attend a Cabinet Council, and about six to-day it was known that a reconciliation had been effected. Has Pitt or Addington yielded? Will Sir C. Middleton remain First Lord of the Admiralty? Voilà ce qu'il faut resoudre et qui sera probablement connu demain. Meanwhile more letters are come from America and none from you, but Lady Hawkesbury tells me such a panegyric of you as gave her the greatest satisfaction. I long to read the letter.

May 2nd.

You will see by the papers all the rumours of the French fleet and of ours. Dieu sait ce qui sera de nous, but if the French can get out when they choose why should our blockading system continue which so fatigues ships and men.... The Duke and all of us are going to see young Roscius to-night in the character of Richard the Third. It is a bold undertaking, but his Genius justifies his daring. God bless you, my dear child, and may you soon quit those inhospitable climes you are in, though I hear that even the Americans are delighted with you, and wonder we don't always send our young men of fashion there rather than to France or Italy.

Lady Elizabeth Foster
    To Augustus Foster.
                    DEVONSHIRE HOUSE, *May* 21, 1805.

... Since my last letter there was another question lost by Ministers, and the motion for taking Lord Melville's name out of the list of Privy Councillors was carried. Indeed Pitt announced that he gave way, and had advised the King to do so. I hope there will be no need of any thing further. He is obliged to sell his house in town, to let Wimbledon, and is going somewhere to the sea side with her. It is a most melancholy vicissitude, and I do feel for him to my heart. Lord Aberdeen comes here to-night. There is a little dance after the Opera. I know not why, but we have not seen so much of him lately, which I regret very much, and am afraid there are plots to keep him away. The day before yesterday Madame Jerome Bonaparte landed at Dover. She had been to Lisbon, and not allowed to land there. I hear she then went to Holland, and orders were sent there not to receive her, and at last the ship put into the Downs, and orders were sent for her landing and every attention to be paid her, though I heard Lord Hawkesbury say he should not allow any of the men to land, but I hope that this is not so, as I see by the papers that her brother and a physician are on board with her. What a strange fate hers seems to be. I should like to see her, but I am afraid they won't let her come to London, which seems to me very extraordinary. I should like to talk to her of you, and I feel inclined to like her from what you said of her and from her unhappy situation. He is supposed to be gone on to Madrid. As to publick affairs, the combined fleets[229] are said certainly to be out of Cadiz, and Lord Nelson certainly to have passed the straits and to be coming homewards. Whether this means that the enemy intend a great junction of all their fleets to make an attack on Ireland, or that some are gone to make a great attack on Jamaica, nobody seems able to guess, but there is a look of anxiety amongst Ministers which gives an idea of alarm, and the total want of information of where the combined fleets are gone adds to that apprehension. However, with Lord Nelson near us, I think we need not fear our own shores, but think what a blow Jamaica would be to Charles Ellis, and indeed to hundreds of others—ma speriamo.... Of private news already I have told you that Caroline Ponsonby[230] is to be married to William Lamb, now an elder brother. It is to be next week, and Lord Cowper's marriage is declared with Emily Lamb, and they are all to be here tonight. These are certainly two as pretty marriages as possible. The Melbournes, as the Queen good-naturedly said, wanted this consolation after their trying misfortunes, and they are very happy with it.

28th.

Madame Jerome is come to London. I wish I knew how to get acquainted with her. We are all very much occupied at present with the story of an American lady, a Mrs. Randolph, who is daughter to English parents, their birth and fortune considerable. They changed their name on going from England to America. She was daughter to a Duchess and married an Earl's second son, and this third daughter married a Mr. Randolph. The estate in Virginia, I think, was disputed; they lost it, and the lawsuit cost a great sum, and they were ruined. The yellow fever carried all off but this young woman, to whom on dying her mother revealed her family name, but made her promise never to reveal it. She came to England, as she supposed, to a friend of her mother, and on her landing read her death in the papers. She wandered about till, fainting through want, she knocked at the door of Mr. Mansbridge to ask him a permission for the parish infirmary. Her appearance and story strongly interested him, and Mr. Trumbull of America was with him. He promised to inquire about her, and has written from America that all she has told is true. I wish you, too, would inquire about her family. They lived chiefly, I think, in Virginia and Philadelphia, and were well known and in great consideration. I never heard a more melancholy story, and Mrs. Randolph is a widow of one and twenty.

June 2.

I have seen Mr. Trumbull's letters, which mention Mrs. Randolph as being known to several persons and very much respected by them, but the mystery is not yet cleared, though, by circulating the paper which gives an account of her, they hope some of her father or mother's family may claim her.

Caroline Ponsonby is to be married to-morrow; she looks prettier than ever I saw her. Sometimes she is very nervous, but in general she appears to be very happy. W. Lamb seems quite devoted to her. They supped here last night, and she received her presents and gave some. Lord Morpeth gave her a beautiful acqua marina clasp. I gave her a little pearl cross with a small diamond in the middle. Caroline gives a hair bracelet with amethyst clasp. Lord Melbourne gave her a beautiful set of amethysts, and Lady M. a diamond wreath. The Duke of Devonshire gives her her wedding gown, and the Duchess a beautiful veil. Harriet gives a beautifull burnt topaz cross, and then, &c. &c. What a comfort to have her so near, and yet what a trial to poor Lady Bessborough.

June 5th.

The marriage was on the 3d at half after seven or 8 in the evening. We went to Cavendish Square, and besides the Devonshire House party were only the Melbournes, Morpeths, Fitzwilliams, Lord Spencer, Lady Sara and Lord Althorpe, Lord Cowper as trustee, and your brother by Caroline's own invitation. They set out about nine; she was dreadfully nervous, but his manner to her was beautifull, so tender and considerate. There was a great crowd assembled, and the favours looked very gay and pretty. They went to Brocket Hall,[231] and will stay there, I believe, about a fortnight. The Melbournes fit up the middle apartment at Whitehall for them. As to poor Corise all goes on the same. She looks thin and ill, I think. He has no money to marry, and his father is obstinate. The family praise her very much....

The only news here is that Lord Melville is to appear at the bar of the House of Commons and make a speech in his own defence. Probably this will save him from being impeached. Yesterday dispatches were received from Nelson, and he was pursuing the combined fleet, yet very unlikely is it that he should meet with it; great movements are seen in all the fleets nearer home, but invasion is scarcely now believed in....

Lord Aberdeen is, I am afraid, in a grand flirtation with Lady Catherine Hamilton. They make him great advances, and a person here whom I had hoped he liked or seemed inclined to like is too proud to seem to care if not certain of being preferred, so the others have champ libre, and as it is a connection as to Politicks that his friends would like I dare say it will do, but he is too good for them; I don't say for her, for she is pretty and, I believe, amiable, but I am very sorry for her. I think him delightful, and I am sure he likes the society here.

Augustus Foster
        To Lady Elizabeth Foster.
                        WASHINGTON, *June* 2, 1805.

Aberdeen's plan of going abroad I was always afraid would be only a
bubble, though I think the Russian scheme would have suited him very
well. I am sorry for this affair of Lord Melville's. He would have held out
a very good ladder for Aberdeen in politics. Now he has only got Mr. Pitt,
but he, you will say, is everything. So Roscius, a boy of 13, has changed
your hours and manner of living in London, brought you down to plain
country five o'clock. Can any of the bishops say as much, I pray? but this
is the age of wonders. Lord Hawkesbury, Lord of the Admiralty, or what
you please, sir. Is it strange or not that he should thus be hopping about
all the stepping-stones of the Administration? The Secretaries here are
astonished that he should have such variegated talents, but I tell them that
with us every Minister of State must be thoroughly acquainted with our
whole system, and it is very true. Here none of the men in office at all
are allowed a seat, and therefore are not obliged to know everything....
It is an absolute sepulchre this hole. I am going next week to the Falls of
Potomac at Harper's Ferry, and to Philadelphia the week after. The season
has been delightful here, and when these degenerate sons of our ancestors
arrive at a little taste this situation will be one of the finest in America.
Mrs. Merry is now recovering fast: she suffers more than I can describe
from this country. The women here are in general a spying, inquisitive,
vulgar, and most ignorant race, and yet as ceremonious as ambassadresses.
Even you with all your resources and powers of self-amusement would
absolutely be puzzled here. You can bear many things, but you cannot
bear vulgarity....

Augustus Foster
        To Lady Elizabeth Foster.
                        WASHINGTON, *June* 30, 1805.

... I made a little excursion to Harper's Ferry where the Shenandoagh and
Potomack join and rush through the mountains, if mountains they can
be called. The country is very woody, but has more cultivated spots than
I expected to find. Population does not increase, however, very rapidly in
this part of the United States. The acquisitions which these absorbers of
land are perpetually making have thrown open such an extensive field
for speculation that the farmers absolutely wanton in the excess of it. An
Irishman, when he first lands, without speaking a word of English, which

few who come here can, makes signs with his spade in his hand that he wants work, and obtains a dollar a day, or 4s. 6d. With such high wages he soon is enabled to buy a little land, and when he has got rich upon that he tires of it and removes some miles farther to a better soil, and so goes on gradually to the Mississippi. This is the process that the settlers of every nation go through except the Germans, who plant themselves at once, and there they stick, good or bad. They tug away jog trot at the soil till they die, when their sons march off to the towns or to the back country. With such a rambling disposition you will easily conceive that they can't have much attachment to home. In fact, you nowhere find the rustic simplicity which pleases so much and is everywhere else found in the world. There are no natural manners, no peculiarities that mark the country. You are always among the inhabitants of towns, though you strike upon a Log House in the most distant woods, and as the houses are of such perishable materials there is nowhere any building to mark long residence. Anywhere but in America I could bear, I think, seclusion, but I cannot bear to be eternally among *knowing* people, and what is worse, too, there is no spot so retired among these "regenerated races", as they are called, where you don't find drunkenness. I always have Mr. Fox in my mind when I think of the United States. I know that he has a strong prejudice in favor of this country, but I should like to know whether it is not confined merely to the theory of the Constitution which they possess. That I think excellent, but they surely have become independent too soon for their own happiness. The strongest Party in this country is now making violent efforts to change that Constitution, as I believe I told you, by limiting the influence of the Senate and making the judges more dependent. The possibility of a division is even openly talked of in the public papers, and recriminations are exchanged between the Eastern and the Southern States; in short, they seem ripe for dissension. Of all the members, about 130 Representatives and 34 Senators assembled here last winter, there really was not a single one that we should look up to as a man of great talent in England, nor is it to be expected that there should, as they most of them exercise two or three professions besides, and are almost all speculators; however, there were some very worthy men, and no doubt of great integrity. It is really too great a sacrifice of the best years of life to remain long here. If the Congress met at Philadelphia one might employ one's time, but here there is absolutely nothing, not even books, to be had. I shall forget almost how to be cheerful in this sink of imagination; however, it will certainly be an interesting country to us at no very distant period, and, therefore, well worth the visit. In a week we go to Philadelphia. The French Minister and his wife have been exposing themselves shamefully here by their domestic quarrels. He, it seems, is of the true Jacobin, Godless and licentious cast, and she, it is said, forced herself into where he was assisting at dancing in his own house of not the most reputable ladies, when he beat her most unmercifully and forced her to fly the house. She has been abusing him from house to house here, even his valet told her that she was a Canaille; in short, they are in complete disgrace with the Americans, and she is to be shipped off for France, I believe. I don't know whether I have asked of you already to send me over the newest Country Dances and Cotillon music, which is what they dance most here....

> *Augustus Foster*
> *To Frederick Foster.*
> WASHINGTON, *July* 1, 1805.

... I don't know whether I have yet transmitted to you an account of the installation of the successor of Montezuma in last March.[232] On the 4th he proceeded on horseback from the Palace, which is of white stone, and the largest building here, and, attended by his secretary and groom, rode up the long Avenue of Pennsylvania to the Capitol, which is an unfinished rival in stone of the Roman building of that name, and dressed in black and silk stockings, delivered a speech of some length, which you have, to a mixed assemblage of Senators, Populace, Representatives, and ladies. It was too low spoken to be heard well; he then kissed the book and swore before the Chief Justice to be faithful to the Constitution, then bowed and retired as before, when he received levee at which all who chose attended, and even towards the close blacks and dirty boys, who drank his wines and lolled upon his couches before us all; the jingling of a few pipes and drums finished the day. There was nothing dignified in the whole affair. He is about 65 years old, and affects great plainness of dress and manners. Au reste he is a philosopher of the politico speculative kind. Unbounded freedom reigns in this unbounded land, and the shameless abuse and [torn, V. F.] in their papers is not at all creditable to the country. I thank you and Duncannon for your exertions about a curricle. I shall wait its arrival with impatience, though the roads are so execrable and the streets worse that I dare say I shall not be able to use it much, particularly as I have not served an apprenticeship of driving in England.

> *Lady Elizabeth Foster*
> *To Augustus Foster.*
> DEVONSHIRE HOUSE, *July* 13, 1805.

... I have this moment received your letter, my dear, dear Augustus, of June 2nd, just two days before our hero of the Nile arrived at Barbadoes to liberate the West Indies.... Lord Aberdeen was wretched during all the business about Lord Melville. He is in Scotland preparing for his marriage with Lady Catherine Hamilton.[233] Never were father and son-in-law so different surely as these two are. Mr. Bennet is miserable at the marriage, and thinks he will be lost to all his friends by it. Lord Enniskillen marries Lady Charlotte Paget, and Lord Grantham Lady Harriet Cole. I suppose letters and papers enough will reach you to tell you that the impeachment was carried, and that Lord Melville will be impeached the opening of next Sessions. Lord Sidmouth resigned a week ago.[234] Pitt has patched up his present administration amongst his own people; no new person is added. The rumour of the day is that he had again spoke to the King about Fox; that the King's objections were done away; that this was to lead to a grand union as proposed last year, and that either active war would be carried on, with Russia to help us, or a grand Congress at which Fox would be Ambassador in his character of Secretary of State.

15th.

... Georgiana is recovered from her fourth lying in, and is well except a cold. Harriet and Caro have their flirtations, and are in extreme good looks. Corise, to whom I shall tell the interest you take in her happiness, is quite satisfied with his conduct; he seems more attached to her than ever, and only wants to borrow a small sum of money to marry her directly. He says Lord Tankerville continues *inflexible*, but Lady T. expressed great interest about her.

... Emily Lamb is to be married next Saturday to Lord Cowper, Caroline and Corise bridesmaids.

I don't wonder the Americans were surprised at the projected changes; however, Lord Hawkesbury has remained as he was, and Sir C. Middleton was made Lord Barham. He is eighty, so he brings the weight of experience. We were in great joy at hearing of Nelson's arrival in the West Indies, and now all is despondency again because he has not overtaken and beat the French and Spaniards, but he drove them away....

> *Augustus Foster*
> *To Lady Elizabeth Foster.*
> WASHINGTON, *July* 30, 1805.

I cannot fancy Lady Caroline married. I cannot be glad of it. How changed she must be—the delicate Ariel, the little Fairy Queen become a wife and soon perhaps a mother. I had just finished a letter to her as Lady Caroline

Ponsonby yesterday in answer to her pretty one of March. I cannot tear it, and so pray do not betray my secret, and let it pass as if I knew nothing in this remote country of her marriage; as it is not a love letter it may go, and if I don't answer so I never can to her now she is under the laws of a Man. It is the first death of a woman. They must die twice, for I am sure all their friends, their male ones at least, receive a pang when they change character so completely. I inclose it under cover to you, as well as one to Caroline, and what you tell me about Aberdeen distresses me. Surely they can't have worked on his feelings about Lord Melville to keep him from Devonshire House. I am grieved at his only having received one letter from me. I have written to him so often. He is very young, but he has shewn some character with regard to the Duchess of Gordon. I only hope in you. Keep him to Devonshire House, where I pride myself on having introduced him, and he will do. It is dreadful to be so distant. Aberdeen appears to me to be of that class of persons that are made to be an honor to their country. Who can you mean at Devonshire House that you thought he loved? Was it Caro or was it Lady Harriet? Only get him to be in love with one of them. I shall write to him by this post, but God knows whether the letter will ever arrive. I am sick of the distance.

I shall inquire about Mrs. Randolph, though I am sure from what I have read that she is an impostor. Believe me, there are not more consummate rascals anywhere than in the United States. I see it more and more, and novel species of villanies in this country. The scum of every nation on earth is the active population here.

August 4th.

I have inquired of Colonel Washington, nephew of the General, of one of the oldest families in Virginia, and he knows nothing of such a lady—but however I will inquire further. The hand of God being introduced by Mr. Mansbridge looks rather canting. Now that I have thought upon the matter, perhaps it might be wrong to send the letter to Lady Car, but I send it under flying seal, so that you may or not, only if you do I am supposed to know nothing of the marriage. She is so amiable that I should like to answer her letter to keep up the acquaintance which would otherwise be quite dead through the distance. Would you choose for me a fur Pelisse to be made up at Schweitzer's? The winters here are much colder than those in England, and I want to teach these creatures to wear something like dress of human beings. Is it possible that Aberdeen should be in love at Lady Abercorn's? but you did not, as well as I recollect, think him a good match for Lady Harriet. Who is Caroline inclined to favor? As for me, a young girl, a phenomenon for this country, has just died of a consumption whom I certainly should have admired *prodigiously*. She said on her death bed that she thought the lower part of my face extremely amiable, but in the forehead something rather too stern. I tell you all the nonsense in the world, because I always have and shall always consider you as my sister. She could not bear the society of this place though she had never been to Europe.... Madame Jerome was supposed to be likely to add to the race of the Gallic Caesars when she left America, so that I suppose you will not see her soon. Her father came over here from Ireland, as Mr. Pichon, the former French Chargé d'Affaires declared, as a Redemptioner, that is a person who sells his services for a certain period to pay for his passage from Europe, and he became an hostler. He is now, however, universally respected as a merchant, and is one of their most honoured dealers in Baltimore. She declared three days before Jerome was won that she would have him. It was veni, vidi, vici. These words resemble our dear Italian so much that I won't insult you with a translation....

Lady Elizabeth Foster
To Augustus Foster.

CHISWICK, *August 5*, 1805.

... We are at present all impatience and expectation and some anxiety about the fleet. Nelson, by the terror of his name, seems to have driven the enemy from the West Indies, and to be pursuing them home. Clifford wrote to me the 12th of May from St. Vincent;[235] the 4th of June from Barbadoes; on the 12th, after having visited six islands, they weighed anchor again, and on the 19th he ended his letter saying they were in full pursuit and hope to be at Cape St. Vincent before them, and perhaps even to come up to the enemy before that. What a wonderful man Nelson is! How rapid and well combined are his operations. On the 21st the combined fleet was seen off Ferrol, and Sir R. Calder attacked them and captured two of the Spanish ships;[236] he kept in sight of them four days and then they disappeared, and he on the 31st resumed his station off Ferrol, so that they are not got into port, and perhaps that Nelson may yet meet with them. Every day, every hour, they expect to hear from him, and the impatience and anxiety is beyond all expression. On the other hand, the public are dissatisfied with Calder for not doing more; yet with 15 ships he attacked the combined fleet of twenty and defeated them. Fog and night came on which prevented his continuing the battle then, and they contrived to escape two days after. It is these two days that the public are dissatisfied with the loss of, and say that a Nelson would not have rested so. They also blame Admiral Cornwallis for not doing something on his part; yet all this may be accounted for satisfactorily, and it is hard to blame an officer who has defeated the enemy and to condemn him unheard, As to home politicks, the impeachment,[237] as I told you, is decided on, and will come on early in the present Sessions. Lord Melville is gone or going to Scotland, and Lord and Lady Aberdeen are now at Wimbledon, which he has, I believe, hired of Lord Melville to put a few hundred pounds into his pocket. Lady Melville is going to the seaside and to Bath. What a melancholy ending to such a career. The rumours are stronger than ever of a grand junction, and the King has spoke in the handsomest manner of (?), and is said to have taken a dislike to Addington. Mr. Pitt is reported to be again very eager for a union with Fox and the principal people of his party. The Duke of Devonshire said here the other day that he thought it would be the best thing for this country that could happen, and we could not help remarking what a glorious triumph it is to Fox's talents and character after all the odium so long endeavoured to be thrown upon him to have his opponent express himself twice in so decided a manner upon the necessity for the publick advantage to have the aid of his councils and that he should be of the Administration. It does Pitt honor also so completely to forget all resentments and to acknowledge this, and I think that if they ever joined it would last. Two such minds once brought to act together would not be in danger of quarrelling from any petty jealousies and selfish views. They would act for the good of the country on great and enlarged views, and perhaps bestow on the age the greatest of all blessings, that of a solid and lasting peace....

> *Lady Elizabeth Foster*
> *To Augustus Foster.*
>
> *August 30, 1805.*

... Several rumours have been and are abroad about a junction of parties, and Pitt has, I believe, certainly again told the King that he thought the admitting of Fox to the Cabinet essential to the welfare of the Country. The King, it is said, spoke highly in praise of Fox, and said the principal objections in his mind were done away. There would be a great difficulty now with several of our friends, for they were so irritated by Pitt's conduct last time that many are totally averse to Fox agreeing to any junction. The King's eyes are rather better, but some say that his health is not so good. The Duke of Gloucester's death will affect him very much, as the illness did....[238]

> *31st.*

Nelson is, I hear, to have a great command: he is delighted with his reception here, but says with great modesty, "They have received me as if I had done some great feat". And so God knows he has.... The Brest fleet came out, but on Cornwallis forming his line of battle and attacking his foremost ships they retreated into their harbour again. Calder is again pursuing the combined squadrons....

Augustus Foster
> *To Lady Elizabeth Foster.*
>> PHILADELPHIA, *September* 2, 1805.

... General Moreau arrived last week with his family, and they are gone about 30 miles off to Morrisville near Trenton, where he has hired a country seat. I shall not see him probably unless by accident, for in my *public* situation it would be improper for me to call on him even with your letter.... Mr. and Mrs. Merry are bored to death with these United States, but Merry is a man so strictly en regle that I know he conceives it to be his duty to stay here in time of war upon his post at least longer than he should do in peace. You have no idea of how miserable the state of society is throughout and radically so, but yet you are to hear their pretensions to manners and to national honor and dignity and at the same time of their meannesses, perpetual breach of faith, and perpetual lying. Talleyrand, who travelled here, said of the country that he did not like it because there was not a man in it but would sell his favourite dog.... I am vexed at Aberdeen's marriage. It never will do. He has a fine imagination, and she told me once that she could not conceive how any body could find a pleasure in reading poetry; besides, she does not look wholesome, and is, I fancy, older than he is. How odd of him to marry so young, and the connection is not the most agreeable....

Augustus Foster
> *To Lady Elizabeth Foster.*
>> ELIZABETH TOWN, NEW JERSEY, *Sept.* 22, 1805.

Long Island is the part of all America that I have seen which would make the most agreeable residence in my opinion, and it is the only part in which the people bow to you and seem to possess simplicity. You see some of the old Dutch dresses there still, and even some of the descendants of the Tuscarora nation of Indians. I dined there with Mr. King, whom I saw for the first time, and who was Minister to England. On my return here, Lord Bolingbroke,[239] who lives a mile off under the name of Mr. Bellasyse with the German lady his wife,[240] now declared so, and married over again to him since the death of Lady B., sent his carriage for me to a ball which he gave on his departure for Niagara. He has been here near ten years now, and as they say means to return to England this year. She is anything but handsome; a little square German with broken teeth, but they say very amiable. Their children are remarkably fine. He flatters himself that he is not known here to be Lord Bolingbroke. As he did not inquire after his friends in England I did not say any thing about them to him, but I dine with him to-day. He is disgusted, I believe, as every man of education must be, with the manners in general of the people of this country, which is so made up of the ragamuffins and adventurers that flock here from all parts of Europe, and particularly the Irish. As no man is thrown out of society here from the badness of his character, you sometimes meet with the meanest and most worthless fellows in free conversation and intimacy with perhaps very respectable men, and I must say this that people sometimes perhaps judge too harshly of the natives from the foreign adventurers that they meet with.... I would not come here as Minister to live at Washington with £10,000 per annum, and if I did I would not take—I was going to say my wife—I would not take my sister for £20,000. A woman of education and feeling suffers dreadfully. It is a land for poor men, single men, I mean, and when they get rich they should go to Europe to enjoy it....

> *The Earl of Aberdeen*
> *To Augustus Foster.*

PRIORY, *Sept.* 24, 1805.

My dear Augustus, ... You must without doubt have heard before this that I am married and to Lady C. H.[241] Repress your astonishment for the present, and it may perhaps cease when we meet.

... You may depend on the papers for the truth of the coalition, which is now certain. I am glad that Nelson had it in his power to shew your peevish children in America that England, old as she may be, is still pretty active; the spirits of your friends in opposition cannot be very high. Mr. Pitt is as firm as ever, and as the troubles on the continent increase will be more so every day. Lord Melville's impeachment will come on the beginning of next Session, the result after all that we have seen it would be vain to predict.... By the way, we are to be bored this year by that wretch called the Young Roscius,[242] who is the greatest impostor since the days of Mohammed.—Yours ever, most affectionately,

ABERDEEN.

I say, Mr. Foster will say, that Aberdeen has not slipped on the noose already, Yours, C. ABERDEEN, otherwise the amiable Lady C. H.

> *Lady Elizabeth Foster*
> *To Augustus Foster.*
>
> CHISWICK, *Sep.* 30, 1805.

... I think from your letter you will regret Lord Aberdeen's fate being so early decided; however, she is very pretty and amiable, and seemed to be very much in love with him, and I hope he will be very happy. He deserves it. I never meant to say that he would not be (taking him such as he is) a good match for Harriet, but perhaps rather said so the more from nervousness because I wished it, but should have hated her marrying except from affection, or he either. The Abercorns never lost sight of him. At first he certainly seemed to like Harriet, but she will never show or feel a preference for any body who is not decided in their liking for her; and she did not indeed give herself time to know if she would have liked him, for, the odious papers having taken it up, she would scarcely speak to him. We continued, however, seeing a good deal of him, and we all liked him. You may retract all your sorrow about Caro Ponsonby's marriage, for she is the same wild, delicate, odd delightful person, unlike every thing, witness her dating to Lady Maria Lane her first letter of congratulation on her marriage with her brother Duncannon from "Brocket Hall, *heaven knows what day*". Lady Maria is very amiable, and Duncannon seems very happy.... Pray don't marry an American, or, if you must, let her be rich—for really the more I see of poverty the more detestable it appears to me.... As to politicks, I believe that Pitt is very happy at having roused the continent, but it seems to me the deepest game that ever people played. What Bonaparte can mean by risking everything only to gain more than he can want is inconceivable, and we too play very deep. It is an awful moment, yet certainly the war seems to begin with better prospect of success than usual. Nelson is gone with a great command, and is, I believe, by this time off Cadiz. Clifford says he is happy enough to be with the in-shore squadron, and that they see the enemy's fleet clearer than their own. The combined fleet are 36 strong and we 26, with which he says we are fully equal to them, and with Nelson to the whole navy of France. I wrote you an account of the disappointment occasioned by Sir R. Calder. Every thing seems now drawing to a crisis on the continent, and it makes one tremble to think what events may happen before this time twelvemonth. It is supposed Lord Hardwick will resign and Mr. Foster be reinstated....

Lady Elizabeth Foster
  To Augustus Foster.

October, 1805.

... Every thing is, if possible, worse than was reported. Bonaparte crossed
the Rhine on the 1st of October, and on the 17th was master of Ulm, and
of above thirty thousand men, besides baggage, &c. The Austrian army
is destroyed. For Heaven's sake see Moreau. I can't conceive any thing
so interesting as his conversation would be at this moment. Do not deny
yourself the satisfaction of visiting a great man in disgrace.... Lord Nelson
is off Cadiz with a great command. Could any thing be done against the
combined fleet, it would rouse the spirits of the country, which are quite
depressed. I have seen nothing like the present moment. You hear nothing
else from the drawing-room to the steward's room, in every street, and
road, and lane; as you walk you hear Bonaparte's name in every mouth.
Mr. James said he believed it was an event unparalleled in history, and
that it roused even him who did not care for politicks. It is shocking, and
in the midst of it they intend sending the Duke of York to command the
expedition to Hanover. I fear that Mr. Fox's words will prove too true, that
a tardy confederacy will enable Bonaparte to beat his enemies one by one.
I hope your new world is more progressive than our old one. L'Europe est
bien vieille, Giambone used to say. We should except the vigorous limb,
France....

Lady Elizabeth Foster
  To Augustus Foster.

CHISWICK, *October 29th*, 1805.

There is a great consternation to-day amongst all people, I hear, in London.
A fishing-boat put off and when Sir Sydney took it it contained news that
Ulm was taken and the Austrian army *annihilated*,[243] General Mack and
his staff made prisoners.[244] It is also said that Bonaparte will not even have
the King of Prussia as an enemy, that he will not join the Confederacy. Our
expedition is stopped by contrary winds, and all is tardy on the part of the
Allies; all rapid like lightning on Bonaparte's.

My dearest, my opinion is that a man in disgrace and in adversity is of
no country, but entitled to every attention that one can pay them, whether
one happens to be in a publick or a private character. Therefore I wish you
by all means to call on Moreau. If, however, Mr. Merry has begged of you
not, then only send my letter with a civil note of your own expressing your
regret at being prevented from profiting of the introduction it would have

been to you. Were we at peace with France it might be wrong to visit an exiled general of hers, but how can it be so being at war, and the exiled a man of spotless character and oppressed? My opinion, I own, is entirely for your visiting him unless, as I said before, Mr. Merry wishes you not, and then certainly you owe it to him, and particularly as he has been very civil to you, to avoid any thing that would distress him: but Ministers made no scruple of visiting Pichegru here,[245] and any objection there could only arise on the part of Moreau, who might scruple the more from his disgrace the receiving any civility from the enemies of his country, but that surely should be left to him. The subject came naturally into my mind, because I remember when Moreau talked to us of Bonaparte's talents as a general, he said, "C'est la foudre; il frappe avant qu'on puisse voir d'ou part le coup".

Nov. 3rd.

I have been interrupted—no news since the taking of Ulm, and even of that no official accounts have arrived; already do some doubt the fact; all believe in some exaggeration; and it is now asserted that the King of Prussia has sent six regiments into Hanover to join the Russians. Lord Harrowby has sailed on his embassy to Berlin; how I should have liked had you been with him. It is supposed that the two Emperors and the Kings of Norway and Sweden will all meet...

> *Augustus Foster*
> *To Lady Elizabeth Foster.*
>
> *Nov., 1805.*

You must all of you in England be almost mad with joy at the glorious victory of poor Lord Nelson. What a drawback, however, is the loss of such a man to us, who with his bare name could chase away our enemies from one hemisphere to another! We can hardly say in the words of Chevy Chase that we have five hundred good as he,[246] but I hope, however, that we shall find several such still if occasions offer for trying them.

In this country I think the majority are glad of the victory, but there are great many of those engaged (?) in public situations who exaggerate upon our loss, and consider it too dear a purchase. Peace to all such! Those who know them care little for their praise or blame. If you knew the meannesses, the littlenesses of the nation which we are in Europe pleased to call great and virtuous! My dearest Ma, I do believe from my soul that from the Province of Maine to the borders of Florida you would not find 30 men of

Truth, Honour, or Integrity. Corruption, Immorality, Irreligion, and, above all, self-interest, have corroded the very pillars on which their Liberty rests. Nothing is wanting but numbers and a Caesar to change this boasting Republick into a despotism of the worst description. They have inherited all our faults without one of our virtues that I know of. They are free more from the nature of their land than from their laws which are not enforced. Were the aristocracy of Venice to be placed in command of America they could not rule otherwise than mildly, for, should they exercise severities, the innumerable rivers which offer navigation for thousands of miles would open easy channels of escape, and of escape to richer countries than they would leave. The plains of Louisiana and of the Ohio will in a few years exceed in population the States on the Atlantic. Believe me, it is better to admire the theory at a distance than to come and see the practice. It never yet was said that the freer a people are the happier they are. It is agreed on all sides that for the good of society it is necessary that bounds should be set to the liberty of individuals. Les Bornes que les Americains y ont mises sont souvent franchies au lieu que les notres, prises de plus haut, ne le sont impunément jamais. Les assassins se promenent souvent en plein jour faute de force dans les lois, but I am quite tired with writing about them. I beg you will let me know if there is any chance of escaping from them in any reasonable time, and if you mean to make peace in your hemisphere soon....

I have had a letter from Aberdeen announcing his marriage. I hope sincerely he may never repent. Ma temo temo ... As for me, were I in London or any town but this, you would run great risque of becoming belle mère. I am a little hard to please, but should I find une personne à mon gout je ne reponds plus de moi même je vous l'avoue. Je me rappellerais toujours de la promesse sacrée que je vous ai donnée en partant de Londres, mais le peril n'est pas grand ici; hors l'attrait de la jeunesse et quelque fraîcheur: il n'y a guère d'autres dans les filles de cette partie de l'Amérique....

The Earl of Aberdeen
    To Augustus Foster.
                        WIMBLEDON, *November* 20, 1805.

My dear Augustus,—I have received yours of the end of September from Philadelphia, inclosing a specimen of the Jacobin print, which has amused me much, but what vulgar ignorance the fellow betrays; however, when such extreme license prevails, you cannot fail occasionally to have many speculations at least entertaining. I have written you before to say that I am married, and am now the veriest Benedick of the age. I do not think I shall ever have cause to repent this step....

You have no idea of the effect which Nelson's death has produced, so great indeed as almost to counteract His Victory, certainly the most glorious ever atchieved. Many people wear silver favours with black in the centre as mourning, and we shall probably have a public mark of this sort when his body arrives, of which, however, there is some danger, for it is strongly believed the Euryalus is lost or taken with it and the French and Spanish Admirals on board. I believe Prussia is really disposed to co-operate, but I doubt much if she will go so far as active war....

I am going to commence actor this Christmas at the Priory, where we have got a very good theatre. I am to perform Oroonoko, Falkland in the Rivals, &c., &c. William Lamb also acts.

Have you no conception of the period to your exile, or must it still be much prolonged? I trust not. There will be active work on the continent, which perhaps may procure you employment. Lord Granville is certainly coming home, tho' Lord Cathcart, who was to succeed him, is ill of the gout. I have heard it said, but mind this is sous la Rose, that Jackson is to be recalled owing to some disagreement with the court of Berlin. Stratton is still at Constantinople, although dieing to get away. There will be some sharp debates in Parliament at the opening of the Session, but these continental alliances and naval victories have come very opportunely to Mr. Pitt's assistance. Lord Melville's business will perhaps be prolonged through the Session. How this persecution will end, God knows....

I hear nothing of Ossulston interesting. Au reste it y a un bruit sourd which says that he is actually married. The Theatre is in great glory.[247] Kemble and Mrs. Siddons every night—fancy after being made sick with an automate of a boy all last year, a girl of 7 or 8 years old is coming out this week at Covent Garden. Ohe jam satis!—Yours most affectionately,

ABERDEEN.

Tell me something about Moreau and Dessalines.[248, 249] What sort of a fellow is Christophe?[250] Adieu. If you see Moreau put him in mind that Jackson introduced me to him at Paris, and that I told him (Jackson) that he was the man I most admired and wished to see in France.

> *Lady Elizabeth Foster*
> *To Augustus Foster.*
>
> *November 29, 1805.*

It was in vain, my dearest Augustus, to have written to you the first days of the news of the victory of Trafalgar,[251] for nothing that I could have said would have conveyed to you any idea of the impression on the public made by the loss of their favourite hero. Great and wonderful as the victory was, the prevailing sentiment in each mind was sorrow, was grief, for Nelson. If it was the most flattering homage that could be paid to worth, to heroism like his; it was also an honour to the nation to feel it as they did. When we arrived at the Admiralty it was crowded, but every countenance was dejected—nor could one have guessed that it was a victory of twenty ships of the line taken from the enemy, only that defeat would have caused tumult, and this was the silence of sorrow and respect. We were shown into Mr. Marsden's room.[252] He was oppressed with the contradictory feelings of triumph for the country, and sorrow for the loss of the greatest hero we ever had, and his friend. As we came away there was a vast rush of people, but all silent, or a murmur of respect and sorrow, some of the common people saying, "It is bad news if Nelson is killed", yet they knew that twenty ships were taken. A man at the turnpike gate said to Charles Ellis, who was going through, "Sir, have you heard the bad news? We have taken twenty ships from the enemy, but Lord Nelson is killed." Illuminations followed, but the first night, as if unable to rejoice, there were none seen but on the public buildings. The two next nights they were general, but chiefly transparencies or mottos relating to the "dear departed hero". Nelson was the only person I ever saw who excited real enthusiasm in the English. Every day makes his victory more precious.

ON THE VICTORY OF TRAFALGAR AND DEATH OF NELSON.

By Georgiana, Duchess of Devonshire

Nelson, by Valour led to deathless fame,
All toils surmounted and all Foes o'ercame,
Met every danger calm and undismay'd,
Whilst some new conquest mark'd each step he made.
Superior Force his ardent soul defied,
He conquer'd, knew it, "blessed his God", and died.

Britannia glorying in her Hero's fame,
On her Victorious shield inscribes his name,
Gratefull proclaims the safety which he gave
Yet midst her Triumphs weeps upon his Grave.

Lady Elizabeth Foster
        To Augustus Foster.

November, 1805.

... How do you like these lines? written by the Duke of Devonshire on the death of Nelson.

> Oft had Britannia sought midst dire alarms
> Divine protection for her sons in arms.
> Britons received from Heaven a mixed decree
> To crown their virtues, but to check their pride
> God gave them victory, but Nelson died.

... Villeneuve and two other admirals are landed prisoners in England.[253]

Augustus Foster
        To Lady Elizabeth Foster.

WASHINGTON, *Dec.* 1, 1805.

... On this day the Congress opens. We expect a boisterous session, for they are angry with us about our regulations in regard to their commerce. They and we are now the two rivals in what has always given power wherever it has extended, Commerce, but I trust that still and for a long time we shall maintain the immense superiority that we do now. They are next us in the race, but in nothing else are they near us. We drove them into being a Nation when they were no more fit for it than the convicts of Botany Bay, though I must say that their leader Washington was a great character,[254] and one or two others whom the tumult of the day drove from their counters, but since that interest and speculation seem to have taken fast hold of the whole country to the exclusion of every generous feeling. Their boasted Constitution is as much a piece of theory as that framed by the French National Assembly, the difference being that here it has had as yet no day of trial; it hangs loosely upon the shoulders of the inhabitants, but we must see it when the reins are drawn close to be sure that nothing is brittle. I think people mistake where the real advantage of this Nation lies. I believe that under a Monarch they have the means of being free and independent from the nature of the land, the scattered manner in which it is peopled, and the immense difficulty that there would be in enforcing harsh mandates, from the want of easy communication through the marshes and forests. Almost all the sensible Americans whom I have conversed with that were not warped by prejudice have allowed that as Colonies, before our oppressive exactions took place, the Country was much happier, and the Government as mild and less burdensome. Their manners, too, were then much simpler, and the laws were enforced. What do you think of a society of Atheists having been formed not very long ago at Philadelphia for the purpose of enlightening the Country? They had undertaken to publish an Atheistical Paper. They were cried down, it is true, but still remember how the simplicity of these good people is cried up and the pure city of Philadelphia. A Mr. Clay,[255] a Member of Congress, lately having occasion to draw on the Bank there, wrote a Draft payable to J—s Ch—t or order. I had myself, as you know, a high opinion of the Constitution and manners of this country before I left England, but I do assure you that disgust, not to use a worse word, is all the feeling I have in respect to them now. The character of a gentleman is very rare to be found, but what has surprized me, the character of an honest man of principle is to the very full as rare.... There is an ambassador from Tunis arrived here with the most splendid dress I ever saw, and the President receives him in yarn stockings and torn slippers, as he does us all.

> *Lady Elizabeth Foster*
>   *To Augustus Foster.*
>   CHISWICK, *December* 1, 1805.

Archduke Charles the same accounts state to be dead "de fatigue et de chagrin". I was in London for an hour or two, and Farquhar told me this news, with which I went to Crauford's. At first M.D. had brought contrary intelligence, and that Woronzow, who was at Lord Macartney's, whence he came, said that there was an army of 15,000 Russians ready and united to act, and that with this help it seemed impossible that the Emperor of Germany should make peace. A few minutes after the Duke of Queensborough sent Crauford a written paper with the intelligence as I have given it you, so that I am afraid it is true, and the evening papers seem to confirm it. It is a campaign which one can compare to nothing. They have fallen before Bonaparte like card soldiers, and he does not seem to have lost an officer of note. My brother still says that the game is not up; but what can they look to? What has war done but make Bonaparte greater and more powerfull each campaign.

                                                              Dec. 2.

The Duchess was in town to-day. She was told that they were betting ten to one in the City that the news was not true, for some papers were received of the same date as the Dutch Admiral's note, and they mentioned neither circumstance; it would be a great relief to know that it was not true, yet Heaven knows if they can make any resistance; but any thing is better than making peace with the enemy at the gates. I hope some certain account will come before I seal my letter.

The Victory is arrived with the remains of our beloved Nelson. Alas, the awful vicissitudes of human life! When I dined with him in London he said to us, "in about two months I hope to have done my duty and to return to England". He is returned in little more than two months, but the Victor is laid low. Four of the prizes were saved; three are arrived; four others were taken by Sir R. Strahan, and the two in the summer makes ten ships of the line taken and sixteen destroyed on the 21st. Of that mighty combined fleet three only are now able to put to sea. Dear Clifford has written the most affecting and interesting letter possible, and is miserable at having been sent with five others on a particular service a fortnight before, but when I look on the number of midshipmen killed and wounded I can but rejoice he was not there.

Now as to the state of your friends here at Chiswick, the Duke has the gout, but is, I hope, getting better; the Duchess is pretty well, so am I. Duncannon and his bride dined here yesterday; we like her very much; some think her pretty, others not. I think her pretty though, with a nose almost as long as Prince D., but she has a fair and soft skin, pretty teeth, good hair, pretty figure, and very pleasing voice and manners. He seems very happy, and they are to come back and stay a few days. Lord Aberdeen is making pendant at the Priory to Caro and W. Lamb, who flirt all day long è face adesso.

Augustus Foster
  To Lady Elizabeth Foster.
                                    WASHINGTON, *Dec.* 27, 1805.

... I am here in the midst of Africans and Savages. We have an Ambassador from Tunis and his suite in the City, and deputies from eight nations beyond the Mississippi are arrived. They passed on horseback by my windows a few days ago in arriving, and made such a Hue and Cry that I thought all Washington was in convulsion. Two of them were naked to the waist, their heads shaved to the Crown, faces red, ears green, and feathers and bills of birds stuck all over them. Others had their faces shaded with black, and streaks of black painted from the crown to the chin, with sack loads of feathers and quills tied to their hair behind. They are 21 in all, generally tall, stout men, but not so much so as I expected to find them.

I have formed an acquaintance with a young man of the Sac nation who is very good looking, about 17, and who is son to a very principal chief of that country.[256] I got him to come to me for three hours to have his portrait taken, and I had an opportunity of studying a little his character, which is very reserved and timid. However, he becomes by degrees at his ease more and more, and I amused him extremely by shewing him caricatures. The figure of Lord Salisbury in the King and Gulliver made him laugh excessively, and he observed that John Bull had very short legs. His name is Wa-Pawni-ha or White Hare. We are great friends, and he shakes my hand with a smile of content when he sees me. He has four men to attend on him, and is now occupied in learning to write English. The first lesson I saw him taking to-day, and he really seems very intelligent. None of them have that ferocious countenance which I had been led to expect, and they behave very decently and with perfect propriety. Another man, an Osage, I was introduced to to-day. His name, for you must have him introduced to you in form, is Pa hu la or beaux cheveux. He told me that when he was young he had fine hair, but on becoming warriors they tear out the hair, a most painful operation in appearance, but which they don't seem to mind. There are no squaws come with them, to my great disappointment.

From this side of the Mississippi there are arrived several Cherokees, who are the most advanced in civilization. They dress like us, and have features like inhabitants of the South of France. They and the Creeks are the only two Nations which are supposed now to increase their number. Division of property has taken place among them within these few years, and, which is a great point, the women are treated with respect. Colonel Hawkins, a very amiable man, who is superintendent of the Southern Indians, told me that ten years ago, when he first settled among the Creeks, the women would leave the pathway for the men to pass, but now, by his example, the men universally give place to the women. He says that the fair sex has been of the greatest assistance to him in civilizing that nation, and that now a woman will not dismount from her horse unless helped off by a man, and that they are fully sensible of the benefit he has been to them. They still, however, throw away their children if deformed, and they show very little outward and visible signs of attachment of any sort....

Our Corps Diplomatique has really been enriched very much from a quarter which one should little expect any thing from—Tunis. Sidi men ne melli, the Ambassador from the Bey of Tunis turns out to be a very intelligent, amiable, and conversible man. He is an old acquaintance of Prince Augustus, to whom he sends a letter by this packet, and of Lady Hamilton, and was of her parties at Naples. He has taken a great fancy to me, and we are the best friends in the world, as I speak Italian, which he also, though imperfectly, understands. As we are at war with

Spain and France he is almost the only one of the Corps with whom we communicate. A nephew of Mr. J. Randolph (a Member of Congress of Virginia, and a young man of considerable merit), a boy about 12 years old, who is deaf and dumb, has just been sent by his uncle to England to try the effects of medical aid. He goes to Mr. Munroe's first, and then to a school at Bermondsey, and if you can be of any service to him in case he should ultimately go to Paris, to Sicard,[257] it would be doing a kind thing, and I should be glad of it, for, though Randolph is an enemy to England, yet he is almost the only gentlemanly man that belongs to the Congress.

You may rest assured that no Randolph such as is described in the paper you sent has ever possessed a town house in Philadelphia, nor has there been one within these 20 years whose estate was disposed of in the manner described. As the lady is so young and the name so aristocratic a one in this country the story of Mrs. Randolph would have been fresh in the memory of every one, and particularly of the Virginians; and the whole family and its branches have been all conned over repeatedly before me, and no individual found to apply the account to.

> *Lady Elizabeth Foster*
> *To Augustus Foster.*
>
> *December 16th(?),1805.*
>
> [Fragment.]

to-day to see the preparations, and in returning your brother stopped me; he had overheard in the streets saying the Mails are come in and the news is not so bad, but when we got to St. James' Square, where we dined, we found how bad the news was thought. It is indeed over with the Continent.[258] The Emperor of Russia is not concerned in the armistice and was ready to go on, but nothing can be more ruined than the Emperor of Austria and Germany. The gloom over Pitt's friends is extreme, and he is himself very ill at Bath.

> *Lady Elizabeth Foster*
> *To Augustus Foster.*
>
> DEVONSHIRE HOUSE, *December* 31, 1805.

... You can't conceive anything like the publick anxiety about the event of the battle of the 2nd, and those said to be given subsequent to it. We have been left without certain intelligence for a length of time, and the reports have been strong of a decisive advantage to the Allies, but a boat has come out with the Argus paper, printed at Paris, saying that the Emperors of Austria and France had concluded an armistice. I do not, cannot believe the Emperor Alexander has to do with it. W. Ponsonby speaks of him with enthusiasm, and his bravery has been conspicuous; but war is Bonaparte's element, and we play his cards for him when we give him an opportunity of making it. Where it will end, God knows.

Meanwhile magnificent preparations are making at home for our loved Hero's funeral. It is to be a national tribute to the favourite of this great nation which has been blessed with many heroes, but surely none so great, so brilliant as Nelson. They have tried to throw difficulties in the way of the Prince of Wales attending, but he is determined. He admired him, he says, as the greatest character England could ever boast of and he loved him as a friend to whom he was bound by every tie that could bind him to another. He was proud that England had produced such a hero. If there is a good life of him I will send it to you. The Bishop of Exeter is to write one, I know, and with original letters....

> *Lady Elizabeth Foster*
> *To Augustus Foster.*
>
> 1805.

... Lord Aberdeen looks dreadfully; he has been at Bath, and he frets so about Lord Melville that I really think he will make himself ill; yet the trial must come on, and I fear new things are come out. Both Lord and Lady Melville are at Bath; she is ill, and the complaint at his heart seems to increase. I pity them from my heart. Poor Lord Aberdeen, he is a delightful person. She is very pretty and likes Petrarch; that is something to redeem her with you. He and I have sparring about Roscius, for since Kemble was at the Priory instructing Lord Aberdeen in acting he has won him from the Boy and made him insist that all merit depends on right emphasis, and think that all acting different from Kemble's is wrong,—but the Boy has had a complete triumph: two nights ago acting Rolla, which he did with great success, Charles Kemble,[259] out of low envy, tried to cast a ridicule on him, and in the prison scene where Rolla gives his disguise to Alonso, Charles Kemble, to mark the difference of their size, threw it round him like a sack, on which the whole House hissed him, crying "off," and hissed him every time he appeared, whilst the applause to the Boy was greater than ever, with shouts of "bravo, excellent". It is a wonderful piece of acting, and his carrying off the child perfect nature and grace. Grassini sang in Cleopatra Tuesday, and excellently, I hear, but alas we lose her this summer.... There is a wax figure of Lord Nelson put up in Westminster Abbey, which is as if he was standing there. Vivra il suo nome mille secoli é mille.

Note from Charles J. Fox
    To Georgiana, Duchess of Devonshire.

1805.

Pray speak to everybody you can to come down or we shall be lost on the Slave Trade. Morpeth, Ossulston, Ld. A.H., Ld. H. Petty all away. Pray, pray send any body you see. Yours,

C. J. F.

½ past seven, H. of C.

INSCRIPTION FOR A BUST OF
CHARLES JAMES FOX,
BY THE HONBLE. WILLIAM LAMB, AFTERWARD
VISCOUNT MELBOURNE, PRIME MINISTER.

Live, Marble, Live, for thine a sacred Trust,
The patriot's face that speaks his noble mind;
Live that our sons may kneel before this Bust,
And hail the Benefactor of Mankind.

This was the man who midst the Tempest's rage
A rock of safety to the nations stood,
Warn'd with prophetic voice a servile age,
And strove to quench the ruthless thirst for blood.

This was the man whose ever deathless name,
Recalls his generous life's illustrious scenes;
To Bless his fellow Creatures was his aim,
And universal Liberty his means.

EPITAPH BY THE DUKE OF DEVONSHIRE
ON THE LATE LORD SPENCER. D. 1805.

If e'er sincerity inscribed the stone,
Giving the dead no merits but their own,

Behold it here. This verse with Sculpture's aid,
Records the debt by Love and Duty paid,
That Strangers and Posterity may know
How pure a Spirit warmed the Dust below.
But they who felt the Virtues of his Life,
Whether the Orphan, Friend, or Child or Wife,
Need not Poets or the Sculptor's Art
To wake the Feelings of a Grateful Heart.
Their Love, their grief, his honour best proclaim,
The Living monuments of Spencer's Fame.

Lady Elizabeth Foster
To Augustus Foster.

January 17, 1806.

The American dispatches have been retarded, and I have delayed also sending or writing even, for really there is such a gloom over every thing. I wanted to have something better to say. Then the procession and the funeral pomp(?) at Greenwich and to town and from the Admiralty to St. Paul's was affecting beyond measure. In short, what with that and seeing people connected with Lord Nelson and collecting a variety of anecdotes about him you cannot conceive how knocked up I feel. We are going—Fred F., Caro, and I—to Brocket to-morrow for a couple of days.[260] I think it will do us good. Nothing has done more honor to the country than the manner in which they have felt the loss of Nelson. In the thousands that were collected on that day it was a stillness which nothing broke through but a sort of murmur of "Hats off!" as the Car passed, and ejaculations of "God bless his soul who died for us to protect us; never shall we see his like again". This show altogether was magnificent, but the common people, when the Crew of the Victory passed, said: "We had rather see them than all the show". The Prince has shown a feeling that did him honor.

Now a new interest arises. Parliament meets on the 21st, and Pitt is so ill that he can't attend, nor will he, I believe, be able for a long time. The King is so blind he can't open the Session, so you see we are in a happy state. Lord Ossulston has just told me that Lord Henry moves the amendment. It is also thought that the Addingtons will vote with opposition. Lord Wellesley is just arrived from India, and is undecided which way to act.[261] They say that he owes everything to Lord Grenville, but I suppose he dreads the Lion recovering,[262] and that he should have turned too soon against him. What a miserable being is a Politician without a heart!

18th.

… I think your letter a very clever one, and I have thoughts of shewing it to Mr. Fox. It is the best picture of America I have had. I hope there will be no war with us…. Lady Holland inquired a good deal about you last night, and Lord Holland owned he believed your account was a true one…

Lady Elizabeth Foster
To Augustus Foster.

Thursday, January 23, 1806.

The papers will tell you of Mr. Pitt's death,[263] but none of them can do justice to the generous regret that is felt by opposition. On the Tuesday we were stopped at Devonshire House and told that at the moment the amendment was to be made Pitt's death would probably be announced. This, however, was not so, but now it is over; it is past; that name that filled so vast a space in the world is gone! He was calm and resigned, and his fortitude unshaken! It is an awful moment, and I will write more another time.

Saturday.

Nothing can paint better the feelings of a generous mind than the conversation which passed between Fox and the Duke. The Duke was saying that he thought it impossible not to be shocked at the death of a man of such superior abilities, even though one differed from him in political opinion. "Shocked," answered Mr. Fox; "yes, certainly it feels as if something was missing in the world!" I can't tell you the effect these few words had upon me—so simple, so sublime in their simplicity. It is reported that the King has sent to Lord Grenville; if so, I am sure he will not come in without Fox.

Monday, 27th.

Lord Grenville has been with the King. The King said to him, "I wish you, my Lord, to help me to make a new administration". "I must first, Sire, consult with Mr. Fox." "Yes, certainly," said the King, "I supposed so." So the conference ended, and now is indeed an anxious moment. I was sure, from a conversation I had with Lady Hawkesbury, that this was likely. The whole tenor of her conversation went to extol the King's purity of intention and devotion to whatever he thought the good of the country. We shall see. The King only added, "Let me have it by Wednesday or Thursday". Today was Mr. Lascelles' motion of publick honor to Pitt.[264] The motion is to be framed, they say, on the one made for Lord Chatham. Fox wished it might have been so worded as that he may agree, and even said before in the House that if it was not so worded as to be a gross violation of all his principles to support it that it would meet with no opposition from that side of the House, but I hear Mr. Lascelles was obstinate. It, however, gave rise to the most beautiful speech Fox ever made. The Morning Chronicle gave it very ill; instead of his saying "perhaps it was an honor," Fox said, "people had done him the honor to call him that Right Honourable Gentleman's Rival" (and a great honor it was), but you will have seen it in the papers. Mr. Wyndham's no body liked; however, all Pitt's relations and friends were pleased with Mr. Fox's. How happy shall I be if I can promote your advantage and happiness.

30th.

Lord Grenville has asked for another day. The King came to town and has seen Lord Hawkesbury, but I don't suspect any trick. Fox won't tell us any arrangements, and says they ought not to be known till the King has seen them. General Fitzpatrick was resisting our invitations to Devonshire House, saying we should be trying to get secrets from him. "That's a good one," said Fox laughing, "he has none to tell." You may conceive the busy look of St. James's Street. Mr. Fox asked me in the kindest manner about you, and whether you liked America. La risposta era facile. I long for tomorrow.

Friday.

The King said he should make no observations, but should send to Lord Grenville when he wanted him: different comments are made on this.

The King saw Lord Grenville this evening; he seemed surprized at the article about the Duke of York. "Is it", he said, "meant as a slur on the Duke of York?" "Nothing, Sire, further from our intentions." The King then said he must reconsider of it. He asked if it had not always been as now since the Duke of Cumberland. Lord Grenville assured His Majesty that if he inquired he would find it had not, and the article at bottom of the list was in the most respectful terms, saying that, as the revision of the measures for the defence of the Country must be the first that would come into consideration, it was humbly hoped that the Commander in Chief would submit to concert his measures with the Council at a time when the state of the Country required so much that they should act in concert. As nearly as I can ascertain, it was expressed these people had been prepared to think it had been intended to remove the Duke of York, or that something harsh had been said, but it was not so; and when this was understood there seemed to be but one voice that the King ought to be advised to consent to it.

Monday, Feb. 3.

It is said that the King wrote to Lord Grenville yesterday, and that he is to see him to-day. Before the ship goes I hope I shall have some decided intelligence to send you. Yesterday London was in a fever, for it was soon circulated at the Opera that it was off. Fox was there in his usual good spirits, at which, I suppose, people were surprised, but he is unlike any thing and superior to every body. I have heard that some people were for letting the subject of the Army rest for the present, but he, with his noble sincerity and integrity, said that it was more fair and much handsomer to state all their intentions now; to take no advantage. It has risked the whole thing being off, but it is with honor if it is so, and if the King has a heart to appreciate Fox, what honor this must do him with the King. I shan't dare send this letter by the merchant ship, but I will write a line by it to tell you of this.

Wednesday, 5th.

… To-day they were to kiss hands. I left off Monday. That was a day of fever. About one we knew Lord Grenville was with the King; about three or four that all was doing well; and about six a note from Arlington Street told us that all was settled. Lord Grenville was to see the King again in the evening for the final arrangements, and that the new Ministers were to kiss hands, and to-day I believe there is some delay about Lord Grenville on account of some plan he has which may delay it till to-morrow, but on Friday this packet goes, and with it I will send you the correct list. What a change! You will hear, I suppose, and so do we here, some abuse of letting in some of the Addingtons. Yesterday all was discontent amongst some of our minor friends on this account, but it is very different from the manner in which Mr. Pitt came in, leaving all the Addingtonians whom he had abused and tacking himself on to them, or coming in a great body, as Fox and Lord Grenville do, and then admitting Lord Sidmouth and one other to the Cabinet, and a few to other places—to form, in short, a *broad bottomed* administration, placing people there where their talents can be of use—thus Lord Auckland is at the Board of Trade—he, and almost he only, understands trade.

Wednesday night.

Fox says the order of the day is content, and the Duchess incloses you a list of the new administration as far as it goes, I mean as is finally settled. Several kissed hands to-day, and the King was very gracious, but so blind, poor man, that it was painfull to see him. The report is Sir R. Strachan is in sight of a squadron of the Brest fleet, and pray God we may have a victory, though that of Trafalgar might suffice for a century...

> *Augustus Foster*
> *To Lady Elizabeth Foster.*
> WASHINGTON, *Feb.* 1, 1806.

Our disputes and concerns with this country are becoming greater and greater every day, and our business becomes consequently greater likewise. The two greatest commercial nations on the globe cannot move in the same sphere without jostling one another a little while we are aiming blows at the French Marine. We want elbow room and these good neutrals won't give it to us, and therefore they get a few side pushes which makes them grumble. However, I hope they will see their interests better than to seriously quarrel with us for the benefit of the foreign adventurers who carry on an unlawful trade from their ports with the West Indies...

> *Lady Elizabeth Foster*
> *To Augustus Foster.*
> DEVONSHIRE HOUSE, *Feb.* 3, 1806.

I send you this merely to say that all our friends are coming in, and I believe are to kiss hands the day after to-morrow. You will see by the papers the loss the Country has again sustained in the death of Mr. Pitt! that name, so great, so known, which occupied so vast a space, is gone! ... On Thursday Mr. Pitt died; on Saturday the King sent for Lord Grenville and told him he wished his assistance to form a new Administration. Lord Grenville said the first thing he must do must be to consult Mr. Fox. "I supposed so," answered the King," let me have the list by Wednesday or

Thursday." "By Thursday, Sir,"—so it ended. They asked a day more, and gave it on Friday. An article at the end about the Commander in Chief made a difficulty, and the king said he must reconsider of it. I mistake— the King took it Friday and said he should send for Lord G., and on Saturday evening it was that the article about the Army made a hitch: it was reported at the opera to be off: most of Sunday passed without any thing; Sunday evening another message to Lord Grenville, and on Monday (yesterday) the King saw and settled every thing with Lord G., and we were told about five that Wednesday (to-morrow) they were to kiss hands. What a change! and what hopes, my Augustus, does it give me for you! but of this another time. Lord Hawkesbury has the Cinque Ports. Some blame him, and certainly Mr. Fox had wished it for Lord Chatham, to whom he would have given it. Fox made a beautiful speech yesterday on the motion to pay Mr. Pitt's debts. I send you a paper, The most beautiful was that on the motion for public honors. Mrs. Fox is happy, but has the most perfect good sense as well as good nature in her new situation. One of her first ideas was to ask me about you. I sha'n't forget that. The Duchess' friendship you know too well to doubt it—so a little patience, dearest child, go on improving yourself in French and Italian. I have seen no faults lately in French, and Italian I am afraid you now know better than me....

Georgiana, Duchess of Devonshire
To Augustus Foster.

March, (?) 1806.

Dear Augustus,—Mr. Pitt's death was felt by his opponents in a manner that did equal honor to him and them. They regretted his loss and his talents, and I may venture to say Mr. Fox would be well pleased indeed could he recall him to life and place him in his Cabinet. At any other time I should rejoice and exult in the assemblage of talent and integrity which we now can boast of, but alas, in these times what is to be done; it is uphill labour, and it must be the regret of every one that the proposed junction was not suffered to take place when it might have saved Europe.... I have sent you a remembrance—a memorial of Lord Nelson, but I trust, as you do, that he will have left us some of his élèves and comrades who will emulate his glory....

Augustus Foster
    To Lady Elizabeth Foster.
            WASHINGTON, *March* 10, 1806.

... Our news is not later than the 19th of December from London, and
we only know up to the reports of the battle of the 5th, and the heroism
of the Emperor Alexander. You may have had peace long ago for ought
we know here. I wish sincerely you may if it be a good one, for I long
very much to return. Nevertheless, I must own that this Mission is very
interesting during war time. Our disputes about Neutral rights have been
under discussion in the Congress, and I have heard their best speakers.
One of them, Mr. J. Randolph, the uncle of the deaf and dumb boy whom
I recommended to you, who is with Mr. Munroe, took up the argument
favorable to England, and managed it with a great deal of brilliancy and
success, though hitherto considered as the leader of the Democratic party
in opposition to the Federalists. He has now taken his stand as head of
the landed interest as opposed to the carrying part of the Commercial
interest. He is a very singular character, and has the extraordinary merit of
having taught himself. He lost his father when a boy, and was indulged in
idleness by his mother till he was 16 or 17, when he was sent to a college,
where he learned very little. He is now 33, has the voice of a boy, and the
appearance. He is extremely thin, and from bodily infirmities scarce can
know an hour's ease. He is a good deal at times at Mr. Merry's, and as he
is very gentlemanlike and full of imagination I like him very much. As he is
certainly the first in point of brilliancy in either house, I have given you this
account of him. He has, besides, as who has not who has heard of her, a
most sincere veneration for your Duchess and for your mutual friendship.
Being a direct descendant from Pocahontas, he values nobility of birth
very highly, and is intimately acquainted with all our great families, even
to their estates, and their distances from London and each other: he has
taken me en amitié, and we often ride together.

For about a fortnight during the winter Washington was as gay as it can
be, that is, we met parties crowded in little rooms in the different houses
here, by going 3 or 4 miles, sometimes 6 miles, every evening. There
were several strangers, and some very pretty girls. There was one with as
handsome a face as any I have ever seen. Mrs. Merry gave a little dance,
which was pronounced *feiner* and more *charmin'* than any thing of the
sort ever seen. I wore the Prince's uniform, which is very popular here,
though I was obliged to shew a little resentment at a reason which was
insinuated for its being so.... I congratulate you on the defeat of the French
fleet in the West Indies. We seem to sweep the Ocean. General Moreau I
have not seen. I must obey Mr. Merry about him, unless I should meet him

in private society. He is very communicative, I understand, at Philadelphia, where he now is. He gives as his opinion that Bonaparte has got into a Cul de sac, and must be destroyed if the Austrian generals manage the matter skilfully. Madame Moreau is enchanting the Americans. Her dancing is said to be superior to any thing ever seen of the sort in the United States. Moreau wears plain clothes and a round hat: he won't come down here, as he says, for fear of embarrassing the Administration. General Miranda has gone on an expedition to South America,[265] as is supposed, and has carried ammunition and men in four ships to revolutionize the Caraccas. He has provided printers and printing presses among other things. General Turreau burst into tears, as is said, on hearing of the battle of Trafalgar....

> *Augustus Foster*
>> *To Lady Elizabeth Foster.*
>>> WASHINGTON, *March* 25, 1806.

Still no packet arrives, and five months are fast going by since the date of your last letter to me. I almost dread its arrival now, and wait for the Post every evening with nearly more fear than hope. Our public news has been so bad that I scarce dare to think what our letters may bring. When such a man as Pitt dies in the full vigour of life, and such campaigns are fought as the one of last winter, one cannot guess what may next happen. However, if I only had letters from you of February in my pocket, I should not grieve much about our National Affairs. We are pretty safe, I think, from French fleets and French invasion. Such men as Lord Grenville and Mr. Fox, I dare say, will not sacrifice our rights, and Alexander may yet find the Usurper a good deal to do in the Levant. Pitt has haunted me ever since his death. I think I see his figure every hour thundering over poor little Addington. At such a distance as this, when one hears of the death of so great a man as he, one really cannot conceive it; it only serves to call him more forcibly to one's mind, and to place him in the strongest point of view in which one has ever seen him. He and Nelson have been indeed great losses to us, and Lord Cornwallis, as Viceroy of India, was surely a loss to us, but to compare small things with great, they say that no man should long be *under* the same valet de chambre, and perhaps it was necessary we should know by proof that our whole dependence was not upon one person, however pre-eminent.... If they make peace, we shall, we must be ruined. Give him a year, 'tis all he wants to fill his dockyards with materials, and our only safeguard will be in jeopardy. We have only now to look to our wooden walls, and I trust they won't be sacrificed. The moment our right arm is bent we are gone...

LINES WRITTEN BY THE EARL OF CARLISLE
ON THE DEATH OF GEORGIANA, DUCHESS OF
DEVONSHIRE, MARCH 30, 1806.

Bright eminence and worth have seemed of late,
For cold extinction to be marked by fate:
Soaring with higher flight, Death wings his way,
And, like the eagle, strikes the noblest prey.
Valour's first-born, lamented Nelson, dies:
Next o'er Pitt's corse we hang with weeping eyes.

Now, at the insatiate Tyrant's savage call,
The most attractive of her Sex must fall.
O! tenderest Parent! O! sincerest Friend!
Can it be Thee, o'er whose pale form we bend;
Thee, whom so late on Health's elastic bound,
We saw diffusing pleasure all around.

Is that the forehead, where each Grace and Muse
Twined their joint garland of a thousand hues?
Are those the eyes which beam'd with vivid sense,
And spoke the soul of pure benevolence?
That the warm breast, where mild Affection chose
To graft on Meekness stern Compassion's rose?

Peace to thy fleeting soul! Tho' here below
Malice at all direct the assassin's blow.
Nor even Thee the accursed fiend should spare,
Yet where All's justice thou hast least to fear,
For leagued with mercy at the Almighty's throne,
Shall Charity unbend the accusing frown,
Sustain thy trembling head, and claim thee for her own.

George Prince of Wales (afterwards King George the Fourth)[266]
To Lady Elizabeth Foster.

Dear Lady Elizabeth,—I am really quite asham'd of intruding upon you and upon the Duke under any circumstances at the present moment, but particularly so when it is respecting a trifle. To take up as little as possible of your time, I will immediately come to the point, and will beg of you to borrow from the Duke for a few days his Collar of the Order of the Garter.

By some misfortune my Brother Augustus cannot find his, and if you will have the goodness to send it to me to Carlton House this evening, I will take care of it and return it when the Trial is over.[267] Forgive me all the trouble I am giving you, and believe me ever, Dearest Lady Elizabeth, most affectionately yours,

GEORGE.
CARLTON HOUSE, *April 28th*, 1806.

The Hon. Mrs. Lamb
To Augustus Foster.

1806.

You must feel so very anxious to know how your dear Mother's health and spirits have borne the dreadful misfortune we all deplore, that I will write to you a line to tell you that she is better than I could have expected, and than her misery seemed to give any hope for, but as to spirits, what, my dear Augustus, can ever restore them since time that soothes and heals common afflictions seems but to add to this? Each new day brings some new proofs of its extent, and how very very irreparable it is. All who knew her loved her, but it was adoration that she inspired to her nearest friends, and thus to have her torn from them, to watch her through a suffering illness and in the awful moments of death, is a lesson so striking, yet so heartbreaking, that we must have sunk under it had not God Almighty supported us through it, and in the height of misery given us strength and resignation to bear it; but I need not and cannot describe to you all that we have gone through, scenes of misery and horror rendered more dreadful by the contrast to a life of happiness, to the thoughtless security of a few weeks past...

Lady Elizabeth Foster
To Augustus Foster.
DEVONSHIRE HOUSE, *May* 18, 1806.

One of the cruel circumstances attending on distance is the unconsciousness of our nearest friends to what is most nearly influencing the happiness or misery of those they love. Thus, my dearest Augustus, I read your three letters, which otherwise would have been delightful to me, with agony of heart. Alas, that friendship which could excite enthusiasm even in an American is lost to me for ever. The recollection alone remains, and regrets, never ceasing regrets, regrets only to be equalled by the angelick, the unequalled qualities of the friend of my heart, my dear, my loved, my adored friend. Frederick wrote to you what I could not. Since then I have lived in a kind of stupor; all seems like a dream; we have never left the house; we live amongst ourselves, so that as yet I am not awake to the certainty of the horrid event. Oh, my dear Augustus, what a blank in my future life! I am and ought to be grateful for the friend that is preserved to me, and for such affectionate sons, but she was the only female friend I ever had. Our hearts were united in the closest bonds of confidence and love, and the charm of her society, which you so well know how to appreciate, could only be equalled by the divine, the truly angelick qualities of her heart and soul. Oh, could you see how sad poor Devonshire House looks. All are well in health.

... I wrote you a journal of all, and my loved friend wrote you a list of the new Administration...

> *Augustus Foster*
> *To Lady Elizabeth Foster.*
> WASHINGTON, *May* 28, 1806.

I thank God that you are well, my ever dearest mother, and I am very much obliged to Frederick for his kind consideration for writing so in the first line of his melancholy letter. Oh, my poor Ma, what a loss, what a dreadful loss! How keenly, how bitterly must you feel, to be severed from such a tie. The sad news reached me almost all at once. I had scarcely read in a paper the day before of her illness, when in another the next day I saw we had lost her for ever. I still had some hopes till Frederick's letter proved it but too true. What a cruel addition to the losses of the last winter! It seems as if we were to be deprived of all that is good and great in our country to prepare us for some heavy calamity. There is no part of this world, I believe, where the angelic Duchess will not be deeply regretted; her kindness and beneficence were wound up with the happiness of so many. Such a high and exalted character, such unbounded nobleness of soul, such excellence of heart, so totally free from all selfishness, and so absorbed in thinking only for the good of others, with every charm and every means to throw lustre on her excellent qualities, will, I fear, never again be met with in the same woman. How kindly she ever treated me, who had no other recommendation to her than that of being son to her dearest friend. She is an angel, my dear mother; you must think of her now as in the enjoyment of the greatest bliss which the most virtuous mortal can be rewarded with in the uncontaminated abode, where your own dear soul will meet with her again. You have seen her suffer under long and dreadful pains before her death. It must surely be a consolation to you that you were with her, and that all the offices of the purest and most unsullied friendship were performed by you from the first to the very last. It must have been a great relief to her to be eased of her cruel sufferings. These considerations will, I trust, enable you to bear up with a fortitude that becomes you. You are too necessary to the happiness of your own and your adopted children, and from such a loss doubly so to the happiness of us all, not to make it our common cause to solicit you to bear up. I hope and trust Frederic will write to me by Merchant Vessels frequently to say how you are. How sadly I regret the distance I am from you at such a moment, when I might be of some little comfort to you. My only consolation is that you have Caroline, who understands you, with you, and Frederick, who is ever affectionate. Poor Lady Harriet! she has strong claims on you for your taking care of yourself.... Confide in me, my dearest Ma. The affliction you must be suffering is my greatest anxiety.

> *Lady Elizabeth Foster*
> *To Augustus Foster.*
> DEVONSHIRE HOUSE, *June* 6, 1806.

... We try to be grateful for the blessings left, but yet

> My heart so late of many joys possessed
> Laments for many lost and trembles for the rest.

Take care of yourself therefore, my dearest Augustus, for my sake. I really have suffered so much lately that I feel as if I had scarcely strength for anxiety. I look to your return with great delight, and hope the period is not very distant. I have already told you that I had written to you constantly, and from December that we came to town had taken pleasure in writing you journals that you might know exactly how things went on and the opinions and expectations of the day—all during Pitt's illness and the forming of the new Administration, and my beloved friend had written to you the list of the new Ministers and Mr. Fox's message about you.... As to the present moment I can say but little, for I have had no heart to attend to politicks, or to see those could tell them to me.... Russia seems more inclined to peace, and has given up the Cattaro to Austria to be yielded to France.[268] Sweden is chevaleresque, and is worthy of admiration. England still triumphant at sea, and the publick just now very curious about Miranda, so pray write to me all about him. Lord Elgin, Lord Yarmouth, and Col. Abercromie are come home. My brother supports Government, which is delightful to me; he approves Mr. Wyndham's plan, and meant to speak in support of it.... I do not wonder at all you felt about Pitt's death. I had written to you Mr. Fox's expression about that event. He said, "It feels as if something was missing in the world". Oh Heavens! how truly may that be said of my dear, dear Georgiana, who ever filled such a space as she did in society? To whom was she as she was to me? ... I have not seen Lord Aberdeen since my misfortune, but I hear that it is thought that the trial of Lord Melville will end well. The day is not known, but I suppose that it will be in about ten days. He bears up amazingly well...

Lady Elizabeth Foster
To Augustus Foster.
DEVONSHIRE HOUSE, *July* 2, 1806.

... It is believed that there is a negotiation going on between this country and France, but all is kept a profound secret. Meanwhile several of the persons that were detained have returned to England. The next thing that occupies the publick mind is the affairs of the Princess of Wales, and Sir I. or Lady Douglas has deposed on oath assertions of her ill conduct. The Prince told the King, and the King ordered a committee of the Privy Council to examine the evidence. Lord Grenville, Spencer, the Chancellor, and Lord Ellenborough are the persons so empowered. The report is to be given in to-day.... The Session is now nearly over. Scotland is, I believe, henceforth to have her juries and decide her own causes. Irish Elections are to be put on the same footing as the English ones, and other regulations of that kind, which tend to civilize the country and give it a little more political morality. To-day, also, we are to know who goes to India. The day before yesterday the Duke dined with Charles Fox, who was very cheerful, and Lady Bessborough and I have generally gone in the evening. Never was any thing more perfect than all Lord Grenville's conduct towards Fox, and as to the question which in one of your letters you say is put of who is first: Is Fox under Lord Grenville or Lord Grenville under Fox? I really believe their great and good minds despise the form. They have united for the publick service and act cordially together...

Lady Elizabeth Foster
To Augustus Foster.
DEVONSHIRE HOUSE, *July* 3, 1806.

... Mr. Fox continues mending. The Duke of Devonshire dined with him the other day, and Fox sent to him again for to-day. The rumour of the day is peace, and Lord Holland to go to Paris. The truer are Lord Minto to India and Mr. T. Grenville to the Board of Controul. Mr. Erskine does at last go to America, so the speculating Lord Selkirk you are rid of....[269] Lord Ossulston I really believe very soon will marry Corise. As to poor Devonshire House, we have as yet gone no where, seen no body but the nearest friends. I have had no heart, no courage, to do any thing, nor will you be surprised at it. The constant charm of my life is gone. She doubled every joy, lessened every grief. Her society had an attraction I never met with in any other being. Her love for me was really "passing the love of woman "—povero cor mio quanto hai sofferto.... As to the affair of the Princess of Wales which the papers are full of, the report of the Committee was given in to the Council yesterday, but it is said will not be made publick. It is a strange business altogether, but I can't believe her really guilty. You tell me nothing about Miranda, yet he excites publick curiosity to the greatest degree. Lord St. Vincent called on me yesterday, and went to Portsmouth to-day. He said he would not come on shore again till there was a peace or change of Ministers, and then he would cut them....

> *Lady Elizabeth Foster*
> *To Augustus Foster.*
> DEVONSHIRE HOUSE, *July* 9, 1806.

Thank you, my dearest child, for your anxiety about me. No wonder that you thought I could not support myself under such a blow, but God is merciful and gives a strength we know not we possess. How I went through it, as my angel friend herself said, or how I am alive to tell it, I know not—such a loss! Oh, Dearest Augustus, She was the charm of my existence, my constant support in all my sorrows, the doubler and sharer of every joy. There is no giving you any idea of the three weeks we passed, or rather the fortnight, for the first week she recovered so much I thought not of danger, though Farquhar from the first was uneasy. I scarcely left her room or her bed, yet she was almost in a continual lethargy; still almost to the last she knew her sister and me, and her last words were to tell me she did not mind it. Oh, heavens! my dear Augustus, how is it that one goes through certain trials that but to think of at a distance seems impossible to bear. We felt stunned and unable to conceive what had passed. I am told it is the case always in great and deep afflictions. The Duke and I were saying one day it appeared to us like a dream. On saying this to Farquhar he told us it was always so. We have as yet seen scarcely any body; we have lived with each other; travelling was impossible on the Duke's account, who was not quite well, and wished to remain in London; it was equally so to me to whom she had left all her papers and affairs, and this trust, so sad and sacred, still occupies almost all my mornings. It is, I feel it, a comfort as you say, to have been with her, to have watched her looks, her words, to have been there, as I was, hanging over her in breathless anxiety, for in each interval of stupor there she saw me; but it was heart-rending, it was agony, and it seems to have shut my heart to all joy. Yet the interest of my dear children, their happiness and welfare, must still give me pleasure and all the happiness I can know.

I feel by your letter all that you are to me. Dearest Caro has been to me what you wished her. Fred really overcame himself with sorrow. Dear Clifford has come to support and cheer us all a little; poor Hartington said it could alone give him a feeling of pleasure at being again in Devonshire House,[270] and he has been much better since; poor Lady Bessborough is, as you may suppose, wretched; Georgiana and Harriet are indeed deserving of all one's compassion. Georgiana is just recovered from her lying in, and looks well. The kindness and feeling of Lord Morpeth I can never forget. You never saw such a scene as Devonshire House. The anxiety of people was extreme; the crowds that inquired immense, and the silence and solitude of the succeeding one horrid. Hartington I had sent for; he shewed a manliness beyond his age, and saw his adored mother every day, even afterwards; so did I! and I am alive to tell it you.

I do indeed trust that I shall meet her again in "another and a better world" as the Stranger says. Never, I believe, were two hearts and minds so united; never did two people think and feel so alike. She is so present to me, and I am so constantly occupied for her that I feel as if she was absent on a journey, and I catch myself saying "I'll tell her this", nor feel all my loss till some person speaking or some circumstance makes the whole rush upon me with fatal conviction of the truth....

We are all in sad anxiety about Mr. Fox. He has a tendency to dropsy, which is alarming at his age and with his size; he has been better, but was worse yesterday. The Duke dines often with him, and is very uneasy, I think, about him. It would be too shocking to have him wrested from us just as his wonderful abilities were best calculated to do good. He has been too ill for me to speak to him latterly about you, and indeed I had so firm a reliance on what he said to me that I have felt convinced he only waited for an opportunity of doing what was for your advantage. If we lose him we have nothing left but secondary characters. Except D.D. I know not one very pre-eminent one. However, there is no cause for despair, and I will try to hope for the best ... I am not ill, I do assure you. I go on occupying myself with her affairs, and in all I can doing what I hope would please her dear Spirit if it can look down upon us, and may we meet never to part....

Augustus Foster
        To Lady Elizabeth Foster.
                                    WASHINGTON, *July* 20, 1806.

Your affecting letter I have just received, and shall ever preserve it as a last memento of the truest friendship that ever existed.... Who has a claim to the attention of every body if you have not, who are so considerate about every body? She was indeed to you what she was to nobody else she has left behind her, and by none is the cruel loss so fully estimated as by you; of this I am sure. Thank Heaven you had so many about you who could feel with you, and that you were able to support one another....

Frederick Foster
        To Augustus Foster.
                                    LONDON, *July* 30, 1806.

... I am sorry to tell you that Fox is still very ill, and I fear that his recovery is very doubtful. It is dropsy, and I am afraid not alone, but he has great strength of constitution and his lungs appear to be sound, so that we can't help entertaining hopes of his recovery. I must think that it would be a most amazing loss, and it's really frightful to see almost all the talent, genius, and worth of the country dying before one's eyes—Nelson, Pitt, Cornwallis, and our beloved, amiable Duchess. Heavens! what a change since this time last year; you will scarcely know the country at your return....

                                    August 1st.

Fox still continues very ill, but Lady Holland told me to-day that he was better, and that the doctors had entered upon a new system. In short, they have hopes and no more. Fox is *really* better....

Augustus Foster
        To Lady Elizabeth Foster.
                    LANCASTER, PENNSYLVANIA, *July* (?), 1806.

... I thank you sincerely. for your details about that Heavenly Woman, and the more so as I know what it must have cost you to write them. I should be sorry indeed if Mr. Fox was to be wrested from us, and particularly now that he is engaged in negotiations for Peace. His great and enlarged mind is necessary to enable us to find out our real interests at this gloomy period. I don't, however, quite agree in our having none but secondary characters to take his place. Lord Grenville, our English Cato, and Lord Howick, I think we might with confidence rely on....

LINES BY GEORGIANA, DUCHESS OF DEVONSHIRE ON THE BUST OF CHARLES FOX, AT WOOBURN.[271]

Here 'midst the friends he loves the Man behold
In Truth unshaken and in Virtue bold,
Whose ardent Zeal and uncorrupted mind,
Dares to assert the Freedom of Mankind.
For whilst contending factions raged afar,
And fell Ambition spread the flames of War,
Fearless of blame and eloquent to save,
'Twas He, 'twas Fox, the warning council gave,
Oppos'd, but ah, how Vain! the Tide of blood,
And to the Nations as a Sea Mark stood!
Yet still propitious might his voice avail,
And happy Realms returning freedom hail.
His Wisdom still might bid fierce discord cease,
And give the world humanity and Peace.
But should he fail, our gratefull sons will here
Their tribute pay, regret, admire, revere,
Uphold his worth, bear witness to his fame,
And in their annals proudly boast his name.

Lady Elizabeth Foster
　To Augustus Foster.
　　　　　DEVONSHIRE HOUSE, *September*, 1806.

I have scarcely courage to write to you, and to announce the great, the irreparable loss which the World has sustained—the sad, sad loss to friends more attached than almost ever man was blessed with. Good God! what a change in England since you left it. It is frightful to think of, and makes me tremble for those precious lives which still must attach me to life. The probability, however, is that I shall not have that misfortune added to the rest; the uncertainty of my own health may secure me from that. Do not, however, take any alarm, my dear child, from this expression, for I really am pretty well, but these events make one low. Nothing can give an idea of the anxiety about Mr. Fox, for though his health was seriously affected, he had recovered so much strength at Chiswick, and was so happy here, that it was impossible not to flatter oneself that he might yet recover a considerable degree of health. The change was sudden and dreadfull; he had slept pretty well, was cheerfull, went to look at his favourite pictures in the drawing-room, and returned to his room to dress and go out; his secretary was reading to him; he suddenly fell back; an extreme weakness came on which, with the interval of one day, when hopes were revived, continued from Monday till Saturday, when he died.[272] He had his senses to the last, knew his situation. Mrs. Fox asked him if he would have prayers read, and he said, "Yes, my love". Whilst they were reading he joined his hands. He gave ample directions to poor Lord Holland; to Mrs. Fox he turned with unceasing tenderness in his countenance, and an hour before his death said to her, "I die happy, but I pity you". Most of his intimate friends were at Chiswick. It was a touching scene to see all those men unable to suppress their grief, and careless to conceal their tears. How they can attend the funeral I know not; it is to be the tenth of October, and I own I dread it for the Duke.

October 1st.

... The Paris papers say that Jerome is made a Prince, and divorced that he may marry a Princess of Wirtemberg. Poor Madame Jerome! Can it be true also that Moreau is returned to Lisbon; it would seem very imprudent. The capture of Buenos Ayres has made a great sensation here, and the treasure has been lodged at the Bank with great show and pomp. I hope we shall not lightly give up that settlement or Miranda.... Town will be full for a few days on account of the funeral of our loved Patriot. Heavens, that the same year should have witnessed four of such persons! all, all pre-eminent, for my loved friend was pre-eminent in beauty, goodness, and all that can attach or attract. May God preserve those we love, and are still so necessary to our happiness....

> *Lady Elizabeth Foster*
> > *To Augustus Foster.*
> > > DEVONSHIRE HOUSE, *October* 28, 1806.

I have much such accounts to give you as I sent last year. Scarcely had Lord Morpeth reached Erfurt when he found that the Queen and the Ministers were obliged to fly for safety; of course he did the same, and with great difficulty got back to Weimar and Brunswick. The beaten army were flying in all directions,[273] and he was obliged to walk 14 miles, and then to get a sort of cart for the rest of the journey. At Brunswick they confirmed the terrible tidings, and the Dutch papers are since come with horrid details, such as 200 pieces of cannon, five or six of their best generals wounded and made prisoners, and, in short, unless it is true that Hohenlohe defeated the right wing of the French,[274] I don't see what is to enable them to make a stand; it is too shocking, really.

29th.

There was an account that the Prussians fought from three in the morning till five in the evening, and yet retreated in good order; now the loss of the French must have been very great also, and if the Duke of Brunswick is not too much wounded to direct the retreat,[275] perhaps they may still make some resistance. Lord Morpeth is, I believe, to proceed to head quarters, wherever they are. This is not pleasant to dear Georgiana, who is, of course, very anxious. At home the elections are going on all over the country. Sir Francis Burdett has put in an advertisement that has offended all parties but a few Horne Tookists,[276] and I believe he will lose his election. T. Sheridan will lose his at Stafford.[277] Sheridan is opposed by Paul,[278] but I do not suppose he can succeed. Fred Ponsonby stands for Kilkenny. Duncannon refused, and the Duke brings in Lord Ossulston for Knaresborough. There is a Mr. Faukes who stands for Yorkshire, who Lord Fitzwilliam is anxious should succeed. He is a man of large property, and of uncommon eloquence...

Nov. 3.

Lord Morpeth is returned, and I am afraid Bonaparte is master of Berlin and Potsdam, and of Sans Souci. What times! Lord Morpeth went to Erfurt and Weimar, but was forced to return after the battle of the 14th had proved so disastrous. He over took Haugnitz and Luchesini, who were flying also. The King is gone to Custrin, and the Queen has joined him there. Where will all this end?

Augustus Foster
   To Lady Elizabeth Foster.
               WASHINGTON, *Nov.* 27, 1806.

... Madame J. Bonaparte is in great distress at Jerome's divorce. She goes no longer out, though just before he had sent her a great many presents and desired her to go to all amusements. She lives at Baltimore, 45 miles from here. The ill-natured Americans don't pity her. They say she deserved it for her vanity, and yet not one but had done the same. The French Minister speaks of her as Mlle. Patterson. When Jerome first landed she declared she would have him, and that she had rather be Madame Jer. B. one year, though she was to be nothing afterwards, than marry anyone else. She did not know she was so near the real event. Moreau is in New York, and is said to be about going westward. Miranda is an old woman. A new character is busy in the Western World—Mr. Burr,[279] the late Vice President of the United States, of whom you probably will hear more. The public papers are full of him. No less than a separation of the Union is said to be his object. Thus for the last thirty years Revolution will seem to have been brought on by Revolution, till there remains nothing to revolutionize. The hope of Peace, I suppose, is buried with Mr. Fox. To have been present at his last hours, to have almost caught the last breath of so great a man expiring in the very house where you were, must have been very affecting to you. It is melancholy to see our greatest men cut off in such numbers just when we have most occasion for them. However, the spirit of the nation is still high, and I am convinced that we have more men of integrity and talent in prominent situations to boast of than there are in all the world besides. Here we are feared and respected more than the rabble Republicans choose to believe or allow of; but in fact a mere face of anger is all we need shew to these Democrats, for a long time to come.

Lady Elizabeth Foster
To Augustus Foster.
DEVONSHIRE HOUSE, *December* 2, 1806.

Frederick tells me that he has written all the great events to you, and I have been doubly glad of it, as, from an unavoidable association of ideas, I have felt lower than usual; the beginning of winter, so different to every other; the thousand, thousand circumstances that recall the daily occurrences of so many years past; the blank, the sad blank, now left to me; all this presses upon me, and has made me unfit for writing my dispatch to you. But you, of all people, almost understand me, and know how to feel for me.

This year's events have surpassed the last. No person even knows where the poor King of Prussia and his beautiful Queen now are. If you had been told when you was there that Bonaparte would have been in the Palace at Berlin, possessed of that and all that country, how little you would have believed it. He is said to be beyond the Vistula, I mean the King of Prussia, and that an army of Russians is hastily approaching; but meanwhile Bonaparte will give a King to Poland, and perhaps march on to Petersburgh. He is said to have asked for ships of the line of the Danes, and that the Sound should be shut against us. This, I believe, our Lord Nelson has proved they can't do; but indeed the state of things is terrible. However, I hope that we shall extend our conquests in the new world, and so keep a balance.

Parliament meets the 15th, and they are to have no holidays at Christmas. Lord Morpeth is come in for Cumberland and W. Howard for Morpeth. William Lamb moves the address. I should think that he would do it well, but Caroline will be very nervous. Fred Ponsonby is come in for Kilkenny. Duncannon idly refused.... The clamour of the hustings is all against Sheridan, and for Paull; he came here to-day, and was very low. I have the promise of several votes for him. The Duke makes his steward exert himself. Even Sir S. Hood is unpopular. Duncannon was to have been proposed for Middlesex, but it was thought of too late, and Mr. Mellish stands.

4th, Midnight.

Sheridan gives up, and Tierney. Sheridan was struck at and wounded yesterday evening. Mr. Rhodes' son defended him, and knocked the man down. He can't stand this unpopularity, and means to give up. They wanted Duncannon in for it, but it is too expensive.

A messenger and a Dr. Brown are come from the King of Prussia, and they report that the King is in a strong position behind the Oder. The King sent word he was as well as under his misfortunes he could be. The army, about 20,000 strong, are there also. It is said Luchesini went to solicit peace, and that Bonaparte would not hear of it; that the Duke of Brunswick sent to ask the neutrality of his country, and that Bonaparte answered that he did not recognize such a person as the Duke of Brunswick, and had ordered him to be seized wherever he was found. This ferocious answer has obliged the poor Duke of Brunswick to fly, and he was going from Hamburgh to Denmark. I wish he was coming to England, that every attention and respect might be shown him. Lord Morpeth offered to go again, and was the person they would have sent again, but they think it best to send a military person, and Lord Hutchinson goes. It is truly anxious and interesting....

Lady Elizabeth Foster
 To Ausustus Foster.

December, 1806.

... One line only. They talked here yesterday, some company who dined at Devonshire House, of a plan of sequestration of foreign property in retaliation for the British seized at Hamburgh. hope it won't be. I would not have a stain on the public faith for worlds of gold. Let us conquer Spanish America with all my heart, but all good faith in publick as in private actions. Say nothing of it unless you hear it elsewhere, and I hope it won't be so. The Duchess of Brunswick is, it is said, out of her senses. No wonder; his death,[280] poor man, was fortunate for himself, for his life must have been misery. The Duke goes with me to Chiswick to-day which hurries me so. Poor Chiswick, Chiswick, where my angel friend delighted to live, and where that great man Charles Fox breathed his last! How has this world been impoverished!

Augustus Foster
 To Lady Elizabeth Foster.

WASHINGTON, *Dec.* 29, 1806.

... Buenos Ayres I fear,[281] is retaken. What will Sir H. Popham be thought of now that the Spaniards have felt their strength. What 5000 men might have done a few months back with ease will, I am afraid, be very problematical. He had good information as to the state of the place, as his success proved, but to retain a town of 70,000 inhabitants required more than 1500 men. Miranda, whom you seem to be anxious about, is and was to all appearance when here a mere old woman of a man, as I believe I wrote long ago to you.

A man of superior abilities is plotting Revolution in the western part of these States, and occupies very much the public mind here. Colonel Burr is a notoriously profligate man, but of very great address. He has chosen a singularly situated country as the scene of his ambitious projects, and I suppose we shall soon see their development or confusion. The public rumours are that he is engaged in a plot to sever the whole country west of the Alleghany mountains, in extent near 3000 miles, from Lake Michigan to New Orleans, from the rest of the Union, and to form an expedition for the plunder of Mexico, which is a City of 130,000 inhabitants, defenceless, and in one of the finest countries in the world. The Western Country contains not above a few hundred thousand inhabitants, and those scattered in swamps and villages. New Orleans, the largest town, has about 8000 inhabitants, but it has the singular advantage of being, as it were, the key to all the countries connected with the Mississippi, Ohio, Missouri, &c., the only outlet for the commerce of those immense territories, and bids fair to be one of the very finest Capitals in the Universe. Immense emigration annually takes place to those Countries from the Atlantic States. A Senator of the United States, who travelled last year in Ohio, told me that in two days he had counted 105 waggons, each containing a family, on their way to settle in the woods of the State of Ohio. They were chiefly families from beyond the Hudson river. The Americans give me the idea of Locusts. They ruin the land as they pass on, and are eternally changing their soil. The mode of cultivation among them exhausts the earth, and they must shift their crops every now and then into timber land in order to have them good. Mr. Burr was Vice-President of the United States or President of the Senate when I arrived. It was he who killed Mr. Hamilton in a duel which was detailed in all the English papers a little time before I left England. It will be a sad thing if he succeeds, for the whole Country will then fall in pieces. I have written thus much, as you will very likely be interested about him from the accounts you will probably see in the papers. The Government are taking measures, and will probably prevent his conspiracy from going on, and save these States from the horrors of a revolution. Nothing has yet been done openly by Mr. Burr.

Lady Elizabeth Foster
To Augustus F.

DEVONSHIRE HOUSE, *Jan.* 6, 1807.

… We had yesterday our great debate on the negotiation.[282] It was a curious one, from two circumstances. Lord Yarmouth and Lord Howick spoke in direct contradiction to one another, and Mr. Whitbread thought fit to express his opinion that peace might have been made. Lord Howick opened his speech admirably, and his reply, I hear, was excellent. It was to a malicious, odious speech of Mr. Perceval,[283] and I dare say his Hotspur blood was boiling in his veins. I long to have you acquainted with Lord Howick, and to be employed by him; he is a true Foxite. The debate lasted till near five in the morning. We supped at Caroline Lamb's at Whitehall, and about half after one Lord Morpeth, Lord Granville, Lord Ossulston, and William Lamb came from the House, the debate then going on. Fred Ponsonby took the oaths, and when the Speaker asked him the name of the estate which was to qualify him he could not tell it, which occasioned a laugh.[284] … I have been twice to the Opera. Catalani is as near perfection as any thing can be,[285] not quite so touching or so handsome as Grassini,[286] but sufficiently so to please, and she is as wonderful and more so than Mrs. Billington.[287] ... I know how you will feel it, coming to this dear house, where *she*, my angel friend, used ever to receive you as if you were her son. I believe sometimes the greatness of the blow prevents our having the power of dwelling upon it....

I send you the French publication of the State papers. It differs from ours in several things. They omit the extract from the Emperor's speech, and they put in a great deal of Talleyrand's answer to Mr. Fox. I suppose you have the negotiation as published here. A rumour prevails that Buenos Ayres is retaken, and though an expedition is gone which may take it again, yet it would cause dreadful loss to the merchants here; it would be bad, too, for poor Sir Home Popham.

Night.

Fred Ponsonby has given us a very good account of the debate; he is in raptures with Lord Howick, and I never heard anything so liberal as his conduct. Perceval in the last debate had remarked upon some private letter of Fox's which could not, Ministers said, be shewn; well, Lord Howick, as soon as he went home, sent Perceval that letter, which he owned could not be shewn to the House. Could anything be more liberal? Yet Perceval last night began again as though he had not seen that letter, and with base insinuations. Lord Howick, almost trembling with rage, vindicated his lost friend, and reminded Perceval that he had sent him the papers, which he had refused the House. The House quite murmured at Perceval's conduct, and Canning was most liberal in his praise of Lord Howick's conduct and nobleness of mind. The papers have given the debate wretchedly....

> *The Earl of Aberdeen*
> *To Augustus Foster.*

THE PRIORY, *Jan.* 13, 1807.

Dear Augustus,—Although I am quite persuaded that there is no chance of my silence, however long, being interpreted by you to signify in the slightest degree intentional neglect, yet I will honestly mention a few facts, although they tend very little to a justification. Mr. Pitt's death quite rendered me incapable at the usual time; the poor Duchess soon followed, and then came the anxieties of Lord Melville's trial. On his acquittal I should indeed have written. The summer passed I do not know how in Scotland, and the dissolution of Parliament gave me full employment. You may have heard of my success,[288] which was somewhat remarkable, being the only candidate who came in against the exertions of Government.

Very little has as yet been done in Parliament, but we shall shortly be very active; there will be motions of Inquiry on several subjects, and from all we hear it is very probable the late treaty between this country and America will furnish matter, for, although the particulars are still unknown, it is by no means popular, the general opinion being that we shall be found to have made too great concessions; indeed, what has transpired tends to confirm this.

The final discussions respecting the slave trade will come on in about a fortnight; no doubt is entertained of the abolition being carried, which, I should think, would materially affect the Americans one way or other.

I give you joy of a new Emperor in your neighbourhood; do on your return take a view of Christophe and his capital. Your old friend Jerome is acting a considerable part in Poland, where matters are very near a crisis. Bonaparte is in a most perilous situation. If the Russians continue wise he cannot hold out till spring, and there is a fair chance of his destruction. Reports of sickness in his army, though probably much exaggerated, are believed. Some faint hopes are entertained of Austria. No one apprehends much from the declaration of a blockade. You cannot easily imagine how great my pleasure was on your brother's telling me the other day that you were coming home. My desire of seeing you again has been now so much increased by the time of your absence, in addition to the great distance which separated you from us. When you return I will not say that you are to find me with a son and heir, but in two or three weeks something will certainly be produced, but of what gender it would not be so easy to determine. Pray let me hear from you about the reality of your motions, and believe me, most affectionately,

ABERDEEN.

Lady Elizabeth Foster
To Augustus Foster.
DEVONSHIRE HOUSE, *Jan.* 21, 1807.

... The papers are filled merely with rumours, first of a Russian victory, and then of Buenos Ayres being taken and not being taken, so that bets are nearly even on the subject. Ministers have been abused for sending the telegraphic account of its recapture, but how could they do otherwise. However, it has caused great alarm in the city and provincial towns. The reports are various, too, about the disposition of America towards England....

Caroline Lamb is with child, but her uncertain health prevents one's knowing what is her state, or almost what to hope.

> *Lady Elizabeth Foster*
> > *To Augustus Foster.*
> > > DEVONSHIRE HOUSE, *March* 3, 1807.

Corisande is already very big—come ti sta it cuore? placido e sicuro io spero. We have nearly finished the grand work of abolition of the Slave Trade; it was carried 283 to 16. The remaining discussions are merely for compensation and such things. Yesterday an uncommon degree of anxiety and curiosity was excited by Paull's Petition against Sheridan,[289] which went to accusing him of tampering with the witness, but such a set as Paull brought in, so low, so vulgar, so contradictory in their accounts, that it turned the whole thing in Sheridan's favor, and if nothing unforeseen happens, two days hence he will be triumphant. There is a report of the French having beat the Russians. This is a sad disappointment, but it is also said that the Turks have made peace again with the Russians, so there is bad and good. We have a squadron opposite the Seraglio....

> *Augustus Foster*
> > *To Lady Elizabeth Foster.*
> > > WASHINGTON, *March* 31, 1807.

... The President means to retire after the next year. He is wonderfully popular at present, and may do nearly what he likes. Burr, the conspirator, is arrested, and to be tried at Richmond, in Virginia. His grand plot ended in the seizure of his nine boats and fifty men and boys. He was betrayed, as is said, by some of his accomplices, and as he had assembled them from amongst the ruined and the unprincipled, it was what he might expect. The opposition in England seem miserably weak in their attacks. Lord Castlereagh's argument that if France included America in her Decree, England should punish her, and if America was not included in the Decree, that she should be equally punished for connivance, was not lost here. To advance such nonsense can proceed from nothing but impatience at being out of office; it cannot be surely from any sound principles of opposition. Were I an oppositionist before, the shallowness visible in such paltry attacks would induce me to cling to the Government. Lord Hawkesbury seems more manly. Canning is all froth and smoke and noise. I cannot see the statesman in his speeches. His wit and stories and pleasantry seem to me misplaced in debating gravely upon great National questions. Lord Howick's speech is indeed very manly and dignified, just what the organ of a great Nation, such as, I trust, we still consider ourselves to be, should be....

> *Lady Elizabeth Foster*
>   *To Augustus Foster.*
>   DEVONSHIRE HOUSE, *May* 6, 1807.

We are in the midst of elections again, and London scarcely possesses a Beau worth speaking to. What is worse, the Ministers have raised a cry about Popery, which has taken possession of the lower class, and blinded them to their best interests. I think it an unworthy measure of the Ministers, and one they will some day repent of. In Derbyshire they told Lord George C. they would vote for him, but they would worship no golden images; in Liverpool Roscoe has given up the contest. A friend of his was on horseback, and a man from the opposite crowd rushed out and stabbed the horse of the other to the heart: the man was hurt, and another wounded. At St. Albans, where Duncannon is candidate, they say it is a pity so good a lady as Lady Spencer should wish to bring the Pope to England; it is really shocking to see Religion made such a tool of, and the King's speech an electioneering cry. Your brother is at St. Albans canvassing for Duncannon; so is George Lamb.... You will see by the papers Sir F. Burdett's duel with Mr. Paull. It has hurt Paull's interest, and I believe he has no chance of succeeding for Westminster, but that Sir F. Burdett will come in with acclamation. Sheridan has played his cards ill. He can't attempt Westminster,[290] and having forsaken Stafford before, he now only comes in for a borough in the Prince's interest. His overweening vanity has been his ruin. Pray read Lord Grenville's letter to the Society for propagating the Christian Religion; it is reckoned a very fair one.

... We have failed at Constantinople, and the negotiation seems to have been sadly mismanaged. There should be no threatening or bullying, but when anchored, like Nelson, close to the walls of the Enemy's Capital, you can destroy it, but to menace and not do it is sad business.

Lady Aberdeen is recovered in great beauty from her lying in. Lord Grenville goes to Russia as soon as his election is over. I am afraid Duncannon will lose his.

Lady Elizabeth Foster
To Augustus Foster.

DEVONSHIRE HOUSE, *Oct.* 18, 1807.

... Your friend Merry is gone, as I told you, to Copenhagen, but I believe we must make up our minds to have the Danes our enemies, nor should I much regret it. The quantity of stores seem to indicate most forcibly for what reason they were collected, and their own conduct to Hamburgh in 1801 takes from them the title of an innocent and unoffending people, since with far less pretext they did by Hamburgh what we have done by them. I hope Russia is favourable to us. The Country certainly is, but Alexander has been duped by Bonaparte, and given up his conquests just as he had nearly destroyed the Turks. The fate of Portugal is at present the prominent interest. Suza told Mr. Motteux that he believed that his Government meant to go to South America, and that six sail of the line were to sail from Plymouth to escort them; but people still think that they will make their peace. How extraordinary it would be if they should migrate to the Brazils! At home party is likely to be violent and Ministers secure, since the success of the Baltic expedition. The Prince has given up politicks, is good friends with the King, and lives but for Lady Hertford. C'est vrai je t'assure; à 50 ans près elle a captivé le Prince. Il ne vit, ne respire que pour elle et par elle; la ci-devant arnie est inquiète et triste. Je la plains, car c'est une bonne personne qui n'a jamais abusé de son pouvoir; as to the Duchess of Brunswick, you hear no more of her than if she was in Holstein.

Lady Elizabeth Foster
To Augustus Foster.

CHISWICK, *Jan.* 1, 1808.

... Nothing but Spain hardly is talked or thought of. The moment is to us interesting beyond all former periods, as besides the great interest which every body feels about the Spaniards, the having an English Army now actually joined, and with, and ready to co-operate with them, brings the war home to every body's feelings. I had letters from Penn to-night, which state that Opadaca had accounts of Madrid having resisted for three days. The French were repulsed over and over, and lost a great many men. Ch. and Morla retreated with the regulars, who with Castanos,[291] it is hoped, will make a strong army. From Galicia you will see accounts are every day expected of an action. In the English army, of persons whom we all know, are two Cavendishes, three Bentincks, Fred Howard, and though last not least in interest, Corise's brother. The Duke of Rutland's two brothers also are there, and, in short, many of our English nobility. Lord Morpeth is in a state of great nervousness about his brother, and, indeed, the moment is a most anxious one...

Lady Elizabeth Foster
    To Augustus Foster.

CHISWICK, *Nov.* 9, 1808.

... We are all struck with the style of Bonaparte's speech to the Legislative Body and of their reply. They express a kind of foreboding of ill which, if not dictated by himself as a loophole to him, would have made him angry.

10*th.*

I have just seen two very interesting letters of Mr. Gell's, and he confirms all my hopes. The report of to-night is that Austria has declared war, and that Bonaparte is returned to Paris, but this I can scarcely believe. Blake is said to have had a sharp engagement with Ney,[292] and that the latter retreated eight leagues. How I long to hear of Vittoria or Pampluna being taken or some of the strong passes of the Pyrenees.

Lady Elizabeth Foster
    To Augustus Foster.

CHISWICK, *Nov.* 28, 1808.

... I have had little heart or pleasure in writing latterly, as our dear Spaniards have met with sad reverses. I hope, however, that all may be retrieved, and since our troops are gone, that we may turn again the tide of affairs. We have now been a terrible length of time without hearing, and that is always, I think, a bad sign. Oh, dear, it is too hard really, and when one sees the nook into which they were driven, I could sit down and cry to see the strides that they have made towards Madrid again. Still, however, if the Spaniards bear being beat they will ultimately conquer. I think they must. You have, I hope, arrived to hear of some advantages gained by the Swedes, who certainly are the next most interesting people.

Lady Elizabeth Foster
   To Augustus Foster.

CHISWICK, *December* 7, 1808.

I had hoped to have something favourable to send you, my dearest Augustus, regarding Spain, but all is anxiety, and to a great degree doubt in that quarter; yet I hope still, so does Lady Melbourne, so does, which is better worth attending to, General Ferguson. Blake, it is certain, has shewed great skill, and his army great courage and steadiness, and if this spirit continues I have no doubt of the result. Bonaparte has made some of his rapid movements, but I do not think that he has gone on with a pas de géant as he used to do. Never, however, was there greater anxiety felt than now, for it is supposed that he means to push forward in order to prevent the junction of our armies, and this may expose both to be attacked by a very superior force. Lord Morpeth is very anxious about his brother, who is with Baird.

8th.

I had better send this off, for bad news comes so quick now that the sooner it goes the better. Our dear Spaniards fight bravely, but I fear that skill and numbers are on the side of the French. The detested Bonaparte has advanced, and meanwhile has directed a blow against Castanos, which, I fear, has been successful. They still hold firm at Madrid, and it is said that General Hope's Brigade has reached the Escurial, and has joined the army of defence for Madrid, but will they be able to stop Bonaparte's career? Oh, dear Augustus, what a sad reverse, and what reason one had to dread the arrival in Spain of that Tyrant....

Lady Elizabeth Foster
   To Augustus Foster.

CHISWICK, *Dec.* 10, 1808.

... I trust that there are good hopes about Finland; that the brave Swedes may resist the barbarous Russians. If Turkey makes peace with us perhaps they may make a powerful diversion and occupy the Russian troops. How you will grieve over the dear Spaniards. God knows what will be done if yet they can make a stand, but next to the misery which they are exposed to, one feels for the National disgrace to us of boasting for three months of the great armed force we send to their assistance, and then these armies retreating without firing a gun in their defence. I can't bear to think of it. The only accounts received have been from General Baird.[293] He mentions Sir J. Moore sending him word:[294] his account from Madrid was that Castanos had been entirely defeated and his army dispersed. In this dilemma it was supposed that the Central Government would move to Toledo. General Hope was said to be at the Escurial, and that Moore, who had separated himself from his artillery, had ordered Baird to fall back on Vigo. Think of leaving Romana and his army to the mercy of Bonaparte; this cannot surely be. No, though we are tardy and fools in the art of war compared with Bonaparte, I am sure we shall not do a dishonourable thing. I understand from G. Lamb, who came this evening, that more troops are going out to Portugal. There we are to make a stand, and to act again in spring if possible, and, I hope, preserve even now the south of Spain.

> *Lady Elizabeth Foster*
> *To Augustus Foster.*
>
> CHISWICK, *Dec.* 20, 1808.

I see that Liberty is not more befriended in your part of the world by fortune than she has been in the South. Why despotism and oppression are thus everywhere to succeed I know not, but I trust that we may yet see Liberty triumph again in Finland and in Spain.... I hear that there are hopes of some stand being still to be made, and that Moore is concentrating his forces. God only knows what will be the result; we must hope for the best; and I suppose that Bonaparte does not think himself quite secure by his ordering so many more troops.

> *23rd.*

... More troops are going, and if we send at all we should certainly send largely. We fight and dispute: I mean Lady Bessborough and me. Some accuse generals, others ministers. Some say Spanish enthusiasm is less, but if it is it is our fault, who have not yet fired one gun in their defence except at Rosas, and even that we have allowed to be taken. However, I am not so much in suspicion of ministers' want of activity as Moore. He seems to be over cautious, a bad quality with Bonaparte for an enemy. I hope there is no danger for Sweden itself. They are a fine race of people, and their King deserves to have his fortunes favored with success.... Lord Liverpool is dead, and, I suppose, died very rich.... I hear that he has left this Lord L.[295] at least £10,000 a year.

Lady Elizabeth Foster
    To Augustus Foster.

CHISWICK, *January* 29, 1809.

... Great and brilliant as was the victory which we gained at Corunna, yet the having been obliged to retreat, and the North of Spain being in this manner almost entirely conquered by the French, we must consider the Campaign as a most unfortunate one. To you, who will know the result of the different operations, and have not passed the interval of dreadfull anxiety which we all did during the retreat of our army, every thing will, I suppose, seem as bad as possible, except that there is this fact, put out of all doubt, that when we do meet the French we always beat them, even with an inferior force, and even Bonaparte can't deny our having obtained the victory; and all military men say no retreating army can embark if it is not victorious at the point of embarkation. Sir John Moore is a great loss, and is sincerely and generally regretted; but, unwilling as one feels to say any thing against an officer who died so bravely, yet people seem to think that his plan was a bad one, and that to the decision of marching 400 miles to the army he was to co-operate with instead of landing close to them has been the cause of all the reverses. The troops have returned exhausted with fatigue, but their spirit and bravery at the battle of Corunna exceeds all belief. The Cavalry distinguished themselves in the retreat, always attacking and defeating the enemy. The infantry hung their heads and murmured whilst retreating and not allowed to fight. At Corunna they had their revenge, and literally drove the French before them, who for 14 hours never appeared, and they embarked without leaving a man or a piece of artillery behind them. I am told that troops are to go to Cadiz and Minorca and Gibraltar to assist the South. When Moore in his dying moments asked who the command fell on, he was told General Hope. He said, "I am satisfied; there does not exist an abler officer". I am afraid, poor man, that he knew that the people of England had been dissatisfied at the army not having ever joined the Spaniards or encountered the French, but he shewed, as all say, the utmost skill in his retreat and in the order of battle. Lord Paget ...

Lady Elizabeth Foster
    To Augustus Foster.

CHISWICK, *Feb.* 5, 1809.

... All goes on ill, and the new year ushers itself in with a bad grace. Barcelona is relieved, and I am afraid Zaragossa is reduced to the last extremity, though all that can be done will be accomplished by Palafox.[296] I think that even those who regret General Moore the most, and all do regret him, are sorry that he adopted so inactive a line of conduct. The great subject of dispute now is his last dispatch; opposition have asked for it, and Mr. Whitbread told me to-day that Ministers said, that is, Canning told him, that they would publish all or nothing, and that he advised him, Mr. Whitbread, to consult with his friends and be fully aware of the consequence, for that one half of the letter was abuse of the Spaniards, and the other half of his own army; that at the end he says that when there was fighting he ever found them at their post, and with a determined bravery. Whitbread still seemed inclined to have the letter published, and General Stewart seems to have answered without consulting with his brother, and to have encouraged the giving of the letter. I do like General Stewart; he seems to be such a spirited creature, so brave and yet so mild and affectionate.

6th.

The Morpeths dined with us to-day. There was no news. The expedition had been dispersed, and we have no accounts from Spain. I always dread a bulletin after a pause.... The Duke of York's business you will see enough of in the papers. I do not believe that any body thinks that he shared in her profit, but one regrets seeing him in such bad company, and not being so generous as he ought to be to a woman who had lived with him. It seems strange that there should be no account of the French entering Portugal yet, and in Spain their tyranny is intolerable. Would that we had sent succour sooner to Catalonia and every-where. I hear that Ministers answer to this that they could not send our army before their Government was formed, and that they quarrelled among themselves.

15th.

I have waited in hopes of hearing from you, and of something being decided about the Duke of York. Neither of these things have happened. I suppose the ice still incloses you, and the examinations still go on about Mrs. Clark. I can't help hoping that something favourable may come out for the Duke of York, at least that her character is so bad that her accusations may be doubted, and if not proved I shall doubt. Cavallos is arrived, and Opadaca's wife.[297] I hope that the Spaniards have had some success in Catalonia, and that Romana is safe in Portugal. Does not his retreat show that we could have retreated had General Moore adopted that plan?

Lady Elizabeth Foster
> *To Augustus Foster.*

CHISWICK, *Feb.* 25, 1809.

... We have had an eventfull time. You were not advised, I think, in your news beyond the retreat of our army, and bad as the retreat was, yet you will be pleased with the battle of Corunna and proud of the valour displayed by our army. Since that the French have done little. Saragossa, it is said, still holds out, and not only that, but that the immortal Palafox, the noble Palafox, has again repulsed the French. I trust, therefore, that all is not desperate, and that a nation of brave peasants may yet check and withstand the disciplined barbarians of France. The preparations of Austria have occupied the attention of Bonaparte, and may, I hope, lessen his armies in Spain. I hope, too, that we are sending more troops there, and with a more active commander, though perhaps not a better officer, and there could not be a braver. Sweden, Austria, and Spain have, however, all been forgot in the inquiry that has taken place in consequence of Mr. Wardle's and Mrs. Clarke's accusation of the Duke of York. Nothing I ever remember made the sensation which this has done; opinions are very different, and, what is more extraordinary, parties are violent in favor of Mrs. Clarke, and yet, as Lord Grey justly says, however people may differ about the Duke of York, who can doubt of her being a most malignant and profligate woman? Yet subscriptions are open for her in the city and amongst gentlemen. It is really disgusting.

March 1st.

The Brest fleet was out, and the croakers had already talked of it as on its way to Ireland, but today accounts are received of its having slunk into Basque roads on seeing our squadron at Rochefort. Poor Lord Falkland is killed in a duel with a Mr. Powel, a man whom every body was in the habit of scoffing at, and who at last revenged all his quarrels on Lord Falkland.

Lady Elizabeth Foster
> *To Augustus Foster.*

DEVONSHIRE HOUSE, *March*, 1809.

The examination of Mrs. Clarke has proved a more serious thing than you seem to think it, for it is now said, even by those who wish best to the Duke of York, and who acquit him of all corruption, that his remaining Commander in Chief is impossible from the weakness with which he was governed and influenced by so base a woman. Your brother and some others rejoice in this proof of the strength of the democracy in England, others regret all that has passed, and most think it a hard fate for a little blindness pour les beaux yeux.... They expect to take the King's opinion Wednesday, if they can carry the acquittal of corruption. They then, I hear, want the Duke to resign.[298] This I should think best. Saragossa's fate is still, I believe, undecided....

DEVONSHIRE HOUSE, *April* 17, 1809.

The papers mention Armfeldt being Commander in Chief,[299] and that he had sent word to Sir T. Hood that they wished to remain at peace with us. Is this so? His poor friend Ruggerdorff has been sent away, to his great inconvenience and sorrow. I wish I knew the truth about him. I can't help pitying the poor King, but I really believe that he was a little mad. We are going on here in a very odd manner. The spirit of reform is abroad and strikes to the right and left.... The Peninsula, I fear, goes ill. In some respects, better so far that Gallicia seems roused, and Romana is again in some force, but to the South the enemy advance, and unless we can defeat them in Portugal I shall also begin to despair of success. I have seen Lord St. Vincent,[300] and he says that Admiral Harvey has demanded a Court Martial on Lord Gambier. Gambier had sent him home to be tried, and he makes this return, and on serious accusations. Gambier is a brave man, but too much of a psalm-singing man, says Lord St. Vincent, though psalm-singing is a good thing, he says; but, as we both agreed, keep to the beautiful doctrine of the Bible, and you will ...

> *Lady Elizabeth Foster*
> *To Augustus Foster.*

DEVONSHIRE HOUSE, *April* 23, 1809.

We go on from one reform to another, till I suppose that we shall be the purest of governments and Parliaments. To-day Lord Archibald makes his motion about Lord Castlereagh,[301] and it is supposed, poor man, that he must resign; had he quitted his situation before, it would have been a good thing as his dilatoriness caused sad delay in the expeditions. He is a good-natured man, and I wish he had been removed for any other reason than that he goes out upon....

Lady Elizabeth Foster
    To Augustus Foster.
            DEVONSHIRE HOUSE, *May* 1, 1809.

In these eventful times I write oftener to you, as you must wish to know all that is passing. The surprise caused by the appointment of Lord Wellesley was very great.[302] I had known it, but dared not say any thing; but from the Opera every body came so full of it, and all expressing great surprise. Last night Lord Ossulston said it was the deepest intrigue possible; never was there such a thing; and as to Lord Grey having been sent for, what could that be for? what good could he do? he had better stay in Northumberland. Mr. Tierney and Lord Robert were with me in the morning. Mr. Tierney thinks that Lord Castlereagh will go out Wednesday. Lord Morpeth saw him in the House to-day, and looking, as he thought, very dismayed. I am sorry for him; he is a good-natured man, and will feel the want of place more than most people; but yet I am afraid he was a corrupt politician, and in this reforming age corruption can't escape. Lord Auckland brings on his famous motion, or rather infamous, not to receive any bill of divorce unless it is clogged with a clause that the parties can't marry. What can this do but encourage men to seduce a woman, and was ever any woman debarred from sacrificing herself from motives of self-interest? They say that the Commons are (in case it is passed) determined to bring in a Bill not to pass any Bill where such a clause is introduced, so that there can be no divorce. That something should be done all agree, but not what that should be. As to news there was a firing heard, which it is feared was for a victory over the Austrians. This would be sad indeed. In Spain things go better, and some people are sanguine enough to look to Soults's being taken.

                                                    2nd.

Here is Daniel come with an account from Brooks that the division was 78 to 98, but he don't know which way; how provoking, and the papers are not out. If Lord Castlereagh should go out, I dare say there will be some further changes still to surprise Lord Ossulston, and it is acknowledged that the Administration was too weak for it to go on.

After all, the debate on Lord Auckland's motion, or rather Lord A.'s motion, was not that day. It was carried by twelve only, I think. Lord Castlereagh is not out yet, but as Lord Temple's motion about Spain was put off, it is supposed to be owing to that. Lady Castlereagh gives a party to-morrow, and invites all *her foes*. Nothing further from Germany. In Sweden we hear that you mean to try the King.

Lady Elizabeth Foster
   To Augustus Foster.

BROCKET HALL, *May* 22, 1809.

... To-day the Tower guns fired for the taking of Oporto and defeating Soult.[303] Lord Arthur is said to be pursuing him.[304] The passage of the river was, I hear, one of the most brilliant things ever done; as usual, however, opposition, I am sorry to say, are depreciating it. What a pity it is always to do this! Ministers have been in a minority two nights running, one on Lord Burgersh's promotion,[305] the other on a further grant to Palmer. I am quite a Wellesleyite. I must say that I am grieving for the poor King of Sweden, whom, if he must be confined, why disinherit his poor children? What times we live in!

Lady Elizabeth Foster
   To Augustus Foster.

May 31, 1809.

Still no accounts; the anxiety is very great; should Soult attack Beresford again before Lord Wellesley's reinforcements reach him,[306] the worst may be apprehended. How shocking it is that we are always obliged to fight with inferiority of numbers.

Lady Elizabeth Foster
   To Augustus Foster.

DEVONSHIRE HOUSE, *June* 1, 1809.

... Bonaparte is again at Vienna. However, I do not think this time that the Emperor will make peace without the Archduke's leave, and the last French bulletin holds out no certainty of being able to destroy the Archduke. In Spain there has been some disaster in the Asturias. I hope our friend Materosa has behaved well, but the Junta, they say, have not. We are very anxious to hear more of Sir A. Wellesley. At home you will see that they have been obliged to rescind Burghersh's promotion, and Col. Shipley in consequence gave up his resolutions. He paid some compliments to Lord Burghersh. Corruptions have been proved that perfectly disgust one, and I hope they will steadily, but with moderation, persevere.

Above left: Frederick Augustus Hervey, 4th Earl of Bristol (1730–1803); and Church of Ireland bishop of Derry, father of Lady Elizabeth Foster. It is said that Lord Bristol's knowledge of fine things in Europe and love of travelling and staying in luxury inspired the fashion for naming a hotel the 'Hotel Bristol'.

Above right: Elizabeth Hervey, née Davers, Countess of Bristol (1733-1800), mother of Lady Elizabeth Foster, by Anton Moran, *c.* 1778.

Below left: Lady Elizabeth Christiana Foster, 'Bess', née Hervey (1759-1824), by Joshua Reynolds, 1787.

Below right: Bess's brother, Frederick William Hervey, 1st Marquess of Bristol (1769-1859), styled Lord Hervey between 1796 and 1803 and known as the 5th Earl of Bristol between 1803 and 1826. He was created 1st Marquess in 1826. He married, 1798, Elizabeth Charlotte Albinia, née Upton (1775–1844), six sons and two daughters. Portrait by John Hoppner.

Above left: John Spencer, 1st Earl Spencer (1734-1783), by Thomas Gainsborough *c.* 1763. John Spencer married, 1754, Georgiana, née Poyntz (1737-1814).

Above right: Margaret Georgiana Spencer, Countess Spencer, née Poyntz, by Thomas Gainsborough. The date is unknown, but probably *c.* 1763,

Below left: Georgiana, Countess Spencer, and her daughter, Georgiana (1757-1806), by Joshua Reynolds, *c.* 1760.

Below right: Another depiction of Georgiana, Countess Spencer, *c.* 1765, this portrait by Pompeo Batoni.

Above left: Lady Georgiana Spencer, by Joshua Reynolds, *c.* 1759-60.

Above right: Lady Georgiana, Lady Henrietta Frances and George John Spencer, Viscount Althorp; the first three children Earl and Countess Spencer; by Angelica Kauffman, 1774.

Below left: Georgiana's brother, George Spencer, 2nd Earl Spencer (1758-1834) at the age of about 20, detail from a portrait by Joshua Reynolds, *c.* 1778.

Below right: William Cavendish, 5th Duke of Devonshire; portrait painted in Rome by Pompeo Batoni, 1768.

Four portraits of Georgiana. *Above left* is by Thomas Gainsborough, 1783, *above right* is the earliest, by Joshua Reynolds, 1775-6. *Below left* is also by Thomas Gainsborough, but later *c.* 1787. *Below right* is probably the most interesting of all; it is by Maria Anna Angelika Katharina Kauffmann, painted in Rome, 1793, and less flattering than Gainsborough. It is remarkably similar in facial features to the portrait on the following page of Georgiana with her infant daughter Lady Georgiana by Reynolds. Perhaps Reynolds and Kauffmann are depicting the true likeness of Georgiana, who is clearly less pretty than Bess Foster, and may be a clue as to why Bess caught the duke's attention, leaving Georgiana to be the uncherished family breeding stock.

Above left: Georgiana, with her infant daughter Lady Georgiana (1783-1858), who was born after nine years of childless marriage. In 1801, Georgiana married George Howard, Viscount Morpeth, later becoming Countess of Carlisle upon her husband's accession in 1825. Portrait by Joshua Reynolds, *c.* 1784.

Above right: Georgiana, Countess of Carlisle, 1853. She and the Earl had twelve children including the 7th and 8th Earls of Carlisle. Another child, the Duchess of Sutherland, was Mistress of the Robes and a close friend to Queen Victoria.

Below left: Portrait of a Gentleman, said to be the young Charles Grey, later 2nd Earl Grey (1764-1845); Prime Minister 1830-34. Grey met Georgiana in the late 1780s while attending a Whig gathering at Devonshire House. Grey and Georgiana became lovers, and she became pregnant. Grey wanted Georgiana to leave the duke and live with him, but the duke told Georgiana if she did, she would never see her children again.

Below right: Eliza Courtney (1792-1859). Georgiana was sent to France, where she gave birth to a daughter, Eliza, on 20 February 1792 at Aix-en-Provence. Eliza was relinquished, shortly after birth, to the care of Grey's parents. She married, 1814, Lt-Col. Robert Charles Ellice; two sons and three daughters.

Above left: Edmund Burke (right) in conversation with Charles James Fox. In Georgiana's family slang, Fox was 'the Eyebrow'.

Above right: George, Prince of Wales by Thomas Gainsborough, *c.* 1783. In Georgiana's family slang the prince was 'Prinny'.

Below left: William Cavendish, 5th Duke of Devonshire (1748-1811), by Anton von Maron.

Below right: A miniature of William Cavendish in the form of an unfinished sketch by Richard Cosway, commissioned by Lady Elizabeth Foster in 1782. This was the same year that Elizabeth, known as 'Bess', met William Cavendish, 5th Duke of Devonshire and his wife, Georgiana at Bath.

Above left: Lady Louisa Theodosia Hervey (1767-1821), as a child, sister of Bess, who married, 1795, Robert Jenkinson, 2nd Earl of Liverpool; a portrait by Johann Friedrich August Tischbein, 1778.

Above right: Robert Jenkinson, 2nd Earl of Liverpool (1770-1828); by Sir Thomas Lawrence *c.* 1795.

Below: Wife & no wife—or—a trip to the Continent, a cartoon by James Gillray, 27 March 1786. Edmund Burke, dressed as a Jesuit, marries the Prince of Wales and Mrs Fitzherbert. The Prince is about to put the ring on her finger. Fox gives her away, holding her left wrist. Beside him (right) stands Louis Weltje, the Prince's cook in back view but looking to the left at the ceremony. A napkin is under his left arm, bottles project from his coat-pockets, and the tags on his shoulder denote the liveried manservant. To the left of Fox appears the profile of George Hanger, a companion of the Prince of Wales. The prince admired Hanger's sense of humour and his exploits, both military and with women, and appointed him Equerry in 1791. On the left Lord North sits, leaning against the altar wall, sound asleep, his legs outstretched.

Above left: The Prince Regent, by William Beechey, 1803. Beechey gave the first version of this portrait to the Royal Academy in 1798 as his 'Diploma Work' (compulsory donation made upon being elected academician). This repetition was painted in 1803 for the sitter's brother and Queen Victoria's father, Edward, Duke of Kent. *The Royal Collection*

Above right: Maria Fitzherbert by Sir Joshua Reynolds, *c.* 1787.

Below: L'Assemblée Nationale. A cartoon by James Gillray, 18 June 1804; a reception given by Mr and Mrs Fox to various groups of the Opposition. Three Grenvilles bow to the host and hostess; the Marquis of Buckingham, wearing his ribbon, holding hat and gold-headed cane and showing a gouty leg and foot, bends low. Next is Lord Grenville, clasping his hat to his breast, more ingratiating but less obsequious than his brother. Next is the stout Lord Temple. Fox, wearing a sword, returns Buckingham's bow; on his right stands Mrs Fox, curtseying, and ogling Grenville. On the extreme right is the Prince of Wales. Behind Mrs Fox is a family group: the Duchess of Devonshire, with a fan inscribed 'The Devonshire Delight or the new Coalition Reel', Lady Bessborough wearing a miniature of 'Nelson', and, behind them, their brother, Lord Spencer. In the foreground on the extreme left, the Duke of Bedford, sits at a small table holding out an open book. Next to him sits the Duke of Norfolk, fat and gouty, resting on his knee a frothing tankard of 'Whitbread's Entire'. Behind Norfolk, Sheridan, gross and conspiratorial, offers his snuff-box to Windham.

Above: A coloured aquatint of Vauxhall Gardens, by Francis Jukes, from a drawing by Thomas Rowlandson. This was published 28 June 1785, but as Dr Johnson had died in December 1784, Rowlandson must have drawn it earlier. It depicts Madame Weichsel on a balcony, with an orchestra behind her. Below is a crowd including some notable personalities of the day. Dining in the box on the left are Boswell, Dr Johnson and Oliver Goldsmith. The two fashionable ladies in the centre are the Duchess of Devonshire and her sister, Lady Bessborough. The Prince of Wales is also in the crowd.

Below left: Charles James Fox, a portrait by Joshua Reynolds, 1783.

Below right: Portrait of a Gentleman, traditionally identified as Richard Brinsley Sheridan (1751–1816), by John Hoppner.

Above left: Harriet, (Henrietta) Ponsonby; by Angelica Kauffman, 1793. Harriet was a leading figure in society and notorious for her affairs with Richard Brinsley Sheridan and Granville Leveson-Gower, 1st Earl Granville, who became her most enduring lover.

Harriet married, 27 November 1780, Frederick Ponsonby, Viscount Duncannon, the Duke's cousin, even though she was unsure of his character. They quickly became part of the Devonshire House set.

Above right: Granville Leveson-Gower (1773-1846), at the time of his mission to St Petersburg, c. 1804, by Sir Thomas Lawrence. His affair with Harriet produced two illegitimate children: Harriet Emma Arundel Stewart and George Stewart.

Left: Harriet, Viscountess Duncannon (later Countess of Bessborough) and her two sons, Frederick and John (later the 4th Earl of Bessborough); by John Hoppner, 1787. Harriet became addicted to gambling and amassed thousands of pounds of debt that she could not afford to pay. Duncannon proved to be an abusive husband, desperate to get his hands on Harriet's financial settlement and frequently Harriet turned to her family for help. They had four children, John William (1781), Frederick Cavendish (1783), Caroline (1785) and William (1787).

Above left: Lady Caroline Lamb née Ponsonby (1785–1828), only daughter of Frederick Ponsonby, 3rd Earl of Bessborough, and Harriet, niece of Georgiana and cousin (by marriage) of Annabella, Lady Byron. She married, 1805, William Lamb, who was later 2nd Viscount Melbourne and Prime Minister. They had one son, George Augustus Frederick, born 1807, and a daughter, born in 1809, who died within 24 hours. From March to August 1812, Lady Caroline embarked on a well-publicised affair with Lord Byron, subsequently giving Byron what became his lasting epitaph when she described him as 'mad, bad, and dangerous to know'. Bryon referred to Lamb as 'Caro', which she adopted as her public nickname. After Byron broke things off, her husband took the disgraced Lady Caroline to Ireland. Detail from a portait by Thomas Phillips.

Above right: Portrait of George, Lord Byron (1788–1824), by Thomas Phillips, 1813.

Right: Elizabeth, 'Bess' Foster, née Hervey (left with basket) and Georgiana Duchess of Devonshire. In 1809, three years after Georgiana's death in 1806, Bess married William Cavendish, to become the new duchess, but it lasted just two years as he died in 1811. She later lived at Rome. A miniature by Jean-Urbain Guérin, 1791. *Wallace Collection*

Above left: Henrietta Elizabeth 'Harriet' Leveson-Gower, Countess Granville, née Cavendish, (1785-1862), 'Harryo' or 'Hary-o'. Harriet was born at Devonshire House, second daughter of William Cavendish, 5th Duke of Devonshire and Georgiana, Duchess of Devonshire. Despite her parents' turbulent marriage, Harriet had a happy childhood. Her mother's death in 1806 led to an unpleasant situation in which her father's long-time mistress Lady Elizabeth Foster took control of the Devonshire household; as the unmarried eldest daughter, this should have been Harriet's role. To help her escape this awkward domestic situation, Harriet's maternal aunt Harriet arranged for her niece to marry her lover of seventeen years, Granville Leveson-Gower, 1st Earl Granville. The couple's marriage proved to be happy, and produced five children.

Above right: Portrait of the Spencer Sisters; Georgiana Duchess of Devonshire and her sister Harriet, by Thomas Rowlandson, 1790.

Right: Charles James Fox, a portrait by Karl Anton Hickel, 1794. *National Portrait Gallery.*

Above left: George John Spencer, 2nd Earl Spencer (1758- 1834), styled Viscount Althorp from 1765 to 1783, was Georgiana's brother and a Whig politician. He notably served as Home Secretary from 1806 to 1807 in the Ministry of All the Talents.

Above right: Lavinia Spencer, Countess Spencer, née Bingham (1762–1831), was the eldest daughter of the Irish peer Charles Bingham, 1st Earl of Lucan and his wife, the portrait miniature painter Margaret, née Smyth. She married George John Spencer on 6 March 1782, and the couple had nine children. A portrait by Joshua Reynolds, 1781-82.

Right: John Charles Spencer, 3rd Earl Spencer (1782–1845), son of George and Lavinia, aged 4, portrait by Joshua Reynolds, 1786.

Above left: William Cavendish, 'Hart' (later 6th Duke of Devonshire) when Marquess of Hartington, *c.* 1805.

Above right: William Spencer Cavendish, 6th Duke of Devonshire (1790-1858), who died unmarried. He intended to marry Lady Caroline Ponsonby, his cousin, but she married William Lamb, which he found devastating. Portrait by Sir Thomas Lawrence.

Below: Granville Leveson-Gower, 1st Earl Granville (1773-1846) and his wife, Lady Harriet Elizabeth Cavendish 'Hary-o' (1785–1862), and their four children; and possibly also his illegitimate son; a portrait by Thomas Phillips, *c.* 1815.

Above left: Lady Elizabeth Foster by Angelica Kauffman, 1786.

Above right: A contemporary hand-coloured print of Bess.

Below left: Bess's second son, Sir Augustus John Foster, 1st baronet (1780-1848). Foster was an attaché at Washington, a minister at Copenhagen, and then British Minister at Washington 1811-1812. He married, 1815, Albinia Jane, née Hobart (1788-1867).

Below right: Admiral Sir Augustus William James Clifford, 1st Baronet (1788-1877). Clifford was the illegitimate son of William Cavendish, 5th Duke of Devonshire and Elizabeth Foster, née Hervey.

Above left: George Hamilton Gordon, 4th Earl of Aberdeen (1784- 1860), styled Lord Haddo from 1791 to 1801, Prime Minister from 1852 until 1855. A portrait by Sir Thomas Lawrence, 1829. Gordon was a close friend of Augustus John Foster and accompanied him on his trip to Weimar in 1799.

Above right: Jean Victor Marie Moreau (1763-1813), was a French general who helped Napoleon to power, but later became a rival and was banished to the United States. He returned to Europe and entered the service of Tsar Alexander I of Russia. Moreau was mortally wounded in the battle of Dresden on 27 August 1813 while he was talking to the Tsar and died a few days later.

Below: The ruins of Glyde Court, County Louth, the ancestral home of the Foster family.

Baron d' Armfelt
    To Augustus Foster.
            ST. PETERSBOURG, *ce* 15 *juin*, 1809.

On m'a dit ici, mon, amiable ami, que vous êtes parti de Stockolm le 7—j'en suis au desespoir, car dans 8 jours *je suis* sûr d'avoir eu des choses importantes à vous communiquer.

Mais je n'ai que le tems de vous dire, que nous sommes dans une crise violente ici. L'Empéreur est à Tver, chez sa soeur la Duchesse d'Oldenbourg, cette Soeur revient ici aussi que l'Empereur dans la semaine prochaine.... La Duchesse est charmante, une bonne tête, détestée de Bonaparte et le détestant de même, elle a tout L'esprit de la grande Catharine mais hélas! pas son experience—On est diablement mal ici pour les finances, mais cette operation-ci rame-neroit le Credit public, et ceux qui cachent aujourd'hui leurs Roubles, les sortiroient alors de leurs coffres forts. Dans 2 ou 10 jours ceci sera decidé ou manqué. Mon affair d'argent l'est, on me recevoit (?) a Berlin, et si je n'étois pas victime de—tous les Diables, j'irois là et je verrois L'Allemagne—partout je suis mieux qu'en Suède jusqu'à ce que les choses ont pris la forme qu'il faut. Gisman est parti sans que j'ai pu l'atteindre, la ville est deserte et j'ecris des memoires—il n'y a que l'ennui qui en profite—Mettez moi aux pieds de Madame votre mère et ne m'oubliez pas.

                                    VAVA.

Lady Elizabeth Foster
    To Augustus Foster.
            DEVONSHIRE HOUSE, *July* 3, 1809.

... I hope the Russians are not advancing upon you. Fortune seems to coquet it a little just now with our allies, and one more good, decided victory of the Archduke Charles, and much may indeed be hoped for. All in the North of Germany are rising, and the Tyrolese have emulated the Spaniards. The accounts from Spain to-day are good. The French are driven out of Ferrol and Corunna. Sir Arthur keeps Victor at Bay,[306] and he will soon, I dare say, proceed to Spain, and I hope they will finally be driven out: now is the time, whilst Bonaparte is in Germany and sending for all the troops that he can from France.

                                    July 5th.

To-day the account is confirmed about Ferrol and Corunna, and the defeat of the French under Ney by the Spaniards under General Curera. Two of our officers were in the action, and speak highly of the Spanish bravery and zeal. Soult's army seems to have been nearly destroyed by Sir Arthur Wellesley. The Duke of Brunswick has an increasing army, and the Duke of Dantzig was defeated by the Tyrolese. At home Col. Wardle has been accused by Mrs. Clarke of bribing her by a promise of fine furniture to accuse the Duke of York and then to have left it unpaid. He lost his suit, and therefore declares that she is perjured and ought not to be believed. This is curious enough.

6th.

Mrs. Clarke is indicted for perjury, but the jury have not decided upon it. If she is perjured it weakens her evidence against the Duke of York; if she is not it more totally is the ruin of Col. Wardle's character and popularity; it is a strange business altogether.

7th.

One more day, but not much of news. All that there is seems good, and the French are, I believe, returning to their former position on the Ebro, but I trust that they will not be allowed to stay there.

> *Lady Elizabeth Foster*
> *To Augustus Foster.*
> DEVONSHIRE HOUSE, *July* 14, 1809.

We are in anxious expectation of more news from the Continent, and conjecture is at work about our own expedition.[308] Heaven knows where it is going. It takes away all the remaining society of London, and is an immense armament. Lord Paget goes with it,[309] which is the best thing that could happen for him after all that has passed. I am in hopes that all goes well for our dear Spaniards, and if the present moment can be profited of, they will, I hope, be free. I have the greatest faith in Sir Arthur Wellesley. At home the only changes perceptible to the vulgar eye are Lord Granville Leveson in the Cabinet and Secretary at War, Lord Harrowby (your friend) an Earl and of the Cabinet, and of the Board of Controul. Lord Wellesley goes to Spain as soon as he is well enough, and at his return is, as is rumoured, to be Minister of War....

Lady Elizabeth Foster
  To Augustus Foster.
        DEVONSHIRE HOUSE, *July* 20, 1809.

We are waiting with the greatest anxiety for more news from the Danube, and the report to-night of a firing on the Dutch and French coast adds very much to our anxiety and apprehensions. It would be too shocking now for the Archduke Charles to be defeated, and yet it is more probable that he should than that Bonaparte should. Our expedition is expected to sail to-morrow or next day, but where is the question.

                  21*st.*

Still the report of a firing continues, and I am terrified. I wish that we could have sent a powerful diversion sooner, and why now to stop to take Capri and Ischia instead of sending succour to Catalonia; however, I hope and suppose that they know better than I do. Mr. Wardle is a wreck of popularity; his is all gone, and I rejoice at it. I always thought that his conduct was odious, and it has now been proved so....

Lady Elizabeth Foster
  To Augustus Foster.
        DEVONSHIRE HOUSE, *July* 29.

You augured too well, dearest Augustus, from the silence and absence of couriers from the Danube. We may consider every thing now as over,[310] I am afraid, and it is difficult to understand even by the French accounts how it could be necessary for the Archduke to solicit an Armistice. You cannot conceive any thing like the gloom which it spread here, and even the success which is expected from our expedition don't seem to afford ground of hope for any good to the Continent. Bonaparte's army did not fight better than the Archduke Charles', but he outwitted him. Your letter was a delightful one, and every expression of your affection to me is a source of comfort and happiness to me. I have great pride in your present situation, as I am sure you are doing yourself credit; it is a difficult one, too, and therefore the more is it to your credit. Much as I admire the Swedes, I can't reconcile myself to their excluding the young Prince, so fine a boy too! Is it true that the King has asked permission to go to Switzerland?

Monday, 31st.

I am assured to-night that accounts are come of Flushing having surrendered and all the Island of Walcheren, and some say that they willingly surrendered, but that the French fleet were gone up the Scheldt. I suppose we shall follow, and Fort (?) Lillo and Antwerp will, I fear, be tougher work. However, our force is a strong one; would that it had gone a month, or even a fortnight sooner.

> *Lady Elizabeth Foster*
> *To Augustus Foster.*

... I have opened my letter to say that I am frightened about Flushing.[311] The French have thrown in reinforcements who made a sortie. We drove them back, but with a loss of 200 men; Major Thornton wounded. Lord Huntly, (and Hope, I think) have taken all South Beveland, but my fear is that by Flushing holding out that Antwerp and Fort (?) Lillo may be reinforced also. Lord W. Bentinck and H. Cavendish are going to Spain.

> *Lady Elizabeth Foster*
> *To Augustus Foster.*

CHISWICK, *August* 14, 1809.

Now, my dear Augustus, walk about the streets of Stockholm with looks of pride and exultation, bear high your head, and glory in being a Briton. The Tower guns have announced to-day the glorious victory gained by our favourite, Sir Arthur Wellesley. It was, as he says himself, a fearful odds, but followed by complete success. Twenty pieces of cannon, four eagles, and 10,000 slain of the French bear testimony to this. Sebastiani wounded,[312] two generals killed, and two others wounded; Joseph a witness to his defeat.[313] The dear English alone were engaged, but it is said that the Spaniards are pursuing the defeated French army. Pray God that they may profit of the confusion and dismay the French seem to have experienced, and if they imitate their countrymen at Zaragossa and Gerona they will do so. F. Ponsonby, who is in the 23rd Dragoons, was in the thickest of the fight, and is safe, Thank Heaven! Lady Bessborough heard the report of the battle before she left Chiswick this morning, and set off, as you will believe, in great anxiety. Only yesterday she and I and Lady Granville had been fighting with Mr. Vernon, and he was saying that he wished Sir Arthur back again, that he believed indeed that he could not advance from want of shoes and money, and that his situation was a most perilous one. To Lady Melbourne he said he hoped she was not John Bull enough to believe that we could fight the French with such inferiority of numbers. She said she longed to see him again to triumph over him. Here were we with about 20,000 against fully forty thousand French. Perhaps you will hear fuller and better accounts, but good news bears a repetition. How it makes one regret that Sir John Moore did not trust more to English valour and hazard a battle sooner. The battle was, you see, at Talavera la Regina.[314] Cuesta was said to be following them and Varegas to have advanced to Toledo and Aranjuez. Is it true your Prince Augustenbourg has refused the sovereignty of Sweden, that the Russians have had a check, and that our squadron has done good service? The weather has been sad for the expedition, and they anxiously wait for news from thence.

> *Lady Elizabeth Foster*
> *To Augustus Foster.*
>
> CHISWICK, *August* 21, 1809.

... I should like your plan of marrying one of our Princesses in Sweden much better if it did not confirm the setting aside the poor young Prince, which I do think a great act of injustice. However, I will say that I should think that the Princess Mary would suit your Prince Regent perfectly,[315] and I should think that she would be a happier person than living to be an old maid.... I hope you have heard by this time of the surrender of Flushing, and got my letter about the battle of Talavera. The French have ventured to talk of it as a victory, and to date from Talavera on the 29th, though Sir Arthur Wellesley, who writes his last dispatch on the first of August, states that the French had retreated beyond St. Olalla. This is the most extraordinary lie they have yet ventured on. The report of to-day is that the Armistice is broke, that the Archduke Charles has resigned, and that Prince John of Lichtenstein is to command the army. I think that Russia ought to be jealous of French colours in Galicia...

> *Lady Elizabeth Foster*
> *To Augustus Foster.*
>
> CHISWICK, *August* 28, 1809.

... As to news I am almost in despair. It seems to me that by thus dividing our forces we do nothing well or effectually, and the only large one which we have sent was commanded by so dull and slow a man that it must fail, while dear Sir Arthur, who should command hundreds of thousands, has a small army of 20,000 to meet 70,000 French, for I much fear that as yet we can only reckon on the Spaniards when behind walls or for cutting off small parties. Sir Arthur, it is said, went to meet Soult, relying on Cuesta's promise to guard Talavera, but that very evening Cuesta arrived, leaving our sick and wounded behind. If this is really so Cuesta ought to be displaced. Lord Robert Spencer, Mr. Vaughan, and the Baron de Rolla are here. They say that the opinion is that nothing can be done against Antwerp. In short, this expedition, which was to have been a coup de main, has already lasted a month, and only Flushing, Walcheren, and South Beveland taken.

> *Lady Elizabeth Foster*
> *To Augustus Foster.*
>
> CHISWICK, *September 5*, 1809.

Every thing every where goes so ill that I have had no courage to write to you. Lord Chatham deserves signal punishment,[316] I think, first for the presumption of asking for such a command, and then for the failure of the measures he pretended to be equal to command. It really was too bad to give such a man such an army whilst the heroic Lord Arthur had three French armies to encounter with 20,000 English, the Spanish commander thwarting him in every plan and attempt. I don't know what we are to look to or hope for. Mr. Tierney is just come,[317] but being one who will triumph in the justness of his prophecy I have not courage to see....

> *Lady Elizabeth Foster*
> *To Augustus Foster.*
>
> DEVONSHIRE HOUSE, *Sept.* 8, 1809.

... You will grieve to hear of Lord Wellington's retreat. Lord Chatham you prophecied too right about. I feel very anxious about the Swedish expedition, so pray let me hear about it.

> *Lady Elizabeth Foster*
> *To Augustus Foster.*
>
> CHISWICK, *Sept.* 11, 1809.

... I feel so interested about the Swedish expedition, and do so rejoice that though they could not beat the Russians, yet that from losses the latter were forced to abandon Umea. I beg you will go on telling me about them. You will hear of the discontent here on account of Flushing being the only object obtained by the expedition, and that with great loss by sickness. Lord Wellington, too, has retreated to Elvas, but it seems to have been a dignified retreat, and then taking up a strong position and waiting till the Junta are turned, as I hope they will be, into a Regency, and are a little more active and energetic. America, you see, is again discontented with us....

> *Lady Elizabeth Foster*
> *To Augustus Foster.*
>
> *Sept.* 21, 1809.

What strange events happen. These two months I have heard it said that Canning would not stay in if Lord Castlereagh was not turned out.[318] Lord Castlereagh is out, yet Canning's resignation is accepted, and this morning these two fight a duel, in which our dear Canning is wounded, but, though a narrow escape, Vaughan says that it will be of no consequence.... What I can't understand is why Lord Castlereagh is out, why Canning resigns. It is supposed that the King supports Lord Chatham: if so, they will patch up an administration perhaps again with the Doctor:[319] it is too bad. The rumours of the Grenvilles and Lord Grey having been sent for have subsided. I believe the King hates the thought of the Grenvilles.... I have written to Charles Bagot to inquire how Canning does. Fred could not tell me where Charles Ellis lives. Good God! what he must have felt when he saw that Canning was wounded. They say it was some sarcasm of Canning which galled the Viscount, and so he challenged him.

> *22nd.*

Huskisson, Mr. L., and Sturges Bourne have resigned with Canning and Rose—of the Cabinet none certain yet but Lord Granville L. Canning suffered in the night, but is going on well.

> *Lady Elizabeth Foster*
> *To Augustus Foster.*
>
> CHISWICK, *Sept.* 25, 1809.

The strangeness of the times continues. Canning, however, is doing well, but you will be grieved at his resignation, and so am I. Lord Grenville and Lord

Grey have been sent to, but whether in such a manner as to make it possible for them to accept I don't know. Report says that the message is from the King and to join the six remaining Ministers, Liverpool, Harrowby, Eldon, Chatham, &c. I wish that our friends originally had joined with Canning and not with Sidmouth.... Canning, I am told, after the duel, said to Lord Castlereagh, "Now, pray tell me what we have been fighting about". When Home the surgeon came to his house he shook hands with him and joked him about having set C. Ellis' leg crooked. Home said to himself, "It can't be him who is to fight". Charles Ellis shook hands with him, and his hand was cold as marble, on which Home said, "If this is the man who is to fight, what an unfeeling second he has". Poor Charles Ellis! I can't conceive such a situation.

> *Elizabeth, Duchess of Devonshire,*
> *To Augustus Foster.*
>
> CHISWICK, *Sept.* 28, 1809.

Since I wrote to you nothing more has occurred, because they wait for Lord Grey and Lord Grenville's answers. If, as I heard yesterday, Perceval has written to offer to share the Cabinet between them, I don't think they can possibly accept of it, because they think so point blank differently on such principal topics. However, there is so marvellous a facility in men to reconcile things that will secure power, that there is no saying what may happen. If, as I think, opposition don't agree to this, then probably the Doctor will come in for a short reign, and the best result would be the union of opposition and Canning.... The Norwegians seem inclined to be friendly to us, and the Swedes are heroes. Their march to Umea does them honor, and I wish that they could drive every Russian away. Spain is reviving a little, and Lord Wellington is secure in his position, and meditates, I hope, offensive measures. He will do all that can be done. William Ponsonby has been with his brother at head quarters. When he arrived, Col. Seymour, S. T. Colonel, called out to his servant, Look out for two spare trees for Mr. Ponsonby to lodge in. They say Lord Grenville don't accept, and that Lord Grey won't come to town. This is very odd indeed.

> *Elizabeth, Duchess of Devonshire,*
> *To Augustus Foster.*
>
> CHISWICK, *October* 5, 1809.

I think Canning has been ill used by Lord Camden and the Duke of Portland. He entrusted to them the telling Lord Castlereagh, which they never did, and now Canning appears as a false person to many, because he continued transacting business with him while he declared him incompetent to that place: perhaps it would have been still better had he told him himself, but still he must have thought himself certain of the communication being made through Lord Castlereagh's uncle and the first Lord of the Treasury.

> *Lady Elizabeth Foster*
> *To Augustus Foster.*
>
> CHISWICK, *Nov.* 9, 1809.

... As to Politicks, they sicken me, for though Bonaparte has failed, for he announced the total destruction of Austria, yet how is a country fallen that can give up such a people as the Tyrolese....

> *Elizabeth, Duchess of Devonshire,*
> *To Augustus Foster.*
>
> CHISWICK, *Nov.* 13, 1809.

... As to politicks, Canning's statement, which is in the form of a letter to Lord Camden, is to be out very soon. He has shewn it to Lord Tichfield and Lord W. Bentinck. The first made scarcely any alteration. The second begged Canning to efface what was really a beautiful character of his father, attributing his conduct to the mildness of his nature and his unwillingness to give pain, and to substitute what he said he knew to be his father's real motive, the wish to keep the Administration together. Strange that Lord W. should prefer his father's conduct being attributed to real downright deception than to the weakness of good nature, increased by illness and age; but this between ourselves alone; but it is certain that they worked upon Canning's good nature, who perhaps has not yet taken the tone his talents entitle him to do. If Lord Wellesley accept under the present Ministers, I think it will lower him much. .

> *Elizabeth, Duchess of Devonshire,*
> *To Augustus Foster.*
>
> CHISWICK, *Dec.* 5, 1809.

... Canning said to me that he had left a written memento in the office to mark his approbation of your conduct, and that you had every thing that would be most likely to make you rise in that line, good sense, good temper, conciliatory manners, &c...

Elizabeth, Duchess of Devonshire,
   To Augustus Foster.

March 1, 1810.

Mr. Cavendish, the philosopher,[320] has died worth, £1,075,000, and though it is a week ago we are still ignorant how he has left his property. The Duke and I, however, are quite convinced that he has left him nothing, so the question is how much he has left to Lord George, and what to men of science, and for Charities.

   ... You will see strange things—Lord Chatham's narrative, Joseph Napoleon's advance to Seville and Cadiz; and Lord Wellington's preparations for quitting Portugal; it is melancholy to see the end of this contest for liberty and independence.

Elizabeth, Duchess of Devonshire,
   To Augustus Foster.

CHISWICK, *March* 26, 1810.

To-day is the great discussion of the Scheldt expedition. Lord Wellesley is clear of it certainly, and so is Canning and Lord Castlereagh of the delay in recalling the troops, but no country can see the failure of such an armament, and mourn the loss of so many thousands by sickness and disease and not insist on knowing the cause of such a misfortune. It is supposed that the discussion will last two or three days, but nobody knows how it will end—probably only a near run thing.... What a stroke of policy Bonaparte's marriage seems to be.[321] We hear of nothing but his magnificent preparations for it. He seems to be quarrelling in earnest with America, but they bear with any insult from him....

Baron d'Engelstròm[322]
   To Augustus Foster.

May 31, 1810

Monsieur,—Vous avez voulu une lettre de moi pour justifier votre depart. La voici. Vous connaissez votre position. Je me trouve dans le cas de vous prier de partir jeudi au soir. J'espère l'avantage de vous voir avant que vous quittez Stockholm pour vous renouveller les assurances de la considération distinguée et de l'attachement sincère aux lesquels j'ai l'honneur d'etre.— Monsieur, votre tres humble et très obeissant serviteur,

D'ENGELSTROM.

A M. FOSTER.

Note of Mr. Foster on the above—Ordered out of Sweden by Napoleon's directions.

Elizabeth, Duchess of Devonshire,
To Augustus Foster.
DEVONSHIRE HOUSE, *Jan.* 10, 1811.

I came to town a few days ago, as the Duke of D. was obliged to attend Parliament on the question of restrictions.... I afterwards found that we had beat the ministers on most of the questions, but, lo and behold, the vicissitude of things: the King is now said to be recovering, and that there is an end of the Regency. So be it. I am sure nothing would be so bad for my friends as a three months' administration. I am told that the 1st of Feb. is the time fixed for the Regency if it does take place. The King, however, is so emaciated and reduced that I should not suppose he ever can be equal to business again; and after what has come out of Lord Sidmouth having been appointed with two mad doctors in the room, it will make people slow to believe in H. M.'s perfect recovery....

The Prince Regent
To Elizabeth, Duchess of Devonshire.
February 14, 1811.

I have the pleasure to announce to you, my dearest Duchess, that I have this day assented to the nomination of Mr. Augustus Foster as Minister to the United States of America. I hope this will meet with your approbation, as nothing can ever afford me more pleasure than whatever I know can convey satisfaction both to yourself as well as the dear Duke.—I remain, ever most truly and sincerely, your affectionate Friend and humble Servant,

GEORGE, P.R.

CARLTON HOUSE, *February* 14, 1811.

Elizabeth, Duchess of Devonshire,
    To Augustus Foster.

DEVONSHIRE HOUSE, *Feb.* 15,1811.

I inclose you the Prince Regent's letter, which I received at the Play last night. You will believe that I never said one word about you to him or any body else. I was obliged to answer the Prince, but this I did merely by expressing my thanks to him for his unvarying kindness to me, and by saying that you was in Ireland. The Prince announcing this nomination to me himself makes me suppose that in the present situation in which we stand with America it is considered as an important and advantageous mission, and it is one in which you are first, and therefore all the credit will be yours, and distinctions would probably follow. I know, however, your dislike to that country so well that I shall not say any thing to influence you more than it is absolutely my duty to do, and this, that if your dislike to accept of this mission arises from any hope of succeeding with ———,[323] you ought, I think, to bring that to a point by making your situation known. If she has any liking for you, the idea of your going would make her decide in your favor, and you would either then not want to go anywhere or might perhaps get it exchanged for some other Country she would like. If you only relinquish this line for Parliament, pray pause and consider how few people rise to any eminence in it; how very few obtain from Parliamentary merit alone either fame or emolument. You are appointed now Minister to the United States at a period of great consequence to this country. If it all terminates well, considering our connections and friendships, you are likely to receive flattering marks of approbation, and every thing that is pleasantest hereafter in the profession is open to you. Having said what I felt it my duty to do, I can only leave the ultimate decision to you. Your happiness and advantage is all I wish for, but I should be sorry to see you throw away the means of doing yourself credit from an unfounded pursuit of other objects. At all events, I think you ought to return directly...

Elizabeth, Duchess of Devonshire,
    To Augustus Foster.

August 3, 1811.

This is black Monday, so that I have no letters, and rumours prevail. Lord Burgersh told me that it was strongly reported that M'Donald had been defeated at Riga, and my brother read a sixth Bulletin dated still from Wilna, in which Bonaparte complains so much of bad roads that it is suspected he has no victories to boast of. What a blessing a real check to his arms would be! General Graham is come home in good health, but in danger of losing his eyes; he has had Weare's advice, however, who has given him much comfort about them. He has given his horses and wine to Lord Wellington, of whom he is an enthusiastic admirer, I am told—well he may. Several negotiations have been going on for Lord Wellesley and Canning to come in, but it has gone off, and, I believe, because they could not settle about the lead in the House of Commons, and something, it is said, in a letter of Lord Castlereagh's to Lord Liverpool about Canning which Canning could not put up with.[325] It is a pity it is gone off; their names would have done good just now.

Elizabeth, Duchess of Devonshire,
To Augustus Foster.

CHISWICK, *August* 30, 1811.

Knowing your anxiety for me, I have written two or three times since my dreadful misfortune.[326] I hope others have too, for at first I could write but a line or two; calmer now, but as wretched; less stunned, and therefore more competent to feel the full extent of my loss. I can only wonder that my life and intellect have lasted. What is it that enables one to survive such a shock, so sudden, so unexpected, so overwhelming? God has supported me, and given me dear children and kind friends, and I ought to be, and am, grateful for these blessings, but indeed, my dearest Augustus, the husband whom I have lost was the creature of my adoration, and long had been so. He was so eminent in all that is good, amiable, noble, and praiseworthy. I almost wondered at my own happiness in being united to him, and when you was with us here, scarce more than three short months ago, there was not a day, scarcely an hour, I did not thank Heaven for the happiness of belonging to such a man. Oh God, it is too, too much. This place, too, so full of him; his dear, his gracious form in every part of these gardens so present, so fully impressed on my mind, that all appears at times a fearful dream. I will not distress you further, I know how you will feel for me, how you will regret him. Thankful I am, though that moment of misery never can be effaced from my heart, that I had strength to be with him to the last, and that it was in my arms that he expired; yes, expired, and I live to write it....

Elizabeth, Duchess of Devonshire,
To Augustus Foster.

CHISWICK, *Nov.* 3, 1811.

... You must be content for a while to get shabby letters from me, for though I do all I can to bear up in return for all the kindness shewn me, yet it is a hard task, and I feel that no time can give me a happy feel again. I shall be happy at moments when I see you, and the moment of return of those who are dear to me must be one of enjoyment to me, but life has lost that which gave it its great value, that which made me for a short time the happiest of human beings, for such a being as him surely never existed. What a wreck in these last few years! All that is pre-eminent is gone. To me it is as a desert, and but for my children what an exile should I feel in this world.... The King is worse and worse. The Duke of Clarence has proposed to Miss Long,[327] and has been rejected, but they say that he don't despair.

> *Elizabeth, Duchess of Devonshire,*
> *To Augustus Foster.*
>
> *November 4, 1812.*

Every thing is now so melancholy that nothing that can be said upon it can be too much, or even increase my misery, but I am happy in you, Augustus, Caro, and Clifford; but life has lost its charm, and the world the noblest creature that ever adorned it. To have been his; to bear his name is still my pride and comfort.... Lord Byron is come back,[328] Mr. Rogers told me, and very much improved, and regretting his satirical poem, which he wrote, he says, writhing with anger at the Edinburgh Review....

> *The Honble. Mrs. George Lamb*
> *To Augustus Foster.*
>
> LONDON, *November 6, 1812.*

My dear Augustus,—I have delayed answering your letter till half an hour before the time, and inexcusable as it is, with a month between each post day, to plead the want of time, I must make use of it to-day. I am now writing at a very melancholy moment. The Duchess is come to town to pack up all her things and to leave this house for ever. It is a moment I have always dreaded for her. I think a widow's situation at all times a most dreadful one; at the time that she wants most comfort and care she is obliged to leave her home and the comforts she has been used to all her life. There are a thousand little things, too, which have annoyed and worried her. It grieves me to the heart to see her unhappy. We are going to the seaside for a little while. The Liverpools have, I believe, lent her Walmer, and we shall go there till she has got a house in town, and she will then settle in London. I think it is the best place for her, for she is not very fond of the country, and, so used to Society as she has been all her life, I am sure that great retirement would be the worst thing for her. I have seen nothing of your friends in the north,[329] but I have heard nothing that need alarm you; great coldness to all the admirers.

I hope you received a letter I sent you from Lady Milbanke. She has persuaded, or rather forced, poor Sir Ralph to stand again for Durham, and I am afraid it will be absolute ruin, besides which, I hear he has no chance of carrying it. His opponents are Lord Barnard and Sir Harry Vane. I am just come from Brocket Hall. They are all going on very jollily there, and Caroe is a little less mad than usual....[330]

C. J. LAMB.

Elizabeth, Duchess of Devonshire,
To Augustus Foster.

January, 1812.

The restrictions end the 17th, and the King is worse than ever. You will see that the Catholick question has been brought on; dear Hartington seconded. Lord Fitzwilliam was very much frightened, but did it well, and ended with a true Cavendish sentiment, that, thinking this measure right, he supported it, and always would. Lord Morpeth spoke uncommonly well yesterday, but the question will go on for three days together. In Spain, Valencia has fallen, but so, I believe, has Ciudad Rodrigo to Lord Wellington. There never was surely so unfortunate a general as Blake. Lord Wellington has raised our military fame high, yet, I fear, if opposition came in they would cramp his means. God bless you, my dearest Augustus. I as yet see no body but the friends, the immediate friends, of him I know not how to live without, nor do I feel as if I ever could. Dear Georgiana is lying in. Harriet is absorbed in Lord G. L. Hartington is affectionate and kind, but very young and surrounded. Your brother and Caroline seldom leave me, but to-day I made them dine at Lord Cowper's. How shocked you will be to hear of poor William Cavendish's death.[331] I never heard of so dreadfull and awfull an accident, three minutes before they were all together the happiest family possible—poor wretched Mrs. Cavendish adored him; she is with child, which, I believe, alone supports her. Your correspondence is moved for, and, when produced, ministers say will do you the greatest credit. Oh! the comfort of that. I thank God for the children he has given me.

The Earl of Liverpool
         To

January, 1812.

Thursday, January.—My dear Lord,—I send you the correspondence with Sir James Craig on the subject of the Indians. The inclosures which contain the reasons and inducements to the Indians not to engage in hostilities with the United States it would not be desirable should be published, and need not perhaps be forwarded to Mr. Foster. The following facts appear clear, however, from Sir J. Craig's letter, that as soon as he knew of any intentions on the part of the Indians to commence hostilities he informed Mr. Morier of the circumstance in order that he might make a communication thereupon to the American Government, that he at the same time and subsequently used every endeavour to dissuade the Indians from their projects of hostilities, and that his conduct was approved from home in the month of July last, and Sir George Prevost directed to pursue the same course of procedure,—Ever yours sincerely,

LIVERPOOL.

The Earl of Aberdeen
         To Augustus Foster.

ARGYLL HOUSE, *Feb.* 5, 1812.

My dear Augustus,—I wish it was in my power to give you some positive information concerning that which must interest you very much, as well as it does us. I mean the formation of the Ministry after the expiration of the restrictions. Until very lately no one doubted that every thing would remain as it is. It is certain, however, that Lord Wellesley has given in his resignation, and only holds the seals pro tempore. The cause is assigned to some radical difference of opinion between him and Perceval on several subjects, but principally on the conduct of the war. It is thought that this step will shake the foundations of the present Government, and indeed destroy its existence altogether. This is also my belief. We have a report of a Government being formed, of which Wellesley and Canning are to be the principal members, but this is highly improbable. If any change takes place it will be for the purpose of bringing in the opposition.

I read with great satisfaction your correspondence with Mr. Monroe, and, although it is possible that I might view it with partial eyes, I find the general impression is just that which I could desire. We are at least come to believe in the possibility of a war; perhaps even now it is not intended, but the language recently adopted certainly threatens it.

I received your barrels of apples, which are said to be excellent. Thinking that all apples are turnips growing on trees, I am not an apple-eater.

You will probably hear many reports about the Prince's health: in order that you may not be deceived, I can tell you that he is in reality well. There is a strange numbness in his hands, but even if it gets worse there is no sort of danger, for I understand it is a very common thing. Believe me, very affectly.

yours,

ABERDEEN.

Elizabeth, Duchess of Devonshire,
To Augustus Foster.
PICCADILLY TERRACE, *Feb.* 29, 1812.

I begin before the regular day, my dearest Augustus, because I want to tell you without delay how much I feel the kindness of your letters, and of how great a comfort they are to me. They are the greatest possible comfort, first, because they prove you feel my misfortune, as it soothes me that it should be felt, great and terrible even to think of; then that you shew me how you know how he deserved, and saw how I adored him I have lost, my dear, dear husband, and yet that you try to turn my thoughts to that which I should be and am gratefull for, the affection of you all, my dear children, and of his children, and that, since grief did not kill me at first, that I must try to live in health for them to whom I am yet a source of comfort. To your affection, to your conduct, publick and private, dearest Augustus, I look for much of what I can yet experience of pleasure and comfort.... Caro means to see la bella Anabella before she writes to you. I don't like the last letter which you received, and I shall almost hate her if she is blind to the merits of one who would make her so happy.... As to politicks, they are in a state as novel as distressing. Dear Lord Wellesley has resigned. Lord Castlereagh succeeds. The Prince Regent quarrels with his old friends, and abuses his new ones. Sheridan and Lord Lauderdale declare in his name to G. Ponsonby that the Catholick question shall not be made a Cabinet one, and Perceval contradicts this in his speech in Parliament the next day. It is all inconceivable.

March 3rd.

To-night on Orders in Council it is expected to divide so strong as to leave Ministers a majority only of 40. This in common times would have been reckoned a defeat, and Lord North would have resigned on it, but Perceval, I believe, would stay in at all risks. I shall add a few lines to-morrow. It is since I began this letter, I believe, that the Ministers were beat on Banks' motion for not granting Col. M'Mahon the place which the Prince Regent had given him. People say it is the first instance of Parliament refusing to confirm the first act of favour of a new reign. To me, who really love the Prince, this is melancholy; but he sits all evening in Manchester Square, and loses sight of all but the politicks of that little circle. Now, though I do believe that there is no cry for the opposition in the country, yet the people dislike his having forsaken his friends of 25 years in that way, and I could have wished that he had sent to them, and fairly said that, being determined to go on with the war in Spain, that he would not now call them to his Councils, but having the same friendship and esteem for them, that he should still look to them when circumstances allowed him to do so. No half measure or trickery ever did credit to the person or service to their cause....

> Lord Palmerston
>> To Sir Augustus Foster.
>>> WAR OFFICE, *March* 25, 1812.

Dear Foster,—Mr. Lawrence, the bearer of this, is connected with my brother in law, Mr. Sulivan, and, being bound to America, is desirous of having the advantage of being made known to you. I know too well the extent of business which you must have upon your hands at the present moment to do more than write two lines to say that if you should have it in your power officially to be of any use to him without much inconvenience to yourself, I should be very much obliged to you for any attention which you may shew him.

I hope Buonaparte's last communications with his Conservative Senate may be of use to you as to the question of the existence of the French Decrees. If you make musick of the Americans you will accomplish what appears next to impossible, and yet you seem to be making progress. I suppose the Suaviter in Modo fortiter in Re tells with them as it does with others.[332]—Yours very truly,

> PALMERSTON.

> *Augustus Foster*
>> *To Elizabeth, Duchess of Devonshire.*
>>> WASHINGTON, *April* 18, 1812.

... I am afraid my chance is small with Miss Milbanke. Indeed, staying as long as I do here, it is scarce just to think I can keep an interest with her sufficient to balance in any degree against the daily assiduities she must listen to. I wish, however, very much that I could go home, for I cannot consent to add to the number of diplomatic old bachelors.... Here they talk more loudly than before of war. The French Minister, on being told that France was threatened as well as England, said he must in that case solicit an interview with the British Minister, in order for us to concert together measures of defence against so alarming a power. A great many people are afraid of being laughed at if they don't fight. It is really a curious state of things. They even refer to me occasionally to ask what we should think of them. I am on good terms with almost all. Good living, you are very right in saying, has its effect here.

Elizabeth, Duchess of Devonshire,
To Augustus Foster.

LONDON, *May* 4, 1812.

... I have sent you a very beautiful poem by Lord Byron, who continues to be made the greatest fuss with. The Edinburgh Review is just come out with their critique on it. They praise it because they cannot help doing so; but whilst they accuse him of bitterness in resenting their former illiberal review of his "Minor Poems", they, I think, betray how much they smarted, and still smart, under the keenness of his lash in the "English Bards and Scotch Reviewers": Your brother read it to me, which is a favor most rare, I assure you; but it was very pleasant, and I wish he did it oftener. The *Character* is really all written by Adair, but I own to you I thought with you that it was superior to his usual powers; but it is his and his alone; he did it at my request, and in two days' time. I will send you two or three that if there is anybody you think worthy to possess one that you may give it to them—to Randolph, for instance.... As to that particular *object*, you will have had letters from Caroline and me, which will have, to our great regret, put an end to all our hopes on that subject. The only comfort is that it was, on her part, though not on her mother's, over before you went. She persists in saying that she never suspected your attachment to her, but she is so odd a girl that though she has for some time rather liked another, she has decidedly refused them, because she thinks she ought to marry a person with a good fortune, and this is partly, I believe from generosity to her parents, and partly owning that fortune is an object to herself for happiness. In short, she is good, amiable, and sensible, but cold, prudent, and reflecting. What I have told you is a great secret; you must not breathe it, and I will let you know if there is any change. She is at present with Lady Gosford, but expects her parents this week: we must look out for something better. Lord Byron makes up to her a little, but she don't seem to admire him except as a poet, nor he her, except for a wife. Your little friend, Caro William,[333] as usual, is doing all sorts of imprudent things for him and with him; he admires her very much, but is supposed by some to admire our Caroline more; he says she is like Thyrsa, and her singing is enchantment to him. Dearest life! don't fret about Annabella. I don't think you will, as Lady Selina made a little episode—only guard against American beauties, and we must seek for something more glowing than Annabella; and when you return, who knows what we may meet with. You will have heard of the fall of Badajoz, and the hope of liberating the South West of Spain from Ballesteros being, as it is said, at Seville. Lord Wellington is indeed an eminent Man, and all parties agree in their praise of him. Marmont is said to have invested Ciudad Rodrigo,[334] which must cripple Lord Wellington's movements to the South, but it must be hoped not more than this; and he is said to have taken Badajoz four days sooner than he said, and to have sent divisions off to Ciudad Rodrigo two days after its fall. I hope there may be some news to send you before the letter goes.

5th.

Ministers were beat last night on Mr. Banks' motion on sinecure places. To-night is Lord Holland's motion about America, Mr. Henry's business, and I understand that Lord Liverpool will deny it, though they won't give up the correspondence. Pray Heaven that they may be able to do so, and that dear England may remain with unblemished honor. The accounts from Spain seem good (the French retired from Almeida and C. Rodrigo), and doubly good, in that the Portuguese troops have learnt to fight well, even when not in the presence of the hero Wellington. The accounts of riots in France are confirmed, I am told, and "Bread, Peace, or the head of the Tyrant" was stuck upon the Tuilleries.... Things are in an uncomfortable state, for though the riots are amongst the manufacturers, there is no doubt but that there are ill-intentioned people stirring them up, and that there is a good deal of alarm, all which would be increased by the sort of unpopularity attending the Royal family from the want of state and show which all communities like, and which the people think their due. I trust, however, that the good sense of the English, and the example of the French will keep all things quiet.... I told Adair how much you liked his character, and how much Randolph liked it, and he came to me this morning to thank me, and he expressed how flattered he was.

Elizabeth, Duchess of Devonshire,
   To Augustus Foster.

LONDON, *May* 10, 1812.

... You will see with pleasure that F. Ponsonby has distinguished himself, and I think you must be proud of your Country's Victories, and heroick valour. What say the Americans to it.... With all this I fear we have a weak administration at home, and a systematized spirit of riot difficult to subdue. Every body regrets Lord Wellesley.[335] I sent you by the last messenger Lord Byron's beautifull poem. The parts about Greece will be doubly interesting to you: he continues to be the great attraction at all parties and suppers. The ladies, I hear, spoil him, and the gentlemen are jealous of him. He is going back to Naxos, and then the husbands may sleep in peace. I should not be surprized if Caro William were to go with him, she is so wild and imprudent.

May 11

I am sorry to have to add to my parcel the horrid news that Perceval was just now shot dead in the lobby of the House of Commons.[336] I never felt more horror at any thing. A murder of that kind has not happened in England since Queen Anne's time, and in the midst of the horror and concern for the particular event, one can't help dreading its opening a new epoch in the English character. I trust not, and it really is most horrid. Think of his poor wife and children. If I hear more I will add it to this. Your brother told me when I came home from a quiet, melancholy walk. He had been walking with Colonel Foster. They saw several people riding full speed towards the House, and soon after, this, which they thought idle rumour, was confirmed.

Augustus Foster
   To Elizabeth, Duchess of Devonshire.

WASHINGTON, *May* 26, 1812.

I see you don't like Annabella much.[337] She is certainly rather too cold in her manners, and gives to reason too much empire over her mind, but she has good eyes, is fair, has right ideas, and sense, and mildness. I don't think she will ever be able to love very warmly; but yet I believe she thinks she ought to wait till the spirit moves her, and the spirit perhaps may never come, as I fancy happens to many of her temperament. I long most anxiously to get back to settle that point, good or bad. No Minister ever had such temptations to break up a negotiation. I would give the world to go back for six months, and am miserable that I can't do so, but I can't leave these members to themselves two days together.

From General Moreau
    To Augustus Foster, Esq., then at Mentone.
                                NEW YORK, 26th Mai, 1812.

Monsieur,—J'ai reçu la lettre que vous m'avez fait l'honneur de m'écrire & les passeports que vous avez eu la Complaisance de m'envoyer. Mad^e· Moreau vous prie de vouloir bien agreer tous ses Remercimens. Messres le Roy & Rayard Croyent que le navire le *powhatan* allant sur son Lest & muni de votre recommendation n'est pas susceptible d'étre pris: si cependant ces Mess se ravisent & desirent que le navire y soit mentionné J'aurai l'honneur de vous en faire part.

Je suis très reconnoisant des Reproches que vous me faites d'avoir Resté si peu de tems à Washington, mais que pouvait y faire un ministere entre les decrès de Milan & de Berlin, les ordres en Conseil, L'acte de non importation, L'ambargo & productions bizarres, dont tout le monde parle, que peu de personne comprennent & sur lesquelles on ne s'entendra jamais, & puis j'etais pressé de jouir de l'importance que donne le Retour de la Capitale, Aurons nous la guerre me demandoit on de toute part? Je repondois que n'ayant vu que des gens très tranquilles, très pacifiques, & très éloignés les uns des autres (vous savez que les maisons ne se touchent pas) on devoit presumer qu'on ne se battroit pas: que Cependant, ayant entendu tout le monde Se plaindre de l'ennui, ce qui à la longue donne de l'humeur, it étoit possible qu'on finit par se facher tout de bon.

Avec cette maniere de repondre on se trompe rarement, on n'ote L'esperance a personne, & on acquiere des droits a devenir prophete.

Je prie v. ex. d'agreer l'assurance des sentimens de la consideration la plus distingués avec lesquels je suis. Monsieur, Votre très humble and très obeissant serviteur,

                                        V. MOREAU.

Elizabeth, Duchess of Devonshire,
    To Augustus Foster.
                                        May 28, 1812.

... The Prince Regent was there, and in pretty good spirits, the crowd and heat enormous;—but now your eyes have wandered over this for a name more interesting. Well, Annabella was there; Annabella looked well; Annabella and I got more acquainted than I have done yet. Caroline called her to sit by her. I made room, and we all three sat on a couch. I liked her countenance and manners. Old twaddle Ralph and I are all cordiality,[338] and Lady Milbanke called her daughter to speak to me, who said, "I had the honor of talking to the Duchess"—which we had in the further room. She did not ask me about you, which I was glad of; indifference would have made her inquire out of civility; the father did.

June 1.

The accounts have confirmed the Jersey telegraph account. Soult is defeated with immense loss....[339] Lady Milbanke came up to me last night at Mrs. Siddons', and inquired most kindly about you—said she should hear from you as soon as you arrived, and said that if you could adjust things in America you would come home to honor and distinction, and how delightful that would be. The girl still never names you to me—tant mieux.

Elizabeth, Duchess of Devonshire,
To Augustus Foster.

June 2,1812.

I wrote to you about a fortnight ago, just after poor Mr. Perceval's horrid assassination, and we have continued since that without an administration. Lord Liverpool was named first Lord of the Treasury, but not kissed hands, and Mr. Wortley's motion obliged them to resign. The Regent then sent to Lord Wellesley to form or propose a plan for a new administration, and Lord Wellesley brought about a reconciliation between the Regent and Lord Moira. Both these Peers have tried to make arrangements for opposition to come in, but the Prince could not be prevailed on to admit them. Down to the 30th nothing was done. The Prince saw all parties, except Grey and Grenville, but nothing could be fixed on. The ex-Ministers, except Lord Melville, declare that they won't serve with Lord Wellesley. At last, yesterday, Canning announced in the House that Lord Wellesley had the Prince's authority to proceed to the forming of a new administration, and he did submit a paper to them. The Prince expressed a wish to have Moira, Erskine, and Ellenborough in the Cabinet; they were (Grey and Grenville) to name the others of their party, making five opposition Cabinet Ministers if the number was 12, and six if it was 13—Lord Wellesley, of course, to name the others. Well, all appeared smooth and promising when, behold! opposition find out that it is unconstitutional for the Sovereign to name any of the Ministers except the first Lord who is to form it; and so they refuse. My brother says that the talk of the streets was to blame the opposition; to say that the Sovereign has a right to name his Ministers, and that the opposition have refused on grounds of personal ambition. This is a most provoking denouement. I will hope that something may yet be done, but it is a faint hope; however, I will add to-morrow what I hear; it must, I think, be decided one way or another. The Liverpools have been very much hurt with Wortley, but he went to him first, and did it in a feeling and gentlemanlike manner. The truth is, the administration have been weak to a criminal degree.

Lady Erne was so fretted and vexed that she went back to Hampton Court. Lady Hervey is with me, cheerful and good-humoured as she always is. Caroline W. Lamb is quietly, thank heaven! at Brocket with William and all of them. My Caroline is more than ever liked and admired—pur non è felice. Your Annabella is a mystery; liking, not liking; generous minded, yet afraid of poverty; there is no making her out. I hope you don't make yourself unhappy about her; she is really an icicle. Lady Milbanke will make Sir Ralph stand the next election, which, as it will be a contested one, will ruin him, and he is with one foot in the grave; so it is doubly ill-judged. The rest of your friends are well, and I am better, and only wondering that I live.

> *General Moreau*
> > *To Augustus Foster.*
>
> > > NEW YORK, *le 7 juin*, 1812.

Monsieur,—J'ai reçu la lettre que vous m'avez fait l'honneur de m'écrire le 2 de ce mois celle du 3 m'avoit soulagé d'un fardeau. Bien pesant puisque comme vous l'observez vous même ma femme se trouvoit hors de grans ambaras et eviter un detour et des retards d'au moins 40 jours.

Votre derniere m'a replongé dans des inquietudes d'autant plus grandes que la santé de Madame Moreau epuisée par une fatigue consecutive de six jours—Employés a faire en hatte paquets la met presque dans l'impossibilité de profiter du paquebot qui surement fera voile cette semaine—au moins ses medecins le pensent ainsi, Jugez comme elle se trouvoit soulagée par l'espoir d'aller sur le powhatan.

J'ai vu Messres le Roy and Rayard; ils n'ont jamais pensé a porter une Cargaison sous la protection de votre recommendation, et m'ont assuré que quelque soit la Speculation du retour du navire ils n'avoient jamais pensé à en profiter—il me semble au reste que pour L'empecher vous pouvez specifier que le navire doit etre sur son Lest et n'avoir que des passagers, marchandise dont la Capture ne l'embarassent guerres.

Au reste si le vaisseau etoit conduit en Angleterre elle n'auroit pour se rendre en france que la même peine qu'elle auroit en y allant par le paquebot. Une circonstance dont je n'ai pu vous faire part dans ma lettre de Samedi, C'est que quelque personnes de New York avoient Reçu des lettres de Washington ou on leur Mentionnoit Le depart du powhatan avec des depeches du gouvernement americain, un passeport de vous et que vous m'en aviez donné avis.

Je desirerois Bien que Mr. Monroe persistat dans cette opinion, mais s'il y a guerre tous les Beaux Reves peuvent etre detruits, hier on n'y Croyoit pas, aujourd'hui on la craint; C'est comme la fievre intermittente, au reste on pourrait dire à ces Mess. il y a justement 20 ans que quelques Scervelés de L'assemblée de france (1792) declarerent la guerre à l'autriche et a la prusse, elle dure encore!

J'attends avec Bien de l'impatience une reponse à la lettre que j'eus l'honneur de vous ecrire le 6, elle decidera de nos esperances, Je presume que Mr. Monroe me repondra aussi.

Dans le cas ou ma femme ne pourroit partir ni par le powhatan ni par le paquebot, croyez vous qu'il en viendra un autre, ou Supposez vous qu'il y aura quelqu'autre occasion pour l'Angleterre au commencement du mois prochain; la guerre pourroit elle y apporter quelqu' obstacle.—Monsieur, votre très humble and très obeissant Serviteur,

V. MOREAU.

Elizabeth, Duchess of Devonshire,
    To Augustus Foster.

July 4, 1812.

On the 8th I go to Portland Place. We are very good friends, and la madre is anxious about you.[340] Annabella is silent still. I hear of no one likely to be favoured by her, so I shall still live in hope for you.

Augustus Foster
    To Elizabeth, Duchess of Devonshire.
        COPENHAGEN, *August* 10, 1812.

... Never was Minister's arrival so grateful to a people as mine here. The Queen said such things to me as proved how delighted they are. Fortunately I had to use my own discretion in a great measure, and had to use all the grace of conferring the greatest obligation on a Country that it can receive. I was first in recognizing the state of peace here, and the Queen said to-day my coming was the first moment of happiness they have known for a long time....

The Honble. Mrs. George Lamb
    To Augustus Foster.

CHISWICK, *August* 31.

My dear Augustus,—I wrote to you last at a most melancholy moment, and you will feel anxious, I am sure, to hear from us again, and particularly to know how your dear mother is. We have now been at Chiswick near a month, and I think the fresh air and quiet of this place has done her good, and though, of course, after all she has gone through, her recovery must be slow, yet it is a great deal to have been free from fever and regaining strength. Her spirits are very bad, and here there are a thousand recollections which, though they endear the place to us all, yet keep up the dreadful recollection that what made us once so happy is gone for ever. It gave us the greatest pleasure to hear that ministers are very much pleased with your dispatches: the only comfort she can now receive is from the affection of those that are left to her, and we must exert ourselves to the utmost for her.

I am glad to hear that you have written to Lady Milbanke. I think it ought to keep up the interest which she certainly feels for you. I saw a good deal of Annabella this year, and liked her very much indeed. At first she constantly enquired after you, but one day I talked of you as knowing of your attachment to her, and she was much embarrassed, and has never mentioned you since. Another thing which speaks very well for you is that Sir Ralph, whose judgment is, I believe, entirely formed upon that of the female part of his family, praises you, I hear, beyond any thing. I should think it wrong, my dear Augustus, to make you too sanguine by telling you these things, but that I think that at such distance and parted for such a length of time it would be cruel not to give you all the comfort I can. Besides, I feel great horror at the possibility of an American Mrs. Foster. God bless you, dear Augustus. I hope we shall soon have you amongst us again. Yours very aff.,

C. J. LAMB.

VERSES ADDRESSED BY LORD BYRON
IN THE YEAR 1812 TO THE HONBLE. MRS. GEORGE
LAMB.

The sacred song that on my ear
Yet vibrates from that voice of thine,
I heard before from one so dear,
'Tis strange it still appears divine.
But oh! so sweet that *look* and *tone*
To her and thee alike is given;
It seemed as if for me alone
That *both* had been recalled from Heaven.
And though I never can redeem
The vision thus endeared to me,
I scarcely can regret my dream
When realized again by thee.

Elizabeth, Duchess of Devonshire,
    To Augustus Foster.

1812. (?)

... I always say that you don't tell me what is going on, but I make it a rule not to ask you. I am most anxious for it if it is possible without a sacrifice of national honor. It does seem as if it were more for the interest of America to be friends with us, who are masters of the sea, than with France, who has no fleet. Sweden seems determined to be independent. It is said Russia is going to war, and Armfeldt to have a command, but Bonaparte means, they say, to command in person, and if so, the odds are in his favor. Meanwhile dear Spain maintains the conflict, and perhaps may profit of the war between Russia and France.

The subject of conversation, of curiosity, of enthusiasm almost, one might say, of the moment is not Spain or Portugal, Warriors or Patriots, but Lord Byron! You probably read the Edinburgh Review's criticism of his "Minor Poems", published in 1808, not merely severe, but flippant. They prophesied and entreated never to hear more as a Poet of this young Lord. On this, stung to the quick, he published, without a name, his "English Bards and Scotch Reviewers". The prodigious success of this made him publish a second edition with his name and additional lines and notes, and, going abroad, said that on his return he would answer to any who called on him. He returned sorry for the severity of some of his lines, and with a new poem, "*Childe Harold*", which he published. This poem is on every table, and himself courted, visited, flattered, and praised whenever he appears. He has a pale, sickly, but handsome countenance, a bad figure, animated and amusing conversation, and, in short, he is really the only topic almost of every conversation—the men jealous of him, the women of each other. I have my accounts from Caroline, Caro William, and Lady Bessborough—all agree in their accounts. The misery is that his severest lines were on Lord Carlisle, and therefore Lord Morpeth has not yet and can't bear to meet him. But Lord Byron has bought up all the third edition, which is a great sacrifice to have made, and ought to conciliate everybody....

> *General Moreau*
> *To his Wife.*

LAUN, 30 *août*, 1813.

Ma chere amie,—A la bataille de Dresde il y a trois jours j'ai eu les deux jambes emportés d'un boulet de canon.

Ce coquin de Bonaparte est toujours heureux. On m'a fait l'emputation aussi bien que possible quoique l'armée ait foit un mouvement retrograde ce n'est nullement par revers mais par décousu, et pour se rapprocher du Gal Blucher excuse mon griffonage je t'aime et t'embrasse de tout mon coeur je charge Rapatel de finir.[341]

V. M.

This copy of Gen. Moreau's letter to his wife was given to me by her.
E. DEVONSHIRE. Richmond, 1813.

Madam Moreau gave me this copy of General Moreau's letter' to his wife. I saw the original at her house.

E. D.

> *Alexander I, Emperor of Russia,*
> *To Madame Moreau.*

Madame,—Lorsque l'affreux malheur qui atteignit à mes côtes le général Moreau me priva des lumières et de l'expérience de ce grand homme je nourissois l'espoir qu'a force de soins on parviendroit à le conserver à sa famille et à mon amitié—la providence en a disposé autrement—il est mort comme il a vécu dans la pleine énergie d'un âme fort et constant—il n'est qu'un remède aux grandes peines de la vie celui de les voir partager—en

Russie Madame vous trouverez partout ce sentiment et s'il vous convient je rechercherai tous les moyens d'embellir l'existence d'une personne dont je me fais un devoir sacré d'être le consolateur et l'appui. Je vous prie d'y compter irrevocablement de ne me laisser ignorer aucune circonstance ou je pourrai vous être de quelqu' utilité et de m'écrire toujours directement—prevenir vos desirs sera une jouissance pour moi—l'amitié que j'avois voué à votre époux va au dela du tombeau et je n'ai pas d'autre moyen de m'acquitter du moins en partie envers lui que parceque je serai en même de faire pour assurer le bien être de sa famille—recevez Madame dans ces tristes et cruelles circonstances les témoignages et l'assurance de mes sentiments,

ALEXANDRE.

toplitz C C., 7bre, 1813.

Copy of the Emperor of Russia's letter to Mad. Moreau. She gave it to me.

E. D.

Augustus Foster
To Elizabeth, Duchess of Devonshire.
December 13, 1813.

... I dined at the Hollands' yesterday, where were the Cowpers, Ossulstons, Abercrombies, Courtenays, &c. Lord Byron came in the evening. Madame de Stael was attacked at dinner for taking up so much of Sir James M'Intosh's time, and impeding the progress of the history. Allen, in the evening, maintained that she did not understand many of the systems of the Germans she undertook to explain, that she was very confused, and he could get no further than Fichte.... I went from there rather late to Madame de Stael's, where a few remained till past 12 discussing Pitt and Fox's comparative merits with Tacitus and Demosthenes. Madame de Stael strenuously argued Tacitus to be superior to all the rest, and Ward as strenuously put Pitt and Fox above Tacitus and Demosthenes. Madame de Stael said Burke shot above the heads of his auditors, which was agreed to, while Pitt was said to have fired point blank. Madame de Stael was indignant at an orator being put above the historian, and it must be owned to have been disinterestedness in Sir James not to have agreed with her.

Augustus Foster
   To Elizabeth, Duchess of Devonshire.

                       March 31, 1814.

Mr. Dicot is come from Paris....[342] He has much to relate of the public spirit in Paris. He came away on the 14th; he says the National Guard of Paris refused, both collectively and individually, to join Bonaparte's army; that it was proposed to eight hundred of the officers in a body one by one. He says they are resolved to capitulate if any corps of the Allies approach the gates. He laughs at the attempt to fortify the town. It seems part of the Bois de Vincennes and Boulogne was cut for chevaux de frise to protect the town against the Cossacks. Bonaparte has been très grossier in his language: he told the Council of State that Robespierre was the only great man produced by the Revolution; that he knows not why himself is detested so much, as he has not been as yet assez malheureux pour être cruel, and abuses them for their cry of Peace, Peace.

Augustus Foster
   To Elizabeth, Duchess of Devonshire.

                       March 31, 1814.

... I hear there is a Royalist Committee at Paris, and that Talleyrand communicates with them through a relation. D'Ellioto sounds Augereau,[343] who professed to hate Bonaparte, but to be for a Regency. Monni goes to Nanci, and Louis 18 waits the certain account of the rupture of negotiations to set off for Bordeaux. At Paris they shot people in the Bois de Vincennes and filled the prisons, but now the police dare not act, for the agents are known and would be put to death immediately. This is very like insurrection.

Letter from the Countess of Liverpool.

                      Friday, April 18, 1814.

Moniteurs are just arrived with most excellent news. A provisional Government has been formed at Paris, and their first act has been to set aside Bonaparte and his family. Les Dames de la Halle had waited on the Emperor Alexander, and had called out, "Vive les Bourbons". God bless you.—
Yrs.,
                              LOUISA LIVERPOOL.

Frederick Foster
> *To Augustus Foster.*

PARIS, *May* 1, 1814.

My dearest Augustus,—I miss you sadly. The noise drove me away from the Hotel de Bruxelles, and I am now at the Hotel des Ministres de l'Universite, still more noisy, but in a different way. Madame de Stael is arrived. I called on her yesterday, and found her in high spirits, surrounded by a crowd of admirers, and all talking, of course, of Bonaparte. They say he took opium, but, the dose having failed, he considers himself as preserved by Destiny for great things yet; says he was formed to rule the World, and as that failed, it little signifies between France and Elba; that France with the old limits could never have done, the army would not have borne it. On the 24th March the inhabitants of St. Dizier, I think, came to some of the Marshals to know if they were to obey Bonaparte's order of rising en masse. They replied, Oh, non; cette farce est finie.

F. TH. F.

Augustus Foster
> *To Elizabeth, Duchess of Devonshire.*

PARIS, *May* 3, 1814.

... To-day there was a great review of all the foreign troops, from 25,000 to 30,000, composing the garrison. The Russian Guards are really magnificent. Louis XVIII. was at a window to see them pass. The Emperor of Austria in the centre, with Alexander on his left and Frederick on his right, passed by me and joined the King to-night to go to Sir Charles Stuart's ball given to Alexander....[344] The old Guards certainly looked very brisk, and it is not to be disguised that Bonaparte is much regretted by the troops of the line. Count Meister, who used to be so sanguine, now occupies himself with the King, is in transports of joy, and thinks the Bourbons not so extremely severe; nevertheless so many general officers are committed, and so strong is the feeling against Napoleon in the middle orders, that I cannot think there is cause for apprehension. What has surprised everybody is the conduct of the Milanese, for Eugene was really believed to have been a favourite with them.[345]

5th.

The ball was highly interesting.... The Emperor Alexander was there in an English uniform for compliment; he was in stockings and shoes, a thing rare for him, and yet he did not wear the Garter, which we were surprised at; he puts the Garter round his own Star zigzag, which makes us English a little angry with him, as considering it is too great a liberty thus to alter an order: he was observed to pay great Court to La Marechale Ney; he danced with her and spoke a great deal to Ney; it is surmized that he wants to get as many Marshals as he can into his Service; there is not half so much fuss made with him at an assembly as with our Prince (the Prince Regent); he had scarcely room to pass, and backs were very often seen by him. The Emperor of Austria and King of Prussia have no fancy for balls it seems, but we had the two sons of the King and hosts of German Princes, besides Schwartzenberg,[346] un gros de très bonne physionomie; he has great frankness of countenance: there was also old Blucher,[347] with eight orders, looking like an old Satyr: he frequents a gambling-house every night and wins money: he is by no means so much esteemed for his military talents here as he is in London—indeed none of them are. An English officer who was with the army of Blucher says if he was to write his memoirs they would contain a succession of their blunders. I saw my old Weimar schoolfellow, Mounier's son, yesterday. He was made private secretary to Napoleon, and was employed by him to translate the English and German papers, of which the Courier, Times, and Morning-Chronicle were constantly received. He said the Emperor treated him "quelquefois de Philosophe, d' Anglomane", and was proceeding to give Sir Charles Stuart, with whom I went to see him, some interesting details when Berthier entered en frac.[348] ... Augereau himself gives the account I wrote to you in my last: it was at Porte l'Isere he met Napoleon, and M. De Fitzjames tells me an officer who was with Augereau saw Bonaparte take out of his pocket a copy of Augereau's proclamation to his soldiers, and heard him ask, "Ah comment avez vous pu dire ceci de moi", but he heard nothing more. Augereau took Bonaparte apart; they walked together some time, and on parting embraced. The soldiers of the Old Guard are very loud in their discontent, and make no secret of their reproaches of the generals for having betrayed them. Their joy was very considerable, and no doubt they feel the conquest at Paris, and there have been several duels between them and the foreign troops. However, they are too few, and it would be too desperate for them to attempt anything. General Drouet,[349] who, like Bertrand,[350] was brought up by Bonaparte and pushed into a high situation, has accompanied him, but everybody says it is "par point d'honneur et par principe", and not from attachment, that they accompany him. He bought the Bible at Lyons, and told the bookseller to address it to him as Empereur Napoleon.... Think of Lord Wellington arriving yesterday all at once like a great bomb just before the review; he was then on a grey horse, en chapeau rond, and people as soon as they knew it were almost estropiés in hurrying to see him. The Emperor Alexander had called on him immediately. He looks worn and older than Mr. Pole... To-day we made a party to St. Cloud. Its having been the favourite residence of Bonaparte was to me its greatest attraction, though the view is delightful and the rooms pretty magnificent. The concierge said he kicked his servants, and the gardener thought him amiable, and regretted him. They have taken away Bonaparte's family pictures which were there, and which Gerard supposes are to be sent to him in lieu of the originals, as he cannot have them.

> *Augustus Foster*
> > *To Elizabeth, Duchess of Devonshire.*
> > > > PARIS, *May* 5, 1814.

Napoleon is off: he embarked at Fréjus: he has Elba in soveraineté: he was obliged to put on a white cockade near Avignon; to ride and to pass as Lord Burghersh or Colonel Cambell, and even to cry Louis 18. Lord Wellington came yesterday before the review, where he was in plain clothes; crowds pressed to see him.... All the world was at Stewart's ball last night, and Alexander danced with Madame Ney. People think he wants to get as many Marshals as he can into his service.

> *Augustus Foster*
> > *To Elizabeth, Duchess of Devonshire.*
> > > > PARIS, *May* 7, 1814.

Paris, May 7, 1814..... We are just come from being presented to the King of Prussia. The Duke of Wellington was there in the Blue Ribbon. Yesterday the messenger arrived with the *Gazette*, and in time for him to be presented as Duke to the Emperor of Austria, who invested him with the Grand Order of Maria Theresa, which he wore at the opera. He was loudly applauded; hats taken off; all stood up and hurrahed. The applause was even greater than that given to the Duke of Berri,[351] who had come into the Royal box, and who was repeatedly obliged to bow during the evening, the piece given—"Colenetti"—having many allusions to the Bourbons....[352] Yesterday we went to St. Cloud. The Concierge says there is no servant with Bonaparte but Ali, a Mamelouk,[353] who had been sent away through the jealousy of Rustan, and whom Napoleon is too happy now to have. He can shave himself, fortunately. I suppose the account of his journey will be in all the papers. He cried a good deal, I hear; but how flattering to us his confidence in us. He was so taken up with saving himself and baggage he did not seem to pay attention to the circumstance of embarking at Frejus, which took place there as more convenient than St. Trogues. At St. Cloud the gardener seemed to regret him, and described him as walking very amicably with the Empress in an avenue every morning, when they would embrace and separate. An Austrian who was on guard there expressed surprise at the Empress loving him as she did. He said all the Austrian and Russian armies were firmly convinced the child was not his son. We see very few of the French, and at the opera there were not ten ladies to a hundred men.

> *Elizabeth, Duchess of Devonshire,*
> *To Augustus Foster.*
>
> *May 8, 1814.*

... I did not suspect Bonaparte to have been reduced to ride for his life, and to pass for an Englishman to save himself, and cry vive Louis 18! What a lesson for ill weaned ambition! I am delighted that the ceremony of the 3rd was so fine, and the feeling so general for the King. We must expect some sadness amongst the troops, who, accustomed for so long to war and plunder, almost dread a state of quiet...

> *Augustus Foster*
> *To Elizabeth, Duchess of Devonshire.*
>
> PARIS, *May 8, 1814.*

May 8.—We went to Gerard's to-day. He is the last who made a picture of Napoleon, and it bears the mark of the Russian and Spanish campaigns. There is a savage ferocity in the countenance that is quite disgusting. I was much pleased at Gerard's account of Drouet, who was a man hardly ever seen at Court, but, having been advanced by Napoleon, has thought it dishonourable to quit him. He even told him that, having a few thousand livres of his own, he should not be a burden upon him, but pay his own expenses. What a contrast to his own family! Pauline having refused to follow him,[354] and even his mother not coming forward to comfort him. She was a most avaricious old jade, Gerard says, that was always putting by, as she thought things would not last. Gerard says the Oueen of Naples is the best of the sisters, and Eliza the most like him. His face was covered with tears on his journey at one place, and the next day he talked of the Powers of Europe as if he was at the Tuileries.... I find Bernadotte had a great party here,[355] as had Maria Louisa,[356] and as the former missed stays (excuse a sea term) the latter would have had his men had she stayed here. I saw Madame De Coigny to-day, who thought so too....[357] I saw Weissenberg at Castlereagh's last night.[358] He says Bonaparte did tell him he should have fared better had he married a Russian, and thinks had Maria Louisa stayed at Paris she would have much embarrassed him. Bonaparte had commissioned Weissenberg to abdicate for him in favour of his son. Madame De Coigny and another lady I saw at her house think there is no doubt she would be Regent had she stayed. Throughout the Austrian and Russian army it is believed the King of Rome is not his son, but Weissenberg declares he is very like him, and it is "malheureusement trop vrai".

> *Augustus Foster*
> > *To Elizabeth, Duchess of Devonshire.*
>
> > > > *June*, 1814.

... I am sure you must have been sorry for poor Josephine's death.[359] It seems to have been very sudden, and I dare say will afflict Napoleon if he ever had any feeling. They say he is very busy arranging his Court. I suppose he will actually leave no stone unturned in his whole island....

> *Augustus Foster*
> > *To Elizabeth, Duchess of Devonshire.*

[Fragment of a letter written from Paris in 1814.]

Mr. —— saw Napoleon often after the retreat from Leipzig, and says he was not changed in manner, as could be perceived, except that he took larger doses of snuff than was usual, and in a more hurried manner; and when the Legislative Body met he hurried across the hall to his throne and back again in rather a precipitate manner. You know Captain Usher kept a regular journal while on board; it must be very curious: a general Montoro and family have been to see Elba: they saw Napoleon, who invited them to return in a few hours, and they would find him surrounded by his Court. In effect, he had a little theatre fitted up for the mock assemblage of his Elba courtiers. Lord Liverpool says nothing surprizes him but this mania of being sovereign in little; to me, however, it appears reconcilable to the general feature of his character, namely, contempt of the whole human race, whom he uses as the servile instruments of his power, or of his amusements. I wish you could see my schoolfellow, Le Mounier,[360] who was his private secretary for six years.

Augustus Foster
       To Elizabeth, Duchess of Devonshire.

1814.

Bernadotte is quite fallen with every body. One half Paris seems to blame his conduct to Bonaparte, and the other his slowness. He had it in his power to act a magnificent part, and he has ruined himself by too nice calculations: however, Alexander will still help him in Norway. *He* stands as high as it is possible for man; every body praises him. The Parisians, however, are not yet quite rid of their fears for the Museum; he was observed to be noting several articles a few days ago which has excited alarm. Madame de Stael called here yesterday, and was full of contempt for the French character and of blame of Bernadotte. There is a great soreness at the having a foreign garrison in Paris. One meets with all colours of foreign uniforms galloping in every direction, and Germans and Russians standing sentinels in almost every street. The generals and Ministers are quartered upon French houses. Castlereagh was put into that of the Ministre du tresor publique, Cathcart into Berthier's at first,[361] afterwards into Junot's,[362] Lord Aberdeen into Arrighi's.[363] The latter's Aide de Camp swore at first he should not come in, but Aberdeen very spiritedly threatened to send a party of Cossacks to bivouack in his yard; then they surrendered, though he carried away every article of furniture till he found Aberdeen was a quiet gentlemanlike man, and then he sent a few articles of furniture, and came back to lodge in the *second* story himself. The foreign troops are going soon, and the King of Prussia is to set off in a week for England. Last night at the Théâtre des Varietes they acted Le Souper de Henry IV.,[364] in which there is a great deal inserted for the occasion and with great judgment, full of moderation and of menagement for the military glory of the Nation, and it was received with great applause. It is impossible to stand higher than the English do here; people of all sorts are striving which shall best express the feeling to us. The French, too, open themselves to us without scruple upon their affairs. One man at Amiens absolutely shed tears at the degradation of his country when he found himself alone with Frederick. The Prussians behave well in the great towns, but commit a great deal of injustice in the villages; one told me they had Champagne enough to bathe in in Champagne.... I should add here that Bernadotte is well satisfied with his allies, but when a levée he was to have had was put off, ill natured persons endeavoured to make out it was because few persons were likely to attend.

> *Frederick Foster*
> > *To Augustus Foster.*
>
> MARSEILLES, *Dec.* 27, 1814.

My dearest Augustus…. We have seen Massena. He is, I believe, stingy, but very civil, and very interesting to see. Bonaparte on embarking for Elba sent him his amitiés, c'est un brave homme je l'aime fort—but Massena says he, Bonaparte, loves nobody; that once when he was ill, Bonaparte never took the least notice of him, never even sent to enquire, and that at another time, when he was also unwell, and that Bonaparte had need of his services, he used to come and see him three or four times a day. He thinks he was a man *de grandes conceptions*, particularly when things went on well, but that in adverse fortune he failed. Believes that Austria wishes to have it in her power to "*lacher un tel dogue*" against Russia and France; yet Massena seemed to have a kind of liking for him; said that it was him who had named him *l'enfant de la Victoire*, and pointing to his great coat said he was happier when he bought that, it was at Vienna. He wishes for war, if it was only to push forward his son. Massena is much broken and altered from what I remember him at the peace of Amiens. He and Wellington met at Paris, and after a stare Massena said, "Milord, *vous m'avez fait bien penser*". "*Et vous Monsieur le Maréchal vous m'avez souvent empêche, de dormir.*" We have heard here the same account of Bonaparte's southern journey as we did at Paris in May. At Dijon they gave L—— B—— the same *Bidet* that poor Napoleon rode when disguised as a courier. M—— told that at Orgon he got out of the carriage pour ——, and trembled excessively: had he passed through here they tell us he could not have escaped—and indeed this is far the most Bourbon town we have seen.

> F. T. F.

> *Elizabeth, Duchess of Devonshire,*
> > *To Augustus Foster.*
>
> MARSEILLES, *December* 30, 1814.

Massena lives in the same street with us; he is full of attention to us,[365] and, though broken in health and spirits, animates on topicks which interest him. I heard that he would not talk about Bonaparte, and I was fearful, though very anxious, to name the subject. Last night we went to the prefect's, who has a fine house, and gave a very pretty ball. Massena sat between Lady Bessborough and me; he said something about Grassini. "Oh," I said, too happy to find an occasion, "Etoit ce quand Bonaparte fut si amoureux d'elle?" "Bonaparte," his eye assuming a stern expression, "Bonaparte n'a jamais aimé personne, personne." I then went on from one thing to another, I found I could do so, and it was very interesting. "Quelle impression, Monsieur le Marechale, vous fit il, quand vous le connûtes premièrement?" "Un grand orgueil, Madame la Duchesse. Je l'ai connu qu'il n'étoit que Lieutenant colonel—des moyens, et pour cela de grand moyens, surtout dans la prosperité; dans l'adversité il manquoit de tête, il n'avoit rien de grand." Of himself he said, "il m'aimoit ou en faisoit semblant, car jamais il n'a rien aimé que son ambition; il me tutoya c'étoit a Milan quand il commandoit en chef qu'il me dit, 'Massena ne voudroit tu être un des directeurs?' 'Non,' je lui répondit, 'je ne me connais pas en politique, je ne sais faire que la guerre—mais toi ne voudrais tu pas en être?' Il me repondit *'avec quatre imbéciles, non, moi seul oui'*." He continued, "C'est lui qui m'a baptisé enfant de la victoire—et bien, avec cela je fis une chute qui m'empêchoit d'être avec l'arméee; il vint quatre fois la nuit me voir." "Mais cela," I said, "marquoit quelque sensibilité." "Il avoit besoin de moi. Je fis une maladie après, non seulement il ne vint pas; il n'envoya pas même savoir de mes nouvelles." Many other things he told us, and we talked about, and it was very interesting. I'm afraid he don't live as he ought to do, but to us, &c., &c.

> *Augustus Foster*
> *To Elizabeth, Duchess of Devonshire.*
>   Date? 1814.

... I hope to get a letter from you at Gothenburg, and long to know if you think that Audrey Townsend will be prevailed upon to change her mind, or if you advise me to renounce all hope. If she will but authorize me I would write for leave on my return from Norway and go and meet her where-ever she is. I am sure we should be very happy, though she would only laugh at me if I was to say I was in love with her, yet I think of her every day and in every arrangement I make, and have her beautiful clean hair and light little figure continually before my eyes. If you think a line from me would have any effect pray send the inclosed. She must have now settled her mind about it, and I should not wish to be kept merely in hope....

Augustus Foster
  To Elizabeth, Duchess of Devonshire.
                                        January 10, 1815.

... Mr. Bourke tells me that Masséna three years ago was very ill, but would not be persuaded by his wife to consult a physician, on which she went to Bourgon, a physician, and told him the reason was Massena's unwillingness to pay the necessary fee, begging the physician to come and see him as a friend, which he did, and recommended him to change his climate: then he went to Nice. This he told me à propos to your observation about his cuisine. Madame Massena described him to Bourgon as having des millions, but being more chary of an écu now than he was when he had scarcely one.

Frederick Foster
  To Augustus Foster.
                                        MARSEILLES, *March* 4, 1815.

My dearest Augustus,—Here's pretty news indeed. I was woke this morning out of a sweet sleep with "You had better get up, Sir, there are crowds of soldiers and people in the streets. Bonaparte is landed at Cannes." I got up in a hurry and rushed to the Prefect's, and, in short, the history is that the Emperor Napoleon has, in four or five transports, and a zebeck carrying himself and his staff, landed at Cannes on the first or early the second March with about 1200 or 2000 men. He attempted to surprize Antibes, but the Governor was firm, and at Cannes the mayor behaved very well. Bonaparte asked him why he wore a white cockade; he replied he had taken an oath to be faithful to Louis 18, and would remain so, and that he might do with him as he pleased. He is gone in the direction of Dauphiny. Troops are gone from Toulon in pursuit, and from this place they have been marching all night. The Prefect's Proclamation don't name him, but says that quelques salariés de l'Isle d'Elba have landed, and that they ought to be glad of this mad attempt of the Exile de l'Isle d'Elba, as he will now receive the punishment due to his forfaits. Bonaparte has distributed Proclamations. I have not as yet seen any of them, but I am told they contain great abuse of Marmont and Augereau.[366] They are in General Bertrand's name. The whole of Marseilles is, of course, in great anxiety; it is a very Bourbon place, and the white flag waves almost from every window; the National Guards are all out, and we are in a great bustle. The conduct of the French Government seems inconceivable. Colonel Campbell, on leaving the island, warned them to be on their guard, and they had only two frigates to cruise. At Grasse he stopped and bought stores and paid for them; his six pieces of cannon he has been forced to leave behind him from the badness of the roads. What a noise this will make in England! What second editions of the Courier! O you wise Ministers, to send him to such a place as Elba; several soldiers landed from there lately and were from suspicious conduct arrested, and a great deal of money found on them, with which they had been endeavouring to bribe their former comrades. I forgot to tell you that the Prince de Monaco was met plump by Bonaparte, who stopped him for a couple of hours and then let him go. Estafettes are gone off in all directions; it's inconceivable, I think, his hazarding this without being pretty sure of a strong party to support him. Flahault, a son of the famous Madame de Souza, was suspected of intriguing for him. Did you hear of a sarcasm of Talleyrand to him? F. was talking of the difficulties of his position; that, in his position, favoured as he had been by the Emperor, he did not know what to do, and that in short his position embarrassed him very much. Talleyrand with his cold sneer said, vous avez donc une position, Monsieur de Flahault. I wonder what will be Talleyrand's position now at the Congress, and when will that eternal Congress end?...

> *Elizabeth, Duchess of Devonshire,*
> *To Augustus Foster.*
>
> MARSEILLES, *March 7, 1815.*

Caro will tell you about Bonaparte. Was there ever any thing so extraordinary! The spirit here is excellent, and late last night a traveller who saw him at Sisteron says his force was reduced to 400. People generally seem to think it a desperate effort made on the idea that he was to be removed from Elba—that the great mass of the Nation is against him—a part of the army for him, and even they would hesitate at fighting against friends and relations. Eight hundred marched from here yesterday—Guards, volunteers, troops of the line; the concourse which accompanied them was immense and touching to see. Monsieur de Riviera dined with us on Saturday, and at the Prefect's Sunday: he saw Massena late Sunday, and was quite satisfied with him. My love to Albinia,[367] who, I hope, will be my daughter by the time you receive my letter.

Frederick Foster
To Augustus Foster.

MARSEILLES, *March* 8, 1815.

I wrote to you a day or two ago with the first account of Bonaparte's landing, and I now will add the few details I have heard since. He was so sure of having possession of Antibes that his manuscript proclamations are dated thence. He has had the wicked cunning of dressing two or three of his officers in English uniforms, and as he has gone on he has given out that the English are for him, that he landed from an English frigate, and that all France recalls him to the throne. He appears to be almost sunburnt black, and to be excessively fat; his men are said to be in a wretched state, and some have deserted. Nothing can be more active and fine than the conduct of the Prefect Marquis d'Allecetas or of Comte de Panisse, Commander of the National Guards. The spirit of the people is quite perfect. Many of the principal young men of the place have marched as common soldiers. Some merchants here have dismissed all their workmen to enable them to march, and still continue their pay or wages; yet the confusion this fellow has created is very great. They had just received their franchise, and every thing was reviving, and now every thing is at a stand. Bonaparte seems to proceed with the greatest coolness; at least, he affects it. He has brought his cook with him, and left his carriage at Grasse, to wait, as he said, for his mother and sister Pauline. At any town he comes to he orders rations for six or seven thousand men, so that the inhabitants are terrified and stupefied; however, his freaks that way will be soon found out; the whole country is in arms, high and low, rich and poor, and, excepting a few stupid or treacherous public functionaries, every body behaves perfectly. We expect one of the Princes here to take the command in the South. Precy has marched from Lyons, and Lecourbe, they say, from Briançon, and the King of Sardinia has granted the passes of his mountains. If the worst comes to the worst, and he gets the upper hand, they are determined to make a Spanish war of it, and never to submit. However, I think it will be soon over with him. I am sorry to interrupt your Hymeneal Pleasures with wars and rumours of wars, and hope Albinia will forgive me.

Frederick Foster,
To Augustus Foster.

MARSEILLES, *March* 9, 1815.

You will be too much engrossed with one another to care about news; yet the extraordinary event of Bonaparte's being in France will rouse your attention. Three times to-day have we been told that Bonaparte has been taken, and the whole town has poured out with acclamations of joy; but, alas, it is not so; the news, however, is satisfactory as far as it goes.... The only thing for us to mention is the excellent spirit of the people, the noble conduct of the gentlemen and noblesse, and the rapid marches which the National Guard have made with the troops. They are now within two leagues of Bonaparte. Monsieur arrived at Lyons yesterday with Marshal Ney and Comte de Dumas.[368] Bonaparte speaks with astonishing assurance of the numbers that will join him, but none of whom have done so. He enters a village and orders rations for six thousand men, having only eight hundred. He tells the people that Massena is manoeuvring with twenty-five thousand men near Paris, and that the King has fled to Lisle. It looks well his telling such falsehoods. The people here were growing dissatisfied with Massena: he has at last published a proclamation, in which he ends by saying that he shall spill the last drop of his blood to defend the lawful King. It had an immediate effect on the funds, which rose. Bonaparte left his horse lamed at Sisteron, and forgot a fine spying glass there. He wears a cuirass over his coat.

> *Augustus Foster*
> *To Elizabeth, Duchess of Devonshire.*
>   WHITEHALL, *March* 10, 1815.

We have just heard of Bonaparte's having landed between Antibes and Nice with a thousand, and of the King of France's proclamation. Lord Fitzroy Somerset sent it. I own I am confounded with this news. The worst is the uncertainty of knowing who is and who is not a friend. I trust Marshal Massena will take care of you, and let you set off for Paris and the north; and I trust in your admirable good sense and decision, or I should be greatly alarmed.... People look thunderstruck at this news.... Your house will be let on Monday for a year—viz., to March 12, 1816. I cannot alter it now, for Lord Byron is in the country.

> *W. H. Hill (H. M. Minister at Turin)*
> *To Elizabeth, Duchess of Devonshire.*
>   TURIN, *April* 12, 1815.

Dear Duchess,—I have just received your letter of the 9th, and, having discharged my conscience as to the little danger of being shut up in Genoa (and I think it is but little), I will tell you all I know of Murat. By our last accounts he was still at Guastalla, but we expect every hour to hear of his moving. You are very right, I hope, in your calculation of one great defeat destroying him, and not the Austrians. The latter will not have less than 175 thousand troops in Italy when all their reinforcements arrive, but they have scarcely a third of that number at present. Murat has beat the Austrians once in a pretty smart though not general affair (Don't quote me for this bad news), but if he does not beat them most decisively in a pitched battle within three weeks, I trust he has no chance, for by that time a great body of Austrian reinforcements will arrive. So prevalent is the idea of Murat's reaching Milan that the Marquis D'O. has just been telling me it is universally reported here that he is already there. This is ridiculous. There is the Po between him and the Austrians, i.e., the great force of the latter is on the other side. If you are determined to go to Genoa you had better make haste, and you will be at the head-quarters of all news. It was full of English, but they are beginning to move. The Col di Tenda is very passable. Mr. Burrell came over it and went to Genoa this morning, but if you have set your heart upon going there now I can only hope there is no danger. Murat's army is increasing; he has been joined by many old soldiers. Italy discontented, and his proclamations revolutionary. The news from Vienna is good—eight hundred thousand troops to be ready next month. Many European Powers appear to have signed against Bonaparte. The Emperor Alexander at Prague hurrying his troops through Bohemia. The Sovereigns have not yet met at Frankfort, but are still, it is said, to meet there.

It is reported the King of France, after arriving at Ostend, was invited to join them at Frankfort. In the meanwhile, what is to become of the South of France? We are in the greatest distress upon that subject. Yours ever,

W. H.

Augustus Foster
To Elizabeth, Duchess of Devonshire.
WHITEHALL, *April* 22, 1815.

... Caro has got yours of the 6th. What an interesting diary! and how Massena deceived you! How covered with crimes and disgraceful perjuries are almost all Bonaparte's generals and followers, and how they render the race of Frenchmen detestable and disgusting! I have seen D'Aumont,[369] who was cheated and thwarted by Augereau at Caen. D'Aumont had his volunteers in the Castle, but Augereau was his superior, and sent an order for the admission of some artillery, and D'Aumont could not refuse. When matters were becoming desperate, D'Aumont wanted to carry off the caisses for the King, but Augereau sent an order that not a sous should be touched without his signature. He found gens d'armes following him and preceding him wherever he went, and two at his door. At length Augereau, who had been in the habit of dining with him, advised him to be off, and when he said, But you run as much risk as me, oh! non, the scoundrel answered, C'est différent pour moi, mais peut être que demain je recevrais l'ordre de vous arrêter. So he embarked in a boat in the river, and came in a storm to England...

> *Elizabeth, Duchess of Devonshire,*
> *To Augustus Foster.*
>
> MILAN, *June* 21, 1815.

... Madame de Stael has shown a great deal of character. Bonaparte sent to tell her he would pay her the debt which Louis 18 had acknowledged, but on condition that she would return to Paris. She has resisted, which is the more remarkable, as B. Constant and Sismondi are both won over.[370] What a crisis we are at! It is fearful to think of. Your King, the papers say, is going to join the other Sovereigns. Murat dethroned makes Italy quiet, I think, for some time at least....

> *The Honble. Mrs. George Lamb*
> *To Augustus Foster.*
>
> RICHMOND, *June* 30, 1815.

What wonderful events,[371] my dear Augustus, since I last wrote to you; how glorious to England, but how dearly bought. Poor Frederick Howard! his death,[372] as you may imagine, has affected his family very much. Mrs. Howard is miserable, and has scarcely spoken since. Frederick Ponsonby happily is doing well, and is out of danger, but his wounds very bad ones: both arms were shot, and three stabs in the body. In this dreadful state he lay all night, and was, besides, rode over by the Prussian Cavalry, and, of course, is bruised all over; it is wonderful, I think, that he survived it; but he is, thank God, recovering rapidly. The consequences, too, of the victory are so great that it heightens the glory of it. Bonaparte's abdication, it must be hoped, will stop all further bloodshed. What is to be done with him is the puzzling question now, and who is to succeed? The forcing the Bourbons back upon them seems a violent measure, and one they are strongly against, but yet one dreads their electing young Napoleon unless Bonaparte was out of the way. All sorts of reports are afloat to-day. It was said he had put himself under Lord Wellington's protection. He had better. I dare say he would have more honour towards him than those treacherous Frenchmen, who make it a system to give up one Sovereign after the other the moment they are in adversity. As to private affairs, I suppose you have heard of your friend Lord Aberdeen's marriage to Lady Hamilton—*two* miserable creatures.[373] He says, *What else have we to do?* The truth is, she is beautiful and he is very much in love with her.

> *Augustus Foster*
> 　　*To Elizabeth, Duchess of Devonshire.*
> 　　　　　　COPENHAGEN, *July* 11, 1815.

... Gordon is said to have lost his life in screening Lord Wellington. Having in vain urged the Duke to quit the place where he was, he rode up to put himself before him, and so received the ball. Other letters say he was pulling the bridle of the horse to get him out of the way. What a tremendous contest, but what a decisive overthrow! Boney's own account does us justice as much almost as one could wish. How curious if he really has gone from Havre to England. I hope we shall give refuge to none of his dastardly generals who have so often perjured themselves.

... The King of Denmark sends the Elephant to Wellington and Blucher and to our Prince Regent.[374] It is a right thing to do, and it is, I suppose, the order Hamlet wore. A propos to the latter, there is an old chronicle about him by the Danish historian, Saxo Grammaticus, who flourished in the thirteenth century, and it is probably from this that Shakespeare took his story; but I am sorry to say the Danish Ophelia was an improper lady employed to betray Hamlet, though she deserves to be called proper, for notwithstanding she consented to his wishes she kept his secret. The Danish Hamlet feigns madness, and manages the death of Rosencranz and Guilderstern, as Shakespeare says, but he marries both an English and a Scotch Princess, and, returning to Denmark, feigns madness again, then sets fire to the palace, stabs the King, and gets possession of the throne, when he reigns gloriously for several years, and at last is killed in a duel with the King of Jutland. The Danish historian makes him out a fine character, and, particularly, says he never told an untruth during his madness. His speech to his mother is real, and so is the killing of Polonius, though the latter is killed under a heap of straw instead of behind tapestry. The story of the Ghost seems to be Shakespeare's, as also the manner of the murder. The whole is a long story, and there are several eloquent speeches of Hamlet to the Troops.

Augustus Foster
> *To Elizabeth, Duchess of Devonshire.*
>> COPENHAGEN, *July* 23, 1815.

... I hope you received my account of Hamlet. I have to add that the story of Hamlet belongs to about the year 550, and I was mistaken about the history, which was written in the beginning of the thirteenth century, but only printed in the sixteenth. I must add the remark of Saxo-Grammaticus, the historian, on Amleth's death, which was caused by his fighting with inferior forces against Vigletus, chief of the Scandians and Zeelanders. He says such was the end of Amleth, who, if he had experienced an equal kindness from fortune as from nature, would have equalled the Gods in brilliancy of deeds, and surpassed Hercules in the acts of virtue. He adds that his burial was magnificent, and that there exists a field in Jutland called after him.

The Hon. Mrs Lamb
> *To Augustus Foster.*
>> HOLLAND HOUSE, *Sept.*, 1815.

... One day Captain Maitland of the Bellerophon dined here, and you may believe we questioned him very much about Napoleon. He has been very much hurt at being accused of being too civil to him, as he merely treated him with the usual forms of civility, which surely it would have been very wrong to refuse to any great man in adversity. He was delighted at the crowds who came to see him, and always shewed himself whenever he might be about. Madame Bertrand attempted to drown herself upon finding they were to go to St. Helena, saying she was the cause of his coming on board that ship. Frederick Ponsonby has been here too, who is quite well again, and grown very fat. He has not recovered the use of his arms, but is in hopes that he shall in time. His quiet and simple account of all he suffered is very interesting. He never lost his recollection, and says it was not pleasant to see the Prussian cavalry advancing, and that *it hurt a good deal.* Lord and Lady Byron have also been here. She is to lie in in November. He appears very happy, and is very much improved by his marriage. George and he are two of the new managers of Drury Lane,[375] very eager about it, and, as it has hitherto gone on very well, it is only a great amusement to them.

Elizabeth, Duchess of Devonshire,
  To Augustus Foster.

FLORENCE, *October* 21, 1815.

Some of my letters, I think, must have missed, or you would have seen my indignation at Massena's conduct before I left Marseilles, and I told dear Riviera so at Toulon. You will soon hear of Murat's fate.[376] Mr. Sneyd brought the news from Rome today that he had been shot. It was so reported last night at Mme. Apponis', and people thought it was very unfeeling of Lady Oxford to be there,[377] and as merry as if he was still on the throne of Naples. She asked me if I was going to Naples, adding that she thought it quite a paradise, and that she lived in friendship with the former Government. I said that I should not go to Naples, but that my friendship was with the present King, to whom my brother had been much attached and most kindly treated. She is a strange woman. I suppose it will make some sensation. He must have been mad. He sailed from Corsica, telling them to steer for Tunis: arrived at a certain point he told them to steer for Calabria: a storm dispersed two of his feluccas; with the third he arrived on the coast of Calabria: he called to the people to shout Viva Giacchino, that he was come to re-enter his kingdom. The peasants fought him; he defended himself stoutly, but was overpowered, bound, and carried to a Sicilian general, who had him shot; and so, I think, that dynasty is at an end. He was such a false, shabby fellow, except in personal courage, that I can hardly pity him....[378]

Augustus Foster
  To Elizabeth, Duchess of Devonshire.

DUBLIN, *December* 31, 1815.

... I hope Massena will get well that you may see him. I hear the Duke de Richlieu is likely all in favor at the Tuilleries, and that the Duke de Choiseul Gouffier is also in great favor. You don't mention to whom Napoleon spoke about the Simplon, &c. Caro says it only prejudices her in favor of Napoleon to hear of the calm with which he bears his misfortunes. One cannot certainly help pitying a fallen man, but he seems to have more of apathy than calm, and he surely ought to be repentant or shew some remorse for the evils he has done. I fear he despises men too much to think them worth caring about. He told Vernon the opposition was very low, and Vernon answered it was because they had predicted the conquest of Spain by him. You don't say any thing of Mme. de Stael's reported ? with Rocca,[379] so I conclude it is a report you despise, though some will have it your silence argues that there is something in it. She told a friend of mine in speaking of Ward "quel dommage qu'avec un si beau talent il soit si egoiste et si incapable d'une veritable amitié".

> *Augustus Foster*
> *To Elizabeth, Duchess of Devonshire.*
>
> COPENHAGEN, *Jan* 6, 1816.

Albinia has made me a Papa. The event happened at 1 P.M. on the 3rd....

> *Elizabeth, Duchess of Devonshire,*
> *To Augustus Foster.*
>
> ROME, *Jan.* 26, 1816.

... I see Canova often.[380] He is delightful, and gives the idea of what the great artists were in 1500. He says he believes his statue of Bonaparte which is at Paris is to be ceded to the Prince Regent, and that he means to place it in the house to be built for Wellington.[381] His own favourite statue, a nymph which is here, he wants to give to the Prince, for Canova is the most liberal person ever known.... I hope the powers mean in earnest to do something to protect their coasts from the Barbaresques. It is dreadfull to have whole families carried off and sold in Africa; besides, as we have taken Malta, we are called upon to supply the place of the Knights who used to protect them. How happy Sir Sidney must have been—knighted by the Duke of Wellington....

> *Elizabeth, Duchess of Devonshire,*
> *To Augustus Foster.*
>
> ROME, *February* 9, 1816.

Rome is too, too beautiful. Gonsalvil and I are such friends that when we are at the same place the crowd gives way for him to come up to me.[382] He is doing much here, and it is delightfull to see the encouragement given to improvements of all kinds, and the publick walks are finishing. An interesting scavato is to take place next month at Preneste.... Bonaparte used to say of his sisters that Madame Murat was l'ambitieuse;[383] Madame Bajocchi, la spirituelle; and the Princess Borghese, la jolie; but they said, "après son mariage avec l'Autrichienne il paroissoit avoir honte de nous"....

Augustus Foster
      To Elizabeth, Duchess of Devonshire.
                              COPENHAGEN, *Feb.* 27, 1816.

... I hear a report that Lord and Lady Byron have separated from incompatibility. I should not be surprised, but hope it is not so....

      Elizabeth, Duchess of Devonshire,
            To Mrs. Foster.
                              ROME, *March* 8, 1816.

... We have a squadron, I hear, arrived at Leghorn, which, I hope, is to protect these coasts against the barbaresques. It is very shocking that there should be a vessel left them to carry off whole families from these countries, and whilst we are forcing all countries to abolish the slave trade, we allow, for the sake of gain, of this worst of all slavery of Christians to the Algerines. If Augustus was in Parliament, and in England, I should like him to take up this cause. What a fair one for a young and ardent mind! We are all astonished here at the separation of Lord and Lady Byron. You will have heard of it from England. Nobody knew the cause when my last letters were written, but every body seemed to pity her. So do I too; but yet I think that, had I married a profligate man, knowing that he was so, and that I had a child, and was not ill used by him, I would not part from him...

      Elizabeth, Duchess of Devonshire,
            To Augustus Foster.
                              March 22, 1816.

Lady Byron's fate is the most melancholy I ever heard, and he must be mad or a Caligula. Caro will have told you some of the stories. It is too shocking, and her life seems to have been endangered whilst with him from his cruelty, and now by her sufferings. I pity her from my heart: she might have been a happy person.... I am sure I have mentioned Thorwaldsen,[384] whom I admire very much, but when they attempt to place him above, or equal to, Canova, I think it is like comparing cinque cento to the antique; but he is very good, and full of genius, but idle.... England seems in an odd state: opposition strong, and making shabby obstacles to publick monuments; foolish remonstrances against guards at the Prince Regent's levee; and an odd marriage decided on for the future Queen of England;

yet every body speaks well of Prince Leopold of Saxe Cobourg, and he is very handsome. Some say that Lord Liverpool is out of favour....

> *Augustus Foster*
> *To Elizabeth, Duchess of Devonshire.*
> *March* 23, 1816.

... Caroline seems quite shocked at Lord Byron's conduct to poor Annabel, but don't give me the particulars. They were certainly two very opposite people to come together, but she *would* marry a poet and *reform* a rake. As to him, he has at length proved himself the true Childe Harold.

> *Elizabeth, Duchess of Devonshire,*
> *To Augustus Foster.*
> *April* 6, 1816.

Thorwaldsen is very clever, but terribly lazy.... Poor Lady Byron's fate is enough to alarm all parents. She is wretched, ill, and persecuted by him, who now refuses to sign the deeds of separation.

> *Elizabeth, Duchess of Devonshire,*
> *To Augustus Foster.*
> ROME, *April* 6, 1816.

... Canova is delightful, and has the enthusiasm so necessary to make a good artist...

> *The Countess of Liverpool*
> *To Elizabeth, Duchess of Devonshire.*
> FIFE HOUSE, *May* 3rd, 1816.

I must write one line to you, dearest sister, to tell you that I was at the Royal marriage yesterday,[385] and not the worse for the exertion, though I had a return of ?, and had been bled two days before. Lord Liverpool did not venture, though nearly well. Dr. Pemberton was afraid the heat and the standing might have brought on a relapse of his complaint. Nothing could go off better than the whole ceremony did in all its parts. The Bride and Bridegroom looked very handsome, and every body was very struck and pleased with the very uncommon manner in which they both followed through the service in their prayer books and distinctly and earnestly pronounced their mutual vows. May they be happy! I wish it from my very heart! They are gone to Oatlands for about a week. When the ceremony was over the Princess knelt to her father for his blessing, which he gave her, and then raised and gave her a good hearty, paternal hug that delighted me, and took her up to the Queen, who kissed her, as did her Aunts. The Prince Regent then embraced his son-in-law, and afterwards took him up to the Queen, who embraced him, as did the Princesses. They all like him extremely, and, indeed, it is impossible not to like him. His manners are perfect, particularly quiet, and mildly dignified without any affectation, but great self-possession. They say he is as truly amiable as he is pleasing, and very religious, which gives the greatest satisfaction here....

> *Augustus Foster*
>> *To Elizabeth, Duchess of Devonshire.*
>>> COPENHAGEN, *May* 18, 1816.

Caroline relieved me much about poor Lady Caroline Lamb. I was afraid it had been madness, but, though bad enough, it seems to have been a passionate fit against her page, and will probably be a good lesson to her. It is impossible not to feel some regard for her from old times, and it is really painful to see so delightful a person as she once was in absolute danger of committing so horrid a crime, and so entirely unmanageable. I must say I think her husband is a great deal to blame, for, had he studied a little more Shakespeare's taming of the shrew, he might have checked her, at least so as to prevent such dreadful and shameful excesses in a disposition not naturally wicked. I cannot conceive what it was Lord Byron did to his wife. You thought her wrong at first, but now you find her grossly injured....

> *Countess of Liverpool*
>> *To Elizabeth, Duchess of Devonshire.*
>>> COOMBE WOOD, *July* 17, 1816.

... I saw the Bishop of London two days ago, and he gave me some comfort about poor Sheridan.[386] The Bishop assured me that during his last visit Mr. Sheridan, though too weak to speak, most decidedly joined in prayer, and by very expressive gestures applied to himself every word which particularly mentioned the mercy of God, the mediation of our Saviour, the great sinfulness of his own life, and the blessed hope of pardon founded on repentance through the merits of our Redeemer. Poor man! his terror of death had been *dreadful*, but that his last feelings were those of *humble hope*. The good dear Bishop has taken Mrs. Sheridan home to his own house. She has scarce left her bed since her husband's death. She has some hopeless inward complaint—it was *her* who first sent for the Bishop.

> *Augustus Foster*
> > *To Elizabeth, Duchess of Devonshire.*
> > > COPENHAGEN, *August* 13, 1816.

... I have read Glenarvon,[387] and only just read it.... As for the story, I had not patience to get through it, it is so disordered and confused, but the traits of character, the sentiments, and the uncommon impudence that runs through it is to me astonishing; yet, if Lord Avondale reads it, he must be a little conscience struck at his character of a free thinker, for I am convinced that, with all his good and noble qualities, he was used to scout at all fixed principles, and taught her, or helped her, to do the same. Glenarvon seems almost too bad for nature, yet agrees very much with the being it is meant for,[388] and squares in with his own portrait in the Corsair, Childe Harold, &c. She don't give me the idea of being at all cured, notwithstanding her confessions. I had a letter from Adair the other day, who says he has made it a matter of conscience not to read the book, and talks of her as going on the same as ever. I sadly fear some bad end for her; she certainly is past all advice....

> *Antonio Canova*
> > *To Elizabeth, Duchess of Devonshire.*
> > > ROMA, 23 *Settembre*, 1816.

Excellenza,—Dall Emi. Card. Gonsalvi ho ricevuto la gentilissima Letterina di S. E. per la quale vengo nuovamente confermato nella speranza, anzi nella certezza, di ritenere qualche parte nella sua memoria, cosa che sommamente desidero e che riconosco quale prezioso ornamento del viver mio. Ho seguito il di lei aviso di scrivere al Principe Reggente sul proposito dei Gessi dei marmi Elginiani e ne ho consegnata la lettera alla lodata Eminenza sua. Spero che avremo il bene di rivederla fra noi nel prossimo inverno come odo che da molti viene asseverato. Se altri cio desidera di cuore io sono uno di questi, e credo che non mi bisognino gran parole a rendernela persuaso. Ella conosce abbastanza la sincerità e il carattere candido di miei sentimenti onde far justizia alle mie asserzioni, ma non potrebbe mai formarsi idea adequata del sentimento di stima e di affezionata considerazione ed ossequio con cui mi onero essere. —di V. E.,

ANTONIO CANOVA.

Translation of the above.
ROME, *September* 23, 1816.

Your Excellency,—I have received from his Eminence, Cardinal Gonsalvi, your Excellency's most esteemed note, which confirms anew the hope, and indeed the certainty, of my retaining some place in your memory, which I greatly desire and prize as a precious ornament of my existence. I have followed your advice by writing to the Prince Regent on the subject of the plaster casts of the Elgin marbles, and have consigned my letter to the care of his Eminence. I hope we shall have the happiness of seeing you again among us next winter, a wish which I hear uttered by many. If any persons heartily desire your return I am of the number, and I think I do not need to use many words to persuade you of this. You are sufficiently aware of the sincerity and candid character of my sentiments to do justice to my assertions, but you could never form an adequate idea of the sentiments of esteem and affectionate consideration with which I have the honor to be your Excellency's, &c., &c.

ANTONIO CANOVA.

Antonio Canova
To Elizabeth, Duchess of Devonshire.
ROMA, 12 *Ottobre*, 1816.

Preclarissima Signora Duchessa,—Le sono infinitamento obbligato della graziosa lettera di cui le piacque onorarmi. L'espressioni di amorevolezza che fa use a mio riguardo mi adornano é lusingano troppo perche io non abbia á sentirne tutto it valore e la riconossenza che meritano. Duolmi che la sua brama di far collocare nel Panteon it ritratto del Cavaliere di Reynolds non possa adempirsi; io pure dentro di me stesso sentiva il dubbio é il peso di quella considerazione ch'ella mi dichiaro. Sono lietissimo della dolce novella da lei datami del suo vicino ritorno a Roma. Ne aspeto il momento colla piu viva impazienza conforme ed equale al sentimento dell' alta forma che le professo.

Io non ho mai fatto nulla che abbia rapporto al poeta Virgilio, nè statua nè ritratto.

Mi conservi la preziosa sua benevolenza e credami cogli offizii del fratello pieno di venerazione e di osservanza.—Di Lei aff.

ANTONIO CANOVA.

Translation of the above.

ROME, *October* 12, 1816.

Most Illustrious Lady Duchess,—I am infinitely obliged to you for the gracious letter with which you have been pleased to honor me. The kind expressions which you make use of towards me are too complimentary and flattering for me not to feel the full force of the acknowledgment which is their due. I am sorry that it is not in my power to carry out your wish that the portrait of the cavaliere Reynolds should be placed in the collection of the Pantheon. I had indeed my own doubts on the subject, and felt the weight of the considerations which you laid before me.

I am very glad of the good news which you announce to me of your proposed early return to Rome. I look forward to that moment with the most lively impatience proportioned to the high regard which I entertain for you.

I have never done any thing having any reference to the poet Virgil— neither statue nor portrait.

Pray continue your precious friendship to me, and believe my brother and myself to be full of veneration and respect.—Yours, &c.,

ANTONIO CANOVA.

G. Thorwaldsen
  To Frederick Foster.

COPENHAGEN, *October* 25, 1816.

My dear Sir,—Yesterday at length the proprietor of the Rosenborgen Pluto appointed the hour tomorrow 1 afternoon. At the same time I was unfortunately decoyed into company of Highnesses, Excellencies, Ribbands, stars and keys. I thought myself in holy place; but alas! two villains, infamous by their very names, *Cold* and fever—these wretches seized me and carried me off, though I made strong protestations. They told me that precedents published by one of the greatest nations upon earth warranted this proceeding. Not entirely free from violence, yet impelled by knavery, my enemies have stretched me on my bed, where I am alternately tortured by heat and cold. My state is that of a volcano.

However, I hope soon to outwit my enemies, to throw them out of doors, and banish them for ever. To-morrow my son Frederick will pay mine and his owne homage to you, and request the honour to be in your guide to Pluto's metropolis, one of the great Inigo Jones' works. Pray give my best respects to your brother, the ambassador, whom I will ever love and admire. Conceal my sufferings from the ladies; their generous feelings can not bear incident misfortunes to their fellow creatures. Above all, bid God to have mercy on me; so doing I shall be benefited without your loss. I am for ever, my dear Sir, your faithfull and very humble servant,

G. THORWALDSEN.

Monsieur FREDERICK DE FOSTER,
Senateur de l'Angleterre.

Elizabeth, Duchess of Devonshire,
To Mrs. Foster.

ROME, *Nov.* 16, 1816.

... Before I forget it, I must tell Augustus that the Danish sculptor Thorwaldsen is grown excellent. Some of his works are really admirable, and he is so modest and so excellent a man that he is liked and esteemed by all. He hopes to go to Denmark this next year, and they have good reason to be proud of him...

Elizabeth, Duchess of Devonshire,
To Augustus Foster.

ROME, *Dec.* 10, 1816.

... Mr. Playfair, Mr. Elmsley, Mr. Sotheby are among the clever men of science and literature at Rome, and Mr. Brougham[368] and Vernon—Lord Henry, the clever men of the set now here, and all almost alike flock to the Princess Borghese, and the grave Lord Lansdowne, the silent Lord Jersey,[390] the politician Mr. Brougham, all go and play aux petits jeux with Pauline. Forfeits condemned Lord Jersey to recite; he got off by promising to waltz. Lord Cowper was to soupirer pour une dame and so on. She shows her fine plate with the eagle, &c., and gets dozens of fine dresses from Paris. I admire the Pope's firmness in letting them all of that family remain at Rome, but I think that the English should put a little reason in their eagerness to go to her. Were it Josephine, who did thousands of benevolent generous acts; Maria Louisa, who was twice a sacrifice to politicks; Madame Lucien,[391] who is an excellent mother and wife, I think the attentions would be natural and commendable, but this person has only been cited for extreme arrogance in prosperity, extreme gallantry, and a good deal of beauty. Louis Buonaparte inspires great esteem,[392] I think, but he is sickly and, I believe, scarcely goes to his sisters....

Elizabeth, Duchess of Devonshire,
To Augustus Foster.

ROME, *Dec.* 16, 1816.

... I hear from England that Lord Byron's third canto of Childe Harold is beautiful, but Lord Cowper don't like it so much, and Lady Bessborough is sending it to me, and I long for it, as, however odious his character, he is a great Poet. M. Lewis told me that he believed he was gone to Venice in order to embark for Dalmatia.[393] M. Lewis till last night has never appeared. Here, as at Florence, he shuts himself up to hold converse only with the departed. I have begun a little excavation in the Foro Romano, and they found a little cup or calice. In digging close to the single Pillar, they found it to be a column to Phocas.[394] I am having the Cup cleaned a little and put together. At the great excavation they found a part of the Plan of Rome, which joins on to that which is preserved in the Capitol Museum. Nothing can be greater than the interest which this excites. I have employed poor labourers instead of forçats, which is a charity. I saw it particularly pleased my friend Cardinal Gonsalvi, and therefore I was doubly pleased to do it....

Elizabeth, Duchess of Devonshire,
To Augustus Foster.

ROME, *December* 29, 1816.

I have told you, I think, what a prodigious improvement Thorwaldsen has made in his works. He really is excellent, and a very interesting person in himself. He has had a great deal to do, and Mr. Hope, his great patron, has desired that he will finish his Jason for him; but Canova's group for the Prince, Mars and Venus, is the most beautiful thing I ever saw, and the best of his works, I do think. This is done by order, and he is finishing for the Prince his Nymph and Amorino, which he means as an offering. He has works ordered that will take up twelve years. I would give any thing for a small work of his, but it is hopeless, and a group or figure I can't afford.

Lord Byron
> *To Elizabeth, Duchess of Devonshire.*
>> VENICE, *November* 3, 1817.

I was yesterday honoured by your Grace's letter of the 19th ult. The newspapers have, I fear, deceived your Grace, in common with many others, for, up to my last letters from England, Newstead Abbey has not been sold, and, should it be so at this moment, I shall be agreeably surprized.

Amongst the many unpleasant consequences of my residence in Piccadilly, or rather the cause of that residence, I can assure your Grace that I by no means look upon it as the least painful that my inconvenience should have contributed to yours. Whatever measures Mr. Denen might find it proper to take were probably what he deemed his duty, and, though I regret that they were necessary, ... I am still more sorry to find that they seem to have been inefficacious. Indeed, till very lately, I was not aware that your Grace was so unlucky as to have me still among the number of your debtors. I shall write to the person who has the management of my affairs in England, and although I have but little controul over either at present, I will do the best I can to have the remaining balance liquidated.—I have the honour to be, with great respect, Your Grace's most obedient, Very humble servant,

BYRON.

Augustus Foster
> *To Elizabeth, Duchess of Devonshire.*
>> COPENHAGEN, *August* 25, 1818.

... I find M. la ferronays a great resource here. I do not know if you are acquainted with him. He has been nearly caught and hung by Bonaparte's creatures; often on the coast of France disguised as a smuggler, and for six years a common soldier in the Austrian army, frequently without enough to eat. His brother was killed as a common soldier at the battle of Lutzen, being then in the French service as a conscript. He was with Korsakow at the tremendous battle of Zurich, and saw the ditches of Waterloo strewed with French and English soldiers. Freddy and Cavendish are flourishing, the latter as fat as ever.

Augustus Foster
> *To Elizabeth, Duchess of Devonshire.*
>> COPENHAGEN, *Sept.* 1, 1818.

... Albinia has something more than a suspicion that a third little being is on its way up to the regions of light. This, I know, will be looked on as

a misfortune by you, and I think so too, unless it should be of the female
sex this time, which would be some consolation. We shall not know this,
however, till about April, so there may be time to make an Italian of the
little creature...

Augustus Foster
        To Elizabeth, Duchess of Devonshire.
                                COPENHAGEN, *Jan.* 9, 1819.

... Cavendish is all fat as yet, but speaks at an earlier age than his brother
did....

Augustus Foster
        To Elizabeth, Duchess of Devonshire.
                                COPENHAGEN, *April* 27, 1819.

I am happy to tell you that Albinia has at last been safely delivered, but it is
of a son instead of the wished for daughter; however, as I assisted this time
and witnessed her sufferings, the little delivered was made welcome. The
event happened yesterday, early in the morning.... You never mentioned
the affair of poor Mr. Colycar: he was a descendant of the Dukes of
Ancaster, and, as such, one out of the way of Freddy's succession to the
situation of Great Chamberlain (?) of England, formerly belonging to
the Veres. As younger sons should have good names, we mean to give the
newcomer that of Vere to shew that he is a link in that chain of descent.[395]

Augustus Foster
        To Elizabeth, Duchess of Devonshire.
                                KROKKEDAHL, *June* 7, 1819.

... What you say of A'Court I think very just.[396] Why, with a good estate
and right if necessary to a pension, dawdle out his days in foreign missions.
It is well enough for us younger brothers who have nor house nor home,
but the Lords of the Soil might stay in their castles, particularly when, like
him, they have boroughs at their disposition. Peel has certainly now come
very forward on the Bullion question,[397] and will no doubt soon verify his
father's prediction of him. It is really interesting to see the success that has
attended old Sir Robert Peel's plan of education. He was himself a common
mill boy, made a fortune by some invention in the manufactory, I believe,

of cotton, and determined to bring up his son to the imitation of Pitt, and behold that very son now at 3 or 4 and 20, putting his foot into the stirrup, and this in his father's lifetime, and in spite of his father's opposition on the Bullion question. Methinks I see Freddy at a distance on the selfsame road, and Cavendish, and Vere Henry Louis following at full gallop: what a prospective for John Bull.... Matters go on better at Paris, thanks to De Serre. It was necessary to stop somewhere, and shew that Louis 18 was not as weak as poor Louis 16, and the Ministers may now have a little more confidence since they have learned that Benjamin Constant, Lafayette,[398] & Co., are really only Jaseurs, and that their friends the Regicides are not popular. I like your saying that the difficulties were not so great at Naples when poor Lady Shaftesbury, with all her money, could not get lodged there, but was obliged to invade the Duke's apartments.... Lady Liverpool seems better; she has consented to be Godmother to the child, so, besides the names of Vere Henry, we have called him, from her, Louis.

> *The Hon. Mrs. Lamb*
> *To Augustus Foster.*
> TUNBRIDGE WELLS, *July* 31, 1819.

... I like this place very much. The walks and drives are beautiful, and I drive in the little gigs of the place with quiet, steady ponies who know every turn. The Noels and Lady Byron are my only acquaintances here,[399] but as I am very fond of the latter, it satisfies me. She has been very much abused in Lord Byron's new poem of Don Juan under the name of Donna Inez. It is very bad in him, and the whole poem is in a very bad style, improper, and flippant, and very odious, but it is reckoned clever.

... I never saw so clever and entertaining a child as little Ada,[400] Lord Byron's child. She is full of fun, but very good-tempered and good, and I hope she will inherit none of his faults. Poor little thing! she is early celebrated in verse, and I have no doubt he will be always trying to work on her mind by his writings....

> *Augustus Foster*
> *To Elizabeth, Duchess of Devonshire.*
> COPENHAGEN, *August* 14, 1819.

... Vere is like Freddy, and is a very fine child. Cavy shews much character, but is too fat still.

Augustus Foster
> *To Elizabeth, Duchess of Devonshire.*
>> COPENHAGEN, *October* 12, 1819.

Thorwaldsen at last arrived here ten days ago, but only called here yesterday. He has been so discoursed to and drank to, praised and panegyrized, that the poor man seems quite bothered; but he was at Albinia's conversazione last night and appeared delighted to find an old Roman acquaintance to talk to in Italian.... Thorwaldsen says he must have occupation and means to model through the winter; he left them a model in Alto Rilievo for the public walk at Lucerne to be cut out of the rock. I dare say it will be very fine, but he leaves it to the Swiss to execute his design; so the Mercury which you admire so much is not yet in marble. He talks of the work in marble as mere mechanical. It certainly is the chief thing, however, else we might be satisfied with what the ancients have left us.

Augustus Foster
> *To Elizabeth, Duchess of Devonshire.*
>> COPENHAGEN, *Nov.* 6, 1819.

... Lord Strangford was necessarily employed to treat with Sweden because it was only at Stockholm that the Convention could be negotiated.[401] To answer your question as to what share I had in it, I have only to send you the extract from Lord Castlereagh's Despatch, which follows:—"There remains for me only the gratifying task of signifying to you His Royal Highness' full approbation of your conduct in the share which you have taken in the discussions which have produced the settlement". This I look upon as a proof of bienveillance in Lord Castlereagh, for the business was, of course, mainly carried on at Stockholm. Let me add from Planta's private letter of October 7, in stating that Lord Castlereagh acquiesced in my request to remain here, he says, "and that he is very well pleased that you should, for the present, remain where you have done so very well and are so deservedly esteemed. In conveying to you this intelligence I use Lord Castlereagh's own words." ... Freddy is much admired here, Cavy less so, though he improves. Vere is like Freddy, but has not cut teeth yet.

Augustus Foster
> *To Elizabeth, Duchess of Devonshire.*
>> COPENHAGEN, *January* 29, 1820.

Cavendish is very well on his legs, fat and stout, but no beauty—he has, however, got a dimple or two and a pleasing smile. The little Vere is a beautiful child.

Frederick Foster
> *To Augustus Foster.*
>> LONDON, *Feb.* 29, 1820.

My dear Augustus,—What do you think of our Conspiracy?[402] Were you not very much surprized? Pallé came running in to tell me of the horrid massacre that was to have taken place, and I went immediately to Miss H., where I found her and Lady Erne still very nervous. Ministers had information all along. It was to have taken place at Lord Westmoreland's dinner some weeks ago, but was deferred; several of them, however, were seen watching about the door. At last they fixed on Lord Harrowby's Cabinet Dinner for the massacre. They were to have broken into the house, first giving a knock, and on the Porter's opening it to have rushed in, killed every thing that opposed them, flung hand grenades into the Rooms, and, in short, to have murdered them all; then to have endeavoured to raise the lowest mob, and so made a Jacobin Revolution of it. A man, one of the Party who repented, stopped Lord Harrowby in the Park and gave him full information of their designs. He agreed with his brother ministers to say nothing to the servants about putting off the Dinner, so it was ordered as usual. He himself slipped out and dined with Lord Liverpool and Lady Erne. He got Lady Harrowby and the children out of the house, telling her the reason—that she was to be quite secret—the constables and soldiers, as you will see, surrounded the house, and after a desperate resistance took nine of them. Owing to some blunder the soldiers did not arrive quite in time, and several of them escaped. It has caused a great sensation in London. Thistlewood is a Lincolnshire man, half gentleman and half yeoman, had about £800 a year, which, I hear, he lost at the gaming table. Poor Lady Liverpool was very much affected, fainted, and was very ill, and so was Lady Erne. The mob, I am told, hissed them as they were taken along the streets. I have not heard when they are to be tried. We are all in a bustle also about the Election. G. Lamb has a good chance for Westminster, and, as a whole, Government will gain, I hear.

F. TH. F.

Baron d'Engestròm
To Augustus Foster.

le *5 juin*, 1820.

Monsieur,—Vous savés Monsieur que le refus constant de Sa Majesté Britannique de reconnaitre le Roi Charles XIII a depuis longtems fait prevoir la necessité de faire cesser les relations Diplomatiques entre les deux Monarques, sans faire naître un etat de guerre entre les deux Nations.

Le Roi a par consequent, sans manquer au Roi d'Angleterre, pû promettre à la France, la cessation de relations qui deja touchaient à leur fin.

Le Traité de paix conclu a Paris le 6 janvier dernier, a eté dans le tems communiqué au Ministère de Sa Majesté, et la Mission de Suède a quitté Londres.

Votre présence quelqu' agréable qu'elle nous soit, pourrait donner lieu à des doutes sur l'intention du Roi, de remplir ses engagemens. Vous savés com-bien Il y est fidêle, et vous ne serés pas étonné que le zêle dont Je suis animé pour Son auguste personne, m'impose le devoir de vous prier de ne pas accrediter en restant plus longtems ici, des soupçons que le caractère loyal de Sa Majesté ne merite nullement.

Je crois être assés connu de Vous Monsieur, pour que Vous soyez persuadé de la parfaite consideration et de l'attachement sincère avec lesquels j'ai l'honneur d'être, Monsieur, Votre tres humble et tres obeisant Serviteur,

LE BARON D'ENGESTRÒM.

The Hon. Mrs. Lamb
To Augustus Foster.

WHITEHALL, *November* 16, 1820.

... Isn't it extraordinary that the Queen has suddenly dismissed Bergamo and all the family upon finding,[403] she says, in the Evidence that they had cheated her in some old money matters. Now that the trial is over, people are wondering what is to be done with her next. I suppose there will be some battling about it in the House of Commons now it is over. It would be handsomer to treat her at once as Queen, and the moment she is no longer persecuted her popularity will cease. Every body here seems to rejoice that the business is at an end without coming to the other house, as it would have been a horrid scene. She burst into tears, I hear, when the news was brought her. It is true that in signing her last protest she said, "Regina still in spite of them". Many of her bon mots are told. I suppose you have heard of her saying she never committed adultery but once, and that was with Mrs. Fitzherbert's husband, and she has repented of it ever since.

Augustus Foster
　　To Elizabeth, Duchess of Devonshire.
　　　　　　COPENHAGEN, *Nov.* 25, 1820.

... We are in the greatest anxiety about poor little Vere, whose teething has, I fear, brought on water on the brain. The little fellow is very strong, and struggles hard with his malady, or rather maladies, for he has several on him, which come on in succession. His nurse has now been up with him for six successive nights. Last night I watched till 7 this morning, and could with difficulty force his Mamma away to take an hour's rest....

Augustus Foster
　　To Elizabeth, Duchess of Devonshire.
　　　　　　COPENHAGEN, *Nov.* 28, 1820.

I must write a line to say that your little grandson Vere has overcome his malady. When we had given him over, I warmed his feet with my hands until the perspiration came, and his nurse put him in a hot bath, which slowly brought back the life into his body. Albinia has had nothing but fatigue and watching, and yet bore it with more strength than I thought she possessed. I believe I wrote by last mail to say the child could not recover, as all the doctors thought...

Lord Byron
　　To Elizabeth, Duchess of Devonshire.
　　　　　　RAVENNA, *July* 15, 1821.

Madame,—I am about to request a favor of Your Grace without the smallest personal pretensions to obtain it. It is not, however, for myself, and yet I err, for surely what we solicit for our friends is, or ought to be, nearest to ourselves. If I fail in this application, my intrusion will be its own reward—if I succeed, Your Grace's reward will consist in having done a good action, and mine in your pardon for my presumption. My reason for applying to you is this: Your Grace has been long at Rome, and could not be long any where without the influence and the inclination to do good.

Amongst the list of exiles on account of the late suspicions, and the intrigues of the Austrian Government (the most infamous in history), there are many of my acquaintances in Romagna, and some of my friends: of these more particularly are the two Counts Gamba,[404] of a noble and respected family in this city. In common with thirty or more of all ranks they have been hurried from their home without process, without hearing, without accusation: the father is universally respected and liked; his family is numerous and mostly young, and these are now left without protection; the son is a very fine young man, with very little of the vices of his age or climate; he has, I believe, the honor of an acquaintance with Your Grace, having been presented by Madame Martinetti. He is but one and twenty, and lately returned from his studies at Rome. Could Your Grace, or would you, ask the repeal of both, or at least of *one* of these, from those in power in the holy city. They are not aware of my solicitation in their behalfs, but I will take it upon me to say that they shall neither dishonour your goodness nor my request. If only one can be obtained, let it be the father, on account of his family. I can assure Your Grace and the very pious Government in question that there can be no danger in this act of—*clemency*, shall I call it? It would be but justice with us—but *here*! Let them call it what they will.... I cannot express the obligation which I should *feel*. I say *feel* only because I do not see how I could repay it to Your Grace. I have not the slightest claim upon you, unless, perhaps, through the memory of our late friend, Lady Melbourne.[405] I say *friend* only, for my *relationship* with her family has not been fortunate for them, nor for me. If, therefore, you should be disposed to grant my request, I shall set it down to your tenderness for her who is gone, and who was to me the best and kindest of friends. The persons for whom I solicit will (in case of success) neither be in ignorance of their protectress nor indisposed to acknowledge their sense of her kindness by a strict observance of such conduct as may justify her interference. If my acquaintance with Your Grace's character was even slighter than it is through the medium of some of our English friends, I had only to turn to the letters of Gibbon (now on my table) for a full testimony to its high and amiable qualities. I have the honor to be, with great respect, Your Grace's most obedient, very humble servant,

BYRON.

P.S.—Pray excuse my scrawl, which perhaps you may be enabled to decypher from a long acquaintance with the handwriting of Lady Bessborough. I omitted to mention that the measures taken here have been as *blind* as impolitic—this I happen to *know*. Out of the *list* in

Ravenna there are at least ten not only innocent but even opposite in principle to the liberals. It has been the work of some blundering Austrian spy, or angry priest, to gratify his private hatred. Once more your pardon.

Augustus Foster
> *To Elizabeth, Duchess of Devonshire.*
>> COPENHAGEN, *July* 20, 1821.

I hear Lord Byron is at Ravenna, deeply in love with the fairest and wealthiest sposa in the place.[406] Is it so? An Italian here tells me he was making love to a Venetian lady when the other came into the room, and instantly he asked to be introduced, followed her to Ravenna, and there fixed himself.

> Of all the cities in Romanian lands,
> The chief and most renowned Ravenna stands

may therefore again be trumpeted forth by another Dryden.

Lord Byron
> *To Elizabeth, Duchess of Devonshire.*
>> RAVENNA, *July* 30, 1821.

Madam,—The inclosed letter, which I had the honor of addressing to Your Grace, unfortunately for the subject of it, and for the writer, arrived after Your Grace's departure. I venture to forward it to Spa, in the hope that you may be perhaps tempted to interest yourself in favour of the persons to whom it refers, by writing a few lines to any of your Roman acquaintances in power. Two words from Your Grace, I cannot help thinking, would be sufficient, even if the request were still more presumptuous. I have the honor to be, with the greatest respect, your most obedient very humble servant,

BYRON.

To Her Grace The Duchess of Devonshire, &c. &c. &c.
Spa. In Allemagne presso Liège, Ibi vel ubi.

Elizabeth, Duchess of Devonshire,
  To Lord Byron.

SPA, *August* 17, 1821.

I regret very much that the letter which your Lordship directed to Rome did not arrive before I left, for it is always easier to explain the subject which one is anxious about in conversation than by writing, unless indeed the pen is held by the author of Childe Harold. I will, however, certainly write to Rome about the persons who interest you so much, and shall be happy if I can be of any use to them. I recollect Madame Martinetti's introducing to me a gentleman of the name of Gamba, but it is the warm interest which you express, my Lord, that will make me particularly anxious to succeed for them. Lady Melbourne had, I know, the greatest regard and friendship for you, and I had ever the sincerest affection for her. Whatever regrets subsequent occurrences might have occasioned her, I believe her friendship for you was unvaried. I have found no difficulty in deciphering your letter without ever being indebted to Lady Bessborough for that advantage, and I have only to wish that I may be successful in my application, and may be able to realize the hopes you have formed from any influence I may possess at Rome. I always wish to do any good I can, and in that poor Gibbon and my other friends have but done me justice, but believe me also that there is a character of justice, goodness, and benevolence in the present Government of Rome which, if they are convinced of the just claim of the Comtes de Gamba, will make them grant their request. Of Cardinal Gonsalvi it is truly said, "Il a établi une nouvelle politique formée sur la verité et la franchise. L'estime de toute l'Europe le paye de ses fatigues." Pray do not judge of the holy City from the reports of others, and, as no one has ever described its monuments with such beauty of poetry as yourself, so no one, I am sure, would do more justice to the merits of its inhabitants if you staid long enough to know them. I beg of you, my Lord, once more to be assured of the pleasure with which I shall undertake, and the satisfaction which I shall feel, if I obtain the recall of your friends to their mother country.

E. DEVONSHIRE.

I give up the Austrian Government to all you choose to say of them.

The Duke of Wellington
  To Elizabeth, Duchess of Devonshire.

LONDON, *Nov.* 25, 1821.

My dear Duchess,—I received your note in Staffordshire, and on my arrival in London your beautiful present. Be assured that I prize the latter much, and that I will have the addition made to it of your own Picture, and keep it in my own Library as a memorial of your kindness to me. I hear that you go on Tuesday, and I call with this note in hopes of seeing you once more before you go, as I am going out of town to stay this evening. Ever yours most sincerely,

WELLINGTON.

Elizabeth, Duchess of Devonshire,
To Augustus Foster.

PARIS, *December* 9, 1821.

… Our affairs seem settled at home, except as to Canning. Never surely did so clever a man so mar his own fortunes; he now declines India. It is only strange that they should ever think of sending him. It is his eloquence which they want and not his government of India....

Augustus Foster
To Elizabeth, Duchess of Devonshire.

RICHMOND, *December* 16, 1821

… I am sorry for Canning, but I certainly think he was right to refuse India; had he accepted it would have been put to the score of necessity. As it is, I think even the Mogul himself must think better of him, and things may turn up better for him hereafter; besides, what would have become of his daughter and other children...

Elizabeth, Duchess of Devonshire,
To Augustus Foster.

May 27, 1823.

There is illness and influenza all over London.[407]

August 20, 1823.

Lord Byron has put into Naples; he is carrying out arms, provisions, and medicines.

February 24, 1824.

… Grecian affairs also promise well, and Byron has given them £10,000, besides arms, medicine, and surgeons.

The Earl of Aberdeen
   To Augustus Foster.

NICE, *January* 19, 1826.

It is a great disappointment to me to be so near without being able to see you. This indeed at present would not be easy from the state of the roads and the quantity of snow, but I fear I shall be obliged to leave Nice in a short time, and before the communication is opened for carriages with Turin. Lady Aberdeen was unwell when I left England, and has been worse since, so that the physicians have forbidden her to think of coming to join me here, and although she is now rather better, she is impatient for my return. I have not quite determined whether to leave my daughter here or take her back with me to England. For myself, I like this place extremely, the climate delightful, and the country very beautiful. I could pass three or four months here every winter with great pleasure. I am very glad that you like your residence; indeed you must be difficult, with two such towns as Turin and Genoa, not to be well pleased. I had never seen Turin until last year, and was quite surprised to find so beautiful a town. It has the reputation of being rather dull, but, compared with this place it must be all liveliness and gaiety, for, notwithstanding the natural charms of Nice, I never knew a place with fewer intellectual resources. It is very full at present; many English, but not such as I know. There are some very good French families and other foreigners. Madame Narischkin arrived here on the very day on which we received the news of the death of the Emperor Alexander. This death has thrown his country into great confusion, for, although matters may be settled for the present, it is to be presumed that at some future period a catastrophe is by no means improbable. Whatever happens, I have only one wish, which is that we may preserve peace; if we succeed in this, it ought to be a matter of indifference to us who is Emperor...

Miss Vere Hobart[408]
   To Mrs Foster.

WHITEHALL, *April* 27, 1827.

Since I wrote to you last Tuesday, I believe what I then told you as positive news has been undone, and (?) twenty times. Lord James Stuart has just been here in great joy saying that Lord Lansdown has *agreed* with Mr. Canning, but what his place will be is not yet declared. It is a grand jumble altogether. We were last night at the Robinsons. After Sarah *desiring* to see us she was too unwell to do so when we arrived;[409] she is to be kept so exceedingly quiet, but I believe her matters are going on perfectly well. Mr.

R.[410] gave us all the history of his Peerage and his Majesty's graciousness, and shewed us the arms and supporters of his new dignity. He is to be gazetted to-night, consequently from this day we must call him,. Viscount *Goderich*. Lady de Grey declared she will spell him *Goodrich*,[411] because elle s'est mise en tête that it should be so, but *he* says not....

Count John Anthony Capo d'Istrias, President of the Greek Republic,
on his embarkation for Greece, to Augustus Foster.[412]

ANCONA, 20 *November*, 3 *December* 1827.

Je ne saurais assez exprimer a Votre-Excellence combien je suis touché de l'interet qu'elle se plait de me temoigner, et dont sa lettre du 26 Novembre m'apporte une nouvelle preuve.

Monsieur le Vice-Consul d'Angleterre, en se conformant a ses ordres, me fit trouver à Bologne une lettre de sa part dans laquelle il me donnait tous les renseignments qui étoit à sa connaissance. La saison orageuse dans ces mers cette année plus que de coutume ne laisse cependant aborder dans le port d'Ancona depuis le 20 novembre aucun batiment ni grand ni petit, et ce fait explique assez le retard qu'eprouve celui que j'attends. Je prends patience, et je tache de me consoler en m'occupant d'avance des affaires très difficiles, et assurément peu agreables, qui me sont reservées; celle de la piraterie, dont Votre Excellence me parle, en est une, et elle reclame sans doute de promptes et fortes mesures;—mais comment s'y atteindre tant que la misère la plus effrayante maitrisera absolument en Grèce tous les hommes et toutes leurs situations. Lorsqu'il en sera autrement, et je l'espère de la justice et de la munificence des cinq cours alliées, je vais repondre qu'une simple proclamation donnée avec pleine connaissance de cause, et soutenue par des forces maritimes *soldés* fera disparaitre le desordre et devoilera à l'Europe les veritable pirates. Jusque la je ne puis que faire des veux, et V. E. ne doute pas de ceux que je forme pour être une heure plutôt sur les lieux. Qu'elle veuille me continuer son amitié, et croire aux sentimens avec les quelles j'ai l'honneur d'être de Votre Excellence le très humble et très obeisant serviteur.

J. CAPO D'ISTRIAS.

À Son Excellence, Mons. de FOSTER, à Turin.

Translation.

Copy of a letter from Count John Anthony Capo d'Istrias, President of the Greek Republic, to Augustus Foster on his embarkation for Greece.

I know not how sufficiently to express to your Excellency how much I am affected by the interest which you are pleased to testify towards me, and of which your letter of November 26 brings me fresh proof.

The English Vice-Consul, in accordance with the instructions received from your Excellency, addressed to me at Bologna a letter, in which he gave me all the information in his possession. The more than usually stormy season, however, of this year in these seas has, ever since November 20, rendered it impossible for any vessel whatever, large or small, to enter the port of Ancona, and this fact sufficiently explains the delay in arrival of the one which I am expecting. I try to be as patient as possible, and endeavour to console myself by occupation in advance with the many difficult and by no means agreeable affairs which await my attention. One of these is the question of piracy, which is referred to in your Excellency's letter, and it no doubt requires prompt and strong measures. But how deal with it so long as the most frightful misery shall continue to dominate absolutely in Greece all the people and all their belongings. Whenever different circumstances shall arise, as I hope will be the case through the justice and munificence of the five allied Courts, I will reply that a simple proclamation, couched in plain language, and backed by a display of armed maritime forces, will cause the disappearance of disorder, and will unveil to Europe the real pirates. Until then I can only form resolutions, and your Excellency cannot doubt my desire to be as early as possible on the ground.

I beg you will continue your friendship and rest assured of the sentiments with which I have the honor to be your Excellency's very humble and very obedient servant,

J. CAPO D'ISTRIAS.

To His Excellency, Mr. de FOSTER, &c., Turin.

Christian 8, King of Denmark,
To Augustus Foster.

COPENHAGEN, le 10 *Avril*, 1840.

Monsieur, vous m'avez sensiblement rejoui en m'adressant vos vœux à l'occasion de mon avènement au trone de mes ancêtres.

Des antécedants qui sont graves dans ma memoire et qui vous reservent une place bien honorable dans mon souvenir ne me laissaient aucune doute sur la part sincère que vous voudriez bien prendre à un evènement aussi important pour moi et pour le Dannemarc, que vous avez appris à cherir durant un long séjour près de nous. Mais il ne m'a pas été moins agréable d'en recevoir l'assurance par la lettre que vous m'avez adressée.

J'aurai d'abord voulu vous reponder, afin de vous porter mes sincères remercimens, mais des occupations assidues m'ont empêché de m'acquitter d'un devoir cher à mon cœur, aussi savais-je que vous étiez occupé à quitter Turin à cet epoque.

Je saisis avec empressement la perspective que vous me donnez d'une visite en Dannemarc; je n'ai pas besoin de vous assurer que vous serez toujours le bienvenu près de moi et que nommement durant cet été la fête du sacre (?) au Chateaux de Frederiksborg, fixé au 28 Juin, presenterait peutêtre un double interêt pour vous. Celui que vous voudrez bien me porter en qualité d'ancien ami, me sera toujours le plus cher, et c'est en vous assurant de l'inviolabilité de mes sentimens pour vous que j'ai le plaisir de [A line torn out].

—Votre, tout affectionné,

CHRISTIAN R.

Madame Foster trouve içi mes complimens et ceux de la Reine, mon epouse.

The Hon. Mrs. Lamb
To Augustus Foster.

D. HOUSE, *Wednesday*, 1845.

You will have heard of poor Lady Holland's death.[413] She will be a great loss to society, and one thinks now only of her kind feelings and steady friendship, and forgets her little whims and failings, and all one disliked before. Her will is much talked of; it is said she has left Lord John Russell £1500 a year, the Kensington estate for his life, and to go at his death to Lady Lilford; to Charles Fox £2000. He was provided for before when Ampthill was sold, and is well off; innumerable little legacies to friends; to Lady Palmerston £300, a picture of Lord Melbourne by Landseer, and all her fans; to Charles Howard her dictionaries and £200; to her doctor £1500 and £50 a year; to Harold, her page, £150 a year; to all her servants something; a picture to the Queen if she would condescend to accept it; her Napoleon box to the National Museum; £300 for a neat monument of herself. How much she seems to have thought of what every body supposed she dreaded the idea, but she met death calmly and with fortitude. Lady Lilford and her younger sons were with her.

The Hon. Mrs. Lamb
    To Augustus Foster.
                DEVONSHIRE HOUSE, *Monday*, July 20, 1846.

My dear Augustus,—Here I am indeed in the tourbillon, such as I never thought to have mixed in again; a great ball to-night—a dinner first to Royalties—this, however, I am not to be at, the tables were full. I don't go to any parties out of the house, and the heat is so overcoming that I shall be happy to find myself at Melbourne again, where I return with Lord Melbourne: he is, of course, not able to come to these parties, though pretty well. Lord Beauvale has suffered much from gout, and wants to go to Buxton. Lady Carlisle goes back Tuesday, and all the world seems on the wing. I am very glad Frederick enjoys himself, and can be driven about. Lady Palmerston says they have nothing *to give*, and are tormented with applications. It is reported Lord Minto is to go to Vienna; he did not wish it originally.

                                                        Tuesday.

I hear things are not quite settled. Ministers were beat on the question of the Bishopricks of Bangor and St. Asaph in the Lords, and will be, very likely, on the sugar duties in the Commons; if so, they mean to dissolve, so, what will come of it all? Nothing, it seems, is ever to be fixed again.

The fête last night was most brilliant. The new fashion of dinners is to have several little round tables instead of one large one, and it seems to answer and to be thought pleasant. Every body's place was settled beforehand, and the lady's name on her plate. Lady Pollington rebelled and tried not to sit in her allotted place; she ran away, but was brought back. Lord Salisbury has been a second time refused by Lady Mary West;[414] there are many jokes about it; he was overheard telling her he should not live above five years, and then she would be a rich widow; she asked him for 24 hours to consider, and was heard to say, "I'll tell you at Lady Shelley's", but, however, it ended in a refusal, and he looks very sheepish. She said there were some things she liked in him, his caring for the poor, and living in the country, and that she could like him better than the idle dandies about town.

Lady Byron
    To Vere Foster.
                BRIGHTON, *February* 14, 1854.

Wishing to contribute anonymously I will trouble you with the inclosed 480 quarts of soup and the use of the tickets. The entrance of a third person prevented me from expressing all the sympathy I felt in your earnest desire for Truth, and my wish that your Life may be the means of promoting it—for "the Life *is* the Light" in no mystical sense, but as matter of fact open to the observation of every one,—Believe me, with sincere esteem, yours,

A. J. NOEL BYRON.

Lady Byron
    To Vere Foster.

October 6, 1855.

I have not as much time to write to you by this post as I could wish. But as your stay at Kirkby,[415] for which I heartily thank you, will be drawing to a close, I will touch on one or two points. Your observations are all of a very useful character.

As to the *difference*, I believe that which is generally recognized as to man and wife is true of most intimate associations—that if the parties cannot settle their own quarrel, nobody can do it for them. Regulations made by authority, even if it were possible to secure their justice, are likely to irritate one side at least. However, I will consider the matter. Congeniality seems to me essential between the two heads of the school. Have you heard Miss F.? I quite agree about the Crochet, and have more than once urged the bread-making occupations in preference to the Lady-like. Brick floor shall be attended to....

Lady Byron
    To Vere Foster.

BRIGHTON, *October* 7, 1855.

On reading your letter again I saw that you *had* heard both plaintiffs. If the wife of the future Incumbent should prove, as I hope, a kind and sensible person, she may have a good influence on such matters, and *present* legislation is so much better than *absent*—or Colonial—that I should willingly waive my rights.

Mr. Noel does much more than could be expected from any regular Land Agent with respect to Schools and plans for the Poor, but it is not the province in which he is specially qualified to judge, and his opinions are not always coincident with my own, though his aims are. The Pastoral Institution, were it properly carried out, would complete the economy of a rural district better than any other means.

What is your opinion of the course which might be most effectual in lessening the temptation to drunkenness in such a Village? Games? Good Readers reading amusing stories to small groups? Little Exhibitions? I dare not propose what I should think best—Dramatic Representations....

> *Lady Byron*
> > *To Vere Foster.*
>
> > > > > > *February 5, 1856.*

Much might be said in answer to Mr. Barnard's enquiry about Preventive Institutions.[416] I wish I know who could say it. Ill as I have been and still am, I can neither attempt to give detailed accounts nor to methodize facts. I will merely express such views as arise without effort in my mind, and you or Mr. Barnard may pick out something from them. Thirty years ago all the Educational Institutions in England might be called "Preventive" in the sense of obstructing Nature.

1stly. The physical demands in the first instance—Fresh Air, Exercise, Relief of Muscles, &c.

2ly. The mental demands—Instruction appropriate to the age, to the powers and aptitude of the Subject.

3ly. The moral demands—Means of exercising the best dispositions and acquiring the best habits, and of putting precepts into practice in mutual relations.

Education was then really, as it is in a great measure still, a plan for preventing health of body and mind. Good Education might perhaps be more justly called Promotive than Preventive according to *these* views.

But, accepting the word "Preventive" in its now popular signification as opposed to the development of Evil, I will put down what I have had reason from an experience with several hundreds of boys since 1834 to believe the great, and if administered before bad habits have become inveterate, the unfailing Prevention of Moral Evil and of Intellectual Perversion.

1st. At least as many hours of the day spent in the open air and in active pursuits as indoors and in sedentary tasks.

2ly. A practical object intelligible and attractive to the young mind connected with the active employment. (This is especially the case when Garden Allotments are rented by boys, and more or less in trade work.)

3ly. Order, for the exercise of Obedience and Self Controul, never passing into severe discipline—violation of Order being a cause of the loss of social or other privilege of the Offender.

4ly. Liberty. Herein De Fellenberg said that the Schoolmaster should imitate Providence,[417] not withdrawing Temptations entirely (were it possible), but ever watching over those exposed to them, often unconsciously to the objects of his care. They will thus learn to know themselves, and be stronger for having failed. The man who acts this Guardian part in the spirit of cheerfulness and hope always attaches boys.

5ly. Variety of Stimuli applied occasionally to discover and test various kinds of ability latent in different Individuals—for Music, Drawing, Building, Moulding, &c., with promise of cultivation to this special talent, directly or indirectly. Every faculty rightly trained is *preventive* of its misuse, and I might have added under each of the former heads how they prevented some form of practical or imaginative error.

6ly. Affectionate reference to Parents (where of a character to meet it) by little acts of kindness. Family feelings in some way to be brought out. Their *preventive* power was well known to Shakespeare when he made Lady Macbeth say, "Had he not resembled *my Father* as he slept I had done it". Among the lower humanizing influences Kindness to Animals is to be made part of the Education. The care of them contributes to this.

7. As Nature is presented to the young Gardener, who has to make a profit of his little Allotment (generally one sixteenth of an Acre) in the Utilitarian point of view *only*, it should be an object to awaken his sense of Natural Beauty by Holiday excursions to scenes which are likely to make such impressions through contrast with the monotony of his common Locale. Coleridge speaks of the ministering influence of Nature even on hardened Criminals, and their *Preventive* influences on the unhardened are too little appreciated. Ruskin says, "The whole force of Education until very lately has been directed in every possible way to the destruction of the love of Nature", and afterwards, "The next character we have to note in the Landscape Instinct (and on this much stress is to be laid) is its total inconsistency with evil passion; its absolute contrariety—whether in the contest it were crushed or not—to all care, hatred, envy, anxiety, and moroseness". He does not say that in certain characters the love of Nature may not *alternate* with evil passion, but they cannot *co-exist*. To refer, however, from theory to fact, De Fellenberg told me that the Mountain excursions of his boys in Switzerland were as conducive to their moral as to their physical improvement. To some of those English boys, now men engaged in active life, the remembrance of those rambles always brings back a purifying and elevating influence. In my own village schools I have traced similar effects, though my means of affording such enjoyments were comparatively very limited. Ought not the Sabbath to be devoted at least occasionally to the opening of the blind eye to "all the glories of the Light". How many of those who sing the Evening Hymn have ever raised their eyes to a Sunset with grateful admiration? Might not such associations be formed with the silvery moon and

countless stars as could not "co-exist" with the purposes of the nocturnal plunderer?

If I have dwelt long on *this* Preventive Culture it is because it is usually thought one of the weakest, and is in my opinion one of the most effectual means. But there must be an Æsthetic touch in the Schoolmaster to elicit any thing beyond Self-interest in connexion with "this goodly Universe" from the minds of his pupils.

8ly. As preventive of extravagance Savings Banks for the boys' pence—habits of care and forethought also called forth with respect to the Garden Produce, either for its preservation from weather and other injury or from decay after being gathered in.

I have said enough to show my principle, which has been most successfully tested in practice, of *leaving no neglected soil for weeds to occupy*. There is a fault which may be called an exaggeration of this principle—the over cultivation of the human mind, and of which there have been sad examples both in private and public Education. But then Nature was utterly disregarded in the kind of culture, and in nothing more palpably and mischievously, as is now recognized, than in the substitution of words for things.

You will learn something of what has been the result of *my*, or rather De Fellenberg's principles during an eighteen years' trial, if you will make searching inquiries of Mr. Atlee, to whom the inclosed is addressed. If there had ever been a "Village Historian" the plan would doubtless have been more generally tried. I was obliged to be content with *doing*, in trust that all is not lost which is not published.—Yours very truly,

A. J. NOEL BYRON.

Lady Byron
　To Vere Foster.

BRIGHTON, February 18, 1856.

Dear Mr. Foster,—I expressed in my letter on education the use which I wished to have made of it, merely to afford suggestions or fragments from which a more complete system might be formed. I did not revise it with a view to its publication in any other way. Never having aimed at Authorship, I got out my ideas just sufficiently for them to be taken up if worth any thing by those better able to give them a popular form.... You will be glad to hear that I am promoted to the Drawing room for a few hours daily. On Sunday last—I don't know whether it was so throughout England—all the preachers in Brighton took the Sabbath for their subject, and abridgments of their discourses are in the Brighton Examiner. Such a heap of Rubbish; but it is, I hope, in the act of being "shot" to form a foundation for something better—not that I am for obliterating Sunday, but I would no longer have it, as Ross called it, the "*vicarious* day", atoning for all the sins of the Week! Griffiths, though very liberal in most things, could not assent to the Recreative or renewing principle of a seventh day, both to health of mind and body.

You will see how little disposed the County of Leicester is, compared with the other Counties of England, to give pecuniary support to a Reformatory. They ought to be stirred up by some eloquent Appeal from a Lawyer, Clergyman, or Layman. £200 per annum more is wanted. Mr. Young undertakes the responsibility of superintending 25 boys—not more, on account of other duties, and, I am sorry to say, delicate health. But with a powerful Master, an Ex-Director would be less needed.
Yours very truly,

A. J. NOEL BYRON.

Mrs. Follen declares that the Southern States are not serious in the threat of War, because they know it would raise the Slave population.

> *Lady Byron*
> *To Vere Foster.*
>
> *February* 28, 1856.

I see that the next Reformatory meeting is to be on the 1st. Shall you attend? I want to find out What course the R. Catholics are taking. Patrick Murray, Catholic Publisher, has just published a pamphlet, which I like, in their favour. As regards Ireland, if there should be a R. Catholic Association in Leicester, I should be inclined to subscribe a trifle to it as a Testimony. I did not consider it a Theological question.

> *Lady Byron*
> *To Vere Foster.*
>
> *March* 18, 1856.

Your letter received to-day contains much which is not only very interesting to me, but which can be turned to good account.... Mr Young is to preach the Visitation Sermon at Leicester, and he means to include the subject of Reformatories. The Rev. Charles Rattcliffe of that County has sent me a pamphlet advocating that object, and addressed to Lord Calthorpe—not very clever. I have no confidence in Reformatories for Adults *in the heart of a Town*.

Have you heard of the attempt made by Mr. C. Buxton in Spitalfields to withdraw the people from the Public House on Sunday evenings by opening a room where they will find *amusing* occupation? I have been talking to some of those best acquainted with the condition of the working class only just above pauperism about the means of affording them some relief *on Sunday* without leaving them more money to spend at the Public House after receiving their wages on Saturday. This is what I *would* do, if it could be made practicable.

On condition of their paying into a deposit Fund, the accumulation of which should belong to them at a certain period—so many pence or farthings, on Saturday they should find ready-dressed for them a Sunday's dinner, to be taken from the Kitchen (wherever appointed) to their homes by Family Men or Women, and perhaps eaten on the spot by the aged or infirm *Single*. I see these advantages in the plan:

1. Relieving the Poor from preparations for the meal and by the *service* of the Rich—a bond of Union.

2. Obviating the Sunday's dealings with Bakers, &c., which many, and I also, think better avoided.[418]

3. Giving to the day an association with Charity, which it has not either in the R. Catholic Church or ours. Perhaps you would accept an invitation from me, as I should have a room to spare next week, before you go to Ireland.

I am much gratified by Mr. Ross's engagement to a daughter of the well known Sterling,[419] whose life was written by Carlisle—a very superior young woman, and calculated to be a real Help-mate. I have borne the severe weather tolerably.

P.S.—I must communicate to you an idea suggested to me by Mr. Ross, that in order to obviate the reasonable objection to having places of amusement and instruction open on the Sabbath, namely, the hardship upon the door-keepers, &c., there should be Sunday Volunteers for that office....

> *Lady Byron*
> *To Vere Foster.*
>
> *March* 28, 1856.

The "Five Points" which I send is chiefly an Appeal for pecuniary aid, and ought to be met. I should like to entrust to you when you go to New York any larger contribution in order to be sure of its proper application, but I will remit a Subscription through Mrs. Follen *now*.[420]

I must also trouble you with money for the postage and purchase in the United States of any printed *retorts*, &c., which might serve my objects here.

I shall have copied for you a sad report of the Peckleton Reformatory, adding another proof of the folly of attempting reformation by the stern retributive course such as the Leicester Magistrates require of the Schoolmaster. Amongst the indirect mischief of Executions is to be reckoned their charm for Law-breakers, to whom what "some deem danger is delight". I doubt whether the Reformatory can succeed under the direction of such Magistrates. Mr. Young himself is too timid and despondent....

> *Lady Byron*
> > *To Vere Foster.*
>
> HAM, *May* 5, 1856.

I sent to ask you to stay to see Lady Annabella, who was expected.

Ockham can't go to the United States, but I have an idea that I can get him, though only on condition of *working*, on board the Atlantic Cable vessel. Ask him if he would like it.

You want a Tour *without* an object, if possible; but I suppose it must be to the Moon. Lord P.[421] won't be allowed to resign by the People.

> *Lady Byron*
> > *To Vere Foster.*
>
> BRIGHTON, *May* 13, 1856.

... I shall be glad to hear what success you have met with in the Girls' Emigration scheme. The value of that article will, I hope, rise in the market in consequence. Believe me, always truly yours.

> *Lady Byron*
> > *To Vere Foster.*
>
> BRIGHTON, *June* 14, 1856.

Dear Mr. Foster,—I am just going to London, No. 4 Cavendish Square, till the 25th inst., and then No. 1 Cambridge Terrace, Regent's Park, a house which I have taken for the summer, thinking it a happy medium between town and country; and when I am tired of my fellow creatures I can find society almost as rational in the Zoological Gardens. I may well say this after reading what you have to endure from the folly of those who prove their knowledge of God by their ignorance of Man! At the same time I am hearing how Mr. Young is reviled in Leicestershire, and *excluded from the Reformatory* as a Papist in disguise. A man's religion seems every where to be his neighbour's business, not his own.

Do not for want of £5, which I shall be happy to give for such a purpose, allow any Emigrant in real need to lose the passage. "The Philanthropist" paper must be given up for want of funds. Believe me, yours very truly,

A. J. NOEL BYRON.

Lady Byron
   To Vere Foster.

HAM COMMON, *March* 18, 1857.

The wish expressed by Mr. West that I should see the printed paper containing his views makes it less presumptuous than it would otherwise be on my part to offer some remarks. I do not know whether you are aware that, notwithstanding my personal intimacy with some of the Abolitionists, I have scrupulously avoided any appearance of concurring in their *mode of action*. It has appeared to me too vehemently antagonistic; but I own that since I have known the cruel course pursued by Slave Owners towards Opponents who had *not* provoked them by any kind of hostility beyond the simple expression of Dissent, I have doubted whether that opinion of mine were not a mistake. It is of little moment whether it be so or not.

As to Mr. West's plan, the chief feature of which, the Emancipation of the Unborn, presumes their Parents to remain in Slavery. We, in England, should think it rather strange if the Owners of Cotton Mills or Collieries, so ill-managed as to shorten the lives or injure the powers of the men employed in them, were merely to give security to those workmen that such evils should not descend to their Children. I sympathize with the living more than with the future generation. The social condition under which the Children of the next twenty years may be born will in all probability be so changed as to frustrate our plans for *then*, but our Cotemporaries belong to us, as part of the World's Common Weal. Ameliorations long talked of are less likely than ever to be carried into effect under the mutual exasperation of Masters and Slaves, and also with the new views promulgated as to the Servile position.

What is to be hoped for? What can be done for the redress or mitigation of actual wrongs? Providence must show the way, either through the agency of some unforeseen political convulsion, or through the influence of some Master-mind. In the mean time let Right Thought spread as widely as possible, supported by Right Action only when a conflict with Wrong Action is inevitable. Oppression has, I fear, never yet been remedied peacefully. The Host must perish in the Red Sea. It was their own doing, however, rather than that of Moses. I quite enter into the horror of civil discord felt by Mr. West. Some American Authorities have contended that more decision on the part of the North would prevent it. Believe me, yours very truly,

A. J. NOEL BYRON.

> *Lady Byron*
> > *To Vere Foster.*

March 25, 1857.

Next month I hope to say something better of myself than I can at present. Happily I can enter into distant interests as well when I am bed-ridden as at any other time, and feel great pleasure in the continued success of your endeavours for the good of those who would otherwise, it appears, have no helper.[422]

I will send you some American papers. Is not Buchanan's "Laissez aller" about the Slave Question very favourable to the free cause.[423]

> *Lady Byron*
> > *To Vere Foster.*

> *Full text of a letter from Lady Byron, inclosing the gift of Two shares in the Original Atlantic Telegraph.*

February 1, 1859.

A bit of Waste paper. I hope Lady Albinia is well; I am not.

> *Lady Byron*
> > *To Vere Foster.*

February 28, 1859.

I wish for your opinion on a question concerning my eldest Grandson, and if you should agree with me, I may ask some assistance from your kindness in promoting the object by kindly communicating it to him, as *your* representations would be likely to have influence.

It is to bring him into Parliament for some Constituency to which an Advocate of the Working Classes would be welcome. On consulting with some of Ockham's best friends, I find that this is thought the only chance for changing his present habits of inertness and self-neglect, not, however, connected, as far as known, with any bad propensities, and he has ceased to be intemperate. If, therefore, at such a moment, a mental stimulus could be given him, it might work probably; and should he not have power to speak in Public, his lineage and prospects would give a certain weight to his Vote.

You will see in to-day's Times, what I had known from a private source, that there will be an Election for Greenwich in April. The proximity to Millwall might be something in his sight, and the Voters are very radical. Admiral Dundas, who was once the Member, is said to have most interest there, and I could obtain help from other (Metropolitan) Members, but the difficulty will be to make Ockham enter into the scheme.

Trusting to your kindness, I send this long story, which could not be shortened.

The *Father* will take no part. I would supply a few hundreds.

The following copy of a letter, which purports to have been written by Napoleon Bonaparte, has been found among the papers of my father, the late Sir Augustus J. Foster, Bart. It appears to have been addressed in the year 1797 to Citizen Barras,[424] a member of the French Republican Directorate. I have not been able to authenticate it, and insert it here merely in the hope that it may fall under the notice of someone who may inform me of its being a true copy of an original really written by Napoleon. There are evidently some faults of transcription, and one word in the copy I have is undecipherable.

VERE FOSTER.

BELFAST, *January* 1, 1897.

4 VENDEMIAIRE.

Citoyen,—Je suis malade, et j'ai besoin de repos. Je demande ma démission. Donnez la si tu es mon ami. 2 ans dans une campagne près de Paris retablira ma santé, et redonnera a mon caractère la popularité que la continuite du pouvoir ... Je suis esclusif dans ma manière de sentir et d'agir, et j'estime le coeur bien plus que la tête.

BONAPARTE.

Je suis au desespoir. Ma femme ne vint pas; elle a quelques amans que la retienne à Paris. Je maudis toutes les femmes mais J'embrase de coeur mes bons amis.

BONAPARTE.

Appendix

The Earl of Bristol, Bishop of Derry

The following obituary of Lord Bristol is taken from *The Gentleman's Magazine* for 1803.

August 8. At Albano, near Rome, of a severe attack of the gout, Frederick Hervey, Earl of Bristol, grandson of the first earl, in which title he succeeded his brother, Augustus John, 1779, and Bishop of Cloyne 1767, of Derry 1768, and a privy-councillor of Ireland. He was born in 1730; educated at Mr Newcome's school at Hackney; admitted of Corpus Christi College, Cambridge, 1747, where he took no degree; but the honorary one of DD was conferred on him by mandamus. He was appointed chaplain-in-ordinary to the king, and a principal clerk of the privy-seal, both which he resigned when appointed a bishop. He married Elizabeth, daughter of Sir Germayn Davers, who died at Ickworth, Suffolk, Dec. 19, 1800, by whom he had two sons, George, late captain of the *Zealous* man-of-war, and Augustus john, and two [three, V.F.] daughters, Mary, married to John Lord Erne, of Ireland, and Elizabeth, married to John Thomas Foster [and Louisa, married to Lord Hawkesbury, afterwards Earl of Liverpool, prime minister from 1812 to 1827, V.F.]. He was among the leaders of the Irish patriots during the American war, and a member of the famous Convention of Volunteer Delegates held in Dublin in 1782 [1783, V.F.], on which occasion he was escorted from Derry to Dublin by a regiment of volunteer cavalry, and received military honours in every town through which he passed on that long journey. His lordship was building at his family seat at Ickworth a villa on the Italian model by Italian architects and artists of every class, to which he had appropriated £12,000 annually, and the ornaments of which are so tender and sharp as to require covering to preserve them from injury by the external air. As an amateur, connoisseur, and indefatigable protector of the fine arts he died at his post surrounded by artists, whose talents his judgment had directed and whose wants his liberality had relieved. His love of the sciences was only surpassed by his love of his country and his generosity to the unfortunate of every country; neither rank nor power escaped his resentment when any illiberal opinion was thrown out against England. In 1798 he was arrested by the French in Italy, and confined in the castle of Milan; was plundered by the republicans of a valuable and well-chosen collection of antiquities, which he had purchased with a view of transmitting to his native country, and was betrayed and cheated by many Italians whose benefactor he had been. But neither the injustice nor the ingratitude of mankind changed his liberal disposition; he no sooner recovered his liberty than new benefactions forced even the ungrateful to repent, and the unjust to acknowledge his elevated mind.

The Earl of Bristol was one of the greatest English travellers (a capacity in which his merits have been duly appreciated by the celebrated Martin Sherlock), and there is not a country in Europe where the distressed have not obtained his succour and the oppressed his protection. He may truly be said to have clothed the naked and fed the hungry, and, as ostentation never constituted real charity, his left hand did not know what his right hand distributed. The tears and lamentations of widows and orphans have discovered his philanthropy when he is no more; and letters from Swiss patriots and French emigrants, from Italian Catholics and German Protestants, prove the noble use his lordship made of his fortune indiscriminately to the poor, destitute, and unprotected of all countries, of all parties, and of all religions. But, as no man is without his enemies, and envy is most busy about the most deserving, some of his lordship's singularities have been the object of calumny, and his pecularities ridiculed as affected; when the former were only the effect of pure conduct, unrestrained by ceremony, because it meant no harm, and the latter the consequence of an entire independence, long enjoyed, serviceable to many, baneful to none.

The late Earl of Bristol, when in Italy, distinguished himself by a peculiarity of dress. He wore a *white* hat edged with *purple*, a coat of crimson silk or velvet (according to the season), a black sash *spangled with silver*, and *purple stockings*. It need hardly be added, what was the fact, that the good inhabitants of Naples and other places looked upon this fanciful suit as the costume of an Irish bishop.

The following is copied from *Memoirs of James Caulfield, Earl of Charlemont*, by Francis Hardy, 1810:—

If this work should chance to survive the present day, those who come after may not be incurious to learn something, however slight, of that singular man. He was the son of Lord Hervey, so generally but so imperfectly known by the malign antithesis and epigrammatic lines of Pope. His mother, Lady Hervey, was also the subject of that poet's muse, but his muse when playful and in good humour. Two noblemen of very distinguished talents, the Earls of Chesterfield and Bath, have also celebrated her in a most witty and popular ballad (see verses on Molly Lepel—Lady Hervey was the daughter of General Lepel). Lord Bristol was a man of considerable parts, but far more brilliant than solid. His family was indeed famous for talents; equally so for eccentricity, and the eccentricity of the whole race shone out and seemed to be concentrated in him. In one respect he was not unlike Villiers, Duke of Buckingham. 'Everything by starts and nothing long'; generous but uncertain; splendid but fantastical; an admirer of the fine arts, without any just selection; engaging, often licentious in conversation; extremely polite, extremely violent;—it is incontestably true that amidst all his erratic course his bounty was not seldom directed to the most proper and deserving objects. His distribution of church livings, as I have been informed, among the older and respectable clergy in his own diocese, must always be mentioned with that warm approbation which it is justly entitled to. It is said (how truly, I know not) that he had applied for the bishopric of Dublin, afterwards for the lieutenancy of Ireland; was refused both, and *hinc illae lacrymae*, hence his opposition. But the inequality, the irregular flow of his mind at every period of his life, sufficiently illustrate his conduct at this peculiar and momentous period. Such, however, was this illustrious prelate, who, notwithstanding he scarcely ever attended Parliament, and spent most of his time in Italy, was now called upon to correct the abuses of Parliament, and direct the vessel of state in that course where statesmen of the most experience and persons of the calmest judgment have had the misfortune totally to fail. His progress from his diocese to the metropolis, and his entrance into it, were perfectly correspondent to the rest of his conduct. Through every town on the road he seemed to court, and was received with, all warlike honours, and I remember seeing him pass by the Parliament House in Dublin (Lords and Commons were then both sitting) escorted by a body of dragoons, full of spirits and talk, apparently enjoying the eager gaze of the surrounding multitude, and displaying altogether the self-complacency of a favourite marshal of France on his way to Versailles, rather than the grave deportment of a prelate of the Church of England.

Richard Brinsley Sheridan

Sheridan, the eminent Irish dramatist, was educated first in Dublin and afterwards at Harrow. He gave no promise as a boy of the brilliancy which he afterwards displayed as a man, being pronounced a hopeless dunce by all his teachers. He does not seem to have been brought up to any regular employment, and after his elopement and marriage in 1773 with a Miss Linley, a public singer of great beauty and accomplishments, his prospects did not seem bright, more especially as he insisted on a point of pride that his wife should give up her profession. As the readiest resource he betook himself to literature, and in January, 1775, his first comedy, *The Rivals*, was produced. Damned on its first appearance through certain deficiencies in the acting, this piece on its repetition found gradually the favour with the public which its wit and vivacity deserved, and made the reputation of the writer. In the course of the year following Sheridan followed up his success by a farce of no very great merit, and a second comedy, *The Duenna*, among the sparkling dialogue of which are interspersed some songs of exquisite merit.

He now became partner of the Drury Lane Theatre, and in 1777 *The School for Scandal* was produced there. This, which is by much his greatest effort, instantly leaped into the popularity it has ever since continued to retain. His other works for the stage were the inimitably clever farce, *The Critic*, in 1779, and, after a long interval, *The Stranger* and *Pizarro*, in 1798, both adapted from the German of Kotzebue. Leigh Hunt observes of *The School for Scandal* that, with the exception of too great a length of dialogue without action in its earlier scenes, it is a very concentration and crystallization of all that is sparkling, clear, and compact in the materials of pure comedy. Through the influence of Fox he was enabled to enter the House of Commons in 1780. He gave a warm and consistent support to the Whig party, and during the Marquis of Rockingham's administration held the office of Under Secretary of State, but he possessed none of the high qualities of a statesman, and as a debater he gradually degenerated into a useless, though amusing speaker, familiarly joked at by the public, admired but disesteemed by his friends. He never failed to amuse the House, and when stirred by the trumpet-call of a great occasion he was capable of rising to heights of noble eloquence. In particular, his famous speech urging the impeachment of Warren Hastings is still traditionally remembered as perhaps the very grandest triumph of oratory in a time prolific of such triumphs. (From *Chambers's Encyclopedia* and *Beeton's Dictionary of Universal Biography*.)

La Comtesse de la Marche

La Comtesse was daughter of Frederick William II, King of Prussia, and Wilhelmina, Countess of Lichtenau, of whom the following account appears in *Meyer's Encyclopedia*, Berlin, 1896:—

Lichtenau (Wilhelmina, Countess of), mistress of Frederick William II of Prussia, was born 29 December 1752, in Potsdam. She died 9 June 1820, in Berlin. She was the daughter of the musician Enke of Hildburghausen.

The then Prince of Prussia, afterwards King Frederick William II, made her acquaintance when she was 13 years old at her sister's house, who was a dancer at the Italian Opera in Berlin. The Prince had her educated in Paris and in Potsdam, where intimate intercourse followed. Five children were born, who received the title of Counts and Countesses of the Mark.

In 1782 she was married to Rietz (Ritz), Groom of the Chamber. When Frederick was crowned King of Prussia Rietz was made Groom of the Privy Chamber. Although Rietz's wife was superseded in the King's favour by the Countess of Voss and the Donhoff, she succeeded in retaining his friendship till 1796, when she received the title of Countess of Lichtenau, which admitted her to Court. The King gave her also the sum of 500,000 thalers, several estates, and a dowry of 200,000 thalers to her daughter, Countess Marianne of the Mark (a son, Count of the Mark, died when nine years old) on the occasion of her marriage with Count Stolberg. She retained the King's affection and confidence, which she never misused, till his death in 1797.

King Frederick William III then arrested and opened proceedings against her, but nothing could be laid to her charge. Nevertheless she was kept prisoner at Glogau, only regaining her liberty by surrendering all her property, in return for which she received a pension of 4,000 thalers a year. A marriage which she contracted with the dramatic poet Holbein in 1802 was dissolved in 1806. In 1811 a portion of her estates were returned to her.

See the *Apologie* of Countess L., edited by Schummel, Breslau, 1808, two volumes; the *Memoirs* put out under her name (1808) are not genuine.

Sir Augustus Foster

Sir Augustus John Foster, Bart., PC, and GCH, of Stonehouse, County Louth, was born in 1780. He was the second son of John Thomas Foster, MP, and Elizabeth, second daughter of Frederick Hervey, third Earl of Bristol and Bishop of Derry. He was educated at Drogheda and Christ

College, Oxford. He entered the army as cornet in the Royal Horse Guards (blue) in 1799, and studied at Weimar under M. Mounier, who afterwards became private secretary to Napoleon. In 1803 he visited Greece in company with his cousin John Leslie Foster and the Earl of Aberdeen. He entered the Diplomatic Service in 1804, being appointed Secretary of Legation at Washington. On his return to Europe in 1808 he was appointed Chargé d'Affaires at Stockholm, whence he was expelled by order of Napoleon in 1810. In February, 1811, he was appointed Minister to the United States, and on the breaking out of war between England and the United States in 1812 he returned to England, and in 1814 received the appointment of Minister to Denmark. He remained at Copenhagen ten years, and in 1824 was appointed in the same capacity at the court of the King of Sardinia. He was created a baronet in 1831, and after a residence of sixteen years at Turin retired from the public service in 1840.

Sir A. married in 1815 Albinia Jane Hobart, daughter of the Hon. George Vere Hobart, second son of George, third Earl of Buckinghamshire, and by her had issue three sons, namely, Frederick John, the Revd Cavendish Hervey, and Vere Henry Louis.

Sir Augustus died in 1848, and his wife Lady Albinia Foster in 1867.

Lord Castlereagh

(Robert Stewart, Viscount Castlereagh, a celebrated diplomatist and minister), eldest son of the first Marquis of Londonderry.

Stewart entered the Irish Parliament in 1789, although then under age. He was made Chief Secretary for Ireland in 1798. It was the year of the Insurrection and of the French Invasion, and therefore some allowance must be made for the terrible severities employed by the Irish Government; yet the cruel part he acted or tolerated in Ireland in suppressing the rebellion and effecting the union always weighed upon his reputation. He afterwards held the positions of President of the Board of Control in the Addington administration, and secretary successively of the War and Colonial Departments under Mr Pitt, until the death of the latter in 1806, when he resigned. He resumed the office of Minister of War in the following year, and in 1812, after the assassination of Mr Perceval, the Prime Minister, he became Secretary for Foreign Affairs in the ministry of Lord Liverpool, which post he held during the period illustrated by the military achievements of the Duke of Wellington.

By this time the general direction of British policy had become unalterably fixed by circumstances, and Lord Castlereagh has at least the merit of having pursued this fixed course with a steadiness, and even obstinacy, which nothing could abate. He was the soul of the coalition against Bonaparte, and it was only by his untiring exertions and through his personal influence that it was kept together.

He represented England at the Congress of Vienna in 1814, and at the Treaty of Paris in 1815. By the death of his father in 1821, he became Marquis of Londonderry, but his mind became deranged, and he died by his own hand in 1822.

This statesman, looked upon by one party as a paragon of perfection, has been characterised by the other party 'as the most intolerable mischief that ever was cast by an angry Providence on a helpless people' —*Chambers's Encyclopaedia*. 1769–1822.

The Earl of Aberdeen

The following particulars are taken from Blackie & Son's *Popular Encyclopedia:*—

George Hamilton Gordon, Earl of Aberdeen, was born at Edinburgh, 28 January 1784. He was educated at Harrow, and afterwards at St John's College, Cambridge, where he graduated in 1804. He had previously, in 1801, accompanied as attaché Lord Cornwall's embassy to France, which resulted in the signing of the treaty of Amiens in the following year. Before returning home he proceeded south to Greece; and, after traversing that ancient land with all the enthusiasm of an ardent classical scholar, retraced his steps to England through Turkey and Russia. Shortly after his return he established the Athenian Society, one indispensable qualification for being a member of which was to have visited Greece, and from this circumstance the epithet of 'Athenian Aberdeen' was affixed to Lord Aberdeen by Lord Byron. As the result of his classical studies and investigations he contributed an article to the *Edinburgh Review* on the topography of Troy, in which he somewhat severely handled Sir William Gell, and also wrote an introduction to Wilkins's translation of *Vitruvius*, giving an account of the progress of architecture in Greece, an essay subsequently published in a separate form in 1822. In 1806 Lord Aberdeen entered Parliament as a Scottish representative peer, and in 1813 was intrusted by the British government with a mission to Austria, for the purpose of inducing the emperor to withdraw from the alliance of his son-in-law, and join the coalition of sovereigns against Bonaparte. In this responsible duty, which was mainly effected through negotiation with Prince Metternich, the young diplomatist acquitted himself with great judgment, and entirely to the satisfaction of the government. At most of the bloody engagements in Northern Germany he was present; and from the experience thus acquired of the horrors of war he appears to have imbibed that aversion to it which at a later period exposed him, in his political administration, to the charges of pusillanimity and want of spirit. On the termination of the war he returned to England, and from this period till 1828 lived in strict retirement. In 1814 he had been created a British peer, in recognition of the services rendered by him in his diplomatic negotiations with Austria. In 1828 he became Foreign Secretary under the Duke of Wellington. He was a warm supporter of the bill repealing the Test and Corporation Acts, a measure effected by the ministry under which he served, and he also advocated the bill for the emancipation of the Roman Catholics. During the short premiership of Sir Robert Peel in 1834–35 he acted as Colonial Secretary, and on the subsequent accession of Sir Robert to the premiership in 1841, again took office as Secretary for Foreign Affairs. Quitting office with his chief in 1846, with whose views on the question of free-trade he thoroughly coincided, he came, on the death of Sir Robert Peel in 1850, to be regarded as the leader of the Conservative free-trade party. On the inability of the Derby ministry to maintain its place, Lord Aberdeen was instructed to form a cabinet, and accordingly returned to office in 1853 as head of a coalition ministry. The principal event which marks his administration is the Russian war; but the tardiness which he displayed, and unwillingness to enter into hostilities, the result of his constitutional aversion to warlike measures, irritated the country. In 1855, a majority of the House of Commons having decided for the appointment of a committee of inquiry into the conduct of the war, a motion which the Aberdeen ministry had uniformly resisted, the resignation of the cabinet ensued, and Lord Palmerston took the post of premier. This event marks the close of Lord Aberdeen's public career; he died, 14 December 1860.

Young Roscius, William Henry West Betty (1791–1874)

Betty's grandfather and father were bleachers of linen at Lisburn, in County Antrim. His mother was the only child of James Stanton, Esq., of Hopton Court, Shropshire. She was a lady of good education and high accomplishments. In the year 1802 the celebrated actress, Mrs Siddons, visited Belfast. Betty had never before been to a theatre. He was so inspired with enthusiasm by her acting that, on his return home from the theatre, he told his father that he should certainly die if he was not to be a player. He was then eleven years old. All his ordinary amusements became wearisome and trivial, and henceforth the theatre became the subject of his morning thoughts and midnight dreams. Mr Aikin, manager of the Belfast theatre, now engaged the boy through his father for a nightly performance commencing 19 August 1803. During the next year, 1804, he acted in the theatres of nearly all the provincial towns of the United Kindgom, culminating in December 1804, in simultaneous engagements at the two great theatres of Covent Garden and Drury Lane, the receipts of these two houses during the first four months of his performance amounting to nearly £40,000. On one occasion, on the motion of William Pitt, the House of Commons adjourned to witness his performance of *Hamlet*. He was usually called Roscius in memory of a celebrated ancient Roman actor of that name.

During 1806 and 1807 Master Betty revisited all the chief towns of the kingdom. At last, after three or four years of hard work, during which the public interest was gradually languishing, and it was recognized that a youth of sixteen or seventeen could no longer be considered a juvenile phenomenon, it was announced at Bath in March, 1808, that he was about to retire from the stage, and in July of that year he withdrew altogether, and entered Cambridge University. It is noteworthy that Mrs Siddons never condescended to act with him, saying that he was a very clever, pretty boy, but nothing more.

On his father's death in 1811, young Betty, then nearly twenty years of age, returned to the stage, and was able to retain his position as a clever and interesting actor for some years longer, but in August 1824, he made his positively last appearance. (The above information is chiefly derived from a lecture delivered at Holywood, County Down, by my friend, Mr. W. H. Malcolm, of that town, in the year 1882.—V. F.)

Caroline Ponsonby (1786–1828).

Caroline, daughter of Frederick Ponsonby, Earl of Bessborough, was married 3 June 1805, to the Honourable William Lamb, afterwards Viscount Melbourne, Her Majesty Queen Victoria's first Prime Minister. She became in March, 1812, passionately infatuated with Lord Byron, of whom she wrote in her diary immediately on her return home after her introduction to him that he was mad, bad, and dangerous to know. He subsequently wrote of *her* that she was the kindest and ablest female he ever met.

After Byron's rupture with her in 1813 her temper became so ungovernable that her husband reluctantly determined upon a separation. While the legal instruments were being prepared, she wrote and sent her first novel, *Glenarvon*, to the press. However, on the day fixed for the execution of the deed of separation a sudden reconciliation took place, and Lady Caroline was found seated beside her husband feeding him with tiny scraps of transparent bread and butter, while the solicitor was waiting below to attest the signatures (see Torrens' *Memoirs of Viscount Melbourne*, vol. i. p. 112).

> In July, 1824, she accidentally met Byron's funeral procession on its way to Newstead. Though she partially recovered from this sudden shock, her mind became more affected, and in the following year she was separated from her husband.

She died at Melbourne House, Whitehall, on 26 January 1828, aged 42, in the presence of her husband, who had hastened over from Ireland. (*Dictionary of National Biography*.)

Mr Jeaffreson, in his *Real Lord Byron*, says of Lady Caroline Lamb that 'it is perhaps no extenuation of her most considerable faults and follies that, in her fantastic and flighty way, she really loved the poet whom she injured so greatly, possibly loved him even when in her jealous wrath she was striking at him with the vicious energy of an enraged tigress'.

Lines on Charles James Fox

On inquiry of His Grace, the Duke of Bedford, I find that the lines written by Georgiana, Duchess of Devonshire, for inscription on the bust of C. J. Fox, now in the Sculpture Gallery of Woburn Abbey, were ultimately slightly altered, and therefore, by His Grace's kind permission, I append the more correct version—

> Here midst the Friends he loved the man behold
> In truth unshaken and in virtue bold.
> Whose Patriot zeal and uncorrupted mind
> Dared to assert the freedom of mankind:
> And whilst, extending desolation far,
> Ambition spread the baneful flames of war,
> Fearless of blame, and eloquent to save,
> 'Twas he—'twas Fox the warning counsel gave:
> Midst jarring conflicts stemmed the tide of blood,

And to the menaced world a sea-mark stood.
Oh! had his voice in mercy's cause prevailed,
What grateful millions had the Statesman hailed!
Whose wisdom bade the broils of nations cease,
And taught the world humanity and peace!
But though he failed successive ages here,
The vain, yet pious, effort shall revere,
Boast in their annals his illustrious name,
Uphold his greatness, and confirm his fame!
—GEORGIANA DUCHESS OF DEVONSHIRE.

Count Capo d'Istrias

Count John Anthony Capo d'Istrias—a patriot, philanthropist, and able diplomatist—was born at Corfu, 11 February 1776. His family originally came from the Illyrian town of Capo d'Istria, near Trieste, but had been settled in Corfu for upwards of four hundred years. He began life as a medical student, devoted himself to political life, and after having held a high position in the Ionian Islands, entered the diplomatic service of Russia. In 1813 he became the minister-plenipotentiary of Russia to Switzerland, and gained the favour of the Swiss by advocating the restoration of all the territory which the French had taken from them, and the re-establishment of Helvetian independence. In 1814 he attended the Congress of Vienna, and in the following year was the plenipotentiary of Russia in the arrangement of the final treaty of peace with France. In 1822 he retired from the public service of Russia and retired to Geneva, whence he plotted the undermining of Turkey; and on the separation of Greece from that power, after the battle of Navarino, in which the Turkish and Egyptian fleets were annihilated by the combined British, French, and Russian fleets, under the command of Sir Edward Codrington, on 20 October 1827, he was elected, in January 1828, President of the Greek Republic for seven years, but was by no means equal to the task which he had undertaken. Everything was in disorder; the people had been long enslaved and knew not how to use their freedom, and the President had been so much imbued with the centralizing principles prevalent at the Courts which he had frequented that some of his measures, especially that restricting the liberty of the press, gave offence to even the most temperate of the enlightened lovers of civil liberty, and his career was cut short by assassination in a church at Nauplia on 9 October 1831, the assassins being George, the son, and Constantine, the brother, of Peter Mauromichali, against whom he was urging on a prosecution for alleged offences against the state. (The above information is culled from the following sources: *Encyclopedia Britannica*, Chambers's *Encyclopedia*, Blackie's *Popular Encyclopedia*, and Beeton's *Dictionary of Universal Biography*.)

Elizabeth Vassall Fox, Lady Holland

Elizabeth, daughter and heir of Richard Vassall of Jamaica, was first married in 1786 to Sir Godfrey Webster. The marriage was dissolved in June 1797, by Act of Parliament, on the ground of adultery committed by her with Henry Richard, Lord Holland, whom she married on the 9th of the following month.

The following notice of Lady Holland is copied from the *Annual Register* of 1845, Appendix to Chronicle, page 314:—

The deceased lady played a very conspicuous part in society, political and literary. Her great attainments, lively wit, her grace and dignity, decidedly placed her at the head of Whig fashion. The charms of the celebrated hospitalities of Holland House in the time of its late revered owners have been made known wherever liberal thought, literary merit, or eminence in the arts are to be found. For the remarkable position occupied by her ladyship during many years of those daily festivals in which genius, wit, and patriotic hope were triumphant, she was eminently gifted. While her own remarks were full of fire, practical sense, and nice observations, her influence was chiefly felt in the discourse of those whom she directed and inspired, and which, as she impelled it, startled by the most animated contrast, or blended in the most graceful harmonies. Beyond any other hostess, and very far beyond any host, she possessed the tact of perceiving, and the power of evoking the various capacities which lurked in every part of the brilliant circles she drew around her. To enkindle the enthusiasm of an artist on the theme over which he had achieved the most facile mastery; to set loose the heart of the rustic poet, and imbue. his speech with the freedom of his native hills; to draw from the adventurous traveller a breathing picture of his most imminent danger; or to embolden the bashful soldier to disclose his own share in the perils and glories of some famous battlefield; to encourage the generous praise of friendship when the speaker and the subject reflected interest on each other, or win the secret history of some effort which had astonished the world, or shed new lights on science; to conduct those brilliant developments to the height of satisfaction, and then to shift the scene by the magic of a word, were among her daily successes. Habituated to a generous partisanship by strong sympathy with a great political cause, she carried the fidelity of her devotion to that cause into her social relations, and was ever the truest and fastest of friends. The tendency, often more idle than malicious, to soften down the intellectual claims of the absent, which so insidiously besets literary conversation, and teaches a superficial insincerity even to substantial esteem and regard, found no favour in her presence. Under her auspices not only all critical, but all personal talk was tinged with kindness; the strong interest which she took in the happiness of her friends shed a peculiar sunniness over the aspects of life presented by the common topics of alliances, and marriages, and promotions; and not a promising engagement, or a wedding, or a promotion of a friend's son, or a new intellectual triumph of any youth with whose name and history she was familiar, but became an event on which she expected and required congratulation, as on a part of her own fortune. If to hail and welcome genius, or even talent, which revered and imitated genius, was one of the greatest pleasures of Lord Holland's life, to search it out, and bring it within the sphere of his noble sympathy, was the delightful study of hers. How often, during the last half century, has the steep ascent of fame been brightened by the genial appreciation she bestowed, and the festal light she cast on its solitude. How often has the assurance of success received its crowning delight amid the genial luxury of her circle, where renown itself has been realized for the first time in all its sweetness.

The remains of Lady Holland were interred at Ampthill, Bedfordshire.

Emanuel De Fellenberg (1771–1844)

De Fellenberg was a philanthropic Swiss nobleman, who, after taking part in the public affairs of his country during the occupation of the French, whom he did all in his power to resist, retired entirely from politics, and devoted his whole life to the cause of literary and agricultural education. In 1799 he purchased an estate near Berne, where he organized a system of tuition, which was designed to show what education could do for humanity. His life from this time is a continual record of benevolent enterprises, labours for the diffusion of knowledge and improvement of the people. He possessed singular tact in disarming the opposition of interested or jealous opponents, and ultimately accomplished a large measure of success for his favourite projects. (Beeton's *Dictionary of Universal Biography*.)

Paul Count de Barras (1755–1829)

De Barras was a most prominent member of the French Revolutionary Convention, in which he voted for the execution of the King, Louis XVI, without delay or appeal. He was appointed by the Convention Commander-in-Chief in 1794, and was mainly instrumental in overthrowing Robespierre and the rest of the terrorists. Being again appointed Commander-in-Chief in the following year, he commissioned his young friend, Napoleon Bonaparte, whose military talents he had learned to admire at Toulon, to crush the Paris sections with merciless discharges of artillery. He next became a member of the Directory, consisting of five members, and appointed Napoleon Commander-in-Chief of the army in Italy, and a few days afterwards arranged the marriage of Napoleon with the widow Beauharnais.

On the overthrow of the Directory by Napoleon, on the 18th Brumaire (9 November), 1799, Barras retired into private life.

Endnotes

1 *The Hon. Mrs. Hervey*—Elizabeth, daughter of Sir Jermyn Davers, Bart., and wife of the Hon. Frederick Hervey, Bishop of Derry, d. 1800.

2 *Mr. J. Th. Foster*—Daughter of the Bishop of Derry and Mrs. Hervey, d. 1824.

3 *Monsieur le Sage*—An allusion to Mrs. Hervey's son-in-law, J. Th. Foster, MP, d. 1796.

4 *16th of December*—Date of Mrs. Fosters marriage in 1776.

5 *your sister*—Mary, Countess of Erne, eldest daughter of the Bishop of Derry, d. 1842.

6 *Doctor Foster*—Thomas Foster, D.D., Rector of Dunleer, father of J. Th. Foster (1709–1784)

7 *Louisa*—Louisa Hervey, youngest daughter of the Bishop of Derry, married afterwards to the second Earl of Liverpool, d. 1821.

8 *Dodd*—The Rev. Wm. Dodd. LL. D., author of *Beauties of Shakespeare* and *Reflections on Death*, found guilty of forgery and executed. His case created a great sensation at the time (1729–1777).

9 *my brother*—Sir Charles Davers, Bart.

10 *Pyrmont*—A noted mineral spring in the north-west of Germany, Principality of Waldeck-Pyrmont.

11 *the foldings*—Portions of the paper folded in so as to serve as an envelope. Before the inauguration of national penny postage there was a separate postage for every separate piece of paper under a quarter of an ounce weight, and therefore both letter and address were usually written on the same piece of paper, which was so folded as to leave a blank space for the address, but when weight alone regulated the postage, in the year 1840, envelopes came into use.

12 *The Padre*—The Bishop of Derry. *See Appendix.*

13 *my sister*—Mrs. Greene.

14 *Sh.*—Sheffield Place or Park in Sussex, country seat of Lord Sheffield.

15 *the young ff's*—A playful designation of Mr. and Mrs. J. Th. Foster.

16 *Our Princess of Brunswick*—Augusta, sister of George III.

17 *Waldeck*—The sovereign principality of Waldeck-Pyrmont.

18 *The Duke*—Duke of Brunswick, d. 1780.
19 *Sheffield*—That is Sheffield place.
20 *from Canada*—From Capt. Hervey, RN, eldest son of the Bishop of Derry, married to Elizabeth Drummond of Quebec, d. 1796.
21 *Mr. F.*—Thomas Foster, DD (1709–1784).
22 *f*—Th. Foster, d. 1796.
23 *Val d'Agno*—A mineral spring in the north of Italy, often mentioned subsequently.
24 *Lord Bessborough*—Wm. Ponsonby, second Earl of Bessborough and Viscount Duncannon (1704–1793).
25 *The Elector*—The Elector of the Rhenish Palatinate in which the town of Pyrmont was situated.
26 *little slimness*—Playful reference to Mr. J. Th. Foster.
27 *mad Sovereign*—Charles Eugene, an extravagant ruler, but a patron of education. The state at this time ranked only as a duchy, but was raised to a kingdom in 1806.
28 *Lou*—His daughter Louisa, as previously explained.
29 *little f*—Th. Foster.
30 *great F*—Thomas Foster, DD.
31 *Dawson Street*—In Dublin.
32 *Dunleer*—A village in Co. Louth, where, as already mentioned, Dr. Foster, her father-in-law, was rector.
33 *Bittio*—A teacher of drawing.
34 *my late brother*—Probably George William, second Earl of Bristol, d. 1775.
35 *Lady Stormont*—wife of the British Ambassador at Paris.
36 *The young senator*—John Thomas Foster, MP, d. 1796.
37 *la Corda*—probably for the punishment known as the strappado.
38 *Voltaire*—François Marie Arouet de Voltaire (1694–1778).
39 *Roussau*—Jean Jacques Rousseau (1712–1778).
40 *Lord Chesterfield*—Philip Dormer Stanhope, Earl of Chesterfield (1694–1773).
41 *Your sister*—Lady Erne.
42 *Slimness*—J. Th. Foster, as already explained.
43 *the dab*—The child Fred. Th. Foster.
44 *Prince of G.*—Prince of Saxe-Gotha.
45 *Lord Stormont*—British Ambassador at Paris.
46 *Monsr. de Noailles*—French Ambassador at London.
47 *Lord Chatham*—William Pitt, Earl of Chatham, (1708–1778); prime minister from 1757 to 1761, and from 1766 to 1768. Lord Chatham had been against harsh measures towards the American colonies, but he was strongly opposed to the Rockingham patty, then in power, and the peace proposed by them as betraying an unworthy fear of France. His last appearance in the House of Lords was on the 7th April—the day after this letter was written—when he protested against the acknowledgment of American independence. He died on May 11th.
48 *the Down Hill*—The Bishop's country seat in Co. Derry.
49 *Castel Gandolfo*—A village near Rome.
50 *Ranizzini*—Cardinal Ranizzini.
51 *Lord Chatham*—The House of Commons voted £20,000 to pay Chatham's debts, and an annuity of £4,000 was settled on his successors.
52 *Cardinal Wolsey*—*Ego et Rex meus* is sufficiently well known (1471–1540)
53 *Bourbon*—The French Royal Family.

54 *Roitelets*—Petty kings, kinglets.

55 *Lady Bristol*—Elizabeth, daughter of Colonel Thomas Chudleigh, and wife (married privately) of Augustus John Hervey, Earl of Bristol and brother of the Bishop of Derry. She married, secondly, E. Pierrepoint, Duke of Kingston, for which offence she was impeached before the House of Lords, and the marriage was declared illegal (1740–1788).

56 *Keppel*—Admiral Lord Keppel (1725–1786). He had been in command of an ill-equipped fleet of twenty ships while the French Brest fleet, with which he was supposed to be able to cope, consisted of thirty-two ships of the line. He accordingly fell back to spithead to wait for reinforcements.

57 *your poor sister*—Lady Erne.

58 *his cousin*—John Foster, (1740–1828), last Speaker of the Irish House of Commons, created in 1821 Lord Oriel.

59 *Duchess Countess*—The so-called Duchess of Kingston.

60 *Jack*—Captain Hervey, the writer's son, Augustus John, who had entered the navy.

61 *his uncle*—John Augustus Hervey, brother of the Bishop of Derry, who had greatly distinguished himself in the naval service of Britain.

62 *poor dear little orphan*—A playful designation of her daughter, Mrs. J. Th. Foster.

63 *Lord Hillsborough*—Lord Hillsborough, afterwards Marquis of Downshire, was a supporter of Lord North, and held more than one office under him.

64 *Lord North*—Frederick North, (1732–1792), Lord North, prime minister from 1770 to 1782.

65 *the King of France*—Louis XVI (1754–1793).

66 *Lady Mulgrave*—The Bishop's sister, who died in March of this year.

67 *the estate*—The estate of Ickworth Park, near Bury St Edmunds. The bishop had succeeded to the tide of Earl of Bristol and to the family estate in December, 1779.

68 *Ch. Governor*—This appears to mean the Lord-Lieutenant.

69 *Duke of Leinster*—William Robert Fitzgerald, second duke of Leinster (1749–1804).

70 *My brother*—Sir Charles Davers, Bart.

71 *the Duke of Devonshire*—William Cavendish, (1748–1811), fifth Duke of Devonshire, who succeeded to the title in 1764.

72 *Duchess of Devonshire*—Georgiana, daughter of John Earl Spencer. She was married to the fifth Duke of Devonshire in 1774, and was one of the two duchesses from whom this volume derives its title; d. 1806.

73 *the general*—General William Hervey, a brother of the Bishop of Derry.

74 *Duke of Portland*—William Henry Cavendish Bentinck, (1738–1809), prime minister in 1787 for a few months; home secretary under Pitt from 1794 to 1801; and again prime minister from 1807 to 1809.

75 *Fred*—The writer's son Frederick Hervey, afterwards successively Earl and Marquis of Bristol. At this time he was only fourteen years of age.

76 *D. of P.*—Duke of Portland.

77 *D. of D.*—Duke of Devonshire.

78 *Lord Rodney*—Lord Rodney, (1718–1792), the famous British admiral, who had defeated the French fleet in the West Indies.

79 *your B.*—The writer's son, already referred to as "Jack" in letter of 12 December 1778.

80 *Birbo*—Italian *birbone*, a worthless fellow.

81 *Barmeath*—A mansion near Dunleer, Co. Louth.

82 *her poor mother*—Margaret Georgiana Poyntz, Countess Spencer, d. 1814. The death of her husband, Earl Spencer, had recently taken place.

83 *Lord Mul*—Lord Mulgrave.

84 *Lady Cow*—Probably for Lady Cowper.

85 *the Emperor*—Alexander I, Emperor of Russia (1777–1825). *Editor note: this is incorrect as the ruler of Russia in 1784 was Catherine the Great; Alexander did not become Tsar until 1801. The Emperor was probably Joseph II, (1741–1790), Holy Roman Emperor, and Emperor of Austria.*

86 King of Sweden—Gustavus III (1746–1792).

87 *Lady Hervey*—Elizabeth, daughter of Colin Campbell of Quebec, and wife, of John Augustus Lord Hervey, (d. 1818), eldest son of the Bishop of Derry. *Editor note: this is incorrect, Elizabeth appears to have been the daughter of Colin Drummond.*

88 *Batoni*—Pompeo Batoni, (1708–1787), Italian painter.

89 *Richard Brinsley Sheridan*—(1751–1816).—*See Appendix. Editor note: this is probably incorrect, for the writer appears to be Eliza Sheridan, née Linley, (1754–1792); she married Richard Brinsley Sheridan in 1773.*

90 *Mr. Hare*—James Hare, wit and politician. See the lines on him on a subsequent page.

91 *muso*—Italian for muzzle, face.

92 *Gibbon*—Edward Gibbon, (1737–1794), author of *The History of the Decline and Fall of the Roman Empire.*

93 *Lady Sheffield*—Abigail Way, wife of the first Earl of Sheffield, Gibbon's most intimate friend, and editor of his posthumous works.

94 *Goodwood*—The country seat of the Duke of Richmond in Sussex.

95 *Lord Macartney*—Lord Macartney, (1737–1806), was at the head of the first British mission ever sent to China, in 1792. The "mock king" here referred to was Louis XVIII, at this time an exile, to whom Lord Macartney was sent on a confidential mission.

96 *Albert Dürer*—(1471–1528).

97 *Angelica Kauffman*—(1742–1807).

98 *Cimabue*—Giovanni C. (1240–1300).

99 *Pompeio Battoni*—Pompeo Batoni (1708–1787).

100 *Rembrandt*—Rembrandt van Ryn (1606–1669).

101 *the author of the Descent from the Cross*—Peter Paul Rubens (1577–1640).

102 *Raphael*—Raffaelle Sanzio (1483–1520).

103 *Garth*—Sir Samuel Garth (1661–1719).

104 *Gay*—John Gay (1685–1732).

105 *Prior*—Matthew Prior (1664–1721).

106 *Shakespeare*—(1564–1616).

107 *Michael Angelo*—Michael Angelo Buonarotti (1475–1564).

108 *Dante*—Dante Alighieri (1265–1321).

109 *your poor brother*—Frederick, (1769–1859), who by the death of his elder brother, also here referred to, had become Lord Hervey. He was afterwards Earl and Marquis of Bristol.

110 *the King of Prussia*—Frederick William II, (1744–1797), king of Prussia 1786–97.

111 *Princess of Wales*—Princess Caroline, (1768–1821), daughter of Charles, Duke of Brunswick.

112 *Duchess of York*—Frederica Charlotte (1767–1820), daughter of Frederick William II, King of Prussia, and wife of the Duke of York, son of George III.

113 *Farquhar*—Sir Walter Farquhar, Bart., a celebrated physician.

114   *Titian*—Tiziano Vecellio (1477–1576).

115   *La Comtesse de la Marche*—*See Appendix.*

116   *Messrs. Gosling*—Bankers in London.

117   *the ablest minister*—William Pitt (1759–1806).

118   *H. Bruce*—Rev. Sir Henry Hervey Aston Bruce, Bart., d. 1822.

119   *Lord Spencer*—The second Earl Spencer, (1758–1831), brother of Georgiana, Duchess of Devonshire; First Lord of the Admiralty in Pitt's government.

120   *Minden*—The French were defeated by an army of Anglo-Hanoverians near Minden, in Westphalia, in 1759.

121   *Rosbach*—Rossbach, in Prussian Saxony. Here Frederick the Great defeated the allied Austrian and French armies in 1757.

122   *Archduke Charles*—Charles, (1771–1847). Third son of Leopold II, Emperor of Austria. He defeated Marshal Jourdan in several battles in 1796. He also defeated Moreau at Rastadt in 1797, Masséna in 1805, and the main French army, commanded by Napoleon in person, at Aspern, May 21st and 22nd, 1809.

123   *Moreau*—The greatest general of the French Republic, except Napoleon (1763–1813).

124   *Alten Kirchen*—in Prussia. The French who had defeated the Austrians here in 1796 were themselves defeated, and their general Marçeau killed on Sept. 19th following.

125   *Fredericks*—The writer's own name, it should be remembered, was Frederick.

126   *Mr. Elliot*—Hugh Elliot a son of Sir Gilbert Elliot, and brother of the first Earl of Minto.

127   *Bishopswerder*—Hans Rodolph B. a Prussian statesman, d. 1803.

128   *Moellendorf*—Richard Joachim Henry, Count de M., a Prussian general (1724–1816).

129   *Lord Elgin*—The seventh Earl of Elgin, (1766–1841).

130   *Thomas Paine*—The well-known anti-Christian writer, author of *The Rights of Man, The Age of Reason*, etc. (1737–1809).

131   *Cicero*—(106–43 BC).

132   *Lucullus*—A wealthy Roman general, a patron of literature and art, and friend of Cicero (115–49 BC).

133   *your eldest son*—Frederick Th. Foster, (1777–1853), now about nineteen years old.

134   *Lord Malmesbury*—James Harris, (1746–1820), the first Earl of Malmesbury, diplomatist.

135   *Bishop Burnet*—Gilbert B., (1643–1715), author of *History of the Reformation* and *History of His Own Times*.

136   *Lord Granville*—William Wyndham G., (1759–1834), created Baron G, in 1790, afterwards Foreign Secretary and Prime Minister in 1806 in succession to Pitt.

137   *house of Brandenburg*—The royal family of Prussia.

138   *Lord Bute*—John Stuart, (1713–1792), third Earl of Bute, best known as being a most unpopular prime minister in the beginning of the reign of George III.

139   *Cromwell*—Oliver (*c.* 1599–1658).

140   *glorious Victory over the Dutch*—At Camperdown, 11 October 1797.

141   *Lord Hawkesbury*—Robert Banks Jenkinson, (1770–1828), son of the first Earl of Liverpool, whom he succeeded as second Earl. He was Prime Minister from 1812 to 1827. He had become (in 1795) the husband of Lady Louisa Hervey, youngest daughter of the Bishop of Derry, and aunt of the young man to whom this letter was written.

142 *Guido*—(1575–1642).

143 *Carracci*—(1555–1619).

144 *General Berthier*—Berthier, (1753–1815), one of Napoleon's marshals. He held the first place in the confidence of Napoleon.

145 *Augustus Foster*—Augustus, (1780–1848), second son of John Thomas Foster, MP, was Chargé d'affaires at Stockholm, 1808–1811; British Minister at Washington, 1811–1812; at Copenhagen, 1814–1824; and at Turin, 1824–1840).

146 *W. Lamb*—William Lamb, (1779–1848), afterwards Viscount Melbourne, and Prime Minister, with exception of a short interval, from 1834–1841).

147 *Lord Castlereagh*—(1769–1822).

148 *Kotzebue*—August K., (1761–1819), well known as a prolific German dramatist.

149 *Lord Howe*—(1725–1799).

150 *Lord Keith*—(1746–1823).

151 *Buonaparte*—(1769–1821).

152 *Aréna*—Barthélemi A., a native of Corsica, was accused with his brother Joseph of conspiracy, and of attempting to stab Napoleon on the 18th Brumaire while dissolving the council of 500 of which B. A. was a member; but he always denied the charge and died in obscurity, though his brother Joseph was executed.

153 *He, Sieyès, and Roger Ducos*—Members of the consulate, Napoleon being First Consul.

154 *Julius Caesar*—(100–44 BC).

155 *the Expedition*—The expedition to Holland under the Duke of York, which was a complete failure.

156 *Schiller*—(1759–1805).

157 *Goethe*—(1749–1832).

158 *Lord St. Vincent*—(1732–1823).

159 *the unfortunate Pope*—Pope Pius VI, (1717–1799), who was taken prisoner by the French general Berthier, and carried away from Rome to Valence, in France, where he died.

160 *the Melbournes*—Viscount and Lady Melbourne, parents of William Lamb, who became afterwards prime minister.

161 *Lady Holland*—Elizabeth Vassall, (1770–1845), daughter of Richard Vassall of Jamaica, and wife of Sir Godfrey Webster, after her divorce from whom, she married, secondly, Henry Richard Fox, Baron Holland. Holland House was for a very lengthened period a hospitable resort for the distinguished in literature and politics.

162 *Lady Bessborough*—Henrietta Frances, (d. 1821), daughter of John, first Earl Spencer.

163 *Lord Morpeth*—Afterwards Earl of Carlisle, (1802–1864).

164 *the Duchess*—of Devonshire.

165 *He*—Bonaparte.

166 *his two inferior Consuls*—When the consulate of three members was first constituted as the supreme power in France, on the 18th Brumaire (November 9th), 1799, it consisted of the Abbé Sieyès, Bonaparte, and Roger Ducos, with equal authority. Sieyès resigned within a month, and on 13 December 1799, Bonaparte, Cambacérès, and Lebrun were elected first, second, and third consuls respectively, each being elected for ten years, and being re-eligible. In May, 1802, Bonaparte was re-elected for ten additional years, and in August of the same year he was made consul for life by

3,568,885 out of a possible total of 3,577,259 votes. Finally, on 18 May 1804, he was made Emperor.

167 *Sir Joseph Banks*—Joseph Banks, (1743–1820), the distinguished naturalist, who had sailed with Captain Cook round the world.

168 *Addington*—Henry A., (1757–1843), Viscount Sidmouth, prime minister from 1801 to 1803.

169 *Canning*—George C., (1770–1827), prime minister in 1827).

170. *the Emperor Paul*—The murder of the Emperor Paul I, (1754–1801), took place on 24 March 1801. His tyrannical rule had caused much discontent.

171 *Benixin*—More correctly Bennigsen.

172 *her*—Corisande de Gramont, daughter of the Duke de Gramont. She became the wife of the Earl of Tankerville.

173 *Madame de Stael*—The celebrated French authoress, (1766–1817), daughter of Necker, the famous financier and minister of France, and wife of Baron de Stael-Holstein, Swedish minister at Paris.

174 *Talleyrand*—Charles-Maurice de Talleyrand, (1754–1838), one of the greatest diplomatists of the period, at one time a warm supporter of Bonaparte.

175 *J. Leslie Foster*—Baron first of the Court of Exchequer in Ireland, and afterwards of the Court of Common Pleas.

176 *Masséna*—André Masséna, (1758–1817), one of the most celebrated of Bonaparte's generals, called by him "Enfant de la Victoire".

177 *Camille Jourdan*—a French writer (1771–1821).

178 *Louis XVIII*—(1755–1824).

179 *M'Donald*—Marshal M'Donald, (1765–1810).

180 *Madame Joseph*—Wife of Joseph Bonaparte.

181 *Madame Murat*—(1782–1839).

182 *Louis Bonaparte*—(1778–1806).

183 *Duchess of Cumberland*—Frederica of Mecklenburg Strelitz.

184 *Grattan*—(1750–1820).

185 *Reis Effendi*—The title of the Turkish minister of foreign affairs.

186 *Charles James Fox*—(1749–1806); Burke called him the greatest debater the world ever saw; and Sir James Mackintosh said he was the most Demosthenic speaker since Demosthenes.

187 *Francis*—Sir Philip F., (1740–1818), supposed author of the celebrated Letters of Junius.

188 *the Doctor*—Henry Addington, (1757–1844), prime minister from 1801 to 1803.

189 *The Earl of Aberdeen*—George Hamilton Gordon, (1784–1860), Earl of Aberdeen, prime minister from 1852 to 1855. He was a man of culture, a student of Greek architecture and antiquities, and had visited Athens by this time; hence Byron designated him as "the travelled thane, Athenian Aberdeen".

190 *Cromarre*—A district of Aberdeenshire, on the Dee.

191 *mountain massacre*—of grouse.

192 *Gell*—Sir William Gell, (1777–1836), a learned classical antiquary.

193 *eis tēn polin*—The Greek words for "to the city". This expression being constantly in people's mouths in ancient times gate origin to the names Istanbul; *Stanbul*, for Constantinople; hence the use of these words in the letter.

194 *Kinrara*—In Inverness-shire, near the Spey, now the property of the Duke of Richmond and Gordon, one of whose titles is Earl of Kinrara.

195 *olive groves of Academia*—That is whether he shall again go to Athens.

196 *Babylon*—London.

197 *Haddo*—The family residence of the Earls of Aberdeen in Aberdeenshire, near the river Ythan.

198 *Tierney*—George Tierney, (1761–1830), statesman and political critic.

199 *young Roscius*—William Betty, the boy actor, *See Appendix*.

200 *General Fitzpatrick*—Wit and politician, the most intimate friend of Charles James Fox.

201 *The Princess Charlotte*—Charlotte, (1796–1817), the only child of the Prince Regent, afterwards George IV. She was married to Leopold, king of the Belgians, but died at the age of twenty-one.

202 *Lord Granville*—Granville Leveson Gower, (1773–1846), Earl Granville, diplomatist.

203 *Ossulston*—Lord Ossulston, (1776–1859), son of the Earl of Tankerville, to which title he succeeded.

204 *Toujours Gai*—A punning designation.

205 *Madame Jerome*—Daughter of Mr. Patterson, a rich Baltimore merchant.

206 *Jerome*—Jérome Bonaparte, (1784–1860), youngest brother of Napoleon. He was king of Westphalia from 1807 to 1813. Me married a princess of Würtemburg while his first wife was still alive, the marriage with Miss Patterson being declared null and void by Napoleon after he had become emperor.

207 *the President*—Thomas Jefferson, (1743–1826), president of the United States from 1801 to 1809.

208 *William Cobbett*—Political and miscellaneous writer (1762–1835).

209 *Mr. Grey*—Afterwards Earl Grey, prime minister when the great Reform Bill of 1832 was passed (1764–1845).

210 *Randolph*—John Randolph, an American statesman distinguished for his eloquence, wit, sarcasm, and eccentricity, and for thirty years more talked and written of than any other American politician. He boasted that the Indian Princess Pocahontas was one of his ancestors (1773–1833). *Editor note: the reference to Republican Democrats has nothing to do with 21st century American political parties, although the eventual current Democratic Party has its roots in this Republican Democrat foundation, even though it seems a misnomer due to having the word 'Republican' at its head.*

211 *Pocahontas*—Daughter of Powhatan, an Indian chief of Virginia, married to John Rolfe in 1613, and baptized by the name of Rebecca (1595–1617).

212 *Lord Bristol*—The Bishop of Derry had died in Italy in 1803, and his son Frederick was now Earl (and afterwards marquis) of Bristol (1769–1859).

213 *Grassini*—Josephina Grassini, the finest Italian singer of her time (1775–1850).

214 *Garrick*—David Garrick; Pope said of him after seeing him act in *Richard II*, 'That young man never had his equal as an actor, and will never have a rival' (1716–1779).

215 *Sir Walter*–Sir Walter Farquhar, the physician mentioned previously; *Dr Blane*—Afterwards Sir Gilbert Blane, a celebrated physician (1749–1834).

216 *poem*—The Lay of the Last Minstrel.

217 *Melville*—Henry Dundas, Viscount Melville, long prominent in the political world. He was impeached for crimes and misdemeanours committed while acting as treasurer of the Navy, but was acquitted. The "tenth report" refers to the proceedings in regard to this trial (1740–1811).

218 *Lord Wellesley*—The Marquis Wellesley, the famous governor-general of India, and eldest brother of the Duke of Wellington. He returned from India in 1805, having been about eight years there (1760–1842).

219 *Holkar*—Jeswunt Rao Holkar, Maratta ruler of Indore, who gave much trouble to the British, and gained a rather important victory over the Colonel Monson mentioned here.

220 *your friend Lord A.*—Lord Aberdeen.

221 *The Duchess of Gordon*—She probably wished him to marry a daughter of her own. The Duchess—Jane Maxwell—was famous as a successful match-maker, and was in several ways somewhat notorious.

222 *Harriet*—Lady Harriet Cavendish, daughter of the fifth Duke of Devonshire—known in the family as Hary-o.

223 *Lord Tankerville*—He appears to have been against the marriage of his son Lord Ossulston with the Corisande several times referred to in the correspondence, but the marriage eventually took place.

224 *Lord Cornwallis*—He was appointed, in 1804, governor-general of India in succession to the Marquis Wellesley, but died in 1805

225 *Your old flame*—Corisande Gramont.

226 *That eventful day*—Eventful in the proceedings against Lord Melville. Mr. Whitbread moved certain resolutions censuring the conduct of Lord M.; Pitt moved the previous question; and the votes being equal the Speaker (Mr Abbot, afterwards Lord Colchester) gave his casting vote in favour of Mr Whitbread's motion. Lord M. at once resigned the post of First Lord of the Admiralty, and his name was erased from the list of members of the Privy Council, but Lord Aberdeen's confidence in his ultimate triumph was not misplaced.

227 *Trotter*—Paymaster of the Navy under Lord Melville.

228 *Duke of Clarence*—Afterwards King William IV (1765–1837).

229 *The combined fleets*—French and Spanish.

230 *Caroline Ponsonby*—See Appendix (d. 1828).

231 *Brocket Hall*—The country seat of Lord Melbourne in Hertfordshire.

232 *The successor of Montezuma*—Meaning Thomas Jefferson, President of the United States, who had now entered on his second term of office (1743–1826).

233 *Lady Catherine Hamilton*—Daughter of the first Marquis of Abercorn (d. 1812).

234 *Lord Sidmouth*—Formerly known as Henry Addington, Prime Minister from 1802 to 1803 (1757–1844).

235 *Clifford*—Augustus C., created a baronet in 1838 (1788–1877).

236 *Calder*—Admiral Sir Robert C., created a baronet in 1798 (1745–1818).

237 *The impeachment*—of Lord Melville.

238 *Duke of Gloucester*—brother of George III (1743–1805).

239 *Lord Bolingbroke*—(1761–1824).

240 *German lady*—Baroness Hompesch.

241 *Lady C. H.*—Lady Catherine Hamilton (d. 1812).

242 *Young Roscius*—William Betty (1791–1874). See Appendix.

243 *Ulm*—In the Duchy of Würtemberg. After a battle between the French and Austrians, in which the latter under General Mack were defeated with dreadful loss by Marshal Ney, Ulm surrendered with 28,000 men on October 20, 1805.

244 *General Mack*—(1752–1829).

245 *Pichegru*—General P., gained great glory as one of the generals of the French Republic, but afterwards sided with the Bourbons. He was transported to Cayenne, but escaped and lived for some time in England (1761–1804).

246 *Editor note: Chevy Chase—this is not to be confused with the actor. The*

Ballad of Chevy Chase is an English ballad, dating from the fifteenth century, relating to the Cheviot Hills, straddling the Anglo-Scottish border, and the frequent battle between English and Scots.

247 *Kemble*—John K. was at this time carrying on Covent Garden theatre (1757–1823), Mrs Siddons was the sister of John and Charles Kemble (1755–1831).

248 *Moreau*—The greatest general of the French Republic except Napoleon (1763–1813).

249 *Dessalines*—Jacques D., first Emperor of Haiti. He was an enslaved black from the Gold Coast of Africa, and was totally uneducated (1760–1806).

250 *Christophe*—Henri C., negro King of Haiti. He began life as cook in a tavern (1767–1820).

251 *Victory of Trafalgar*—On October 21, 1805.

252 *Mr. Marsden*—Chief Secretary of the Admiralty.

253 *Villeneuve*—Admiral V., French commander at Trafalgar. He was released in 1805, and returned to France, but, learning that his reception by Napoleon would be unfavourable, he committed suicide (1763–1805).

254 *Washington*—George W. (1732–1799).

255 *Mr. Clay*—Henry C., Speaker of the American House of Representatives, and afterwards United States Senator. He contested the Presidency three times without success (1771–1852).

256 *Editor note: The Indian was Wa Pawni Ha, a seventeen-year-old Sack chief. At Foster's request the Swiss miniaturist David Boudon—(or Bourdon), active in the United States 1797–1816—took Wa Pawni Ha's portrait in late December, and then presumably either he or Foster donated it to him. Wa Pawni Ha may have presented the image to Jefferson when the delegation visited the President's House on 4 January 1806. It now hangs in the entrance hall of the Jefferson Monticello Rooms.*

257 *Sicard*—The Abbé S., instructor of the deaf and dumb (1742–1822).

258 *It is indeed over with the Continent*—This evidently refers to the battle of Austerlitz on 2 December 1805, which was followed by an armistice a few days after. This victory of Napoleon is said to have given Pitt his death-blow.

259 *Charles Kemble*—Brother of the more famous John Philip K. and of Mrs. Siddons (1775–1854).

260 *Brocket*—Brocket Hall, country seat of Lord Melbourne in Hertfordshire.

261 *Lord Wellesley*—Marquis Wellesley, Governor-general of India (1760–1842).

262 *The Lion*—William Pitt (1759–1806).

263 *Mr. Pitt's death*—He died 23 January 1806, the day on which this letter was written.

264 *Mr. Lascelles' motion*—The motion was for a public funeral and monument to the memory of Pitt. Fox declined to assent to the motion, and Wyndham spoke against it. Among those who supported it were Wilberforce and Lord Castlereagh. On a division the motion was carried by 258 to 89. Pitt's debts, amounting to £40,000, were paid by the nation. He was buried in Westminster Abbey on 22 February 1806.

265 *General Miranda*—Founder of the Independence of Spanish America (1750–1816).

266 George, Prince of Wales, afterwards King George IV (1762–1830).

267 *The trial*—Probably in view of his being present as a peer at the trial of Lord Melville, which began in Westminster Hall on 26 April.

268 *The Cattaro*—An Austrian town and district in Dalmatia which belonged for a few years to the French.

269 *Lord Selkirk*—Thomas Douglas, fifth Earl of S. He assisted in settling emigrants in some parts of Canada, and in particular was the founder of what is now the province of Manitoba. The title is now among those borne by the Duke of Hamilton (1771–1820).

270 *Hartington*—Marquis of H., afterwards sixth Duke of Devonshire. He was at this time sixteen years old. He died unmarried, and was succeeded by his cousin, (1790–1853).

271 G. died 30 March 1806; Fox, 13 September 1806.

272 *When he died*—Fox died on 13 September 1806. He was buried on 10 October 1806 in Westminster Abbey beside Pitt.

273 *The beaten army*—The Prussian army utterly routed by Napoleon in the battle of Jena, 14 October 1806. On the same day another Prussian army was defeated at Auerstadt (about 14 miles distant) by the French under Davoust, and on the 27th Napoleon entered Berlin.

274 *Hohenlohe*—Prince Hohenlohe, the Prussian commander in the battle of Jena, 14 October 1806 (1746–1858).

275 *Duke of Brunswick*—The Prussian commander at Auerstadt.

276 *Sir Francis Burdett*—Prominent as a politician of advanced views, and for thirty years (from 1807) Member of Parliament for Westminster. The election here referred to was for Middlesex, and Sir Francis was defeated (1770–1844).

277 *T. Sheridan*—Son of R. B. Sheridan. Stafford had been at one time represented by his father.

278 *Sheridan*—Richard Brinsley S. The election here referred to was for Westminster, and Sheridan was successful.

279 *Mr. Burr*—Aaron Burr, of whom more will be heard in subsequent letters (1756–1838).

280 *Editor note: The Duke of Brunswick—Charles William Ferdinand, Duke of Brunswick-Lüneburg (1735–1806), he was married to Princess Augusta, a sister of George III. The duke commanded the large Prussian army at Auerstedt during the double Battle of Jena–Auerstedt on 14 October 1806. His forces were defeated by Napoleon's marshal Davout, despite the Prussians outnumbering the French around Auerstedt by two to one. During the battle he was struck by a musket ball and lost both of his eyes. Severely wounded, the Duke was carried with his forces before the advancing French. He died of his wounds in Ottensen, near Hamburg, 10 November 1806.*

281 *Buenos Ayres*—It was retaken by the Spaniards in August. The news was long in travelling.

282 *The negotiation*—Regarding peace with France.

283 *Mr. Perceval*—Spencer P., afterwards Prime Minister from 1809 to 1812 (1762–1812), assassinated 11 May 1812.

284 *To qualify him*—At this time the qualification for a county member was an estate of £600 a year, and for a borough member one of £300.

285 *Catalani*—Angelica Catalani (1780–1849) was an Italian opera soprano.

286 *Grassini*—Giuseppina Maria Camilla Grassini was a noted Italian contralto, and a singing teacher (1773–1850).

287 *Billington*—Mrs. Elizabeth Billington, a British opera singer, born in London, the daughter of German parentage; Carl Weichsel, principal oboist at the King's Theatre and Frederika, née Weirman (c. 1768–1818).

288 *My success*—Lord Aberdeen was elected a Scotch representative peer on 4 December 1806.

289 *Paull's Petition against Sheridan*—In connection with the result of the recent Westminster election, at which Sheridan was returned.

290 *He can't attempt Westminster*—Sheridan was a candidate at this new election, but failed, being behind Sir F. Burdett and Lord Cochrane (afterwards Earl of Dundonald).

291 *Castaños*—Francisco Javier Castaños Aragorri Urioste y Olavide, Count of Castaños y Aragones, 1st Duke of Baylen, the most distinguished of the Spanish generals in the Peninsular War (1758–1852).

292 *Ney*—Marshal of the Empire Michel Ney 1st Duke of Elchingen, 1st Prince of Moscow (1769–1815).

293 *General Baird*—Sir David B., specially famous for his services in India (1757– 1829).

294 *Sir J. Moore*—The hero of Corunna (1761–1809).

295 *This Lord L.*—Robert Banks Jenkinson, 2nd Earl of Liverpool, (1770–1828), Prime Minister (1812–27). He married, 1795, Elizabeth Foster's sister, Louisa, née Hervey.

296 *Palafox*—Spanish general, celebrated for his heroic defence of Saragossa against the French (1780–1847).

297 *Editor note: Opadaca—This appears to refer to Juan Ruiz de Apodaca (1754–1835), Spanish Ambassador to England, 1809.*

298 *Want the Duke to resign*—The Duke of York had to resign his post of Commander-in-Chief, though a select committee of the House of Commons acquitted him of any corrupt practices. His services to the army had been very valuable, and he was reinstated in 1811.

299 *Arnfelt*—Gustav Mauritz A., a celebrated Swede (1757–1814).

300 *Lord St Vincent*—John Jervis, Earl of St Vincent, the celebrated admiral (1734–1823).

301 *Lord Archibald*—Lord A. Hamilton brought forward unsuccessfully a motion of censure upon Lord Castlereagh for his abuse of Indian patronage. *See Appendix.*

302 *The appointment of Lord Wellesley*—As ambassador to Spain.

303 *Soult*—Marshal (1769–1851). The occupation of Oporto, the passage of the Douro, and the retreat of Soult, were the first incidents of Wellington's brilliant career in the Peninsula.

304 *Lord Arthur*—Lord Arthur Wellesley, afterwards Duke of Wellington (1769–1852).

305 *Lord Burgersh*—Afterwards eleventh Earl of Westmoreland (1784–1859).

306 *Beresford*—Viscount B. His chief service in the Peninsular War was the reorganization of the Portuguese army (1768–1354).

307 *Victor*—Marshal V. (1766–1841).

308 *Our own expedition*—The unfortunate Walcheren expedition.

309 *Lord Paget*—Afterwards first Marquis of Anglesey and Field Marshal. He commanded an infantry division in the expedition (1768–1854).

310 This evidently refers to the battle of Wagram.

311 *Flushing*—Taken 16 August 1809.

312 *Sebastiani*—Marshal S., born in Corsica (1776–1851).

313 *Joseph*—Joseph Bonaparte, eldest brother of Napoleon (1768–1844).

314 *Talavera*—The battle was fought on 27 and 28 July 1809.

315 *Princess Mary*—Daughter of George III, afterwards married to her cousin the Duke of Gloucester (1776–1857).

316 *Lord Chatham*—Eldest son of the great Lord Chatham.

317 *Mr. Tierney*—George T., statesman (1762–1830).

318 *If Lord Castlereagh was not turned out*—On account of a difference of
policy, followed by misunderstanding on the subject of the Walcheren
expedition, of which Canning disapproved, wishing that reinforcements
should rather be sent to Lord Arthur Wellesley in Portugal.

319 *The Doctor*—Henry Addington, Lord Sidmouth.

320 *Editor note: Mr. Cavendish, the philosopher—Henry Cavendish FRS*
(1731–1810) was a natural philosopher, scientist, and an important
experimental and theoretical chemist and physicist. Cavendish is noted for
his discovery of hydrogen or what he called 'inflammable air'. He described
the density of inflammable air, which formed water on combustion, in a 1766
paper 'On Factitious Airs'. Antoine Lavoisier later reproduced Cavendish's
experiment and gave the element its name. Cavendish was the son of
Lord Charles Cavendish, third son of William Cavendish, 2nd Duke of
Devonshire. He inherited two fortunes that were so large that Jean Baptiste
Biot called him 'the richest of all the savants and the most knowledgeble of
the rich'; at death he was the largest depositor in the Bank of England.

321 *Bonaparte's marriage*—With Marie Louise, daughter of Francis I, Emperor of
Austria (1791–1847).

322 *Baron d'Engelström*—Swedish Minister of Foreign Affairs.

323 *Succeeding with*—Miss Milbanke.

324 *M'Donald*—Marshal Macdonald (1765–1840).

325 *Lord Liverpool*—Prime Minister from 1812 to 1827 (1770–1828).

326 *My dreadful misfortune*—The death of her husband, William Cavendish, 5th
Duke of Devonshire, KG (14 December 1748–29 July 1811).

327 *The Duke of Clarence*—Afterwards King William IV (1765–1837).

328 *Lord Byron*—(1788–1824).

329 *Your friends in the north*—The Milbankes.

330 *Caro*—Caroline, wife of the Hon. William Lamb.

331 *Editor note: William Cavendish's death—Hon. William Cavendish MP*
(1783–1812), the son of Lord George Cavendish, later Earl of Burlington.
He married, 18 July 1807, Louisa O'Callaghan, daughter of Cornelius
O'Callaghan, 1st Baron Lismore. They had four children, including
William Cavendish, who eventually succeeded as 7th Duke of Devonshire
(1808–1891). William Cavendish was accidentally killed when he was flung
from his curricle driving in Holker Park on his way back from a shooting
excursion, 15 January 1812.

332 *Editor note: Suaviter in Modo fortiter in Re—Pleasantly in manner,*
powerfully in deed.

333 *Caro William*—Caroline, wife of the Hon. William Lamb.

334 *Marmont*—Napoleon's marshal (1774–1852).

335 *Editor note: Wellesley accepted the post of Foreign Secretary in Spencer*
Perceval's cabinet. Unlike his brother Arthur, (later the Duke of Wellington)
he was an eloquent speaker, but was subject to inexplicable 'black-outs' when
he was apparently unaware of his surroundings. He held this office until
February 1812, when he retired, partly from dissatisfaction at the inadequate
support given to Wellington by the ministry, but also because he had become
convinced that the question of Catholic emancipation could no longer
be kept in the background. From early life Wellesley had, like his brother
Arthur, been an advocate of Catholic emancipation, and with the claim of the
Irish Catholics to justice he henceforward identified himself. On Perceval's
assassination he, along with Canning, refused to join Lord Liverpool's
administration, and he remained out of office till 1821. His reputation

never fully recovered from a fiasco in 1812 when he was expected to make a crucial speech denouncing the new Government, but suffered one of his notorious 'black-outs' and sat motionless in his place.

336 *Perceval*—Spencer Perceval (1762–1812) was prime minister from October 1809 until his assassination in May 1812.

337 *Editor note: Anne Isabella Noel Milbanke (1792–1860). She married, 2 January 1815, the poet George Gordon Byron, 6th Baron Byron (1788–1824), and had one child, Augusta Ada (1815–1852), but they separated in 1816.*

338 *Ralph*—Sir Ralph Milbanke, 6th baronet, d. 1825, (Annabella's father).

339 *Soult*—Marshal General Jean-de-Dieu Soult, 1st Duke of Dalmatia, named Marshal of the Empire in 1804 (1769–1851). In 1812, after Wellington's victory of Salamanca, Soult was obliged to evacuate Andalusia.

340 *La madre*—Lady Judith Noel Milbanke, d. 1822.

341 *Editor note: Jean Victor Marie Moreau (1763–1813) was a French general who helped Napoleon Bonaparte to power, but later became a rival and was banished to the United States. Moreau returned to Europe and began to negotiate with an old friend from the circle of republican intriguers, Jean-Baptiste Bernadotte, now known as Crown Prince Charles John of Sweden (later king Charles XIV of Sweden). Charles John and Tsar Alexander I of Russia were now together with the Prussians and the Austrians leading an army against Napoleon. Moreau, who wished to see Napoleon defeated and a republican government installed, gave advice to the Swedish and Russian leaders about how best to defeat France. He was mortally wounded in the Battle of Dresden on 27 August 1813 while he was talking to the tsar and died on 2 September in Louny.*

342 *Editor note: this is probably a transcription error. The name is more likely to be 'Didot' not 'Dicot'. The Didot family were famous printers and publishers in Paris. There were numerous members of the family at this time so precise identification is difficult.*

343 *Editor note: Charles Pierre François Augereau, 1st Duc de Castiglione (1757–1816), general and Marshal of France. After serving in the French Revolutionary Wars he earned rapid promotion while fighting against Spain and soon found himself a division commander under Napoleon Bonaparte in Italy. He fought in all of Bonaparte's battles of 1796 with great distinction. During the Napoleonic Wars, Emperor Napoleon entrusted him with important commands. His life ended under a cloud because of his poor timing in switching sides between Napoleon and King Louis XVIII of France. He served the restored Louis XVIII, but, after reviling Napoleon, he went over to him during the Hundred Days. Louis XVIII, when re-restored to the royal throne, deprived him of his military title and pension. Augereau died at his estate of La Houssaye the following year.*

344 *Sir Charles Stuart*—Charles Stuart, 1st Baron Stuart de Rothesay (1779–1845), known as Sir Charles Stuart between 1812 and 1828. He was twice Ambassador to France and also served as Ambassador to Russia between 1841 and 1844.

345 *Eugene*—Eugène Rose de Beauharnais, Duke of Leuchtenberg (1781–1824) was the first child and only son of Alexandre de Beauharnais and Josephine Tascher de la Pagerie, who later became the first wife of Napoleon as Empress Josephine. After the fall of Napoleon in 1814, Eugène retired to Munich and at the behest of his father-in-law King Maximilian of Bavaria, did not get involved with Napoleon during the 100 days'escapade.

346 *Editor note: Karl Philipp, Prince of Schwarzenberg (1771–1820),*
     Austrian field marshal. He repelled an attack by Napoleon in the Battle of
     Arcis-sur-Aube on 20–21 March and overcame the last barrier before Paris
     by winning the Battle of Fère-Champenoise on 25 March. His capture of the
     French capital on 31 March after the Battle of Paris resulted in the overthrow
     of Napoleon.

347 *Editor note: Gebhard Leberecht von Blücher (1742–1819), Prussian field*
     marshal. He earned his greatest recognition after leading his army against
     Napoleon at the Battle of Leipzig in 1813 and the Battle of Waterloo in
     1815.

348 *Louis-Alexandre Berthier*—(1753–1815), 1st Prince of Wagram, Sovereign
     Prince of Neuchâtel, was a French Marshal and Vice-Constable of the
     Empire, and Chief of Staff under Napoleon. Following Napoleon's first
     abdication, Berthier retired to his estate. He made peace with Louis XVIII
     in 1814, and accompanied the king on his solemn entry into Paris. During
     Napoleon's short exile on Elba, he informed Berthier of his projects. Berthier
     was much perplexed as to his future course and, being unwilling to commit
     to Napoleon, fell under the suspicion both of his old leader and of Louis
     XVIII. On Napoleon's return to France, Berthier withdrew to Bamberg,
     where he died a few weeks later on 1 June 1815 in a fall from an upstairs
     window. The manner of his death is uncertain.

349 *Jean-Baptiste Drouet, Comte d'Erlon*—(1765–1844) was a marshal of France
     and a soldier in Napoleon's Army. He notably commanded the I Corps of the
     Armée du Nord at the battle of Waterloo.

350 *Editor note: Henri Gratien, Comte Bertrand (1773–1844), rose through the*
     ranks to be one of Napoleon's most famed generals. His life was henceforth
     closely bound up with that of Napoleon, who had the fullest confidence in
     him, honoring him in 1808 with the title of count and at the end of 1813,
     with the title of Grand Marshal of the Palace. It was Bertrand who in 1809
     directed the building of the bridges by which the French army crossed the
     Danube at Wagram. In 1811, the Emperor appointed Bertrand governor of
     the Illyrian Provinces and during the German campaign of 1813. After the
     Battle of Leipzig, it was due to his initiative that the French army was not
     totally destroyed. He accompanied the Emperor to Elba in 1814, returned
     with him in 1815, held a command in the Waterloo campaign, and then,
     after the defeat, accompanied Napoleon to St Helena. Condemned to death
     in 1816, he did not return to France until after Napoleon's death, and then
     Louis XVIII granted him amnesty allowing him to retain his rank. In 1840
     he was chosen to accompany the Prince of Joinville to St Helena to retrieve
     and bring Napoleon's remains to France, in what became known as the
     retour des cendres.

351 *Editor Note: The performance that night is not known for certain, but it*
     may have been Œdipe à Colone, a tragic opera in the 'tragédie lyrique' genre
     by Antonio Sacchini first performed at Versailles on 4 January 1786 in the
     presence of King Louis XVI and Marie Antoinette. The opera became one of
     the most popular pieces in the repertoire for several decades, reaching a total
     of almost 600 performances by 1844.

352 *Editor Note: Charles Ferdinand d'Artois, Duke of Berry (1788–1820), was*
     the youngest son of Charles X. The Duke was said to be a jovial, vain, and
     somewhat ill-mannered person, and he was considered the black sheep of the
     family because he constantly attracted trouble. Six years later, on the evening
     of 13 February 1820, the Duke and his wife were attending the Paris Opera.

Near the end of the ballet, as was customary, the Duke, the Duchess, and the Duke's small entourage withdrew and went to the Rue de Rameau where the Duke's carriage was waiting. As the Duke handed his pregnant wife into the carriage, a man came from the shadows and plunged forward with a knife, assassinating him.

353   *Editor note: Ali le Mamelouk was Louis-Etienne Saint-Denis (1811–1856). He was born in Versailles and entered the service of Napoleon in 1806, became his footman in 1811, then followed him in his successive exiles to the islands of Elba and St Helena. In 1840, like Comte Bertrand, he was chosen to accompany the Prince of Joinville to St Helena to retrieve and bring Napoleon's remains to France, in what became known as the retour des cendres.*

354   *Editor note: Pauline Bonaparte (1780–1825), was the sixth child of Letizia Ramolino and Carlo Buonaparte, Corsica's representative to the court of King Louis XVI of France. Napoleon was her elder brother. She married Charles Leclerc, a French general, a union ended by his death in 1802. Later, she married Camillo Borghese, 6th Prince of Sulmona.*

355   *Editor note: Jean-Baptiste Jules Bernadotte (1763–1844) served a long career in the French Army and was appointed as a Marshal of France by Napoleon, though the two had a turbulent relationship. Napoleon made him Prince of Pontecorvo on 5 June 1806, but he stopped using that title in 1810 when his service to France ended and he was elected the heir-presumptive to the childless King Charles XIII of Sweden.*

356   *Marie Louise*—(1791–1847) was the eldest child of Emperor Francis II of Austria and his second wife, Maria Theresa of Naples and Sicily. She was Napoleon's second wife and Empress of the French from 1810 to 1814.

357   *Editor note: Aimée de Coigny (1769 –1820) was a French aristocrat who was known as a great beauty. She was imprisoned during the Revolution and André Chénier's elegy la Jeune Captive, published in 1795, was inspired by her ordeal.*

358   *Editor note: Baron Johann von Wessenberg-Ampringen (1773–1858) was an Austrian diplomat. From 1801 he worked as a secretary at the Austrian embassy in Berlin led by Count Johann Philipp von Stadion and in 1805 was appointed ambassador at Kassel, where he witnessed the occupation by the French troops under General Mortier in 1806. In 1808 Wessenberg returned to Berlin as ambassador at the Prussian court. From 1811 to 1813 on he led the legation at Munich and afterwards travelled as special envoy to London, France and Milan before in 1814 he was appointed second Austrian delegate (after Prince Metternich) at the Congress of Vienna.*

359   *Editor note: Josephine did not bear Napoleon a child. At dinner on 30 November 1809, Napoleon told her that in the interest of France he must find a wife who could produce an heir. Josephine agreed to the divorce so the Emperor could remarry in the hope of having an heir. The divorce ceremony took place on 10 January 1810 and was a grand but solemn social occasion, and each read a statement of devotion to the other. Josephine died in Rueil-Malmaison on 29 May 1814, soon after walking with Tsar Alexander in the gardens of Malmaison. She was buried in the nearby church of Saint Pierre-Saint Paul in Rueil. Napoleon learned of her death via a French journal while in exile on Elba, and stayed locked in his room for two days, refusing to see anyone.*

360   *Editor note: Claude Edouard Philippe, Baron Mounier (1784–1843), Napoleon's secretary.*

361 *Editor note: General William Schaw Cathcart (1755–1843), Scottish soldier and diplomatist. On 1 January 1812 he was promoted to the full rank of general and was sent to Russia as ambassador and military commissioner. He served with the headquarters of the Allies throughout the War of Liberation (1812–1814); and was generally successful in the delicate and difficult task of maintaining harmony and devotion to the common cause amongst the generals of many nationalities.*

362 *Editor note: Jean-Andoche Junot, 1st Duke of Abrantès (1771–1813), a French general during the Revolutionary and Napoleonic Wars.*

363 *Editor note: Jean-Toussaint Arrighi de Casanova, duc de Padova, (1778–1853) a French diplomat and soldier during the Revolutionary and Napoleonic Wars.*

364 *Editor note: Le souper de Henri IV; a comedy of one act in prose and vaudeville by Michel Nicolas Balisson de Rougemont, (1781–1840) and René Perin (1774–1858), first performed 23 April 1814.*

365 *Editor note: André Masséna, 1st duc de Rivoli, 1st Prince d'Essling (1758–1817), was a French military commander during the Revolutionary and Napoleonic Wars. He was one of the original eighteen Marshals of the Empire created by Napoleon, with the nickname l'Enfant chéri de la Victoire (the Dear Child of Victory).*

366 *Editor Note: Auguste Frédéric Louis Viesse de Marmont, duc de Raguse (1774–1852) was a French general and nobleman who rose to the rank of Marshal of France. Marmont stayed loyal to Louis XVIII during the Hundred Days.*

367 *Editor Note: Augustus Foster married, at St Martin In The Fields, Westminster, London, 18 March 1815, Albinia Jane Hobart (1788–1867), daughter of George Vere Hobart, second son of George Hobart, 3rd Earl of Buckinghamshire. Augustus and Albinia had three sons: Frederick George, 2nd baronet (1816–1857), died unmarried: Cavendish Harvey, 3rd baronet (1817–1890) and Vere Henry Louis, the original editor of this book (1819–1900).*

368 *Monsieur*—Louis, brother of Louis XVI, whom he afterwards succeeded as Louis XVIII (1755–1824).

369 *Editor Note: Louis Marie Celeste Aumont, duc d'Aumont (1770–1831). D'Aumont commanded the military district centred on Caen. Being in danger at Caen with rising support for Napoleon, his chief of staff, Colonel Corbett, a British officer, saw him safely aboard a Royal Navy vessel for England.*

370 *Constant*—Benjamin C. (1767–1830), *Sismondi*—John S., historian (1773–1842).

371 *Wonderful events*—The battle of Waterloo, &c.

372 *Editor Note: Major Frederick Howard (1785–1815) was the 3rd son of Frederick Howard, 5th Earl of Carlisle, and Margaret, daughter of Granville Leveson-Gower, 1st Marquess of Stafford. He was killed while leading the last charge at Waterloo. He was buried at Waterloo, but on 3 August 1815 his body was disinterred and re-interred in Streatham. In 1879 his remains were removed from Streatham, and re-interred in the family mausoleum at Castle Howard, Yorkshire.*

373 *Editor Note: Lord Aberdeen married, first, 28 July 1805, Lady Catherine Hamilton (1784–1812), daughter of Lord Abercorn and they had four children. He married secondly, 8 July 1815, his sister-in-law, Harriet Douglas (d. 1833), daughter of Hon. John Douglas and Lady Frances Lascelles, and widow of James Hamilton, Viscount Hamilton (1786–1814), five children.*

374 *Elephant*—The Danish order of the 'Elephant'.

375 *George*—The Hon. George Lamb, brother of William Lamb who succeeded to the title of Viscount Melbourne.

376 *Murat*—Marshal M., King of Naples (1767–1815).

377 *Editor note: Jane Elizabeth Harley, née Scott, Countess of Oxford and Countess Mortimer (1774–1824). In 1794 she married Edward Harley, 5th Earl of Oxford and Earl Mortimer. She frequently took lovers from among the pro-Reform party during her marriage, firstly Francis Burdett and most notably Lord Byron—the affair lasting from 1812, in the aftermath of Byron's affair with Lady Caroline Lamb until 1813. Her marriage was not a love match and her large number of children were known as the 'Harleian Miscellany' due to uncertainties over whether her husband was their father, but the marriage did not break up. Even in the easy-going world of the Regency aristocracy, her affairs were considered to have put her beyond the pale, and few people were prepared to receive her.*

378 *Editor note: Murat fled to Corsica after Napoleon's fall. Joined by around a thousand followers, he hoped to regain control of Naples by fomenting an insurrection in Calabria. Arriving at the port of Pizzo, Murat attempted to rally support in the town square, but his plan turned awry. The crowd was hostile and he was attacked by an old woman blaming him for the loss of her son. Calabria had been badly hit by Murat's repression of local piracy and brigandage during his reign. Soon he was captured by forces of King Ferdinand IV of Naples. He was imprisoned in the Castello di Pizzo, the small castle in the harbor, from where he wrote several letters, especially to his family. He was tried for treason and sentenced to death by firing squad.*

379 *Rocca*—Albert Jean Michel de Rocca (1788–1818) was a French lieutenant during the Napoleonic Wars. He was also the second husband of Anne Louise Germaine de Staël. She had been secretly married to this young man for several years.

380 *Canova*—sculptor Antonio Canova (1757–1822).

381 *Editor note: Napoleon as Mars the Peacemaker is a colossal heroic nude statue by Antonio Canova, of Napoleon in the guise of the Roman god Mars. It was created in 1806 and is at Apsley House, London.*

382 *Gonsalvi*—Cardinal G., Roman Prime Minister.

383 *His sisters*—Carlotta (afterwards named Marie Pauline), married to Prince C. Borghese; Maria Anna (afterwards named Elise), married to Felix Baciocchi, a Corsican soldier; she was created by her brother Princess of Piombino, and is said to have been more respected perhaps than any other member of the Bonaparte family; and Annunziata (afterwards named Caroline), wife of Joachim Murat, whom Napoleon created King of Naples.

384 *Thorwaldsen*—Bertel Thorvaldsen (1770–1844) was a Danish/Icelandic sculptor who spent most of his life (1797–1838) in Italy.

385 *Royal Marriage*—Marriage of the Princess Charlotte, daughter of the Prince of Wales, to Prince Leopold of Saxe-Coburg (afterwards King of the Belgians).

386 *Poor Sheridan*—Richard Brinsley S. (1751–1816). He died 7 July 1816 at 14 Savile Row, London.

387 *Glenarvon*—A novel written by Lady Caroline Lamb.

388 *The being it is meant for*—Lord Byron.

389 *Mr Brougham*—Henry B., afterwards Lord B. (1778–1868).

390 *Editor note: George Child Villiers, 5th Earl of Jersey (1773–1859), married, 23 May 1804, Lady Sarah Sophia Fane, daughter of John Fane, 10th Earl of*

Westmorland. Lady Jersey was one of the great hostesses of English society, a leader of the ton during the Regency era and the reign of George IV, and a patroness of Almack's. Lord Jersey was an ardent fox hunter and a breeder and trainer of horses, owning two Epsom Derby winners. His wife's numerous love affairs did not trouble him: asked why he had never fought a duel in her honour, he replied that he could hardly fight every man in London.

391   *Madame Lucien*—She was widow of Monsieur Jouberthon, a stockbroker, and was second wife of Lucien Bonaparte, to whom she bore nine children, the eldest of whom, Letitia, married Thomas Wyse, Esq., an Irish gentleman, one of whose descendants, Bonaparte Wyse, is a Government Inspector of Irish National Schools.

392   *Louis Bonaparte*—Third brother of Napoleon, who made him King of Holland. He married in 1802 Hortense Eugenie Beauharnais, daughter of Viscount B. and of Josephine, who was daughter of Count Tascher de la Pagerie, and was the first wife of Napoleon. His son, Charles Louis Napoleon Bonaparte, was elected in 1848 President of the French Republic by 5,562,834 votes out of a total of 7,500,000, and again by more than 7,000,000 votes in 1851, and in the following year he assumed the title of Emperor as Napoleon III.

393   *M. Lewis*—M. G. L., novelist, author of *The Monk* (1775–1818).

394   *Phocas*—Emperor of Constantinople, d. 610.

395   *Editor note: this child was Vere Foster (1819–1900), the original transcriber and creator of this book.*

396   *Editor note: William À Court, first Baron Heytesbury (1779–1860). William À Court was educated at Eton and succeeded his father as 2nd baronet, 22 July 1817. Created Baron Heytesbury, 23 January 1828, À Court was secretary of a legation to Naples 1801–07; secretary to a special mission to Vienna in 1807; first commissioner to Malta, 1812; envoy extraordinary to Barbary States January 1813–14; Naples, March 1814–January 1822; Privy Councillor, 1817; envoy to Spain August 1822–September 1824; ambassador to Portugal September 1824–January 1828; Russia June 1828–August 1832. He studied at Weimar M. Mounier;s Academy at the Belvedere. He had been sent to Weimar on the recommendation of Lord Malmesbury, to whom he was distantly related. Before À Court had completed his second year at Weimar a quarrel in which he got involved led to a hostile meeting with a young English nobleman and he was forced to remove himself. He would have known Augustus Foster there, and perhaps he was the young nobleman he quarrelled with.*

397   *Peel*—Sir Robert Peel, second baronet (1788–1850). The statement that the first baronet was once 'a common mill boy' is not quite correct.

398   *Lafayette*—Marquis de la Fayette (1757–1834).

399   *The Noels*—The Milbankes had assumed the surname of Noel.

400   *Little Ada*—Only child of Lord Byron, afterwards married to the Earl of Lovelace (1816–1852).

401   *Lord Strangford*—A distinguished diplomatist (1780–1855).

402   *The Cato Street Conspiracy.*

403   *Caroline of Brunswick*—(1768–1821). Caroline married George Prince of Wales in 1795, and they had one daughter, Charlotte (1796–1817). They separated shortly after Charlotte's birth. In 1820, George became king and insisted on a divorce, which she refused. A legal divorce was possible but difficult to obtain. Caroline returned to Britain to assert her position as

queen. She was wildly popular with the British populace, who sympathised with her and who despised the new king for his immoral behaviour. On the basis of the loose evidence collected against her, George attempted to divorce her by introducing the Pains and Penalties Bill to Parliament, but George and the bill were so unpopular, and Caroline so popular with the masses, that it was withdrawn by the Tory government. In July 1821, Caroline was barred from the coronation on the orders of her husband. She fell ill in London and died three weeks later.

404 *Counts Gamba*—Father and brother of the Countess Guiccioli, whose connection with Byron is sufficiently well known.

405 *Lady Melbourne*—Sister of Sir Ralph Milbanke, and aunt of Lady Byron (1785–1828).

406 *Sposa*—The Countess Guiccioli.

407 *Influenza*—This remark shows that the term influenza is not of recent origin.

408 *Miss Vere Hobart*—Half-sister of Mrs. Foster, and afterwards married to Donald Cameron of Lochiel.

409 *Sarah*—Lady Sarah Robinson.

410 *Mr. R.*—Frederick Robinson, created in 1827 Viscount Goderich. He was Prime Minister for a few months in 1827–28 in succession to Canning, and was created Earl of Ripon in 1833 (1782–1859).

411 *Lady De Grey*—Countess De Grey, sister-in-law of Lord Goderich (1782–1859).

412 *Count Capo d'Istrias—See Appendix.*

413 *Lady Holland—See Appendix.*

414 *Lord Salisbury*—James B. W. G. Cecil, eighth Earl and second Marquis of S. (1791–1868), father of the later Prime Minister. He married first in 1821 Frances Gascoyne, by whom he had seven children, and secondly, in 1847 Lady Mary West (whose second refusal was not final), daughter of the Earl of Delawarr, by whom he had five children.

415 *Kirkby*—Kirkby-Mallory in Leicestershire, where Lady Byron owned an estate.

416 *Mr. Barnard*—The Hon. Henry Barnard, a distinguished American educationist.

417 *De Fellenberg—See Appendix.*

418 *Editor note: Many poor people did not have an oven, and if they could afford a scrap of meat, or even a small joint, took it to the bakery to have it roasted, where for the day the baker used his ovens for this purpose.*

419 *Editor note: Revd Alexander Johnstone Ross (1819–1887) of Brighton married, 1856, Catherine Susan, née Sterling (1834–1860), the daughter of John Coningham Sterling (1806–1844), writer and poet, whose life had been written by Thomas Carlyle, The life of John Sterling (1851).*

420 *Editor note: Eliza Lee Cabot Follen (1787–1860) was an American editor, biographer, novelist, poet, playwright, children's author, and lifelong slavery abolitionist.*

421 *Lord P.*—Viscount Palmerston, Prime Minister from 1855 to 1858, and again from 1859 till his death in 1865 (1784–1865).

422 *Your endeavours*—This refers to two special schemes carried out by Mr Foster from 1849 to 1897, in aiding the building, flooring with boards in lieu of damp clay, or equipment of upwards of 2,000 National Schoolhouses situated in every County in Ireland; and in assisting the emigration of honest poor girls between 18 and 30 years of age from the congested districts of the West of Ireland, with the hearty co-operation of all the Roman Catholic

parish priests and curates without a single exception, in addition to nearly all the Protestant clergy. More than twelve hundred clergymen co-operated with Mr. F., and upwards of 25,000 girls were so assisted, about one-tenth of the expense being met by subscriptions, and the rest supplied by Mr. F.

423   *Buchanan*—James Buchanan, President of the United States from 1857 to 1861(1791–1868).

424   *Barras—See Appendix.*